THE
DAVIDIAN
MASSACRE

Disturbing Questions About Waco
Which Must Be Answered

Randy
For liberty
and Justice
Carol
Moore

Carol Moore

LEGACY COMMUNICATIONS
Franklin, Tennessee
&
GUN OWNERS FOUNDATION
Springfield, Virginia

Co-published by Legacy Communications and Gun Owners Foundation. All trade and bookstore orders should be directed to Legacy Communications, P.O. Box 680365, Franklin, Tennessee 37068. All other inquiries should be sent to Gun Owners Foundation, 8001 Forbes Place, Ste. 102, Springfield, VA 22151. For special sales and bulk orders call 1-800-417-1486.

"These Boots Are Made For Walking" by Lee Haclewood, Copyright 1965, renewed 1993. Used by permission.

Photograph Credits: Treasury Department, Federal Bureau of Investigation, Paul Watson, Carol Moore, Ian Goddard, and Dick Sanford.

Graphic Credits: Treasury Department and Carol Moore.

Cover: FBI aerial photograph shot from the rear of Mount Carmel during the first minutes of the fire shows one-half of the gymnasium collapsed by an FBI Tank.

ISBN 1-880692-22-8

To all Martyrs For Freedom

Table of Contents

Preface

$\mathcal{E}$ven as a long-time libertarian pacifist critical of the United States government, I felt confident telling a friend in early 1993, "At least our government doesn't just go in and attack and kill a lot of people like the Serbs do in Bosnia." And on February 28, 1993, when Bureau of Alcohol, Tobacco, and Firearms (BATF) agents stormed Mount Carmel, I saw nothing but what television commentators told me I was seeing—a bunch of armed "religious fanatics," rumored to be abusers of women and children, "ambushing" federal agents. When I saw the bullets blasting through a wall at an agent on the roof, even I thought, "Sometimes you need a little government to protect you from people like that!"

However, as the siege continued and as I kept up with debates on computer bulletin boards and the news from Waco, I began to suspect that federal agents were up to no good. I began to understand why the Branch Davidians were forced to take up arms in self-defense on February 28. And while as a pacifist I felt uncomfortable with the Davidians' continuing armed resistance, I became intrigued by David Koresh, who I jokingly referred to as "little Jesus in Texas," and his defiant "Wackos in Waco."

I hoped David Koresh would quickly finish his book and surrender so that we could move on to the next stage of the soap opera: watching a television tour of the Mount Carmel "compound" and televised interviews of Koresh and his followers—including his many wives and children; hearing Koresh's newest pronouncements on the fate God planned for the Feds; and observing the inevitable circus of the government's trial of "little Jesus" and his disciples. Would Koresh somehow triumph and go free as he had after his by-now famous trial for the shootout with a past leader of the Davidians? The story was just beginning to get interesting.

Only once, in a moment when I myself became impatient with the drawn out siege, did it occur to me that the siege might end in disaster, some kind of fiery inferno, but I shook off the thought. I told myself, "Our government would never do that!"

On April 19, 1993, I was looking forward to celebrating the 217th anniversary of the first battles of the American Revolution. In 1775 a British expedition to raid Minutemen weapons stockpiles in Concord, Massachusetts resulted in the Battles of Lexington and Concord. Even as an advocate of non-violent action who believes the American Revolution could have been won non-violently, I remain rather proud of the fact that I am the great-great-great-great granddaughter of Colonel James Barrett, commander of the militia at Concord. (His son Colonel Nathan Barrett and Lexington native Mathias Hawes, two of my great-great-great grandfathers, also fought in the battles.) Most of the Minutemen weapons were stored at Barrett's farm, which was the primary target of the British expedition. Barrett later gave the order to fire upon the British, should they fire first.

That morning I was late for work and had only a moment to be shocked by the sight of tanks ramming Mount Carmel's familiar pale walls. Later a coworker alerted me that the building was on fire. For the next half hour I watched CNN's live coverage and waited anxiously to see people fleeing. When it became apparent there were few survivors, I closed myself in a storage room and broke down sobbing in grief for people whom I had never known, and even had mocked, and yet with whom I felt a certain solidarity.

Soon enough I began to get angry—especially as I heard television reports that the Davidians had set the fire. I found these reports dubious, considering the way those tanks had been ramming away at the building. What a way to celebrate Lexington and Concord—burn to death individuals also accused of owning too many weapons. The British actually started a small fire in

Colonel James Barrett's barn, but they had the courtesy to put it out! It was clear that the government's punishment of the Davidians was totally out of proportion to the crimes that it alleged some of them had committed.

Like so many others, I might have allowed the federal government's actions to fade into a disturbing memory, had it not been for two events in September, 1993: seeing Linda Thompson's flawed, but eye-opening video, "Waco, the Big Lie," and making the pilgrimage to Mount Carmel during a trip to Texas. In Waco I met with six surviving Davidian women and had the wrenching experience of watching the video again with them in their temporary home at the Brittney Hotel. I met with other Davidians at a religious conference that November in Washington, D.C. After the Branch Davidian trial was over, I began written and phone contact with the Davidian prisoners.

After returning from Waco, I and several other libertarians and pacifists formed the Committee for Waco Justice, which has worked to remind the public about the government's crimes against the Davidians. With dozens of others I have protested on the anniversaries of these crimes outside the White House, Justice Department, Congress, and the headquarters of the Bureau of Alcohol, Tobacco and Firearms and of the Federal Bureau of Investigation (FBI).

Writing this book has been an angering experience, as I have continued to find more and more evidence of federal crimes and cover-up of those crimes. And it has been a painful experience. I have talked to or read letters from Davidian prisoners and survivors who mourn lost husbands, wives, children, and friends. Considering the trauma Davidians have experienced, it is impressive that survivors, even the prisoners, display little hate toward those who murdered their friends and families. And so I have chosen to begin each chapter with a quote from a Davidian.

Contact with the Davidians has set even me, a former Bible mocker, to studying the Bible. I was especially impressed by the biblical recognition of the "mischief" that can be done by statute, or under color of law (Psalm 94:20). While as a pacifist I would like to see all our swords turned into plowshares, I only can support voluntary disarmament schemes, with the emphasis on disarming governments. No pacifist can support government disarming the people by armed force and killing them when they resist. Unjust laws, not an overflowing of Davidian wickedness, brought on this tragedy of biblical proportions.

My research and experiences have convinced me that the federal government, with full cooperation of the media and press, destroyed a loving, committed, interracial community and family, something all too rare in our isolated, alienated, bigoted world. The community—the family—may not have been perfect. However, its greatest problem seems to have been paranoia induced by a government intent on imposing its law upon families and communities and disdainful of their attempts to cooperate with law enforcement.

This paranoia proved to be justified when the federal government launched a paramilitary attack by seventy-six heavily armed men and women firing submachine guns, including from helicopters, and throwing flash-bang grenades. When the family refused to be broken and dispersed, the Feds resorted to assaults by fifty-ton tanks smashing into the living room and kitchen until the home caught fire, killing the family and destroying the community.

Tragically, it seems that on the second anniversary of the fire at Mount Carmel, one small group of individuals traumatized by the massacre of the Branch Davidians may have responded with terrible vengeance against federal employees in Oklahoma City. Two years after the deaths of so many Davidians, Americans again had to witness a search through burned and mangled ruins for the remains of senselessly murdered men, women, and children. I pray that governments will learn to resolve conflicts with citizens cooperatively and non-violently—and that citizens angered by government tyranny will learn the techniques of assertive and effective non-violent civil disobedience and non-violent direct action.

To end, special thanks to Larry Pratt and Gun Owners Foundation and to members of the Committee for Waco Justice of America: Ian Goddard, James Long, Tim Seims, Andrew Williams, Alan Forschler, Michelle McKneally, and Richard Sanford. Thanks also to other investigators and interested parties who generously shared information, including Jim Bule, Jack DeVault, Ken Fawcett, Sharon Fisher, Debbie Green, Dave Hall, Dean Kelley, Kirk Lyons, Michael McNulty, Gordon

Melton, Dewey Millay, Gordon Novel, Jim Pate, Dick Reavis, Nancy Ross, Rick Sherrow, and Mark Swett. Thanks to participants who shared information and their stories, including Phillip Arnold, Sarah Bain, James Tabor, defense, appeals and civil suit attorneys, and those few Mount Carmel survivors. And most grateful thanks to Davidian prisoners who continue to speak out, despite their captivity, and who remain the continuing victims of these terrible government assaults.

Carol Moore
June 1995

BRANCH DAVIDIAN VICTIMS

Died February 28, 1993
Winston Blake, 28, black, British
Peter Gent, 24, white, Australian
Peter Hipsman, 28, white, American
Perry Jones, 64, white, American
Michael Schroeder, 29, white, American
Jaydean Wendell, 34, Asian, American

Died April 19, 1993
Katherine Andrade, 24, white, Canadian
Chanel Andrade, 1, white, American
Jennifer Andrade, 19, white, Canadian
George Bennett, 35, black, British
Susan Benta, 31, black, British
Mary Jean Borst, 49, white, American
Pablo Cohen, 38, white, Israeli
Abedowalo Davies, 30, black, British
Shari Doyle, 18, white, American
Beverly Elliot, 30, black, British
Yvette Fagan, 32, black, British
Doris Fagan, 51, black, British
Lisa Marie Farris, 24, white, American
Raymond Friesen, 76, white, American
Sandra Hardial, 27, black, British
Zilla Henry, 55, black, British
Vanessa Henry, 19, black, British
Phillip Henry, 22, black, British
Paulina Henry, 24, black, British
Stephen Henry, 26, black, British
Diana Henry, 28, black, British

Novellette Hipsman, 36, black, American
Floyd Houtman, 61, black, American
Sherri Jewell, 43, Asian, American
David M. Jones, 38, white, American
David Koresh, 33, white, American
Rachel Howell, 24, white, American
Cyrus Howell, 8, white, American
Star Howell, 6, white, American
Bobbie Lane Koresh, 2, white, American
Jeffery Little, 32, white, American
Nicole Gent Little, 24, white, Australian, and unborn child
Dayland Gent, 3, white, American
Page Gent, 1, white, American
Livingston Malcolm, 26, black, British
Diane Martin, 41, black, British
Wayne Martin, Sr., 42, black, American
Lisa Martin, 13, black, American
Sheila Martin, Jr., 15, black, American
Anita Martin, 18, black, American
Wayne Martin, Jr., 20, black, American
Julliete Martinez, 30, Mexican American
Crystal Martinez, 3, Mexican American
Isaiah Martinez, 4, Mexican American
Joseph Martinez, 8, Mexican American
Abigail Martinez, 11, Mexican American
Audrey Martinez, 13, Mexican American
John-Mark McBean, 27, black, British
Bernadette Monbelly, 31, black, British
Rosemary Morrison, 29, black, British
Melissa Morrison, 6, black, British
Sonia Murray, 29, black, American
Theresa Norbrega, 48, black, British
James Riddle, 32, white, American

Rebecca Saipaia, 24, Asian, Filipino
Steve Schneider, 43, white, American
Judy Schneider, 41, white, American
Mayanah Schneider, 2, white, American
Clifford Sellors, 33, white, British
Scott Kojiro Sonobe, 35, Asian, American
Floracita Sonobe, 34, Asian, Filipino
Gregory Summers, 28, white, American
Aisha Gyrfas Summers, 17, white, Australian, and unborn child
Startle Summers, 1, white, American
Lorraine Sylvia, 40, white, American
Rachel Sylvia, 12, white, American
Hollywood Sylvia, 1, white, American
Michelle Jones Thibodeau, 18, white, American
Serenity Jones, 4, white, American
Chica Jones, 2, white, American
Little One Jones, 2, white, American
Neal Vaega, 38, Asian, New Zealander
Margarida Vaega, 47, Asian, New Zealander
Mark H. Wendell, 40, Asian, American

Prisoners

Renos Avraam, 31, white, British
Brad Branch, 36, white, American
Jaime Castillo, 27, white, American
Graeme Craddock, 34, white, Australian
Livingstone Fagan, 36, black, British
Paul Fatta, 37, white, American
Ruth Riddle, 31, white, Canadian
Kathryn Schroeder, 35, white, American
Kevin Whitecliff, 34, white, American

1

Why the BATF and the FBI Massacred the Branch Davidians

You need to call the President of the United States and explain to him what you have done. You've ruined this country. You've ruined the nation. This is a democracy, supposedly, a republic.

David Koresh, February 28, 1993, on 911 tape

When David Koresh spoke these words the evening of February 28, 1993, he understood the true meaning of the Bureau of Alcohol, Tobacco, and Firearms' (BATF) attack on the Branch Davidians' home and church, Mount Carmel Center. It is a truth that millions of Americans have come to understand since April 19, 1993, when Koresh and seventy-five of his family members and friends—nineteen men, thirty-four women, and twenty-three children—died a terrible death by fire.[1] It is a truth reflected in the oft-repeated remark, "Whatever they did, they did not deserve this."

David Koresh understood that the BATF attack on Mount Carmel Center and its 120 inhabitants—mostly women, children, and elderly people—represented the breakdown of liberty and democracy in America. He intended to use evidence of government crimes contained within the walls and roof of the still-standing Mount Carmel to expose that breakdown to a jury—and very probably win freedom for himself and his friends.

HELICOPTER ATTACK
REMINISCENT OF VIETNAM

The day after the fire Larry Potts, then Assistant Director of the FBI's Criminal Division, expressed what was surely the FBI's prime public reason for going forward with the April 19, 1993, gas and tank assault, "These people had thumbed their noses at law enforcement."[2] However, there is evidence there was another reason, one the FBI refuses to admit.

Few Americans realize a simple truth about the BATF raid, one that the government has tried to suppress and the press has discounted or ignored: in the first minutes of the raid National Guard helicopters zoomed in on Mount Carmel, guns blazing, like Americans raiding a Vietnam village in that far-off war. Davidians claim that four of their group were killed by firing from these helicopters. David Koresh's unarmed father-in-law, who stood behind him at the front door, was also mortally wounded by gunfire from BATF agents on the ground.

Like Koresh, BATF agents knew that if Mount Carmel, whose roofs and walls contained evidence of this helicopter attack, was left standing, the Davidians stood an excellent chance of being acquitted of murder of federal agents by a sympathetic jury. And, in fact, those who survived *were* acquitted of murder.

Moreover, BATF agents could face prosecution and imprisonment for negligent or even intentional homicide in the deaths of the unarmed Davidians. FBI agents took over from BATF and befriended and sympathized with BATF agents who had seen four comrades killed and twenty wounded. It is likely FBI agents, conspiring either silently or explicitly with BATF agents, deliberately sabotaged negotiations with the Davidians to prevent their exiting Mount Carmel. The ravages of time, wind, and rain alone would destroy some of the evidence of illegal gunfire. Moreover, agents may have hoped to create an incident or situation that would give them an excuse to destroy the building and its incriminating evidence. If that meant the massacre of dozens of men, women, and children—all witnesses to the brutal attack—so be it. The possibility that one or two Davidians, in a foolish act of self-defense, lighted one of the fires that consumed the building is the *least* likely scenario.

Unfortunately, the Davidians played into the BATF's and the FBI's hands by not surrendering. Davidians sincerely believed the BATF attack was God's way of helping them spread His word. They were righteously angered by the unjust attack, especially given David Koresh's earlier invitation to BATF to inspect his guns. They were fearful that federal agents would destroy evidence of BATF crimes once they exited the building. And they worried that over a hundred men, women, and children would be rendered homeless and lose their church if they were to exit without legal reassurances they could keep the property. For all these reasons Davidians stubbornly refused to leave their home—until the FBI made it impossible for them to escape alive.

In the video "The Waco Incident: The True Story," controversial investigator Gordon Novel asserts, "That's America's first Auschwitz right there. They're gassing them prior to cremating them." The massacre of the Branch Davidians was the greatest government massacre of civilians on American soil since the massacre of 300 Native Americans at Wounded Knee in 1890.

IS AMERICA BECOMING A POLICE STATE?

Many Americans see the BATF's paramilitary raid upon the Branch Davidians, and the FBI's harsh fifty-one day siege and brutal April gas and tank attack, as evidence that the United States is far down the road toward becoming a police state. Government critic William Norman Grigg writes: "The government's approach to the Waco confrontation—shoot in haste and invent a justification at leisure—is that of the police state. Once the precipitate assault on the sect had resulted in deaths, the government claimed that those deaths justified the raid, in spite of the fact that the raid had *caused* those deaths." Grigg notes that while in a free society "laws are relatively few and easily understood," in a totalitarian police state "laws are plentiful and frequently unintelligible, and the state can intervene at whim into a person's private affairs."[3]

As we shall see, the Davidians were accused of running afoul of "unintelligible laws" and assaulted *despite* their attempts to cooperate with authorities and make sure they were in compliance with those laws. While the government alleges it discovered a number of illegal weapons in the ruins of the Davidians' home, many Americans suspect these weapons actually were manufactured "at leisure" by the government to "justify" their raid.

The War on Drugs

The government's most successful excuse for violating Americans' rights has been the "War on Drugs," a war which is largely responsible for the government's stepped up "War on Guns." Much of today's violent crime is prohibition related, the prohibition of psychoactive drugs instead of alcohol. The attraction of hefty illegal profits has led to even greater struggles over territory and violence between armed gangs than that during alcohol prohibition. Drug-related crime and the profit-driven promotion of drug use has hit inner cities the hardest, even as law enforcement has concentrated its efforts on arresting and imprisoning African-American and Latino users and dealers.

The War on Drugs has led to serious abuses of Americans' constitutional rights by law enforcement: use of unreliable informants, inadequate investigation of alleged crimes, increasing use of entrapment, judicial rubber stamping of search warrants, growing use of unjustified "no knock" warrants, improper use of deadly force, increasing violations of due process of law, chipping away at the exclusionary rule against using illegally obtained evidence, improper use of forfeiture proceedings to augment law enforcement budgets, unjust mandatory sentencing guidelines, and growing use of the military in domestic law enforcement.

The War on Guns

Drug-prohibition-related gun violence has resulted in more laws and stricter enforcement of laws restricting gun ownership. Gun ownership is being added to a growing list of "victimless" crimes. In 1993, after many years of effort, gun control advocates pushed the Brady Bill handgun registration law through Congress. The 1994 crime bill banned the further manufacture, transfer, or possession of nineteen types of semiautomatic weapons (so-called "assault" weapons), and firearm magazines that exceed ten rounds. However, it permitted transfer or possession of weapons or magazines produced before September 13, 1994, the day President Bill Clinton signed the bill into law. It also outlawed the use of more than two attachments to a semiautomatic rifle that has the ability to accept a detachable magazine. The one exception to these prohibitions, of course, is continued manufacture of semiautomatic weapons for the military and for civilian law enforcement. Gun control advocates continue to propose more restrictive laws and taxes on guns and ammunition, including registration of semiautomatic guns and eventually all guns. They even hope to repeal the Second Amendment.

However, both a federal statute—Firearms Owners' Protection Act of 1986, §21—and a judicial decision—United States vs. Anders, 885 F.2d 1248 [5th Cir. 1989]—hold that there is nothing per se wrong with the ownership of large numbers of legal arms. Obviously, the decision and the statute have not reined in BATF.

During the April 28, 1993, House Judiciary Committee hearing on Waco, then-BATF Director Stephen Higgins defended the tactics used at Waco by stating, "In the eighteen months prior to the Branch Davidian incident, ATF Special Response Teams had carried out 341 actual activations to high risk situations," including "diverse sects and survivalists."[4] What he did not mention, but what is well known among Second Amendment activists, is that *most* of those raided were *not* criminals using guns for illegal purposes, but honest and peaceful citizens. Whether they break gun laws out of ignorance, because they are set up by BATF agents or informants—and even if they have broken no law at all—BATF too often treats American gun owners like dangerous criminals.

Several cases of BATF abuses have gained wide notoriety. In December, 1991, agents raided and trashed John Lawmaster's unoccupied home, found nothing illegal, and left without shutting the door, leaving guns and ammunition strewn about the unsecured home.[5] In May, 1992, the BATF raided the home of Louis Katona, a part-time police officer. Agents confiscated his legal machine guns and abused his wife. Later, a district judge dismissed the charges because he could find no evidence a crime had been committed.[6] In February, 1993, BATF agents raided and ransacked Janice Hart's home and interrogated her for an hour without reading her her rights, only to discover they had the wrong name and address.[7] In a 1994 "fishing expedition," BATF agents raided the home of Harry Lamplugh, the largest gun-show promoter in the northeast, ransacked his home, spilled his cancer medicine across the floor, and caused the deaths of three family cats.[8]

Virginia attorney and weapons expert Stephen Halbrook asserts that in over one hundred cases the BATF actually has manufactured evidence that semiautomatic AR-15s illegally have been converted to automatic. Agents do so because they have quotas of convictions they must fill to protect their jobs and gain promotions and sometimes can do so only by fabricating evidence. By definition, a semiautomatic weapon shoots only one bullet with one pull of the trigger; it "automatically" loads the next bullet. An automatic weapon includes the automatic loading feature *and* fires two or more bullets with one pull of the trigger. BATF agents simply remove disconnectors, or safety switches, that prevent automatic fire. Doing this does not make a very effective weapon. But if the weapon fires only two shots with one pull of the trigger and then permanently jams, the BATF still can claim the weapon is automatic and prosecute the gun owner.[9]

Government's Dangerous Paranoia

In the weeks following the bombing of the Oklahoma City federal building, President Clinton and the establishment media flayed the "paranoia" of "right wing conspiracy theorists." However, it is the United States government which is becoming increasingly paranoid of a citizenry fed up with ever rising taxes and ever encroaching rules and regulations enforced with increasing levels of government violence.

A Treasury Department report states: "The raid by ATF agents on the Branch Davidian compound resulted from its enforcement of contemporary federal firearms laws. In a larger sense, however, the raid fit within an historic, well-established, and well-defended government interest in prohibiting and breaking up all organized groups that sought to arm or fortify themselves."[10]

Tony Cooper, a law enforcement consultant on anti-terrorism and professor of negotiations and conflict resolution at the University of Texas at Dallas, describes "the formation of a curious crusading mentality among certain law enforcement agencies to stamp out what they see as a threat to government generally. It's an exaggerated concern that they are facing a nationwide conspiracy and that somehow this will get out of control unless it is stamped out at a very early stage."[11]

WEAVER WAS PRACTICE FOR WACO

Many consider the BATF setup of white separatist Randy Weaver, the 1992 federal marshal attack that killed his son, the FBI sniper attack that killed his wife, and the FBI's eleven-day siege to have been merely practice for the massive attack against the Davidians. Since the same crew of FBI agents and officials are responsible for the massacre of the Davidians, it is useful to look closely at that case.

White separatist Randy Weaver had retreated to rural Idaho with his wife, Vicki, four children, and a family friend, Kevin Harris.[12] In 1990 a BATF undercover agent entrapped Weaver into selling him two illegally sawed-off shotguns for $300. Weaver alleges the BATF charged him after he refused to inform on other white separatists. The government then gave him the wrong date for a court hearing, March 20, instead of February 20, 1991. Disgusted, Weaver decided to end all contact with the judicial system.

The Eleven-Day Standoff

Rather than take immediate action when Weaver failed to appear, U.S. marshals began almost eighteen months of surveillance. On August 22, 1992, six marshals, one equipped with an assault rifle with a silencer, approached Weaver's cabin in order to observe him and threw rocks at his dog in an effort to lure Weaver closer so they could arrest him. According to Weaver's attorney Gerry Spence, the marshals did not have a warrant—though the U.S. attorney insisted they did—and they never identified themselves.

When the agents shot the dog, Kevin Harris and Weaver's fourteen-year-old son Samuel, not knowing who the attackers were, ran toward them, shooting. Their shots allegedly killed U.S. Marshal William Degan—though some assert friendly fire from another marshal killed him. Samuel was shot in the back and killed as he retreated.

The National Guard and the FBI Hostage Rescue Team—whose motto is "To Save Lives"—were called in. According to court records, the U.S. marshals falsely told the FBI that Weaver himself had ambushed them and that the Weavers and Harris would kill anyone who approached them. U.S. marshals never did tell the FBI that Samuel had been killed by a deputy marshal. They *did* tell them Mrs. Weaver was a fanatic capable of killing herself and her own children as an end to the siege.

Finally, U.S. marshals never told the FBI that they knew that when the adults went outside the cabin they always carried weapons. Larry Potts, Assistant Director of the FBI's Criminal Division, authorized "rules of engagement" which gave snipers the go-ahead to shoot any adult carrying a weapon outside the cabin. The standard FBI rules of engagement are: "Agents are not to use deadly force against any person except as necessary in self-defense or the defense of another, when they have reason to believe they or another are in danger of death or grievous bodily harm. Whenever feasible, verbal warnings should be given before deadly force is applied."[13]

While Weaver may have suspected he was surrounded by law enforcement after the initial shootout, the FBI never officially informed him of it or gave him a chance to surrender. And they certainly never warned his family they would be in jeopardy if any FBI agent saw them armed on the property.

The day after the first shootings, Harris and Weaver, carrying their guns, left the cabin to visit Samuel's body. FBI sniper Lon Horiuchi first shot Weaver in the shoulder and then tried to shoot Harris. However, Horiuchi claims he accidentally shot Vicki Weaver as she stood in the doorway of the cabin holding her baby. She died instantly, dropping the baby to the ground. Harris was wounded by shrapnel. Nevertheless, Weaver and Harris refused to surrender to authorities.

During the standoff Richard Rogers' Hostage Rescue Team used psychological warfare techniques against the Weavers. Court records show that the FBI taunted the Weavers after Vicki Weaver's death, calling out over their loudspeakers: "Good morning, Mrs. Weaver. We had pancakes for breakfast. What did you have?"[14]

Weaver and Harris surrendered nine days later, after the FBI allowed Populist Party presidential candidate Bo Gritz to serve as a third party negotiator. The two men were charged with conspiracy to murder federal officers. Their trial before a federal jury and U.S. District Judge Edward Lodge began just five days before the April 19 fire that killed seventy-six Davidians.

Weaver Acquitted and Prosecutors/FBI Fined

Most of the above disturbing information came to light during the trial. It also was revealed that prosecutors had withheld from the defense for several months the information that FBI agents had fabricated evidence by staging photos. They also withheld a government agent's notes and a police captain's assertion that a U.S. marshal had shot first. Federal agents falsely claimed that Degan had been killed by one of the first shots, but evidence later showed he had fired seven shots before he was shot. Judge Lodge fined prosecutors $3,240 for "inexcusable delay" in providing this information.[15]

Weaver's defense attorney, Gerry Spence, did not call any witnesses or present a defense, but simply told jurors the government had failed to prove its case. In July, 1993, the jury acquitted Weaver and Harris of Degan's murder, saying Harris had acted in self-defense. The jury also rejected charges that the two men conspired to provoke a confrontation with federal officers. Weaver was convicted of failing to appear for the original weapons charge trial and sentenced to eighteen months in prison, with credit for time already served. He was freed in early 1994 and sued the federal government in the summer of 1994 for the deaths of his son and wife.

After the victory attorney Gerry Spence told reporters, "A jury today has said that you can't kill somebody just because you wear badges and then cover up those homicides by prosecuting the innocent." Juror Janet Schmierer of Boise, Idaho, said, "I think they built their whole scenario out of how they perceived someone else should be living their lives, and if someone believed differently . . . they must be abnormal."[16] As we shall see, the Justice Department and FBI merely disciplined the responsible agents and officials.

HOW THE DAVIDIANS BECAME A TARGET

The Branch Davidians became a target of the BATF not because of any solid evidence that they possessed illegal weapons, but because former members alleged Davidian leader David Koresh had expressed interest in owning illegal weapons. However, some see an even larger dynamic at work. James R. Lewis writes: ". . . societies need enemies. External threats provide motivations for people to overcome internal divisiveness in order to work together as a unit . . . where external enemies no longer threaten, a society will find groups of individuals within itself that it can construe as threatening and evil."[17]

Davidians Made Howell Their Leader

The Branch Davidians, an offshoot of the Seventh-Day Adventist Church, believe in the "advent" or "Second Coming" of Jesus Christ, complete with the end of the world in a fiery apocalypse, the death of all sinners, and the salvation of true believers.[18] Davidians believe modern-day living prophets can lead church members toward salvation. David Koresh said in one

David Koresh
1959–1993

sermon, "People like dead religions. They want to hear what the Lord said 2000 years ago—and then they want to cut him off at that specific point in time."[19]

Ben Roden's "Branch Davidian" church evolved out of Victor Houteff's Shepherd's Rod Church in the early 1960s. In 1978 Ben Roden died, and his wife Lois Roden, a woman well-known in evangelical circles because of her pronouncement that the Holy Spirit was female, became the new Branch Davidian prophet.

David Koresh's birthname was Vernon Wayne Howell. He was born August 17, 1959, was the illegitimate son of a fourteen-year-old girl and, as many have noted, the grandson of a carpenter. As a boy, he became a self-taught student of the Bible who could recite long passages from memory. His other passion was country-gospel music, and he became an able guitar player. In 1981, seeking a prophet who could help him grow spiritually, he discovered the Branch Davidians and moved to Mount Carmel Center.

Howell's knowledge of Scripture and personable manner quickly gained him the confidence of other Davidians. However, his popularity earned him the enmity of Lois Roden's son, George Roden, who considered Howell to be his prime rival for the role of leader and prophet. Most Davidians considered George Roden to be too poorly versed in Scripture and too erratic to lead the group and sided with Howell. In 1984 a gun-toting Roden drove Howell and his wife Rachel out of Mount Carmel. Over the next two years most of the remaining Davidians left the Rodens to follow Howell. They established a community in shacks, tents, and buses on property rented in Palestine, Texas, and also had two homes in LaVerne, California.

Howell visited Israel in 1985 and, as he explained in a February 28, 1993, KRLD radio interview, had "an encounter" or, as he told FBI negotiators, "a miraculous meeting with God," which instructed him to study and teach the prophecies of the Seven Seals of the Book of Revelation.[20] (Davidians have not revealed the whole meaning of Seven Seals as taught by David Koresh, believing only Koresh could truly teach the truth.)

During these years, Howell also experienced revelations in which God commanded that he create a "House of David" where his many wives would bear him children who would become the rulers of a purer new world. He began to take young, single Davidians as his unofficial wives.

Half of those who chose to join Vernon Howell were of African, Hispanic, or Asian descent. Davidians deny that Howell preached and practiced racial separatism, as some allege. He had two children by an Asian woman and at least one wife of African descent. Livingstone Fagan, a black minister from England, asserts that Davidians had risen above racial concerns or prejudice.[21]

Meanwhile, George Roden was nearly alone at Mount Carmel's ramshackle houses. He was renting out rooms, and his renters included two alleged drug traffickers.[22] (This fact was used against David Koresh years later.) After Lois Roden's death, George Roden challenged Vernon Howell for leadership of the group. In late 1987, Roden dug up the coffin of a long-dead Davidian and challenged Howell to raise her from the dead. Howell complained to authorities about "corpse abuse," but they demanded photographic proof of a crime.

When Howell and seven armed followers sneaked onto the property to photograph the coffin, Roden caught them and a gunfight ensued. Howell and his followers were charged with attempted murder. Meanwhile, after Roden wrote letters threatening to afflict U.S. District Judge Walter A. Smith with herpes and AIDS, Smith sentenced Roden to six months in jail for contempt of court.

Howell took this opportunity to encourage the county to put a lien on Mount Carmel for sixteen years of unpaid taxes. Howell paid the taxes on March 22, 1988, and he and his followers legally re-took Mount Carmel Center. Under the agreement with the county,

Howell and his Davidians would gain final control of the property if they were to occupy it and pay taxes on it for five years from the date of the agreement. Significantly, that five-year period would end during the 1993 siege.

In April, 1988, Howell and his followers were tried for attempted murder of Roden; seven were acquitted and Howell's trial ended in a hung jury. George Roden continued to verbally threaten the group with violence. Then in 1989 Roden murdered a man with an ax and was incarcerated in a mental institution. Nevertheless, Davidians feared he would escape and attack them. They therefore remained armed and alert. Roden did escape briefly in late 1993.

In a February 28, 1993, KRLD radio interview, David Koresh made the point, "If I say I'm Christ . . . the proof is if I can open the seals or not." Those who believed he could, stayed. In a March, 1993, *New York Times* interview, longtime follower Paul Fatta unabashedly declared: "I believe David is the Messiah. He has shown me over and over that he knows the Book and presented Scripture showing how the last days events would happen."[23]

Livingstone Fagan, a social worker and minister who lost his wife and mother in the April 19 fire, holds that "David Koresh was the prophesied instrument through whom God spake." Fagan writes that in his first three hours of listening to Koresh, "I had perceived more significant biblical truths than I had done, the entire eight years I had been involved with organised [sic] religion." He contends that, like David Koresh, those who lived at Mount Carmel were "remade" in the "fashion of God."[24]

Ruth Riddle described the appeal of Mount Carmel to an interviewer, "We were trying to live together in community like the early apostles did. Sharing all things, having things in common, that's why we lived together, like a family."[25]

At the November 22, 1993, American Academy of Religion panel, Jamaican Davidian Janet McBean, who lost her brother in the April 19 fire, summarized David Koresh's appeal: "We are spiritual people. And we feel that God is watching what happens to this world. That's the reason why David protected his people and David felt the way he did. . . . He felt compelled to give us the revelation as he did."

Former Members Went to Authorities

Marc Breault, a Howell follower from 1986 to 1989, swore in a 1990 affidavit: "At first Vernon Howell appeared to be a conservative person whose only wish was to reform the Seventh-Day Adventist Church. As time progressed, however, Howell became power-hungry and abusive, bent on obtaining and exercising absolute power and authority over the group . . . by 1989, he had lost all restraint."[26] Breault was particularly incensed when, in the fall of 1989, Howell declared that God had commanded him take the married women in the group as his wives.

Soon after, Breault left the Davidians and became what he called a "cult buster," devoted to the destruction of the Branch Davidians. He charged that Howell manipulated members through fear of hellfire,

physically abused adults and children for minor
infractions of capricious rules, seduced and impregnated
young girls, and demanded a willingness to die for him
and his prophecies. However, Davidians who remained
with Howell asserted that Breault's accusations were
based on words and actions taken out of context and/or
blown out of proportion and built into fantastic and
untrue stories. (After conducting an investigation of
these accusations, which is too extensive to detail in this
book, I largely agree.)

Davidian survivors charge that Breault had
challenged Howell for control of the group. Breault
replied in November, 1993, "If I was trying to take over
the group I wouldn't have gone to the authorities. I
wouldn't have tried to have justice done and had the
group dismantled."[27]

Bent on "dismantling" the group, during 1990
Breault managed to convince over a dozen Davidians
around the world to join his efforts. They signed
affidavits alleging that Howell was guilty of the statutory
rape of two teenage girls, tax fraud, immigration
violations, harboring weapons, child abuse, and
exposing children to explicit talk about sex and violence.
They presented these affidavits to local police in
California and Texas, the Texas Department of Public
Safety, the Immigration and Naturalization Service, and
the Internal Revenue Service. However, these agencies
expressed little interest in the allegations. Neither did
U.S. Assistant Attorney Bill Johnston, who later became
a prime motivator of the 1993 BATF raid.[28] However,
Breault did not give up his vendetta, which continued
even after the deaths of most Davidians.

In early 1990 Vernon Howell legally changed his name to David (for King David who united Israel in the Old Testament) Koresh (Hebrew for Cyrus, the Persian king who freed the Jews from Babylon). In October, 1990, Robyn Bunds, who was living in the California home, decided to leave Koresh with her son. Koresh immediately sent the child back to Waco, but he returned him when Bunds reported the child missing to police in California. Bunds also told police that Koresh was having sex with the underage Aisha Gyrfas. When the police returned to investigate, Gyrfas and Koresh had returned to Texas.[29] In September, 1991, Jeannine Bunds, who like her daughter Robyn was Koresh's lover, left the Davidians, claiming that she was upset that Koresh had asked her if she was "capable of killing her children."[30]

In the fall of 1991 Breault brought his allegations to the Australian television producers of "A Current Affair." Reporter Martin King, who cowrote Breault's book, visited Mount Carmel and interviewed Koresh in January of 1992. The program that eventually aired portrayed Koresh as a sex-crazed, gun-loving religious fanatic. It also provides one of the few inside views of Mount Carmel Center and Koresh's preaching style.

In fall 1991 Breault also informed young Kiri Jewell's father, David Jewell, that Kiri was slated to become one of Koresh's wives. Jewell sued for custody, and in January, 1992, Breault and other former Davidians testified at the custody hearing in Michigan. Without admitting any wrongdoing, Kiri's mother Sherri voluntarily relinquished primary custody and promised to keep Kiri away from Koresh during visitations.

Spurred on by Davidian detractors, on February 27, 1992, Texas Department of Human Services social worker Joyce Sparks visited Mount Carmel with two other Human Services employees and two McLennan County Sheriff's deputies. Koresh allowed the visit to be videotaped.[31] They made two more visits and Koresh visited their offices. The case was closed on April 30, 1992, for lack of evidence of abuse.[32]

Davidian "defectors" eagerly cooperated with the BATF and FBI investigators in 1992 and 1993. That as many as twenty former members made various allegations to the government and press certainly suggests that some felt discontent with David Koresh's leadership of the Branch Davidians. However, after federal agents' assaults resulted in the deaths of so many of her friends, Robyn Bunds, who had cooperated with the government, said she urged that responsible BATF officials should be punished. "I know there were things going on there that weren't right. But they're dead now. What's the point? . . . It's okay to save them, try to do something, but what you did was kill them."[33] Bunds later joined in the civil law suit against the government with Koresh's mother, another wife, Dana Okimoto, and other survivors and family members.[34]

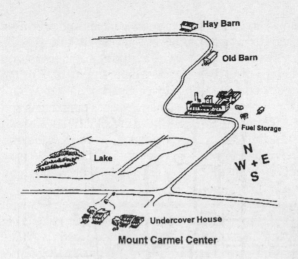

Mount Carmel Center

Koresh Predicted the End was Near

Such continuing attacks might make the most innocent group paranoid. It appears that the mounting pressures on David Koresh in late 1991 and early 1992— the loss of Kiri Jewell, the television exposé, the child abuse investigation, and the knowledge that Marc Breault and others would continue reporting allegedly illegal activities to authorities, convinced Koresh that government agents soon might launch the long-prophesied attack which would signal the beginning of the apocalypse.

Like many today, Davidians believed these were the end times and were preparing for the inevitable tribulation. At trial Davidian Kathryn Schroeder, who

First Floor Layout

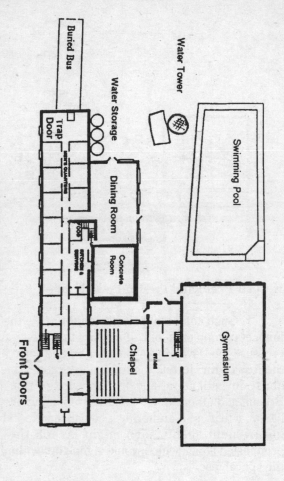

Buried Bus

Trap Door

Water Storage

Water Tower

Dining Room

Concrete Room

Swimming Pool

Front Doors

Chapel

Gymnasium

N
W + E
S

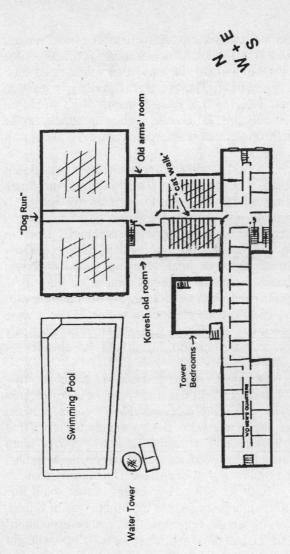

Second Floor Layout

prosecutors bullied into testifying for the government, revealed that Davidians began minimal practice with firearms, but had little idea why they might need such expertise. Marjorie Thomas, also a Davidian prosecution witness, asserted that Koresh taught arms would be needed only for self-defense against an attack, not to attack the government or force anyone to go along with their beliefs.[35]

In 1991 Davidians began tearing down Mount Carmel's separate homes and building one large building where they could be a more tight-knit community, living and studying together. After a neighbor's home was destroyed by a tornado, they also began building the underground tornado shelter— something which could also serve as a shelter should the "beast" burn down Mount Carmel.[36] In early 1992 Davidians reinforced the front wall of the building with a two-foot-high concrete wall to protect them in case someone attacked. (Davidians on the first floor actually *were* protected by this wall during BATF's February 28, 1993, attack.)[37]

Graeme Craddock testified to a grand jury that a few Davidians believed that when welfare workers visited Mount Carmel there were SWAT teams stationed around the property.[38] The government insists that Koresh believed a spring 1992 police SWAT team training near the Davidians' rented garage, the Mag Bag, was the BATF training for an assault on Mount Carmel.[39]

Kathryn Schroeder alleged it was about this time Koresh began to stress the prophecies of Daniel, chapters 11 and 12, regarding the "final confrontation" with the "king of the north," the "beast." Koresh taught that if Davidians were sufficiently faithful to God, they would be "translated" into heaven and the kingdom. This translation did *not* necessarily have to happen through their deaths at the hands of the authorities; if they were obedient to God they could be translated without dying. In fact, after the February 28, 1993, attack Koresh chided Davidians that they had not been so translated during the BATF attack because they were not obedient. (Suicide was not one of the options Koresh taught.)[40]

On July 30, 1992, BATF investigators visited David Koresh's gun dealer Henry McMahon to inquire about Koresh's gun purchases. McMahon called Koresh who invited agents to come out immediately and inspect the weapons. They refused but continued their obvious surveillance, something bound to make Davidians more suspicious.[41]

Kathryn Schroeder testified that Koresh had called in Davidians from all over the world to celebrate Passover of 1992. Predicting that this would be the group's last Passover before the fulfillment of prophecy in the apocalypse, Koresh decreed that they were "going to enjoy this last summer" and bought go-carts, boats, and motorcycles.[42] (It was this gathering which prompted Marc Breault to claim falsely Davidians were preparing for "mass suicide.")

Convinced that these were the "last days," Schroeder and her husband lied about their income to obtain a number of credit cards which they used to buy weapons. While they did make their monthly payments on the debt, they were convinced they would never have to pay it all because they would be "gone by 1995."[43] In

late 1992, perhaps beefing up security, Koresh moved
the gun room and his bedroom from the second story
rooms—something the BATF did not know when they
ordered agents to smash into the second floor rooms,
leading to the deaths of two agents. The guns were
moved inside the first story concrete room (also called
the "walk-in" or the "vault"), and Koresh moved into the
fourth floor room of the four-story tower.[44]

If not for the BATF's unnecessary and
unprovoked attack on the Davidians—and in the event
of no universal apocalypse—it is likely that David Koresh
would have had to change his message to adapt to the
fact that his prophesies were not fulfilled. Koresh surely
would have lost some followers and even might have
experienced a challenge to his leadership from other
Davidians.

However, BATF's attack only confirmed to
Davidians what David Koresh had been preaching all
along—the "beast" would attack the "Lamb" and God's
people and force them to defend themselves. And it
confirmed their belief that these were indeed the last
days—that they should do what they could to help
Koresh spread God's Word to the world to repent before
God made his final judgment upon humanity.

Some have said that Koresh's first prophesying
the government would come to attack him and then
collecting a lot of weapons—including allegedly illegal
ones—just "invited" a government attack; it was a "self-
fulfilling prophecy." However, this is a smokescreen.
The real crime is that the United States government
chose to deal with perceived violations of its laws with

unnecessary and excessive force at the cost of the lives of eighty-two Davidians and four federal agents.

Russian engineer Ilias Abdonlline told a *San Antonio Express-News* reporter why he had come to Waco to see the ruins of Mount Carmel: "Everyone in the world was amazed when this thing happened, but especially when it happened in America. We have a terrible history with Stalin in Russia, and I have a memory with that. When I saw this on television, I was shocked. How could it happen in the U.S.? The U.S. is a democracy."[45] What is so tragic is that in our modern society the Davidians' biblical fear of attack by "the beast" turned out to be a *realistic* fear and not some fantastic interpretation of the Bible!

SEPARATING FACT FROM FICTION

The massacre of the Branch Davidians has spawned a mass of sometimes conflicting "facts," rumors, and "conspiracy" theories. The most infamous of these are those promoted by Indianapolis attorney Linda Thompson in her videos, "Waco, The Big Lie" and "Waco, The Big Lie Continues." These allegations include that the government used a flame-throwing tank to set the fires, that the government set fire to the "underground bunker" and people died there, that a Davidian who escaped from the front roof and another who jumped from a second-story room really are government agents, that the government did not collapse the gymnasium, and that a tank pulled a body away from the building. Flaunting such untruths detracts attention from the more subtle, but more insidious, real truths.

After the Oklahoma City bombing, the national media used Thompson's most flagrant and inaccurate accusations to try to discredit *all* assertions that federal agents committed crimes against Davidians. Despite these faults, the videos do contain enough shocking footage and real truths to have mobilized hundreds of thousands of citizens to seek more information about federal crimes against the Davidians.

This book is a systematic listing and analysis of government crimes against the Branch Davidians, culminating in mass murder, and government cover-up of those crimes. I have attempted to present what, given the evidence available, seem to be the most accurate facts, the most substantive rumors, and the most believable theories. Given my limited resources, some errors inevitably have crept in to the book. This is a story which will be corrected and updated for years.

I have drawn on a variety of sources: wire services, newspaper and magazine reports, books, published reports, electronic mail articles and announcements, government documents, over fifty hours of video tapes, over twenty hours of radio and conference audio tapes, news and government photographs, and personal discussions and interviews with participants in the events and with other investigators and interested parties.

The Treasury Department's September 30, 1993, report and the Justice Department's October 8, 1993, report are little more than internal reviews conducted for public relations purposes—for in neither report were any agents or officials even interviewed under oath. Both reports "redacted," i.e., withheld, information which officials claimed might have affected the prosecution of the Davidian defendants accused of conspiracy to murder, and murder of, federal agents. Much of this redacted information was never disclosed at trial and remains hidden from the American people. These reports are sometimes the *only* sources of some important information and when there seems to be no apparent reason for the government to falsify or distort information, I have relayed it as if it were true. However, very often the government "facts" so blatantly conflict with other, more reliable facts, or with common sense, that the reports provide excellent evidence of cover-up of federal agents and officials' crimes.

The transcripts of 1993 United States Senate and House of Representatives hearings provided other useful evidence of the extent to which devious BATF and FBI agents and officials withheld, falsified, and twisted information to deceive and hoodwink relatively uncritical members of Congress. The two House sub-committees which conducted the 1995 Waco hearings had access to more information than that available in 1993. The hearings were held while this book was in production. Chapter 13 summarizes new information that only supports the interpretation of events described in this book.

Kirk Lyon's Cause Foundation, former attorney general Ramsey Clark, and Houston's Caddell & Conwell are handling most of the family and survivor civil suits against federal agents and officials. These lawsuits provide excellent indications of what attorneys consider to be evidence of criminal action. With their powers of discovery, these attorneys may be able to elicit significant evidence from the government, its agents, and officials.

Unfortunately, as the 1994 trial of eleven Davidians illustrated, the government is eager to withhold from Davidian attorneys information damaging to the BATF, the FBI, and the Treasury and Justice Departments. Important evidence like a bullet-ridden metal door, lethal bullets, video and audio tapes, and autopsy reports, were "missing," damaged, or dubious. While the trial brought out a great deal of information damaging to the government, and much exonerating Davidians, many questions could not be answered because the judge would "not allow the government to be put on trial." He therefore barred admission of important defense evidence and witnesses that might have proved government misconduct.

Of course, because the trial judge promised to throw up procedural barriers to defense attorneys calling important witnesses, the unpaid, overburdened attorneys largely ceased their efforts to bring such important witnesses to the stand.[46] And it is likely some agents lied on the stand to protect themselves and other agents. Referring to BATF supervisors' cover-up of the loss of surprise, one defense attorney said, "While leaders of the ATF, the supervisors, were telling lies to our nation, what was going on? . . . They knew their supervisors were lying, and so their statements, their comments, what they told the Rangers, at that particular time, was cemented, at the time, and it was cemented in an atmosphere, an atmosphere of lies and misrepresentations that they knew were going on, and they went right along with it."[47]

Given the mass of facts, incidents, and personalities involved—and that so much information is being covered up by federal agents and officials protecting themselves and their comrades—it is clear that only the appointment of an independent counsel with a full staff of attorneys and investigators, and full power to subpoena witnesses and grant immunity, will get close to the real truth about government crimes against the Branch Davidians. We must work to assure that the government agents and officials responsible for the massacre and its coverup are brought to justice—and that the nine living victims, the Davidian prisoners, are freed from their prison cells.

Chapter One: Why the BATF and the FBI
Massacred the Branch Davidians

1.   According to several Branch Davidians, in the last few years many in the group had come to call themselves "Students of the Seven Seals." Surviving Davidians have been identifying themselves as "Mount Carmel Survivors." However, most continue to accept the use of the term Branch Davidian. Davidian survivors hold that eighty-two in total died, including two unborn children.

2.   Stephen Labaton, "Officials Contradict One Another on Rationale for Assault on Cult," *New York Times*, April 21, 1993: A1.

3.   William Norman Grigg, "Redefining 'Law and Order'," *The New American*, April 4, 1994: 69, 71.

4.   From BATF Director Stephen Higgins' written statement to the April 28, 1993, House Judiciary Committee hearings. The transcript of this hearing was released just before publication. Because descriptions of comments and quotations come variously from news reports, video footage, and the draft transcript of the hearings, I have not footnoted most references to this hearing.

5.   National Rifle Association April 19, 1993, press release, "NRA Calls for Congressional Inquiry into Waco Raid," and James L. Pate, "No Longer Untouchable," *American Spectator*, August,1993: 35.

6.   James L. Pate, "Katona Gets His Guns," *Soldier of Fortune*, April, 1995: 58.

7.   National Rifle Association May 10, 1995, press release.

8.   Michael Hedges, "Family recounts terror at hands of ATF agents," *Washington Times*, April 13, 1995.

9.   Stephen Halbrook, private communication, September, 1994.

10.   From the *Report of the Department of the Treasury on the Bureau of Alcohol, Tobacco, and Firearms Investigation of Vernon Wayne Howell also known as David Koresh,* September, 1993, Appendix D: 7.

11.   Louis Sahagun and Doug Conner, "Pair Acquitted of Murder in Idaho Mountain Shootout," *Washington Post*, July 9, 1993.

12.   Account in Weaver standoff section drawn from Associated Press wire story, "U.S. plods on in case against 2 white separatists in Idaho," May 10, 1993; Jerry Seper, "White separatist acquitted in marshal's murder," *Washington Times*, July 9, 1993; Jerry Seper, "FBI's Idaho firefight linked to misinformation from marshals," *Washington Times*,

December 1, 1993; Gerry Spence, "First They Came for the Fascists," *Liberty*, January, 1994.

13.   FBI Legal Handbook for Special Agents, Section 3-6.4.

14.   Jerry Seper, "FBI Agents waged war on minds," *Washington Times*, September 22, 1993.

15.   Associated press wire story, "Doctored evidence slows trial," *Washington Times*, May 27, 1993; James Bovard, "No Accountability at the FBI," *Wall Street Journal*, January 10, 1995.

16.   *Washington Times*, May 27, 1993.

17.   Introduction to James R. Lewis, editor, *From the Ashes: Making Sense of Waco* (Lanham, MD: Rowman & Littlefield Publishers, Inc., 1994), xiii.

18.   Except where noted, most information for this section is taken from Clifford L. Linedecker, *Massacre at Waco, Texas* (New York: St. Martin's Press, 1993); Brad Bailey and Bob Darden, *Mad Man in Waco* (Waco, Texas: WRS Publishing, 1993); Kenneth Samples, Erwin de Castro, Richard Abanes, and Robert Lyle, *Prophets of the Apocalypse: David Koresh and Other American Messiahs* (Grand Rapids, MI: Baker Books, 1994).

19.   "Voices of Fire" audio tape, produced by Junior's Motel Records, Otho, Iowa, 1993.

20.   Justice Department report: 43.

21.   Trial transcript: 4127; Livingstone Fagan paper, "Mount Carmel: The Unseen Reality," August, 1994, Appendix A; Dana Okimoto interview, Kenneth Samples, et al.: 182–189; Livingstone Fagan, private communication, April, 1995.

22.   June 9, 1993, House Appropriations Subcommittee hearing transcript on the Treasury, Postal Service, and General Government Appropriations: 189.

23.   Michael deCourcy Hinds, "A believer says cult in Texas is peaceful," *New York Times*, March 6, 1993: A1.

24.   Livingstone Fagan paper, August, 1994: 7; Livingstone Fagan paper, "Christ," 1994.

25.   "Day 51: The True Story of Waco" video, produced by UTV, Houston, Texas.

26.   Brad Bailey and Bob Darden: 134. Unless otherwise noted, most material on or attributed to Marc Breault is from his book, *Inside the Cult,* coauthored by Martin King (New York: Signet Books, 1993).

27. "The Maury Povich Show," November 9, 1993. Povich presented two interview shows about the Branch Davidians on November 8 and 9, 1993.

28. Kenneth Samples, et al.: 72.

29. Clifford L. Linedecker: 144–147.

30. *Newsweek*, May 3, 1993: 27.

31. Trial transcript: 5600.

32. Gustav Nieguhr and Pierre Thomas, "Abuse Allegations Unproven: Koresh was Investigated in Texas, California," *Washington Post*, April 25, 1993: A20.

33. Darlene McCormick, "Agents didn't take cult arrest advice, ex-Davidians say," *Waco Tribune-Herald*, October 1, 1993.

34. Ramsey Clark civil suit (February 25, 1995).

35. Trial transcript: 4524–26, 4559–69; Marjorie Thomas' testimony, November 17–18, 1993: 96–97, 102, 130, 153, 162. (Because of her burn injuries, Thomas' testimony was videotaped in advance of the trial.)

36. Trial transcript: 4518–20.

37. Ibid., 4520, 6392.

38. Ibid., 6368.

39. Treasury Department report, Appendix D: 3; David Aguilera April 18, 1993 affidavit in support of search warrant.

40. Trial transcript: 4479, 4558, 6381.

41. James L. Pate, "Waco: Behind the Cover-Up," *Soldier of Fortune*, November, 1993: 36–41, 71–72.

42. Trial transcript: 4531.

43. Ibid., 4532–34.

44. Ibid., 4472, 4492, 4599.

45. Egon Richard Tausch, court observer article, "The Branch Davidian Trial," 1994.

46. January 6, 1994, trial transcript: 63–67; trial transcript: 5652–53.

47. Trial transcript: 7093–95.

2
The BATF's
Flawed Investigation

Now, we're willing, and we've been willing, all this time, to sit down with anybody. You've sent law enforcement out here before . . . . And I've laid it straight across the table. I said, if you want to know about me, sit down with me and I'll open up a book and show you Seven Seals.

David Koresh, February 28, 1993, on 911 tape

In May of 1992 United Parcel Service (UPS) informed the McLennan County Sheriff's Department that the Branch Davidians were receiving "suspicious" deliveries, including shipments of firearms worth more than $10,000, inert grenade casings, and a substantial quantity of black powder. It is important to understand that a vicious paramilitary raid was conducted on a house filled with women and children *despite* the facts that Davidians ran a legal business, the BATF found no evidence of illegally purchased weapons, and the "probable cause" to obtain a search warrant was based on biased, stale, inaccurate, and misleading information. Moreover, the evidence that illegal guns *were* found remains suspect.

CHRONOLOGY OF INVESTIGATION AND RAID PLANNING

This 1992 chronology is largely drawn from the Treasury Department report's Appendix D or from sources referenced in the following pages.

June—The BATF assigned Special Agent Davy Aguilera to investigate. Assistant U.S. Attorney Bill Johnston, who had shown little interest in former members' complaints in 1990, encouraged Aguilera. Lieutenant Gene Barber provided Aguilera with what the Treasury report calls "a detailed account of Koresh's alleged attempt to kill George Roden."[1]

June–August —Aguilera investigated companies which had sold weapons to David Koresh and discovered the Davidians had purchased almost forty-three thousand dollars' worth of weapons from March 26 to August 12, 1992, after which such purchases virtually ceased.

July—Davidians visited sheriff's office to confirm that their "hell fire" triggers were legal.

July 30—Aguilera and agent Skinner inspected Henry McMahon's records and rejected David Koresh's offer by telephone to show him his guns.

August 8 —Skinner returned to McMahon's and received full documentation prepared by Koresh for the BATF of his weapon purchases.

September–October —Aguilera was assigned to U.S. Secret Service "protective details at three-week intervals," and the case was temporarily dropped.

October—Waco Tribune-Herald reporter contacted Assistant U.S. Attorney Bill Johnston about the paper's planned exposé of the Branch Davidians' alleged child abuse and arms build-up. Aguilera's supervisor Earl Dunagan told him to start work on an affidavit for search and arrest warrants.

November—"60 Minutes" television show contacted BATF about a planned exposé of the agency. BATF officials in Washington demanded more intelligence on Davidians.

November 3 —Aguilera interviewed former members in California who had no information about guns.

November 20 —Assistant U.S. Attorney Bill Johnston held that "there already was sufficient evidence of illegal activity to meet the threshold of probable cause for a search warrant ... and tactical planning for an enforcement operation began in earnest."[2]

December 4 —At first major meeting in Houston, raid commanders discussed logistics and media interest in Davidians. Special Agents Phillip Chojnacki, Chuck Sarabyn, and Ted Royster were given top roles in planning and execution.

December 11 —BATF agent met with Texas National Guard about assistance. Guard went on to overfly Mount Carmel and took photos twice in January, 1993.

December 24 —Meeting in Washington where BATF Associate Director of Enforcement Daniel Hartnett and Deputy Director Edward Conroy demanded that more probable cause be developed and tactical plans slowed down. BATF Director Stephen Higgins told the House Judiciary

Committee on April 28, 1993, that, as of that date: "We had a review here at headquarters' office in December with respect to whether we had probable cause. We decided at that point that we did not, and we continued to gather information," i.e., they started interviewing disgruntled former members in earnest.

January 7–9 —Buford and Aguilera interviewed former members Jeannine, Robyn, and Debbie Bunds, Marc Breault, and others in Los Angeles.

January 11 —Undercover house across from Mount Carmel was opened. Davidians immediately visited it, suspecting those inside were government agents.

January 25 —Buford and Aguilera interviewed former member David Block.

January 27–29 —At meeting in Houston raid planners decided to do paramilitary raid instead of siege.

January 27 —BATF agent posing as a UPS trainee visited Mount Carmel. Koresh complained to sheriff's office about obvious surveillance.

January 28 —Undercover agent Robert Rodriguez made first of several visits to Mount Carmel Center.

February 12 —BATF Director Higgins was first fully briefed on the plan.

February 22 —Aguilera and Dunagan briefed McLennan County sheriff's office about raid support requests. Young Kiri Jewell was interviewed by the District Attorney. *Waco Tribune-Herald* reporter Mark England called David Koresh with questions about "The Sinful Messiah" series.

February 24 —Raid planners learned *Waco Tribune-Herald* would begin running their "Sinful Messiah" series on February 27. BATF rescheduled the raid from Monday,

March 1 to Sunday, February 28. Set up for training of BATF agents began at Fort Hood military base.

February 25 —BATF agents began training at Fort Hood. Aguilera, with the assistance of Assistant U.S. Attorneys Bill Johnston and John Phinizy, produced a "Probable Cause Affidavit in Support of Search Warrant." Magistrate Judge Dennis S. Green signed a search warrant for illegal weapons and explosives for Mount Carmel and the "Mag Bag" garage and an arrest warrant for David Koresh for possession of an unregistered destructive device.[3]

February 26 —The BATF informed Treasury Department officials of the raid plan and officials canceled it. BATF Director Higgins convinced officials that because of the *Waco Tribune-Herald* series on the Branch Davidians, February 28 might be the last opportunity to, as one put it, "catch the cult members unprepared and away from their stockpile of heavy weaponry."[4] Higgins told officials that raid planners had *assured* him that the raid would be called off if the element of surprise was lost. Treasury officials approved the raid.

February 27 —The *Waco Tribune-Herald* published first installment of "The Sinful Messiah" series. BATF agents finished training at Fort Hood and moved into Waco.

Sunday, February 28 —Television cameraman unknowingly informed Davidian about expected "shootout" and Koresh told undercover agent Rodriguez that he knew government agents were "coming." Rodriguez told superiors that Koresh was forewarned, but raid commanders proceeded with raid.

TABLE 2.1
TREASURY DEPARTMENT and BATF
CHAINS OF COMMAND
February 28, 1993

TREASURY DEPARTMENT

Lloyd Bentsen - Secretary of the Treasury
John P. Simpson - Acting Assistant Secretary
Roger Altman - Deputy Treasury Secretary
Ronald K. Noble - unconfirmed Assistant Secretary of the
          Treasury for Enforcement (acting as a consultant)

BUREAU OF ALCOHOL, TOBACCO AND FIREARMS

Stephen Higgins - Director
Daniel Hartnett - Associate Director of Enforcement
Edward Conroy - Deputy Associate Director of Enforcement
David Troy - Chief of Intelligence Division

"NATIONAL RESPONSE PLAN" ASSIGNMENTS FOR "WACO OPERATION"

SAC Phillip Chojnacki - Incident Commander
ASAC Chuck Sarabyn - Tactical Coordinator
SAC Pete Mastin - Deputy Incident Commander
ASAC Jim Cavanaugh - Deputy Tactical Coordinator
SA Sharon Wheeler - Public Information Officer
RAC Bill Buford - Special Response Team 1 leader
SAC Curtis Williams - Special Response Team 2 leader
SAC Gerald Petrilli - Special Response Team 3 leader
SAC Ted Royster - planner, untitled raid coordinator
SA Earl Dunagan - investigator
SA Davy Aguilera - investigator
SA Robert Rodriguez - undercover agent
SAC—Special Agent-in-Charge
          ASAC—Assistant Special Agent-in-Charge
          RAC—Resident Agent-in-Charge
          SA—Special Agent

BATF BYPASSED LOCAL AUTHORITIES

The BATF had little contact with local authorities. Davidian Clive Doyle described Koresh's dealings with local sheriffs: "David always welcomed people in. He had given the invitation to sheriff's deputies to call or come out if they had any questions about anything. A Texas Ranger had come out there. He was welcomed. Deputies came out on a social basis . . . to fish, trade guns or car parts, talk about cars or guns. They would drive by and wave, very friendly."[5]

In fact, it is likely BATF investigators and planners considered the McLennan County Sheriff's Department to be *too* friendly to Koresh. Texas Department of Social Services social worker Joyce Sparks has charged that the Sheriff's Department sabotaged the child-abuse investigation by warning David Koresh she was coming and dissuading her from staying too long. In response, Sheriff Jack Harwell told reporters, "I won't go on someone's property without legal reason to be there. I have to comply with the law. Just go out and talk to them, what's wrong with notifying them?"

The BATF was concerned about alleged leaks when they wanted to question young Kiri Jewell about Koresh's alleged abuse of her in February, 1993. So much so, they first had her flown to Austin and then drove her to Waco to bypass the Sheriff's Department completely.[6]

During a congressional hearing it was revealed that one McLennan County Sheriff's lieutenant, evidently Gene Barber, was assigned full-time to BATF planners.[7] However, I found no evidence that BATF agents consulted anyone else in the department. BATF's ignoring the McLennan County Sheriff's Department seems to be merely one more symbol of federal law enforcement arrogance.

BATF INFLUENCED BY "CULT BUSTERS"

The Cult Awareness Network (CAN) actively urges the press and law enforcement to act against any non-mainstream religious, psychological, or even political movement which it describes as a "cult." These have included groups as diverse as Catholic monasteries, yoga, and karate classes. CAN accuses such groups of sharing similar patterns of mind control, group domination, exploitation and physical and mental abuse.[8] CAN's many critics say "cults" should more properly be called "new religious movements." And they point out that so-called mind control techniques are little different from the education and socialization techniques used by all schools, churches, ideologies, and philosophies.

CAN's former executive director Cynthia Kisser admitted to one reporter that her group would have investigated Jesus Christ Himself. "If he were alive now, we'd take an interest in him because of the great controversy surrounding his fringe activities. We'd ask him for the same information we seek from cults today—financial data, information on his practices, and so on. We'd try to see if there was abuse, unethical behavior, or deceptive practices. And I'd send whatever we could find to reporters."[9]

CAN critic Dr. Gordon Melton charges CAN and its associates have found two successful methods of disrupting groups: first, *false* anonymous charges of child abuse and, second, kidnapping and "deprogramming" members. Because anonymous reports of child abuse are legal under current law, they are a perfect way for a group with its own agenda to disrupt other groups. The Children of God, known in the United States as "The Family," claims CAN members have made many such false accusations, resulting in dozens of arrests—with all charges quickly dropped. They have demanded a congressional investigation of CAN. Deprogramming often involves kidnapping, imprisonment of, and mental—and even physical—abuse of the individual targeted for deprogramming.[10] These deceptive and even violent tactics have given anti-cult activists the reputation of being "cult busters."

CAN's best known deprogrammer, Rick Ross, who once was convicted for involvement in a jewel thievery scam, has boasted of more than two hundred "deprogrammings." Cynthia Kisser has praised him as being "among the half dozen best deprogrammers in the country." In the summer of 1993, Rick Ross was indicted in Washington state for unlawful imprisonment. However, a jury acquitted him in January, 1994, because he testified he had been hired only to deprogram the victim, not to kidnap him. The defense worked the "dangerous cult" angle and called the victim's church, which has 3,600 member churches across the nation, a "cult."[11]

In the summer of 1992, Rick Ross "deprogrammed" former Davidian David Block in the California home of CAN national spokesperson Priscilla Coates. Block had lived at Mount Carmel only three months.[12] Block later gave questionable and damaging evidence to the BATF.

Ross also appeared on the March 10, 1993, "Donahue Show" with David Jewell and his daughter Kiri. Jewell was influenced by amateur cult buster Marc Breault, who first contacted him about Koresh's allegedly evil intentions toward Kiri. They stayed in touch by phone and e-mail. Jewell also seemed devoted to dismantling the Branch Davidian religious group.[13]

Ross provided negative information to the *Waco Tribune-Herald* for its sensationalized February, 1993, "The

Sinful Messiah" series on the Branch Davidians. The paper quotes Ross declaring, "The group is without a doubt, without any doubt whatsoever, a highly destructive, manipulative cult . . . I would liken the group to Jim Jones." The authors write, "Ross said he believes Howell [Koresh] is prone to violence. . . . Speaking out and exposing Howell might bring in the authorities or in some way help those 'being held in that compound through a kind of psychological, emotional slavery and servitude.' "[14]

Rick Ross contends he was in close contact with the BATF before the raid and with the FBI during the siege. Ross bragged on the "Up to the Minute" public television program that he "consulted with ATF agents on the Waco sect and told them about the guns in the compound." On April 19 he told the NBC "Today Show," "I was a consultant offering ideas, input that was filtered by their team and used when they felt it was appropriate."[15]

Nancy Ammerman, a Visiting Scholar at Princeton University's Center for the Study of American Religion, was one of the "outside experts" assigned by the Justice Department to evaluate the BATF's and FBI's actions in Waco. After seeing additional BATF and FBI materials, Ammerman wrote: "The interview transcripts document that Mr. Rick Ross was, in fact, closely involved with both the ATF and the FBI. . . . He clearly had the most extensive access to both agencies of any person on the 'cult expert' list, and he was apparently listened to more attentively."[16]

BATF IGNORED DAVIDIANS'
LEGAL GUN BUSINESS

Davidians had a profitable legal gun business. Davidian Paul Fatta was a regular at Texas gun shows, selling everything from camouflage clothing to military-type ready-to-eat meals, gun grips, and weapons. The Davidians also sewed "David Koresh" brand custom-made magazine vests for sportsmen, shooters, and lawmen and sold them at gun shows. Among the products they marketed were souvenir plaques made of hand grenade casings mounted on wood. Even Marc Breault mentions that of the Davidian businesses, the "most important of all" was trade in weapons.[17]

The widespread rumor that David Koresh, Paul Fatta, or other Davidians had a gun dealer's license is not accurate. Davidians were working with gun dealer Henry McMahon who did have one. His Class III dealer's license allowed him to legally own, sell, and buy any type of weapon. No Davidian held this license. In late April, 1993, McMahon told the Pensacola television show "Lawline" that Koresh had purchased a large number of legal military-style semi-automatics as an investment, assuming that their value would increase if the government restricted their manufacture in the future. McMahon said that most of these guns were kept boxed and never fired to enhance resale value.[18]

At trial, Paul Fatta's attorney Mike DeGeurin (brother of Dick DeGuerin who spells his name differently) told the jury: "Koresh and Fatta saw that a tremendous investment could be made by buying these guns (semiautomatic rifles). They thought the guns may be outlawed in Washington and that they would triple or quadruple in price."[19] (President Bush's ban on the importation of semiautomatics in 1989 already had increased their value.) Between 1992 and 1994 the value of AK-47s had doubled from $150 to $300 and AR-15s from $500 to up to $1,400.[20]

BATF investigator Davy Aguilera's February 25, 1993, affidavit for search and arrest warrants mentions that Koresh attended gun shows with "Henry McMahon who is a federally licensed firearms dealer," despite Aguilera's visit with McMahon, described below. Nevertheless, Aguilera was unable to discover—or refused to acknowledge his knowledge—that Davidians had a legal weapons business.

KORESH INVITED BATF AGENTS TO INSPECT WEAPONS IN 1992

On July 30, 1992, BATF investigators Davy Aguilera and Jim Skinner visited Henry McMahon to inquire about Koresh's gun purchases. Because the agents were asking McMahon a lot of questions about David Koresh, he immediately called Koresh to inform him.

According to a 1993 statement to writer James Pate by McMahon, "[Koresh] said, 'If there's a problem, tell them to come out here. If they want to see my guns, they're more than welcome.' So I walked back in the room, holding the cordless phone and said, 'I've got [Koresh] on the phone. If you'd like to go out there and see those guns, you're more than welcome to.' They looked at each other and Aguilera got real paranoid, shaking his head and whispering, 'No, no!' And so I went back to the phone and told David they wouldn't be coming out."[21]

Despite the emotional objections of prosecutors, at trial Judge Walter J. Smith allowed McMahon's business partner and woman friend Karen Kilpatrick, who witnessed this incident, to describe it. When Kilpatrick waved her hands and shook her head, as had Aguilera, the entire courtroom burst into laughter, annoying and embarrassing the prosecutors.[22] The prejudiced judge agreed to the prosecutor's demand that Henry McMahon not be allowed to take the stand as a defense witness. Instead jurors heard a brief statement stipulated (approved) by prosecutors and read by a defense attorney.[23]

After Koresh's attorney Dick DeGuerin mentioned the incident during a media panel in September, 1993, reporters from two Houston papers contacted Jack Killorin, chief of the BATF's Public Affairs. He told one reporter he was not surprised that a federal agent rejected an offer to inspect weapons. "The preferred method by the law is going with the standard of getting a warrant before entering a home. We execute such warrants."[24] He told the other reporter, "Koresh's learning of the investigation in July, 1992, had no effect on the raid or the resulting standoff between agents and cult members."[25]

During the July 30 visit agents Aguilera and Skinner noticed that McMahon did not have complete paperwork on all of Koresh's purchases. Skinner returned on August 8 and collected documentation which Koresh had faxed to McMahon covering the purchase of lower receivers for AR-15 rifles, and other handguns and rifles.[26]

Davidian David Thibodeau asserts Koresh also tried to reassure BATF undercover agent Robert Rodriquez (who was working under the assumed name "Gonzales") about the Davidians' willingness to cooperate, telling him, "If there are any problems, I've invited the sheriff's department in here a number of times. If they have any questions they can knock on the door and work with me."[27]

BATF FOUND NO EVIDENCE WEAPONS WERE PURCHASED ILLEGALLY

Davy Aguilera's investigation of shipments from various arms vendors to the Mag Bag and of gun dealer Henry McMahon's records indicated that during 1992 the Branch Davidians acquired the following firearms and related explosive paraphernalia: 104 AR-15/M-16, upper-receiver groups with barrels; 8,100 rounds of nine-millimeter and .223 caliber ammunition for AR-15/M-16; 20 one-hundred-round capacity drum magazines for AK-47 rifles; 260 M-16/AR-15, magazines; 30 M-14 magazines; two M-16 EZ kits; two M-16 car kits; one M-76 grenade launcher; 200 M-31 practice rifle grenades; four M-16 parts set kits "A"; two flare launchers; two cases (approximately fifty) inert practice hand grenades; forty to fifty pounds of black gun powder; thirty pounds of potassium nitrate; five pounds of magnesium metal powder; one pound of igniter cord (a class C explosive); 91 AR-15 lower-receiver units; twenty-six various calibers and brands of hand guns and long guns; ninety pounds of aluminum metal powder; thirty to forty cardboard tubes. The amount of expenditures for the above listed firearm paraphernalia, excluding the 91 AR-15 lower receiver units and the 26 complete firearms, was in excess of $44,300.

All these guns, gun parts, powders, inert grenades, and other equipment were lawfully purchased and could be legally owned at that time. None per se established probable cause that Koresh had violated or was about to violate federal laws. As has been noted, the seemingly large amounts are not illegal either according to the Firearms Owners' Protection Act of 1986 and the Supreme Court decision *United States vs. Anders*, nor are they unusual for someone dealing in weapons or holding them as an investment.

At trial, prosecutors could not call even one gun dealer who could provide evidence of illegal purchases of guns. One asserted that Koresh, Fatta, and McMahon's paying thousands of dollars in cash for guns was not unusual among gun buyers.[28]

Aguilera did *not* investigate the one dealer he believed might have sold Koresh illegal arms. In the affidavit he states, "because of the sensitivity of the investigation" he did not contact "vendors with questionable trade practices" who had sold to Koresh, including one merely *suspected* of "unlawful possession of machine guns, silencers, destructive devices, and machine gun conversion kits." (The vendor was Shooters Equipment Company in Greenville, South Carolina, whose owner the BATF prosecuted unsuccessfully after the failed February raid. The judge threw out the case because the parts the man was selling all came from hardware stores.)[29] In effect, Aguilera refused to check to see if Koresh had bought illegal items from this source and instead *inferred* that he had and used this as the basis for probable cause.

Aguilera suspected the Davidians were breaking laws regarding machine guns—otherwise known as automatic weapons—which shoot two or more bullets per pull of the trigger, and laws regarding explosive devices. It is only legal to own a machine gun—or machine gun conversion kit—manufactured *before* May 19, 1986. Both must be registered and one must also pay a $200 transfer tax upon buying the machine gun. Uncertainty arises because the conversion kits can be used to turn semiautomatic guns into automatic machine guns. According to former BATF official turned BATF critic Robert Sanders, this area remains so unclear that, "There are no published rulings telling you what is and what isn't [a violation]."[30]

As of December, 1992, Aguilera's only evidence that the Davidians were committing any such crimes was that they had bought a number of legal weapons and legal gun parts which, with the help of a few parts they had not purchased, can be converted into machine guns. However, the BATF's suspicions remained pure conjecture.

It also was legal at the time to own all the destructive device-related items Aguilera listed—the grenade launcher, M-31 practice rifle grenades, inert practice hand grenades, black gun powder, potassium nitrate, magnesium metal powder, aluminum powder, and igniter cord. What would not be legal is to manufacture these materials into grenades, pipe bombs, or other destructive devices without proper registration. Aguilera asserted in his affidavit that BATF explosives expert Jerry A. Taylor had concluded that these materials could be used to manufacture such devices.

However, according to Paul H. Blackman, Ph.D.: "the assertion that possession of the black powder and inert grenades constitutes an explosive grenade because it is possible to make one is misleading. Not only are more materials needed, along with the machinery to drill and plug a hole, but without intent, there is no violation of the law." Blackman asserts the Davidians were using the explosive materials for construction projects and for refilling ammunition, both legal uses.[31] It was because of this lack of probable cause based on Davidian purchases that in December BATF officials instructed Aguilera to gather information about Koresh's intent and to set up an undercover house and infiltrate Mount Carmel Center.

PROBABLE CAUSE WAS BASED ON BIASED INFORMATION ABOUT INTENT

The credibility and reliability of witnesses in an affidavit is very important. Yet all Aguilera's witnesses as to David Koresh's intent had some credibility problems. Neighbor Robert L. Cervenka, who alleged to Aguilera he actually had *heard* machine-gun fire on the property, had been involved in a property dispute with the Davidians.[32] All other evidence on intent came from disaffected former Davidians influenced by cult busters Rick Ross and Marc Breault.

The BATF Discounted Davidians' Personal Reasons for Owning Guns

The Davidians originally began stockpiling weapons out of fear of George Roden who had driven them off the property with guns, who had been in a firefight with them over the property, and who had vowed revenge. Even after Roden murdered a man and was incarcerated in a mental institution, the Davidians worried he would escape and attack them.

On February 28, 1993, Koresh told KRLD interviewers: "The weapons were bought originally because

in the prophecies. . . . 2000 years ago Christ tried for three
and a half years to present the gospel, right? And the night of
His crucifixion He told His servants, He said, before I sent
you out without cloak nor purse nor sword. So now I say unto
you, if you do not have a sword go sell your cloak and buy
one. The Christian Church was not to stand idly by and be
slaughtered."[33] Nevertheless, Koresh also told CNN
interviewers, "I never planned to use these weapons. The
only problem is that people outside don't understand what
we believe." In fact, the Davidians' whole weapons stockpile
equaled less than three guns per resident, compared to the
Texas average of four per resident.[34]

Cult Buster Rick Ross Provided Information

Aguilera began contacting former members in
November, 1992. He obtained their names from the 1990
affidavits Breault left with the McLennan County Sheriff's
Department and from Rick Ross. Justice Department outside
expert Nancy Ammerman, who had access to relevant BATF
and FBI files, wrote, "The ATF interviewed the persons [Ross]
directed to them and evidently used information from those
interviews in planning their February 28 raid."[35]

Evidence that Rick Ross had a financial motivation
for inciting the BATF against the Davidians is contained in
Marc Breault's January 16, 1993, diary entry where he
describes a conversation with Davidian Steve Schneider's
sister. "Rick [Ross] told Sue that something was about to
happen real soon. He urged her to hire him to deprogram
Steve. Rick has Sue all scared now. The Schneider family
doesn't know what to do. Rick didn't tell them what was about

to happen, but he said they should get Steve out as soon as possible. I know that Rick has talked to the ATF."[36] It is unknown how many other families Ross contacted offering his expensive services "before it's too late."

Former Members' Allegations About Koresh's Intent

Marc Breault, David Block, Poia Vaega, and Jeannine, Robyn, and Debbie Sue Bunds provided Aguilera with the following evidence of intent about illegal machine guns, contained in his affidavit. Robyn Bunds said she found what David Bunds called a "machine-gun conversion kit" in their LaVerne home in 1991, but Aguilera did not interview David himself. Jeannine and Debbie Sue Bunds said they saw a Davidian shooting a gun that must have been a machine gun because it shot so fast. Debbie Sue said she heard Koresh say he wished he owned a machine gun (some machine guns are legal). Poia Vaega said that Koresh had passed an "AK-47 machine gun" around at a meeting (AK-47s also come in legal, semiautomatic versions). Marc Breault said Koresh told him how easy it was to convert a gun to a machine gun. David Block told Aguilera that Donald Bunds, a mechanical engineer who remained with the group after his family left it, operated a metal lathe and milling machine that had the capability to fabricate firearm parts and that he had observed Bunds designing a machine gun on a computer.

Jeannine Bunds, Breault, and Block provided Aguilera with the following evidence of intent to produce illegal explosives. Jeannine Bunds said she had seen one "grenade," but admitted she did not know if it contained explosive materials. Marc Breault said that sometime before 1989

Koresh said he wanted to "obtain and/or manufacture" grenades. David Block said he had heard Koresh ask if anyone "had any knowledge about making hand grenades" and another time he "heard discussion about a shipment of inert hand grenades and Howell's intent to reactivate them." Both Breault and Block asserted that Koresh had expressed interest in the (legally available) *Anarchist Cookbook* which explains how to make explosives.

While such allegations might be credible in most witnesses, they must be regarded skeptically when coming from individuals involved with professional or amateur cult busters. The Treasury report itself notes, "the planners failed to consider how Block's prior relations with Koresh, and his decision to break away from the Branch Davidians at the Compound, might have affected the reliability of his statements. Although the planners knew Block had met with a self-described 'deprogrammer,' Rick Ross, they never had any substantive discussions with him concerning Block's objectivity about and perspective of Koresh and his followers."[37]

PROBABLE CAUSE BASED ON RELIGIOUS AND POLITICAL BELIEFS

In his February 25 affidavit, Aguilera includes secondhand information—from social worker Joyce Sparks to special agent Carlos Torres to himself. "During [Sparks] conversation with Koresh, he told her that he was the 'Messenger' from God, that the world was coming to an end, and that when he 'reveals' himself, the riots in Los Angeles would pale in comparison to what was going to happen in

Waco, Texas. Koresh declared that it would be a 'military type operation' and that all the 'non-believers' would have to suffer." It is possible Sparks misinterpreted Koresh's biblically prophetic statements, statements protected by the First Amendment.

The affidavit also used other statements fully protected under the First Amendment freedom of speech provision as evidence of criminal intent. "David Koresh stated that the Bible gave him the right to bear arms. . . . David Koresh then advised Special Agent Rodriguez that he had something he wanted Special Agent Rodriguez to see. At that point he showed Special Agent Rodriguez a video tape on ATF which was made by the Gun Owners Association (G.O.A.). This film portrayed ATF as an agency who violated the rights of Gun Owners by threats and lies." This was actually the Gun Owners Foundation videotape "Breaking the Law in the Name of the Law: The BATF Story." The video presents interviews with several individuals, including police officers, who charged BATF agents lied to get a search warrant or fabricated evidence to get a conviction.

A later March 9, 1993 affidavit signed by BATF agent Earl Dunagan actually listed as objects for which BATF wanted to search audio and video tapes which criticized "firearms law enforcement and particularly the Bureau of Alcohol, Tobacco and Firearms." The BATF wanted to present these as "evidence of Howell's or other cult members' motive for wanting to shoot and kill ATF agents." During the trial Judge Smith would not allow Robert Rodriguez to testify about Koresh's criticism of BATF,[38] but he did allow Kathryn Schroeder to testify that Koresh had shown members the anti-BATF video.[39]

The affidavit also asserted members watched "extremely violent movies of the Vietnam War which Howell would refer to as training films." However, the movies alluded to were popular Hollywood films *Hamburger Hill, Platoon,* and *Full Metal Jacket.*[40]

OTHER IRREGULARITIES IN THE FEBRUARY 25, 1993, AFFIDAVIT

Davy Aguilera's February 25, 1993, affidavit contains stale, inaccurate, and misleading information and presents an "indefensible" probable cause theory. Considering the sloppiness of Aguilera's February 25, 1993, affidavit, it is not surprising that the Treasury report does not bother to include a copy as one of its several appendixes or that the judge would not allow jurors in the Davidian trial to see it.

Stale Information

All Aguilera's supporting information regarding the purchase of possibly suspicious weapons was more than eight months old. According to David Koresh's attorney Dick DeGuerin, the February 25 affidavit contained "stale information" under the 1932 Supreme Court case *Sgro v. United States* which holds: "the magistrate [has to] conclude that what they are searching for is there now, not that it was there at some time in the past."[41] Similarly, *United States v. Ruff,* 984, F.2d 635 [5th Cir., 1993] holds that evidence must be fresh.[42] Most former members' allegations that they had heard Koresh discuss machine guns or seen Koresh use alleged machine guns came from 1989 and 1991. David Block's allegations that he had heard Koresh discuss a desire to make machine guns and grenades were also more than six months old.

Inaccurate Information

Aguilera's affidavit contained glaring errors of fact that attest to the shoddy nature of the supporting information. Despite Aguilera's swearing to be familiar with federal firearms and explosives laws, he confused the legal definition of "destructive devices" and "firearms." He called E-2 Kits, "E-Z kits" and did not mention that they are legal gun parts kits, not machine-gun conversion kits. He claimed that the AK-47 has an upper and lower receiver, when in fact it has a one-piece receiver.[43] And he claimed the legal .50-caliber rifle Block describes is probably an illegal .52-caliber Boys rifle, though Paul H. Blackman believes it is unlikely such a gun even exists.[44] Aguilera alleged that Koresh was in violation of 26 U.S.C. section 5845(f) regarding destructive devices. However, this code only defines destructive devices; section 5861 actually makes it illegal.[45]

None of the former Davidians who claimed they had seen or heard machine guns were knowledgeable about firearms, nor did Aguilera swear that they were. All identified the guns from pictures and from the fact that they fired more rapidly than normal shotguns. And none seemed to be aware the Davidians owned legal "hellfire" devices that allow more rapid fire but are not automatic. (At trial FBI weapons expert James Cadigan claimed that investigators found no hellfire device among the burned ruins of Mount Carmel.[46] However, these small, spring-like devices easily would have been destroyed by fire.)

Two non-weapons factual errors are of note. The affidavit states a former member "observed at the compound published magazines such as, the 'Shotgun News' and other related clandestine magazines." However, *Shotgun News* is a popular, widely circulated publication with a distribution of 150,000.[47] Also, the affidavit *repeats* Joyce Sparks' inaccurate statement that Koresh made comments about the Los Angeles riots on a date three weeks *before* the riots began. The Treasury report claims that, despite this error, Sparks' records show she did visit Koresh at Mount Carmel the day after the beginning of the riots.[48]

Reporter James Pate asserts that BATF agent Davy Aguilera lied in his affidavit when he alleged that McMahon had referred to Koresh as "my preacher" and when he alleged McMahon tried to hide from him the fact that Howell and Koresh were the same person. McMahon asserts he informed Aguilera truthfully that Koresh was *a* preacher, not *his* preacher. And McMahon asserted he wrote in parentheses after Howell's name on the BATF yellow forms "AKA David Koresh." Pate asserts that Aguilera lied.[49]

Misleading Information

In 1978 the Supreme Court held in *Franks vs. Delaware* that a search warrant is *invalid* if the agent has misled or lied to the magistrate in order to get it. Aguilera's February 25 affidavit contains a number of misrepresentations. It describes child-abuse allegations and the Texas Department of Protection and Regulatory Services investigation, but it does not mention that the case was closed on April 30, 1992, with no evidence of child abuse. Similarly, the affidavit states that a relative of an ex-member alleges "a false imprisonment for a term of three and one half (3 $1/2$) months," but it does not mention that the FBI opened a (probably related) case for "involuntary servitude" in April, 1992, and closed it for lack of evidence in June, 1992.[50]

The affidavit states that Davidian neighbor Robert L. Cervenka reported what sounded like machine-gun fire in February, but it does not mention that the Davidians discussed this allegation with a McLennan County sheriff who assured them the "hellfire" devices they were using were legal. It states that a deputy sheriff heard a large explosion and saw smoke at Mount Carmel on November 6, 1992, but it does not mention that the sheriff didn't consider it important enough to investigate—or that the Davidians were excavating for a large underground tornado shelter at the time.

The affidavit states that Immigration and Naturalization Service records showed most foreign nationals had overstayed their entry permits or visas and that "it is a violation of Title 18, United States Code, Section 922 for an illegal alien to receive a firearm"; it does not provide evidence that any illegal alien was using a firearm. The affidavit states, "Howell forced members to stand guard at the commune twenty-four hours a day with loaded weapons," but it does not mention that in four weeks of observation from the undercover house, agents saw no such armed guards.[51]

The affidavit describes Marc Breault's statements: "While there he participated in physical training and firearm shooting exercises conducted by Howell. He stood guard armed with a loaded weapon." Aguilera and Bill Buford met Breault in person in January, 1993, but they did not note an obvious fact about Breault: he is legally blind, having no vision in one eye, and very little in the other. Therefore it is unlikely that he could have done much in the way of firearms shooting or armed guard duty! Moreover, according to *Waco Tribune-Herald* reporters, "Breault, with his poor vision, was exempt from guard duty."[52] If Breault told the truth to reporters, we must wonder if he lied to BATF agents—or if they simply included these useful "facts" about Breault's activities despite what Breault told them.

According to the Treasury report, BATF experts told Aguilera that Koresh's gunpowder and igniter cord "were themselves explosives requiring proper registration and storage—neither of which Koresh provided."[53] However, Paul H. Blackman writes that since there was no attempt to contact Koresh to ask him what kind of storage he was providing, BATF did not know whether or not it was being legally stored. Moreover, the amount of gunpowder Koresh had was expressly exempt from the law, and no registration is required for igniter cord (U.S. Code, Title 18, §841 et.seq.; Title 26, §5845(f).[54]

Indefensible Probable Cause Theory

Aguilera's February 25 affidavit includes several serious allegations which are not under BATF's authority to investigate: child abuse, involuntary servitude, illegal drugs, and tax evasion. The Treasury report defends Aguilera's presenting this inflammatory material to the magistrate. "While reports that Koresh was permitted to sexually and physically abuse children were not evidence that firearms or explosives violations were occurring, they showed Koresh to have set up a world of his own, where legal prohibitions were disregarded freely."[55] Paul H. Blackman writes, "Such a theory would allow law enforcement agencies to allow any allegations of any serious criminal activity to help to establish probable cause that all other criminal activities were also being engaged in. In law, the theory is currently indefensible."[56]

During the trial defense attorney Mike DeGeurin told attorneys that alleged illegal weapons found after the fire did not justify illegal search warrants. "There's a lot of case law which says that no search can be justified by what it turns up." However, attorneys realized and admitted near the end of trial that in their desperate attempts to try to get information about the BATF's flawed planning introduced into evidence, they had overlooked raising the issue of whether the warrants were legal.[57]

DID DAVIDIANS HAVE ILLEGAL WEAPONS?

It must be remembered that if the Branch Davidians had collected several dozen legal machine guns—manufactured before 1986, on which they had paid the $200 tax—they would have been in the class of machine-gun owners protected by law. Similarly, Americans may possess properly registered silencers and grenades. Of course, that protection does not stop the BATF from violently invading gun owners' homes and confiscating their legal weapons. Because federal law draws arbitrary distinctions between one class of legal gun owners and another class of "outlaw" owners, the federal government has been able to excuse its massacre of eighty-two Davidians by braying, "They had illegal weapons!"

Except for prosecution witness Kathryn Schroeder, surviving Davidians deny they had or knew anything about illegal automatic weapons or machine guns. During allocution before sentencing Kevin Whitecliff asserted, "I've never owned an automatic weapon. I've never fired an automatic weapon. I don't even know what an automatic weapon consists of." Paul Fatta, who ran the Davidians weapons business, denies any knowledge that Davidians converted or manufactured illegal weapons. Even prosecutors admitted there were places like the machine shop and gun rooms that were off limits to most Davidians.[58]

At trial prosecutors presented seemingly convincing physical evidence and witness testimony that after the fire federal agents found unregistered and therefore illegal machine guns, silencers and grenades in the ruins of Mount Carmel. However, many suspect that the BATF, with the help of the FBI, is up to its old tricks of fabricating illegal weapons.

David Koresh told his attorney Dick DeGuerin in a tape recorded March 28, 1993, conversation, "Once we leave the premises here and they come in, I'm just so concerned they are going to twist everything up so much. They're going to—nothing being illegal in here—they're going to put something illegal in here."[59] Many believe Koresh's fears were realized.

Davidians' Legal Weapons

At trial prosecutors tried to overwhelm the jury with the numbers of weapons found in the ruins of Mount Carmel—294 in all, most of them legal. They presented boxes of legal M-16, AK-47, and AR-15 semiautomatic rifles, two .50-caliber rifles, semiautomatic pistols, revolvers, grenade launchers, and more than 100 grenades, none of which were live. The charred and smelly weapons were wrapped in heavy plastic. Texas Ranger Ray L. Coffman said 133 weapons were found in the above ground concrete room; 111 of them were rifles stored in wooden racks.[60] However, FBI weapons expert James Cadigan estimated there were one million rounds of ammunition found throughout the whole site. A defense attorney pointed out, and a Texas Ranger conceded, that one MP-5 submachine gun originally identified as a Davidian gun, actually had been left behind nearby the building by a BATF agent.[61]

The two .50-caliber rifles—which during the siege the government alleged had been converted to machine guns—both were found to be fully legal. However, under cross-examination agent Cadigan revealed that agents found no .50-caliber cartridge cases with firing pin impressions,[62] suggesting no such bullets had been fired.

Allegedly Illegal Machine Guns

On the third day of trial prosecutors presented forty-eight allegedly illegal machine guns. Prosecutors' evidence that these guns were illegal and challenges to that evidence from defense attorneys and others follows.

Agent Cadigan alleged 48 semiautomatics had been modified for full automatic fire: twenty-two AR-15 rifles, twenty AK-47 rifles, two Heckler & Koch SP-89 pistols, and two MAC-11 pistols. He also presented an M-60 U.S. Army light machine gun barrel which, as a part, is not illegal.[63] As previously noted, attorney Stephen Halbrook claims it is AR-15s with which the BATF often tampers to render them illegal automatics.

BATF and FBI agents had both the motive, justifying their actions, and the opportunity to tamper with some, if not all, of the weapons. Agent Cadigan revealed the weapons were forwarded to the FBI laboratories despite the fact that the Texas Rangers were in charge of the investigation and the Texas Department of Public Safety's laboratory was fully qualified to analyze the weapons. Once Texas Rangers handed the weapons over to the FBI after the fire, BATF and FBI agents had exclusive access to them.[64]

Prosecutors would not allow a defense attorney's paid weapons expert to take off the plastic wrapping around the charred guns when he inspected them. This made it more difficult to ascertain whether such alterations had been made, or if they had been made before or after the fire.[65] (However, while the weapons expert, Ken Carter, was originally named as a possible defense witness, he was not called to the stand.[66]) The weapons will remain in storage and, assumedly, they will not be destroyed until after appeals are completed.[67]

Attorneys forced agent Cadigan to concede that Olympic arms, which sold AR-15s to the Davidians, takes extra measures to prevent conversion of their weapons to automatic and that it is difficult to convert them.[68] (According to James Pate, gun owners rarely convert SP-89 pistols, like the two purchased by Paul Fatta, to automatic weapons and their conversion suggests BATF tampering.[69]) They also elicited Cadigan's admission that the FBI had no evidence that automatic weapons were fired on February 28, 1993.[70]

Agent Cadigan claimed that only three of the Davidian automatic weapons still fired and showed a video of that firing. Two were automatic lower receivers found in the fire, with weapons parts supplied by the FBI to replace damaged parts. The other gun was an allegedly fully automatic AK-47 which Texas Rangers stated they found in Michael Schroeder's white van after it had been towed to FBI headquarters at Texas State Technical College after the fire.[71]

It is difficult to believe that Schroeder, who was not at Mount Carmel on February 28, would leave a fully automatic weapon in his unlocked van parked outside a building filled with over two dozen children, including his own. The van evidently was unlocked because BATF agent Barbara Maxwell testified that on February 28, 1993, she and another female agent sought refuge from the firing inside the van. She did not mention having to break into the van.[72] It is possibile that BATF or FBI agents planted that weapon.

Agent Cadigan testified that Davidians had a milling machine and "barrel removal tools" that could have been used to produce illegal weapons parts. And he charged that a book distributor's records indicated deceased Davidian Jeff Little had bought books and a video tape that showed how to convert legal AR-15s to illegal M-16s—and declared that that was the method they had used.[73] However, these machines can be used for other purposes than weapons manufacture, and legal purchase of such books and videos is not definitive evidence of illegal activity.

The government's star witness Kathryn Schroeder testified that she knew David Koresh and his closest followers were illegally converting guns because during Bible studies "he made insinuations very secretively and said, 'I've got a gun that goes rat-tat-tat that I'm going to make go ratatatatat.'

At the end of Bible studies Koresh would say, 'I want my S.S. guys to stick behind. We've got work to do.' Schroeder said, "We knew they were working on guns." Unfortunately, defense attorneys did not clarify whether Schroeder thought illegal guns were being produced before or after the February 28 raid.[74]

Schroeder identified the "S.S. guys" as Scott Sonobe, Peter Hipsman, John McBean, Neal Vaega, and Jeff Little. She named none of the Davidian defendants at trial as "S.S. guys." Desperate prosecutor Bill Johnston, who could not prove that defendants were in any way involved in the alleged weapons conversion, tried to implicate them by stating: "How do you suppose this grinding sounded in their home? How do you suppose this factory sound went over in their home? Certainly, all could hear it. Oh, that's okay, that's just Fatta and Vern making some machine guns. Or they—did they just not care?"[75]

What prosecutors did not respond to was Schroeder's allegation that a surviving Davidian had been involved in weapons conversion. She mentioned, "occasionally, I think he even brought 'Don' Bunds in."[76] As we have seen, Davy Aguilera's February 25, 1993, affidavit includes former Davidian David Block's allegation that Donald Bunds operated machinery capable of fabricating firearm parts and that he had observed Bunds designing a machine gun on a computer. Bunds was arrested and charged with weapons violations as he approached Mount Carmel shortly after the raid and held in "protective custody" by BATF agents for several weeks. He provided information to them.[77]

Davy Aguilera's April 13, 1993, affidavit asserted that within the last "45 days" an unidentified individual—obviously Bunds—had observed the manufacture of silencers and grenades, had seen "100" automatic machine guns, and had "observed that Howell was attempting to construct radio-controlled aircraft which can be used to carry explosives." However, although Bunds was listed as a prosecution witness, prosecutors never called him to testify. That Bunds was not called suggests Davidians are honestly claiming they did not produce illegal weapons.

Schroeder testified it was not until after the raid that Neal Vaega showed her for the first time the difference between automatic and semiautomatic weapons and the process by which semiautomatics could be converted to automatics by cutting out the "safety switch." She testified that the next day she found a fully automatic AR-15 in the gun room. She also claimed that at one point she inventoried such weapons and found more semiautomatics than automatics; she did not mention a specific number. She also claimed she carried an automatic during the standoff.[78] However, at trial agent Cadigan conceded that someone who knew little about guns would have a difficult time distinguishing being an automatic and semiautomatic weapon.[79]

Defense attorneys challenged Schroeder's motives for claiming the guns were automatic, given her limited expertise. At trial, while the jury was outside the courtroom, she confessed that she had pled guilty because the government told her a BATF agent would testify that he or she saw gun shots coming from the window of Schroeder's room. Prosecutors also had letters from Davidian Victorine Hollingsworth in which she alleged Schroeder carried a gun February 28. However, once Schroeder agreed to testify, the BATF agent and Hollingsworth suddenly decided they were too unsure of the facts to testify against Schroeder. She conceded she knew that if prosecutors were not pleased with her testimony they still could choose to prosecute her and, since she had not been granted immunity, use everything she said against her. And she knew evidence against her could lead to life in prison if she were convicted of conspiracy to murder federal agents.

Defense attorneys also forced Schroeder to confess that she had made statements to Texas Rangers about, among other things, what she was doing when the gunfire began, whether she had seen Koresh with a weapon on February 28, whether she heard dogs shot as the gunfire commenced, whether she was allowed to have a gun. Her answers differed from what she told prosecutors. She admitted to lying to Texas Rangers, but attorneys inferred she also might be lying in her current testimony.[80]

Defense attorneys claimed Schroeder's goal was to be with her four children and questioned her about her alleged statement to a cell mate, "I'm going to tell them whatever they want to hear. I just want to be with my children. I've got to get out of prison!" She did not remember making the statement. Defense attorneys made Schroeder confess she stood to make tens of thousands of dollars off a movie deal she had signed.[81]

Davidian defendant Graeme Craddock, who also had little experience with guns, told a grand jury, without consulting an attorney, that he assumed some of the guns were fully automatic. "I think a lot of us assumed that a lot of these arms that we had were full-auto and had that capability, or at least at some stage, might have been converted to full-auto. We were told—the safety switch, there was three positions you could move it, backward to put it on safety, upper, fire, and forward. We were told never under any circumstances we were to push the safety forward." However, defense attorneys, noting that many semiautomatics have three switches, emphasized that the fact the guns were automatic was pure speculation on Craddock's part.[82]

Because nine of the eleven Davidian defendants were not charged specifically with illegal weapons conversion, defense attorneys may not have challenged the authenticity of the allegedly illegal weapons with sufficient vigor. Some attorneys accepted the government's assertions the weapons were illegal and felt it would be more productive to argue that their clients knew nothing about the weapons or that they did not fire them.

Many wonder why Davidians would spend tens of thousands of dollars on semiautomatic weapons, illegally convert them diminishing their value, not use them when they were attacked by federal agents, and not even destroy the evidence just days before they intended to exit Mount Carmel. While it is conceivable that a few Davidian gun enthusiasts did in fact break the capricious machine-gun laws, it seems improbable that they converted forty-eight expensive legal semiautomatics to illegal automatics.

Attorney Mike DeGeurin told reporters, "They can't even show that any of these guns have even been fired. The guns by themselves don't mean anything."[83] Unfortunately, the attorneys were wrong. When it came to sentencing, the presence of these dozens of allegedly illegal guns proved crucial.

Allegedly Illegal Silencers and Live Grenades

Two Texas Rangers testified that in the machine shop they found twenty-two pieces of cut tubing as well as steel wool or wire mesh, all "stock materials" used for the manufacture of sound suppressors or silencers which muffle the sound of a gun shot. These are illegal for civilians to own without proper registration.[84] Defense attorneys did not explore the possibly innocent uses of such materials.

There is evidence that after the February 28 raid the "weapons experts" among the Davidians did bring out live grenades. Jaime Castillo told a Texas Ranger, Graeme Craddock testified to a grand jury, and Kathryn Schroeder testified in court that immediately after the February 28 raid, they saw a half-dozen or more pineapple-shaped grenades on a counter in the kitchen—something they had never seen at Mount Carmel before.[85] However, in his grand jury testimony Craddock also said of the grenades distributed February 28: "I don't think these grenades were ever tested, we didn't know if they would work or not. They were taken back from us a couple of days later because they were concerned that these grenades would probably be rather dangerous, that they would go off accidently. . . . Some of the detonators would unscrew a little bit. One of the pins came out accidently."[86]

All four of the allegedly live grenades identified by Texas Rangers and federal agents were found under suspicious circumstances. The grenade found by Texas Ranger Ray Cano in the cinder block building next to the water tower where Craddock found safety from the fire was not found until six days after the fire—days after Craddock told a Texas Ranger and a grand jury about the grenade and after at least one FBI agent and possibly other federal agents entered the building. Craddock's fingerprints were not found on the grenade.[87]

Ranger Ray Coffman testified he found a live grenade inside the burned out concrete room after the fire.[88] Why a live grenade would not have exploded in temperatures of over 2000 degrees was not explained.

An FBI agent and two Texas Rangers claimed they found two live grenades in clothing Davidian fire survivors dropped near the boat where they gathered after escaping the flames. FBI agent James Atherton said on April 19 he found the grenade in an assault vest which Texas Ranger Marshall Brown described as "a Vietnamese style assault vest," with a small pouch containing the grenade. Texas Ranger George Turner said he found another grenade in the same area the next day in the pocket of a blue jacket.[89]

To end, there certainly is evidence that several deceased and one (unprosecuted) surviving Davidian may have been involved in some conversion of legal weapons without proper registration. However, there is no evidence that Davidian survivors were involved in doing so or that they knew definitively whether their guns and grenade hulls were legal or illegal. And there is ample evidence that "motivated" federal agents could have taken advantage of "opportunity" and tampered with legal Davidian weapons.

Chapter Two: The BATF's Flawed Investigation

1.   Treasury Department report: 19.
2.   Ibid., 37.
3.   Federal Search Warrant, Case Number W93-15M: issued on the probable cause to believe that unregistered machine guns and destructive devices concealed in violation of 18 and 26 USC; Federal arrest warrant for Vernon Wayne Howell, Case Number W93-17m, issued in the belief he was in unlawful possession of an unregistered destructive device in violation of 26 USC. From June 9, 1993, House Appropriations subcommittee hearing: 93.
4.   Michael Isikoff, "Treasury Balked at First at ATF's Raid on Cult," *Washington Post,* May 1, 1993. Assistant Secretary for Law Enforcement, Phillip K. Noble, made the comment.
5.   James L. Pate, "We have the truth on our side: Jailhouse Interviews with Branch Davidians," *Soldier of Fortune,* July, 1994: 47.
6.   Darlene McCormick, "Sheriff says he did not curb probe," *Waco Tribune-Herald,* October 10, 1993.
7.   June 9, 1993 House Appropriations subcommittee hearing transcript: 77, 130, 137–138.
8.   Associated Press wire story, April 23, 1993, 10:25 EDT; Ross and Green report, "What is the Cult Awareness Network and What Role Did It Play in Waco?" 1993. ("Ross" is no relation to Rick Ross.)
9.   Keith Epstein, "Maniac or Messiah?" *Cleveland Plain Dealer,* January 23, 1994.
10.   Dr. Gordon Melton, presentation at American Academy of Religion panel on the Branch Davidians, Washington, D.C., November 22, 1993; December, 1993, letter to the United States Senate from Charles Russell of The Family.
11.   Ross and Green: 12; "Deprogrammer walks," *Royal Teton Ranch News,* February, 1994: 7.
12.   Ross and Green: 12.
13.   Marc Breault and Martin King: 254–56.
14.   Darlene McCormick and Mark England, "Experts: Branch Davidians dangerous, destructive cult," *Waco Tribune-Herald,* March 1, 1993: 7A.
15.   Ross and Green: 12.
16.   Nancy Ammerman, September 10, 1993 addendum to her report to Justice Department.

17.   Jim McGee and William Clairborne, "The Transformation of the Waco 'Messiah'," *Washington Post*, May 9, 1993: A19; Marc Breault and Martin King: 223; Clifford L. Linedecker: 10; Ken Fawcett, Blind Justice: 26.

18.   Paul H. Blackman, Ph.D., report of Institute for Legislative Action of the National Rifle Association, "Affidavit to Kill": 21.

19.   Trial transcript: 525.

20.   Mark Smith, "Firearms dealer says cultists paid with briefcase full of cash," *Houston Chronicle*, February 1, 1994.

21.   James L. Pate, November, 1993: 36–41, 71–72.

22.   Ken Fawcett: 26; trial transcript: 4904.

23.   Trial transcript: 6841–43.

24.   Marc Smith, "Agent allegedly refused Koresh's offer," *Houston Chronicle*, September 11, 1993.

25.   Associated Press, "Gun Dealer Alerted Koresh to ATF Probe, Lawyer Says," *Houston Post*, September 11, 1993.

26.   Livingstone Fagan paper, August, 1994: 12; Treasury Department report, Appendix D: 7; trial transcript: 4889.

27.   David Thibodeau interview, CBS "This Morning," June 10, 1993.

28.   "Gun dealers tell court of sales to Waco cultist," *Washington Times*, February 1, 1994.

29.   Lisa Buie, "Judge throws out charges against gun supply dealer," *Independent Mail*, April 2, 1994; Anna Simon, "Evidence against Oconee gun dealer tossed out," *The News-Greenville, SC*, April 2, 1994.

30.   Daniel Wattenberg, "Gunning for Koresh," *American Spectator*, August, 1993: 33.

31.   Paul H. Blackman report: 51.

32.   Ibid., 23.

33.   Luke 22:33–37.

34.   Daniel Wattenberg: 32.

35.   Nancy Ammerman report to Justice Department, 1993, Addendum.

36.   Marc Breault and Martin King: 317.

37.   Treasury Department report: 143–144.

38.   Trial transcript: 3399.

39.   Ibid., 4518.

40.   Daniel Wattenberg: 36.

41.   Ibid., 33.

42.   Paul H. Blackman report: 10.

43.   Ibid., 12–13.

44.   Ibid., 17.

45.   David B. Kopel and Paul H. Blackman paper, "The God Who Answers by Fire: The Waco Disaster and the Necessity of Federal Criminal Justice Reform": 15.

46.   Trial transcript: 1254.

47.   Larry Pratt report for Gun Owners of America, "Could a Search Warrant Be Your Death Warrant?" 1993: 2.

48.   Treasury Department report: 125–126.

49.   James L. Pate, "Government's Waco Whitewash," *Soldier of Fortune*, January, 1994: 69.

50.   Treasury Department report, Appendix D: 4.

51.   Ibid., 53.

52.   Mark England and Darlene McCormick, March 1, 1993: A10.

53.   Treasury Department report: 124.

54.   Paul H. Blackman report: 6.

55.   Treasury Department report: 27.

56.   Paul H. Blackman report: 21.

57.   "Cult Had Illegal Arms, Expert Says," *New York Times*, January 15, 1994; trial transcript: 1274, 6958–60.

58.   June 16, 1994 trial transcript: 146; Paul Fatta, private communications, 1994 and 1995; trial transcript: 535, 7064.

59.   "Koresh defends actions in tape of interview," *Dallas Morning News*, May 28, 1993: 36A.

60.   Trial transcript: 825–37, 872–875, 905.

61.   Lee Hancock, "FBI video shows capability of Branch Davidian firepower," *Dallas Morning News*, January 15, 1994: 26A; trial transcript: 956, 1194, 1215.

62.   Trial transcript: 1215.

63.   Ibid., 1170, 1179–82.

64.   Ibid., 1244–47.

65.   James L. Pate, private communication, June, 1994.

66.   January 10, 1994 trial transcript: 30.

67.   Teresa Talerico, "Cult trial evidence begins trek to Waco," *Waco Tribune-Herald*, March 1, 1994.

68.   Trial transcript: 1177, 1221–22.

69.   James L. Pate, private communication, June, 1994.

70.   Trial transcript: 1223.

71.   Ibid., 1092–5, 1174, 1192, 1216, 1223.

72.   Ibid., 2266–67.

73.   Ibid., 1185, 1190, 1197, 6122–23, 7338.
74.   "Death and Domesticity Mix at Trial of 11 Cult Members," *New York Times*, February 6, 1994; trial transcript: 4474, 6950–52.
75.   Trial transcript: 4474, 7064–65.
76.   Ibid., 4474.
77.   Don Terry, "Cult Frees Another Child, Raising Hopes in Standoff," *New York Times*, March 5, 1993; Clive Doyle, private communication, May, 1995; Treasury Department report: 110.
78.   "Koresh Follower Pleads Guilty to Resisting Officer," *New York Times*, September 12, 1993; trial transcript: 4471–73, 4501–7.
79.   Trial transcript: 1220.
80.   Ibid., 4425–30, 4588, 4684–87.
81.   Ibid., 4587–88.
82.   Ibid., 6358, 6395–96.
83.   *New York Times*, January 15, 1994.
84.   Trial transcript: 1004–06, 1038, 1186–22.
85.   Ibid., 3057, 4469–70, 6396.
86.   Ibid., 6396.
87.   Ibid., 5466–68, 6057, 6069, 6074, 6075.
88.   Ibid., 915.
89.   Ibid., 5352, 5354, 5363–64, 5683–84.

3

The BATF's
Ruthless Raid Plan

*When they showed up with their armory they
were going to kill us. It wasn't that we had
anything to hide. . . . Those individuals came
to shut us up. It was not about guns, it was
not about search warrants. They came to shut
us up.*

Livingstone Fagan[1]

Despite the Branch Davidians' history of
cooperation with local authorities and with the BATF
itself, the BATF, driven by the bureaucratic imperative
to expand its operations and budget, decided to go
forward with a dangerous paramilitary raid. In the
process it made state and local law enforcement its de
facto partners in crime and abused the *posse comitatus*
law against using military personnel in civilian law
enforcement.

THE BATF IGNORED DAVIDIAN
ATTEMPTS TO COOPERATE

The Treasury report asserts: "Aguilera wisely sought to keep his investigation a secret from David Koresh and his followers . . .[and] . . . sharply circumscribed his inquiries about Koresh to third parties, including arms dealers and former cult members.[2] The report fails to mention Aguilera was not successful. As we have seen, Koresh discovered Aquilera was investigating on July 30, 1992. And the Davidians assumed they remained under surveillance and, through Henry McMahon, invited agents to inspect his weapons immediately. In late January, 1993, after a BATF agent posed as a UPS trainee and attempted to enter the Mag Bag and Mount Carmel Center, David Koresh complained to the local sheriff's department, thinking it was the department trying to infiltrate Mount Carmel.[3]

Koresh Had Cooperated with More Serious Investigations

David Koresh had been investigated on more serious charges than gun law violations and had cooperated fully with law enforcement. In 1987, when Koresh and seven Davidians were indicted for attempted murder after the shootout with George Roden, the sheriff called Koresh and told him they should turn themselves in and surrender their weapons. When deputies showed up to arrest them, they complied.

Former McLennan County District Attorney Vic Feazell, who prosecuted Koresh in that case, criticized federal agents: "If they'd called and talked to them, the Davidians would've given them what they wanted."[4]

In 1991, when LaVerne, California, police demanded Koresh return their child to Robyn Bunds, he did so immediately. Koresh and Sherri Jewell cooperated fully with the Michigan court which awarded primary custody of Kiri Jewell to her father David Jewell. And between February and April, 1992, Koresh allowed Texas Department of Protection and Regulatory Services and McLennan County Sheriff's Department personnel to inspect Mount Carmel on three occasions.

McLennan County Sheriff's Lieutenant Larry Lynch told the June 9, 1993, House Appropriations subcommittee that a few years before the raid sheriffs visited Mount Carmel with only a few officers to serve a warrant on an individual who no longer resided there. BATF Chief of Intelligence David Troy admitted this was the first time he had heard of that service of warrant.[5]

However, the Treasury report falsely claims, "There was, in fact, no evidence that Koresh was prepared to submit to law enforcement authorities or that he had done so in the past" and describes his alleged "disdain for firearms laws and hatred for those charged with their enforcement."[6]

Koresh Invited Sheriff to Inspect Weapons in 1992

In February, 1992, Robert L. Cervenka complained to the sheriff's department that he had heard machine-gun fire at Mount Carmel. According to Aguilera's affidavit, he even "offered to allow the Sheriff to use his property as a surveillance post." Several months later Davidians contacted the local sheriff about this. The *New York Times* reports, "According to Mr. [Paul] Fatta, the weapons the Davidians were firing at that time were legal AK-47s and AR-15s outfitted with a 'hellfire trigger' that allowed for rapid firing without converting the rifles into fully automatic weapons. [Fatta stated] 'We had heard that one of the neighbors had been approached about using their property as a listening post, and we went to the local sheriff's department and asked them if the hellfire triggers were legal, just to make sure. We were told that they were legal.' "[7] According to another article, they told the sheriff, "why don't you come and ask us what we've got."[8]

Koresh Befriended Undercover Agent

On January 11, 1993, eight undercover agents were assigned to pose as students living in the two-bedroom house across the street from Mount Carmel. Davidians immediately visited that house, but undercover agents refused to let them come in.[9] Davidians doubted the men were students because they were too old, their cars were too new, and there was no furniture or clothes in the house.[10] However, the Davidians remained unsure as to which government agency had them under surveillance, thinking it could be the BATF, the FBI, or the INS.[11]

Davidian survivor Clive Doyle said Davidians considered the agents "just like everyone else out there—souls to be saved."[12] Koresh invited agent Robert Rodriguez ("Gonzales") to visit Mount Carmel Center, listen to music, shoot guns on their target range, and attend Bible studies. He even invited him to join the Branch Davidian community.[13] Davidian Livingstone Fagan writes: "It was our hope that, by introducing this agent to our faith, he might communicate its authenticity to his superiors. It was felt that, since they were not listening to us, they might listen to one of their own."[14] Koresh told KRLD radio reporters February 28, 1993, that he was disappointed that after his talks with "Gonzales," he and his superiors did not "understand" that Koresh was a serious religious person worthy of "respect."

After the fire Rodriguez admitted to reporters that Koresh's teachings did affect him. At the trial Rodriguez at first denied being influenced by Koresh, but he then confirmed telling a reporter Koresh was "close" to converting him. "He knew what he was talking about . . . after a while, it gets to you, it affects you. You sit there and listen and it starts to make sense." Discussing the people he had met at Mount Carmel Center, Rodriguez began to weep.[15]

After Raid, Koresh Stated He Would Have Cooperated

The above evidence lends credence to David Koresh's claims on the publicly released February 28, 1993, 911 tape that he would have cooperated with authorities if they had contacted him. On the 911 tape Koresh told McLennan County Sheriff's Lieutenant Larry Lynch, "Now, we're willing, and we've been willing, all this time, to sit down with anybody. You've sent law enforcement out here before."

Immediately after the raid, Koresh told a KRLD radio reporter, "I respect law enforcement. I loved the Waco Sheriff Department. They treated me good. When we had the child accusations against us, some sheriff department guys came out and they treated us with the highest respect. . . . They took the children off where they can talk to them personally. Those kind of people I can deal with." When the reporter asked if he would have gone to town and discussed the weapons with the sheriff's department, Koresh answered, "I would have come. I would have come. I would have come."

The *Houston Chronicle* obtained tapes of telephone conversations between Koresh and BATF agent Jim Cavanaugh shortly after the assault. Koresh told the agent, "It would have been better if you just called me up or talked to me. Then you could have come in and done your work."[16]

When federal prosecutor Ray Jahn asked Davidian Marjorie Thomas, who testified for the prosecution, what the Davidians would have done if agents "had just walked up to the door and turned the knob and started to walk in?", Thomas answered, "We wouldn't do anything."[17] And during a prison interview Renos Avraam asserted, "[Koresh] had let other people in, including policemen. Why wouldn't he let the ATF in? They never gave him the opportunity. So we will never know." Livingstone Fagan agreed, "The ATF could have knocked on the door."[18]

QUESTIONABLE GROUNDS FOR A PARAMILITARY RAID

        Former New York City Police commissioner Benjamin Ward said of BATF's February 28 raid on Mount Carmel, "They did it backwards. The accepted way is to talk first and shoot second."[19] Dr. Robert Cancro, one of the outside experts the Justice Department asked to review BATF and FBI's actions, wrote, "David Koresh asked why they did not serve him the warrant directly rather than through an armed assault. . . . The issue is why was this not considered and evaluated more thoroughly and with adequate behavioral input."[20] While the BATF has given insufficient and conflicting reasons for the raid, it seems clear that the primary reason was the bureaucratic imperative to extend the Bureau's operations and budget.

Questions about U.S. Attorney Johnston's Role

Assistant U.S. Attorney Bill Johnston ignored Marc Breault's complaints against the Davidians for a number of years. It was not until the BATF showed interest in the David Koresh and the Davidians that he began to aggressively pursue the case. He would go on to become one of the trial prosecutors.

According to the Treasury report, Johnston "informed ATF early in the investigation that he would not authorize a search warrant for the Branch Davidian Compound if it was to be executed through a siege-style operation. He, too, feared that a siege strategy would permit Koresh and his followers to destroy evidence and make prosecution more difficult, as happened in the CSA [Covenant, Sword and Arm of the Lord] case. Despite Johnston's views, however, ATF's tactical planners seriously considered a siege plan."[21]

At trial, defense attorneys tried desperately to discover whether Johnston in fact had played such an important role in the decision to go with a dynamic entry (paramilitary raid) instead of a siege (surrounding Mount Carmel until residents surrendered). They argued that if U.S. attorneys were involved in promoting the fatal raid plan, they had a vested interest in showing their actions were proper. Judge Smith repeatedly frustrated attorneys' efforts by ruling the matter irrelevant.[22]

Johnston dismissed the information in the Treasury report saying: "The Treasury Review . . . is a book that was written for release to the public. . . . It is not exactly—it relates to the ATF, as if that had some effect on all of these people, Buford and others in planning, and it's—the full context of that is hard to read."[23] Johnston thereby conceded that the Treasury report was merely a public relations effort, not a serious investigation.

Johnston finally admitted that the Treasury report reference came from another meeting Johnston had with BATF raid planner Chuck Sarabyn. "There was a conversation with Sarabyn, and the quote is not completely accurate, it is just not explained." Johnston did not go on to explain it and asserted he had no intention of calling Sarabyn as a witness.[24]

Although it is widely rumored that Johnston observed the February 28, 1993, raid, he refused to answer specifically defense attorney Mike DeGeurin's question about his presence. He stated, apparently sarcastically, "I wasn't in one of the trailers, Mr. DeGeurin."[25]

Buford Refused to Reveal Real Reason for Raid

At trial defense attorneys sharply questioned the highest raid planner prosecutors brought to the stand, Resident-Agent-in-Charge of Little Rock BATF, Bill Buford. Buford had planned and participated in the 1985 siege of the white supremacist group "The Covenant, the Sword and the Arm of the Lord." By the end of the siege, the group allegedly had destroyed most of its illegal weapons.[26] However, when asked if the Treasury report allegation that this fear influenced the decision to do a paramilitary raid instead of a siege, Buford replied, "Absolutely not."[27]

Buford testified that he originally argued for a siege because it was "the safest way to do it." Buford claimed that he changed his mind and came to support a paramilitary raid "to protect the women and children." However, during cross-examination Buford admitted that he had no idea how many women, children, and elderly lived at Mount Carmel. Moreover, defense attorneys discovered that Buford's rough notes about the planning process contained no mention of concern for women and children.[28]

Defense attorneys sought other planning materials to prove that Buford had lied about his concern for women and children—evidence, in their minds, of his being involved in a BATF coverup. Prosecutors objected vehemently, invoking "privilege as to the other matters, the attachments to the other plans, because they do not reflect the reasoning and internal thought of ATF, this sort of thing, that have nothing to do with guilt or innocence but instead give away strategy and planning, and how these things are arrived at and factors considered by ATF, which involved agent safety and risks, that if they are revealed, it would be detrimental to law enforcement . . . [these] . . . go beyond what's included in the Treasury Report are clearly not discoverable."[29]

First Test of "National Response Plan"

It is well known that forceful execution of search warrants is BATF's preferred modus operandi. The Treasury report acknowledges that BATF planners decided quickly that their only options were a siege or a paramilitary raid.[30] Raid planner Bill Buford confessed at trial that he never had been told that Koresh had invited Aguilera to Mount Carmel to inspect his weapons, something that would have indicated the viability of a non-violent service of warrant.[31]

Two top BATF planners were particularly predisposed to such a raid. Dallas Special Agent-in-Charge Ted Royster had led many high profile, aggressive raids.[32] SAC Chuck Sarabyn, who would become co-commander of the February 28 raid, favored a raid because it would be the first opportunity to test the "National Response Plan" which he had "played a significant role in drafting." This would also be only the fifth time more than one Special Response Team had been used in an operation.[33] Successful completion of the operation would be a big boost to the BATF's credibility in law enforcement circles.

Given these raid planners' military mentality, it is understandable that the BATF named the raid "Operation Trojan Horse."[34] Evidently planners, who were hiding their "troops" in cattle trailers, expected a great surprise victory. David Koresh's attorney Dick DeGuerin explained that the reason the BATF rejected Koresh's offer to cooperate was to excuse a paramilitary raid. "I guess you have to understand the Rambo mentality to understand why these ATF agents and their supervisors wanted to do that."[35]

Publicity Stunt to Bolster BATF's Image and Budget

In early 1993 BATF was a beleaguered agency. Politicians were calling for its abolition, CBS's "60 Minutes" had just done an exposé about female BATF agents who charged routine sexual harassment and even attempted rape, black BATF agents were suing for job discrimination, and the *Waco Tribune-Herald* was calling to find out why the BATF was not doing something about this "dangerous armed cult," the Branch Davidians.[36]

Facing a March 10, 1993, hearing in front of the Senate Appropriations subcommittee on Treasury, Postal Service and General Government, BATF leadership may have felt it needed some good publicity to illustrate its effectiveness, justify its existence, and perhaps increase its budget for the kind of paramilitary operations which it preferred. Arresting dozens of "religious fanatics" and displaying a big weapons caché might be just the thing. Any later story that the guns were found to be legal and that charges had been dropped would never go beyond the local papers. Such publicity also could be used to justify more gun control laws, which would necessitate an even bigger BATF budget—and bigger promotions, perks, and pensions for BATF officials and agents.

Mike Wallace reran the "60 Minutes'" January episode May 23, 1993, and declared, "Almost all the agents we talked to said that they believe the initial attack on that cult in Waco was a publicity stunt—the main goal of which was to improve the ATF's tarnished image." At trial several agents stated that a lead BATF agent yelled the very publicity-conscious phrase "It's showtime!" as they exited the trailers.[37]

During the June 9, 1993, House Appropriations subcommittee hearings lawmakers grilled BATF Public Information Officer Sharon Wheeler to determine if BATF Washington or local offices had been concerned with "the BATF image and whether or not this operation would impact that image." (Her superior, who also appeared and probably knew the answer, did not volunteer an answer.) Wheeler denied two reporters' contentions that when she called them for weekend phone numbers she had told them, "we have something big going down on Sunday."[38] And BATF agents made no attempt to stop the news people following them on the raid—one television crew followed BATF's cattle trailers right up the Mount Carmel driveway.

BATF Paranoia and Hostility

Another explanation for the decision to proceed with a paramilitary raid is the BATF's fear of and hostility towards what *Time* magazine called "determined and fanatical groups." BATF spokesperson Jack Killorin declared, "We've gone about them in a number of different ways—ruse, ambush, siege, and talk. In almost every one we lose law enforcement officers."[39] Marc Breault writes that in December, 1992, BATF investigator Davy Aguilera told him "that he felt Vernon was a lunatic and needed to be put away."[40]

Henry S. Ruth, Jr., one of the Independent Reviewers, asserts: "At least part of the ATF motivation, even if it never rose to the surface, was to enforce the morals of our society. To enforce the psyche of right thinking by retaliating against these odd people."[41] In effect, the Branch Davidians were a strange and alien culture that had to be destroyed.

BATF Desire to Punish BATF Critic

During the January, 1992, interview with Martin King for the Australian television program "Current Affair," David Koresh shared his opinion about guns: "This is not Europe, not where a country overthrows a bunch of people, takes away their weapons so the people cannot argue any issues. Guns are the right of Americans to have. Yeah, we've got a gun here and there. Most of the guns were sold. A lot of people say: 'He's got guns, that makes him bad, that makes him a cult.'" When asked if he would use a gun if "someone" trespassed, Koresh answered, "People trespass all the time. Do we use a gun? No, we don't. Now, they come in here with a gun and they start shooting at us, what would you do? . . . Our constitution states every citizen in American has the right to rebuttal the government. Guns? Yes, we have guns."

Doubtless annoyed, Davy Aguilera in his February 25, 1993, affidavit mentions that Koresh stated that the Bible gave him the right to bear arms and then showed him the Gun Owners Foundation video tape which he wrote "portrayed ATF as an agency who violated the rights of gun owners by threats and lies." And at trial undercover agent Robert Rodriguez described with obvious disgust Koresh's criticism of "silly" gun laws and of the BATF as an organization that violated gun owners' rights.[42] During closing arguments defense attorney Mike DeGeurin explained, "It's because they believe differently and they had guns and they were criticizing ATF that this plan grew."[43]

Davidians' Perceived Separatist Tendencies

The Davidians' perceived separatist or secessionist tendencies also disturbed BATF agents—and later the FBI and prosecutors. Sheriff Jack Harwell said, "They were like living in another little country out there . . . once anyone crossed that property line out there it would be just like someone invading the United States."[44] However, Shannon Bright, a drummer who often visited Mount Carmel, asserted, "They didn't have someone that stood at the gate and checked everyone who walked in. . . . Anyone could walk in peacefully and walk right back out if they wanted to."[45]

Columnist Joseph Sobran wrote: "We are already being told how threatening David Koresh is to society at large, when apparently all he ever wanted to do was to secede from it. And this, I think, is the real nature of a cult: its desire to withdraw."[46]

At trial Robert Rodriguez described Koresh's comments that the United States was a "dragon" that would be destroyed by God and said Koresh "denounced its laws and said that he did not believe in paying taxes."[47] Twice during the trial prosecutors played Wayne Martin's 911 statement, "We don't want any help from your country." Bill Johnston asked the jury, "Can a group arm themselves and secede from the union, kill agents, and claim self-defense?"[48] Dave Hollaway, associate director of the Cause Foundation, commented: "The government cannot allow these kinds of separatist groups, whether they be white separatist groups or religious separatist groups. They cannot allow this so they target these individuals."[49] (Even the Democratic Party-affiliated law firm of Caddell & Conwell, which is filing civil suits for Davidian survivors and family, noted that BATF was prejudiced against the Davidians because of their "separatist" beliefs.)[50]

BATF Shoddy Intelligence

BATF planners decided they only could consider a siege if Koresh was arrested away from Mount Carmel when he was out jogging or in town. Agents believed that without Koresh's leadership, the other members would offer little resistance to a BATF search of Mount Carmel. The Treasury report admits agents received inaccurate information from social worker Joyce Sparks and undercover agent Robert Rodriguez that Koresh rarely left Mount Carmel. It also acknowledges that the agents at the undercover house could not identify who left and entered by automobile.[51] Only after the raid did the BATF receive information that Koresh had left Mount Carmel a number of times during December, 1992, and January and February, 1993, visiting places like Wal-Mart, Whataburger, a wrecking yard, and a local bar.[52]

Cult Busters Advised Against Simple Search

Considering the BATF's bias toward paramilitary raids and its desire for a publicity coup, it is easy to understand why the BATF investigators Davy Aguilera and Bill Buford accepted so uncritically cult-buster "scare stories" which reinforced their commitment to such a raid. Marc Breault writes in his diary entry of January 8, 1993, that "ATF" asked him, "If Vernon received a summons to answer questions regarding firearms, would he show up?" Breault answered, "No way." ATF asked, "If the good guys came with a search warrant, would Vernon allow it?" Breault gave a false version of Koresh's theology when he answered: "There is a considerable amount of danger because Vernon feels that since he is Jesus Christ, he has already died. Therefore he can skip that phase of things. Since he does not have to die, there is no resurrection, and therefore he may well feel he can start shooting beforehand."[53] Social worker Joyce Sparks had warned the BATF, "If you try to serve your warrant with force they are going to get your guns and they are going to shoot you."[54] Breault falsely insisted Davidians would resist any service.

Breault similarly had informed the U.S. Embassy in Australia in February, 1992, that "there would be a shootout with authorities if they attempt to enter the cult's Waco property to take away any of the children now living there, or investigate living conditions."[55] This had not happened when social workers and local sheriffs visited Mount Carmel, yet the BATF heeded Breault's questionable advice.

Doubtless, cult buster Rick Ross also was telling BATF investigators what he told the *Waco Tribune-Herald*—that Koresh was violent and dangerous.

The BATF also was spooked by Ross-influenced David Block's allegation that Koresh urged Davidians to be "ready to fight and resist" any armed attack.[56] BATF agent Lowell Sprague testified during the trial that "raid planners" were convinced that since they had weapons, the Davidians would "make a stand based on their religious beliefs."[57]

This cult buster-induced belief that Koresh would not cooperate was communicated all the way to the top. Chief of Public Relations Jack Killorin claimed after the raid that Koresh was "sworn to resistance" and it was only prudent to have firepower.[58] And David C. Troy, chief of BATF's intelligence division, told a House Ways and Means subcommittee: "Once we had probable cause [to arrest him], he was so kinked up over government. . . . that he would not come off the compound. . . . And the people behind Vernon Howell were just as violent."[59] However, it is clear that cult busters were the ones who had BATF "kinked up" over David Koresh!

Cult Busters' Mass Suicide Scare Stories

The Treasury report asserts that one major reason for a paramilitary raid was former Davidians' assertions current Davidians might commit "mass suicide" should the government attempt a siege. Not surprisingly, Marc Breault promoted this idea "most forcefully."[60] In fact, the Treasury report asserts, "The planners ultimately rejected the siege option mainly because [of] the intelligence obtained in January from former cult members.... Most significantly, they noted the distinct danger that Koresh would respond to a siege by leading his followers in mass suicide."[61] Doubtless, Rick Ross also promoted his "Jim Jones" comparison. However, at trial raid planner Bill Buford never mentioned mass suicide as a serious consideration.

Failed Cult Buster Child Abuse Allegation

According to the Treasury report, BATF attempted to convince Texas Department of Protective and Regulatory Services to summon Koresh to town for a meeting so that BATF could arrest him, but they refused to become involved. The BATF then tried to obtain a Texas arrest warrant for Koresh for sexual activities with a young girl, but that fell through when she refused to testify.[62]

While official documents conceal her identity, an article in the *Waco Tribune-Herald* revealed that it was twelve-year-old Kiri Jewell's allegations against David Koresh which were investigated in February, 1993, by Texas Child Protective Services.[63]

According to the Justice Department report, on February 22, 1993, this young girl told Texas Child Protective Services social worker Joyce Sparks "that on one occasion, when she was ten years old, her mother left her in a motel room with David Koresh. He was in bed and he told [her] to come over to him. She got into the bed. David had no pants on. He took off her panties and touched her and got on top of her. . . . We talked about how she was feeling when this happened and she responded . . . scared . . . scared, but privileged." The report concedes, "This evidence was insufficient to establish probable cause to indict or prove beyond a reasonable doubt to convict."[64]

Not only did her father David Jewell take Kiri to state and federal authorities to tell this story, he exposed her to public scrutiny by allowing her to appear on a March, 1993, "Donahue" show to talk about her experiences with the Davidians. On the show Kiri asserted she knew she would become Koresh's wife when she turned thirteen. David Jewell then interjected, "Quite frankly, there are other incidents that we just really aren't ready to talk about right now."

One wonders if Jewell was holding back only because even in those first ten days of the siege he was negotiating to sell Kiri's alleged story—a young girl having sex with David Koresh is rescued by her father and talks to BATF agents—to television. It was an important story line in the NBC television movie, "In the Line of Duty: Ambush at Waco." Two years later Jewell again exposed his daughter to public scrutiny on the May 4, 1995, special "Where Are They Now?" Prosecutors obviously did not consider Kiri Jewell sufficiently credible to bring her to the stand to speak about Koresh's allegedly abusing her, despite the judge's ruling such evidence was relevant to proving conspiracy.[65]

GOVERNMENT MULTI-TASK FORCE MADE FOR PARTNERS IN CRIME

The Treasury report describes the "multi-task force" of federal, state, and local authorities used to carry out the BATF's February 28 raid. While BATF agents from three Special Response Teams, supported by National Guard helicopters, carried out the actual raid, the Texas Rangers were relegated to setting up roadblocks and the McLennan County Sheriff's Department provided support.[66] (This consisted of three lieutenants assigned to what were considered "minor" duties—like answering raid-related 911 calls to the Waco police.) At the June 9, 1993, House Appropriations subcommittee hearings, BATF Associate Director Hartnett explained that a Drug Enforcement Agency (DEA) team was on hand to disassemble any methamphetamine laboratory which might be found, something not mentioned in the Treasury report. He also said that the INS and the U.S Marshals Service were involved.[67]

The problem with such federal, state, and local "multi-task forces" is that they make all participants de facto "partners in crime," should crimes be committed against citizens—especially if federal agents commit the crimes. National legislation and federal funding for state and local law enforcement ensure that many state and local authorities are not very aggressive in preventing or investigating federal crimes against citizens.

ABUSE OF THE *POSSE COMITATUS* LAW

The 1878 *posse comitatus* law, Title 10, Section 1385 of the U.S. code, states U.S. military forces and state national guards cannot be used as police forces against civilians. However, courts have given law enforcement wide leeway in using military and national guard equipment, facilities, and support personnel.[68] More recent modifications of the *posse comitatus* law (32 U.S.C. §112 and 10 U.S.C. §371) allow the military and national guard to provide "non-reimbursable," i.e., free, support to civilian law enforcement if they are engaged in counter-drug operations. This is just one more example of how the War on Drugs has chipped away at our liberties.

False Drug Manufacturing Allegations

The Treasury report states the BATF wanted to use military training facilities and equipment at Fort Hood—and Texas National Guard aerial reconnaissance before and diversionary helicopters during—the raid. The report goes on to say, "However, in the absence of a drug nexus, the ATF was told by both the U.S. military and the National Guard that the assistance would be reimbursable."[69] To get that free assistance, the BATF constructed drug allegations from dubious and dated evidence.

Marc Breault had told BATF agents that David Koresh claimed that after he took over Mount Carmel from George Roden, "he had found methamphetamine

manufacturing facilities and recipes on the premises."
Koresh told Breault he had asked the local sheriff to
take them away, but the sheriff had no record of doing
so.[70] The BATF revealed to Congress it knew the
identity of the individuals most likely responsible for
building this lab: "convicted narcotics trafficker Donny
Joe Harvey and his associate, Roy Lee Wells, Jr., were
verified by the McLennan County Sheriff's Department
as residing at the compound" during the time Roden
was in charge.[71]

      Undercover agent Robert Rodriguez told the
BATF, "Koresh had told him that the compound would
be a great place for a methamphetamine laboratory
because of its location." (This allegation is mentioned in
the Treasury report—but not in the all-important
affidavit for search warrant.) However, if Koresh made
such a comment, it might have been within the context
of the drug activities of George Roden's former tenants.[72]

      According to information the BATF submitted
to Congress, the last Davidian to be convicted on drug
charges was Brad Branch, back in 1983. Two of the
BATF's other accusations, against Kathryn Schroeder
and Margaret Lawson, were cases of mistaken identity.[73]

      On the basis of this dubious information, Army
Lieutenant Colonel Walker, who advised the BATF on
obtaining "training or equipment or support in a counter-
drug operation," recommended the BATF solicit Texas
National Guard services.[74] The BATF convinced the
Texas National Guard to do two overflights of the
buildings to look for "hot spots" that might indicate drug
laboratory activity. A hot spot was found but, since it
could indicate construction, cooking or other activities

requiring heat, "no official interpretation of the 'hot spot' " was provided.[75] In March, 1993, Davidian Rita Riddle told reporters that hot spots indicated where there were heaters in the house and denied the existence of any drug labs.[76]

Given this dubious evidence, it is not surprising that in the month after the raid, the BATF denied to reporters that it had used allegations of a drug laboratory to obtain Texas National Guard helicopters. Press reports that the BATF had obtained the helicopters under "false pretenses" angered Texas Governor Ann Richards. BATF Associate Director Hartnett sent Governor Richards a March 27, 1993, memo to assure her that there had been sufficient evidence to invoke the drug "nexus" exception to the *posse comitatus* law and obtain free use of National Guard helicopters.

BATF used the same false information to obtain training support from the Army. In the May, 1995, issue of *Soldier of Fortune*, James Pate reveals that the classified teletype message order from then-Brigadier General John M. Pickler that authorized the use of Special Forces Green Berets to train BATF agents was based on the BATF's assertion Davidians were manufacturing methamphetamines. It specifies that "intelligence indicates an active methamphetamine lab and deliveries of the required chemicals to produce synthetic methamphetamine." Another classified message reveals that the BATF told the army that "one of the separate buildings [is] suspected of containing a meth lab."[77]

Questions about Original Written Plan

Also troubling is the BATF's and the Treasury Department's claims that there was no written plan for the raid on Mount Carmel until February 23, 1993, five days before the raid. BATF agent Darrell Dyer, who had past military experience, took it upon himself to write one with agent William Krone. This plan was not distributed before the raid.[78] Those familiar with military bureaucracy find it difficult to believe that military commanders would have advised the BATF on obtaining National Guard and army support without such written documentation.

James Pate presents evidence that there was indeed a written plan, but that it was such a patent violation of the *posse comitatus* law that the military, BATF, and Treasury purposely covered up its existence. Pate notes that BATF spokesperson Jack Killorin referred to a plan that was "months" old. Also, BATF Deputy Assistant Director Dan Conroy stated, "I want to once and for all, unequivocally state—the raid plan was submitted. . . . It was granted 100 percent by headquarters." Then-Brigadier General John M. Pickler's order authorizing the use of Green Berets to train BATF agents notes "ATF has already planned their operation."

Pate goes on to describe what he believes are the details of the suppressed original raid plan. A memorandum by Army Major Philip W. Lindley criticizes the BATF's plan for proposing to illegally use Special Forces trainers in a plan where "civilian targets" are "to be attacked." The BATF also requested Special

Forces to be "in proximity" to "the target" during the raid. The original plan anticipated a significant number of casualties and the BATF wanted access to Bradley vehicles from the start in order to remove them. Moreover, immediately after the failed raid, the BATF again requested Bradley vehicles and did in fact contemplate a second assault on Mount Carmel on February 28 with them, something 911 tapes reveal that Davidians feared. The FBI prevented such an assault.[79]

Questions about Illegal Training

The Treasury report describes the involvement of Army Special Forces from Fort Bragg in South Carolina in training BATF agents at Fort Hood. It asserts they simply constructed stand-alone windows for practicing breaking and entering, outlined the dimensions of Mount Carmel with marking tape, and gave agents medical and communications training.[80] In a May, 1994, article James Pate revealed "military sources" told him that Special Forces trained BATF agents in the use of flash-bang grenades. Moreover, they allegedly trained them "after hours" in techniques of "room-clearing, fire-and-maneuver, and building takedown," methods of indiscriminate killing of uncooperative enemy forces—and "subjects Special Forces are forbidden to teach civilian law enforcement." Pate writes that a source said to him: "Are we worried about being found out? Of course we're worried. . . . The army engaged in a coverup on this from the moment the news hit the fan about that [ATF] raid."[81]

In May, 1995, Pate asserted he had further evidence that Special Forces illegally taught "Close Quarter Combat" to BATF agents, that Green Berets helped write a specific assault scenario and that after the failed raid they all wrote "cover your ass" statements denying any culpability. He also named four Green Berets who were present at Mount Carmel—wearing "civvies"—during the February 28th raid.[82]

At trial BATF raid planner Bill Buford confirmed that Special Forces trained agents but asserted that "to the best of my knowledge" no Special Forces had observed the February 28 raid. However, he said that at least one army medic had told him he wished he could do so.[83]

All this military and law enforcement activity seems particularly unnecessary and even frightening, given David Koresh's exasperated statement on the March 8 home video: "You could have arrested me jogging as I jogged up and down the road. You could have arrested me at Wal-Mart. . . . Cause this ain't America any more when the ATF has that kind of power to come into anybody's home and kick doors down."

Chapter Three: The BATF's Ruthless Raid Plan

1.   "Fagan still irritant for ATF," *Waco Tribune-Herald*, January 27, 1994.
2.   Treasury Department report: 123.
3.   Ibid., 187–188.
4.   Roy Bragg, "Ex-prosecutor laments agents' 'storm trooper' tactics," *Houston Chronicle*, March 2, 1993; Clifford Linedecker: 72–73.
5.   June 9, 1994, House Appropriations Subcommittee hearing: 164.
6.   Treasury Department report: 135.
7.   Dirk Johnson, "40 Bodies of Cult Members are Found in Charred Ruins," *New York Times*, April 22, 1993: B12.
8.   *Lexington (KY) Herald-Leader*, March 7, 1993: A2.
9.   Treasury Department report, Appendix D: 8–9.
10. Clive Doyle interview, "American Justice" program, "Attack at Waco," August 3, 1994.
11. Treasury Department report: 187; trial transcript: 4069.
12. James L. Pate, July, 1994: 48.
13. Treasury Department report, Appendix D: 11.
14. Livingstone Fagan paper, August, 1994: 13.
15. Lee Hancock, *Dallas Morning News*, May 13, 1993: 8A; James L. Pate, July, 1994: 48; trial transcript: 3441–44.
16. "Koresh to agents: Should have called me," *Washington Times*, May 26, 1993.
17. Majorie Thomas testimony, November 17–18, 1993: 207.
18. James L. Pate, July, 1994: 48, 49.
19. *Newsweek*, March 15, 1993: 55.
20. Dr. Robert Cancro report to the Justice Department in *Recommendations of Experts for Improvements in Federal Law Enforcement after Waco*, October 8, 1993: 2.
21. Treasury Department report: 38.
22. Trial transcript: 2925–37.
23. Ibid., 2934–35.
24. Ibid., 2934–35.
25. Ibid., 2716.
26. Treasury Department report: 38.

27.   Ibid., 53; trial transcript: 2831.

28.   Trial transcript: 2687–8, 2756, 2798, 2830.

29.   Ibid., 2927–28.

30.   Treasury Department report: 38–43.

31.   Trial transcript: 2831.

32.   Larry Pratt report: 15.

33.   Treasury Department report: 62.

34.   Ibid., Appendix B: 40.

35.   Steve McVicker, "Interview with Dick DeGuerin," *Houston Press*, July 22, 1993.

36.   Stephen Labaton, "Firearms Agency Struggles to Rise From Ashes of Waco Raid," *New York Times*, November 5, 1993: A21.

37.   Trial transcript: 2387, 2506.

38.   June 9, 1993, House Appropriations Subcommittee hearing transcript: 144–5.

39.   *Time*, March 15, 1993: 39.

40.   Marc Breault and Martin King: 299.

41.   "American Justice" program, "Attack at Waco," August 3, 1994.

42.   Trial transcript: 3385–90.

43.   Ibid., 7279.

44.   Daniel Wattenberg: 32.

45.   Mark England, "Still Having Doubts," *Waco Tribune-Herald*, April 17, 1993.

46.   Joseph Sobran, "Applying the Cult Label," *Washington Times*, March 22, 1993.

47.   Trial transcript: 3385–86.

48.   Ibid., 7083–84.

49.   Marc R. Masferrer, "Lessons from the botched Mount Carmel raid," *Waco Tribune-Herald*, February 27, 1994: 4A.

50.   Caddell & Conwell lawsuit, July 26, 1994: 78.

51.   Treasury Department report: 136–40.

52.   Margy G. Gotschall, "A Marriage Made in Hell," *National Review*, April 4, 1994; trial transcript: 6713–14.

53.   Marc Breault and Martin King: 306–07.

54.   Joyce Sparks interview on ABC's "Primetime Live" television show, January 6, 1994.

55.   Gustav Nieguhr and Pierre Thomas, April 25, 1993: A20.

56.   Treasury Department report: 45.

57.   Trial transcript: 2251.

58. "A Botched Mission in Waco, Texas," *U.S. News and World Report*, March 5, 1993.

59. Associated Press wire story, April 22, 1993, 13:04 EDT.

60. Treasury Department report: 46.

61. Ibid., 141.

62. Ibid., 64.

63. Darlene McCormick, October 10, 1993.

64. Justice Department report: 219.

65. Trial transcript: 4421–22, 4716.

66. Treasury Department report: 79.

67. June 9, 1993, House Appropriations Subcommittee hearing transcript: 77–78.

68. June 9, 1993, House Appropriations Subcommittee hearing transcript: 342.

69. Treasury Department report: 213.

70. Ibid., 30.

71. June 9, 1993, House Appropriations Subcommittee hearing transcript: 188–189.

72. Treasury Department report: 212.

73. June 9, 1993 House Appropriations Subcommittee hearing transcript: 188–189; family member, private communication.

74. Ibid., 177–178.

75. Treasury Department report, 213.

76. J. Michael Kennedy and Louis Sahagun, "Sect member says helicopters shot at compound in gun battle," *Los Angeles Times*, March 30, 1993: A17.

77. James L. Pate, "No Peace without Justice," *Soldier of Fortune*, May, 1995: 82.

78. Treasury report: 207–208.

79. James L. Pate: 58–61.

80. Treasury Department report: 73, 78, and Appendix B: 56.

81. James L. Pate, "Special Forces Involved In Waco Raid!" *Soldier of Fortune*, May, 1994: 35–36.

82. James L. Pate: 60–61, 94–95.

83. Trial transcript: 2811–12.

4

The BATF Initiated
Violent Raid

*There are about seventy-five men around our
building shooting at us in Mount Carmel. Tell
them there are children and women in here and
to call if off! Call it off!*

**Wayne Martin on 911 tape one
minute after BATF attacked**

The 1994 trial of eleven Branch Davidians raised
as many questions as it answered about BATF's
February 28, 1993, raid on Mont Carmel. Questions
that remain unanswered about the raid, include the
following: Who shot first? Did BATF agents shoot from
helicopters? How many unarmed Davidians and BATF
agents fell victim to BATF fire? Did BATF agents simply
murder Davidian Michael Schroeder hours after the
raid? The most likely answers point to negligent and
even criminal action by BATF agents.

FEBRUARY 28 CHRONOLOGY

*This 1993 chronology is largely drawn from
the Treasury Department report's Appendix D or
from sources referenced in the following pages.*

7:45 A.M.—KWTX-TV reporter and cameraman arrive near Mount Carmel.

8:00—Undercover agent Robert Rodriguez enters Mount Carmel for Bible study. Raid Commander Chuck Sarabyn briefs BATF convoy at Bellmead Civic Center.

8:30—A second KWTX-TV cameraman warns postman David Jones, a Branch Davidian, that a "shootout" with helicopters is about to occur. Jones returns to Mount Carmel and warns Koresh.

8:45—Three *Waco Tribune-Herald* cars arrive nearby Mount Carmel.

9:05—Rodriguez leaves Mount Carmel, hurries to undercover house across the street, calls raid Commander Sarabyn, and tells him that Koresh knows about the impending raid. Commanders Sarabyn and Phillip Chojnacki and SAC Ted Royster decide to go ahead with raid.

9:10—Chojnacki calls the BATF National Command Center in Washington and informs them operation is beginning.

9:25—Sarabyn arrives at Bellmead, announces operation is to proceed, tells agents "Hurry. They know we're coming." BATF agents, board cattle trailers.

9:26—Three helicopters carrying Chojnacki, Royster, and Aguilera, and six other agents are on the way to Mount Carmel to create a diversion. KWTX-TV's

reporter and cameraman allege helicopters circle Mount
Carmel three times shortly thereafter.

9:45—Cattle trailers enter driveway of Mount Carmel,
followed by KWTX-TV vehicle.

9:47—Unarmed David Koresh and Perry Jones come
to front door (actually a set of double doors) and BATF
agents fire on them. Helicopters approach back of
building and start shooting at Davidians. KWTX-TV
crew takes cover behind bus.

9:48—Wayne Martin calls 911 to report seventy-five
armed men are attacking Mount Carmel. Sheriff's
Lieutenant Larry Lynch responds. Nineteen attempts
to reach ATF fail because the BATF contact had turned
off his radio.

9:55—Associate Director Hartnett and Director Higgins
are informed agents are under fire.

10:03—Lynch calls back Mount Carmel after
disconnection and talks continue. Martin complains
about shooting from helicopters.

10:20—When a patrolman drives to the command post
to alert Chojnacki, Lynch finally is put in contact with
the BATF and begins negotiating between Davidians
and BATF agents.

10:49—911 call disconnects. Lynch gives Koresh's
cellular phone number to Royster who passes it to agent
Cavanaugh at the undercover house.*

10:59—Lynch negotiates with Martin and Schneider
on one line and Chojnacki and Royster on the other.

11:27—Cavanaugh finds telephone number on
undercover house refrigerator door and calls into Mount
Carmel and continues negotiations.*

11:30—Hartnett unilaterally requests FBI Hostage Rescue Team support.

11:39—Agents move in to pick up wounded and dead agents.

11:54—Ambulance moves in to pick up agents.

12:37 P.M.—Lynch gives Davidian Steve Schneider Cavanaugh's phone number and direct contact is established.*

12:45 approx—BATF agents physically assault KWTX-TV cameraman taking pictures of dead agents.

Mid-afternoon—Davidian Donald Bunds arrested as tries to return to Mount Carmel by car.

4:55—Agents fire on three Davidians trying to re-enter the Mount Carmel property. Michael Schroeder is killed, Norman Allison is arrested, Bob Kendrick escapes.

6:00—Armored vehicles enter the property.

March 1, 1993
5:30 A.M.—FBI Special Agent-in-Charge Jeffrey Jamar arrives at command post. Royster holds first BATF press conference.

10:00—Hartnett and FBI Hostage Rescue Team arrive via FBI Hostage Rescue Team plane. FBI takes charge.

*Seeming conflicts occur between accounts in Treasury report text and chronology in Appendix D.

BATF AGENTS EXPECTED A SHOOTOUT

There is ample evidence that BATF agents expected a shootout—something that only would have made them nervous and possibly trigger happy as they approached Mount Carmel Center.

BATF Commanders Warned Agents Davidians "Dangerous"

The morning of the raid many agents read the *Waco Tribune-Herald's* February 27 "The Sinful Messiah" story and raid co-commander Chuck Sarabyn discussed the article with them during a briefing.[1] The story was filled with cult buster accusations that the Davidians were dangerous fanatics. In closing trial arguments attorney Steve Rosen stressed that BATF raid planners kept telling agents they would be dealing with "cultists" in a "compound" not residents of a home and church and that agents had been "trained to hate."[2]

During the trial BATF agent Eric Evers testified that he remembered a briefing before the raid in which agents were told that a number of the people at Mount Carmel wanted to "come out" of Mount Carmel but were somehow being prevented.[3] Agent Lowell Sprague testified that the raid planners thought there were weapons in the compound and that Davidians would "make a stand based on their religious beliefs."[4] And agent Ballesteros disclosed that BATF agents had been briefed that they would encounter twenty to thirty or more "Mighty Men." He said, "We anticipated we would be met with force."[5]

Perhaps the clearest evidence that raid planners expected a shootout is that BATF agents were told to mark their blood types on their necks for medical purposes if they were wounded, an instruction they had never received before. Treasury report reviewer Captain John Kolman noted that this had an "adverse psychological effect on team members."[6]

Newsman Warned Davidian About Expected Shootout

Just before the raid, Davidians learned that they were facing not a service of warrants, but a "shootout." KWTX-TV cameraman James Peeler asked directions of Davidian David Jones, who was driving his postal truck. Koresh's attorney Dick DeGuerin stated to reporters that Peeler told Jones, "Well, you better get out of here because there's a National Guard helicopter over at TSTC [Texas State Technical College] and they're going to have a big shootout with the religious nuts." [7] Peeler was distressed to see Jones immediately drive to Mount Carmel Center and left the area to call his superiors.[8]

According to the Treasury report, Jones told DeGuerin that "Peeler warned him not to go near the Compound as there were going to be 'sixty to seventy TABC [Texas Alcohol Beverage Commission] guys in helicopters and a shootout would occur.' " And Peeler himself confessed to the Treasury review team that he had told Jones there would be "some type of law enforcement action" and that "the action was likely to be a raid of some type and that there might be shooting."[9]

KWTX-TV cameraman Dan Mulloney testified that KWTX-TV's initial information came from law enforcement agents he refused to name—something the Treasury report failed to reveal—as well as from a private ambulance driver working with the BATF. Similarly, BATF agent Ballesteros admitted that it was non-BATF law enforcement that tipped off the *Waco Tribune-Herald*.[10] Therefore, BATF agents' expectations of a shootout were directly transmitted to the Davidians.

Most Agents Knew About "Loss of Surprise"

After Jones discovered that a raid was imminent, he rushed back to Mount Carmel and told Koresh. Undercover agent Robert Rodriguez alleged that after Koresh learned of the impending assault, Koresh told him "they're coming" and mentioned the BATF and the National Guard. Rodriguez hurried across the street to the undercover house, called raid co-commander Chuck Sarabyn, and repeated these statements.

After consulting with co-commander Phillip Chojnacki, Sarabyn decided to go forward with the raid anyway. He dashed out to the staging area shouting, "Get ready to go, they know we're coming!" and "Koresh knows the ATF and National Guard are coming!"[11] According to the Treasury report, "Over sixty agents who heard Sarabyn on the day have since recounted" that they heard him give these warnings.[12] On top of the propaganda they had absorbed about the Davidians' "ferocity," this information must have unnerved many agents.

BATF AGENTS DID NOT BRING OR ANNOUNCE WARRANTS

During the trial it became evident that none of the more than two dozen BATF agents who took the stand had a copy of the warrants, had seen them, knew what was in them, knew what they were searching for, or had any idea who did![13] One defense attorney asked an agent if they were supposed to just "rummage around" since they did not even know what they were looking for.[14] The government never has revealed if BATF observers or prosecutors had the warrants, and many suspect the warrants were left behind.

Right after the raid BATF spokesperson Jack Killorin told *USA Today*, "We needed sixty seconds of them not being prepared and we would have neutralized the compound and gotten the children out."[15] However, sixty seconds is barely time for an agent to walk to the front door of a large building, knock, wait for an adult to answer the door, and formally announce that he was there to serve warrants.

BATF agent Roland Ballesteros, the first to approach the front door, revealed that *no* agent had been designated to announce the purpose of the raid. "Basically, we all announced. We practiced knocking,

announcing, and then going through the front door."
Ballesteros testified he saw Koresh in the doorway, and
yelled, "Police, lay down!" He said Koresh answered,
"What's going on?" He yelled back, "Search warrant,
lay down." However, defense attorneys pointed out that
this was the *first* time he had mentioned announcing
he was serving a search warrant.

During Ballesteros' February 28, 1993,
interview with the Waco police, his March 10 interview
with the Texas Rangers, and a September 30 pre-trial
hearing, he did not mention these "facts." Ballesteros
testified that he had changed his story because during
earlier testimony pain killers from a raid-related wound
had dulled his memory.[16]

While several agents asserted they had yelled,
"Police!" or "ATF," at least three—Clay Alexander,
Lowell Sprague, and Kenneth King—conceded they had
not done so—nor had they heard anyone else do so. In
fact, Alexander admitted he had never been instructed
to announce anything, despite the fact he would be
among the first to get to the front door.[17]

BATF agent Robert Champion also testified at
trial that agents had identified themselves as police with
a search warrant. Again, he had not told this to Texas
Rangers in March. When questioned by defense
attorneys, Champion said the Texas Rangers had not
specifically queried him about that issue.[18] Agent Kris
Mayfield, who was close to the front door, said he did
not hear such an announcement.[19]

It is clear the Davidians had no idea who was
attacking them. Koresh had heard it was either BATF
or TABC that was about to raid him. (Undercover agent

Rodriguez says he mentioned the National Guard, and Davidian Graeme Craddock is sure he mentioned the FBI.[20]) On the 911 tape Koresh infers that he believes it is local law enforcement attacking him: "We told you we wanted to talk. No. How come you guys try to be ATF agents?" On the same 911 tape Davidian attorney Wayne Martin complains, "They never told us who they were. . . . They never I.D.'d themselves."

The government's star witness, Davidian Kathryn Schroeder, testified at trial that although her room was on the first floor, near the front door, she did not hear shouts of "police" or "federal agents." Nor could she see any writing or badges on the uniforms until the agents began leaving and she saw the "ATF" letters on the back of their coats.[21] Davidian prisoner Kevin Whitecliff stated at sentencing, "I thought they must be some kind of renegades, some kind of anti-Christian group."[22]

Agent Bill Buford, who was in the team that went in the second story window, disclosed that agents were authorized to shoot anyone inside who was carrying a weapon—even though agents had not announced that they were police or serving a search warrant. Buford revealed he did in fact shoot a Davidian who approached him carrying a gun.[23]

BATF USED EXCESSIVE FORCE

BATF's executing search and arrest warrants upon the Branch Davidians with seventy-six heavily armed agents utilizing a plan which provided no opportunity for peaceful cooperation by itself constituted an excessive use of force, regardless of who shot first. Nevertheless, during the trial BATF agent Gerald Petrilli declared there should have been more agents, stating he felt twenty agents for each 2,500 square feet of building is appropriate.[24]

BATF Had No Plan to Serve Warrants Peacefully

Nothing in Aguilera's affidavit indicated that Koresh or his followers would use force to resist service of search and arrest warrants. Nor did the magistrate give the necessary explicit permission for such a "no knock" warrant which would permit agents to bypass giving notice that they were serving a search warrant. Title 18, U.S.C. 3109, states that an officer must give notice of his legal authority and purpose before attempting to enter the premises.

Early in the trial BATF agent Ballesteros acknowledged that BATF planners never had a plan for peacefully serving the search and arrest warrants. Specifically asked by a defense attorney if he ever rehearsed a peaceful entry, he answered, "No, we did not." Instead in their fifteen to twenty practice raids on a mock-up of Mount Carmel, agents only had been instructed in how to scale ladders, smash into rooms, throw concussion grenades, and shoot. Ballesteros himself was armed with a 12-gauge shotgun, 9-millimeter pistol and a .38-caliber handgun. One agent carried a battering ram.[25]

Even if Koresh had thrown himself to the ground in surrender, the assault would have continued. Agent Kenneth King admitted that the two roof teams—which never announced that they were BATF agents or had a search warrant—had received no instructions to stop their assault on the second floor arms room.[26]

Agents Carried High Powered Weapons

BATF Chief of Special Operations Richard L. Garner described to a congressional committee the arms carried by seventy-six agents: every agent had a Sig Sauer 9-millimeter semiautomatic pistol; snipers were equipped with .308-caliber high power sniper rifles; agents also carried eight AR-15s and twelve shotguns.[27] Twenty-seven agents carried tactical carbine Heckler & Koch MP-5 9-millimeter "semiautomatics" or "submachine guns." During the trial several BATF agents adamantly refused to acknowledge that the MP-5s they carried were fully automatic. However, because it fires a two-shot burst, under law it is a machine gun.[28] Only law enforcement is allowed to use silencers on these weapons, which gives agents the ability to shoot first and deny it.

The 9-millimeter hydroshock bullets BATF used in the MP-5s are highly penetrating rounds available only to law enforcement special operations teams and the military. They expand when they hit the human body, destroying large areas of flesh, as opposed to merely passing through the body.[29] During the trial a defense attorney repeatedly questioned FBI agent

James Cadigan about hydroshock bullets. Finally, he gave a testy response. "They're designed to kill, disable, wound, destroy whatever they hit."[30] According to two Davidian attorneys, Dick DeGuerin and Douglas Tinker, hydroshocks are outlawed for use by the military. These hydroshock bullets killed Davidians Jaydean Wendell, Peter Gent, Michael Schroeder, and probably Perry Jones.[31]

Agents Mounted Terrifying Attack

News reports describe the attack: "According to witnesses, federal agents hid in livestock trailers as they drove up to the compound. As three National Guard helicopters approached, the 100 law officers stormed the main home, throwing concussion grenades and screaming 'Come out!' "[32]

Attorney Dick DeGuerin asserted: "These two cattle trailers roar up, and people start screaming out of the back of them, screaming at the tops of their lungs, not anything like, 'This is a search' or 'We're agents' or 'Put up your hands' or anything like that. It was just screaming, yelling, like Marines storming the beach."[33]

During the trial the three Davidian women who cooperated with prosecutors all supported the central defense contention: that Davidians were terrified of the raid and acted in self-defense. All three women testified about dark-clad men rushing the building, guns blazing, and unprepared and terrified women and children screaming and running for safety under beds and into hallways.[34]

Agents Threw Flash-Bang Grenades into Building

Agents also carried flash-bang grenades which explode with noise, smoke, and flashes of light. The BATF claims they are harmless "diversionary devices" which cause only temporary discomfort. Nevertheless, civilians can be prosecuted for having flash-bangs. At trial defense attorneys called Sandra Sawyer of Denver, Colorado, who testified about injuries she received when a flash-bang device was used by police during a raid on a friend's home—the device nearly severed Sawyer's right arm.[35]

Agents threw at least five flash-bangs into the building on February 28. KWTX-TV video tape shows an agent on the roof throwing a flash-bang into the second floor arms room moments after three agents entered it. Agent Kenneth King disclosed that throwing a flash-bang into the windows of both second-story rooms was part of their original plan, though he never got a chance to throw his.[36]

KWTX-TV video tape also shows an agent breaking the ground-floor window of the church chapel and throwing two such flash-bangs into it—possibly a first in American history. Agent Mayfield testified during the trial that he tried to throw a flash-bang into a lower-story window in the front of the building, but it bounced back out and exploded in the yard beside him. He was successful in lobbing a second flash-bang into the building.[37] And agent Kevin Richardson also admitted to "placing" a flash-bang in the same window into which Mayfield had thrown one.[38]

At trial agent Bill Buford conceded that flash-bangs could start a fire and that agents had a fire extinguisher on the ground just in case.[39] Davidians claim that the flash-bang grenade thrown into the second-floor window made a big, jagged hole and did in fact start a small fire which they had to put out.[40] Colonel Jack Zimmermann, deceased Davidian Steve Schneider's attorney, inspected that hole when he visited Mount Carmel during the siege. From his extensive military experience he concluded, and testified at trial, that BATF agent Kenneth King threw not a flash-bang but an even more dangerous and destructive concussion grenade into the room. He believed only that kind of grenade could have created such a large hole.[41] If BATF agents had in fact used a concussion grenade, that would be one more piece of evidence that BATF would have wanted destroyed.

Agents Shot Dogs

The Davidians kept five family dogs—Fawn, Bear, Bandit, Wolfie, and Rascal—in a pen to the west side of the front door. Even though none of the dogs were vicious, BATF's original plan was to shoot the dogs if they could not be subdued—even if Davidians surrendered immediately. Once the gunfire started, agents testified to shooting at dogs they thought were trying to escape from the pen.[42] One aerial photo taken right after the raid shows a line of five dead dogs in the front yard.[43]

EVIDENCE BATF SHOT FIRST

The original BATF plan for ground agents was that while helicopters created a diversion, one team of three agents would smash through the front door while another team of three agents would spray a fire extinguisher at or, if necessary shoot, the dogs in the dog pen near the front door. A second team would go to the tornado shelter to arrest men working there, and two more would climb to Koresh's second-floor rooms, break the windows, throw in flash-bangs, and enter.[44]

Evidence provided during the trial did not answer definitively the question of who shot first or where in the front of the building. However, it does suggest that first shots came either from agents in helicopters at the back of the building or from an agent accidently shooting a bullet as he exited a trailer—these shots (or the sound of agents spraying dogs with the fire extinquishers) probably prompted nervous agents to shoot at the unarmed David Koresh as he stood in the front door.[45] This chapter will deal with the shooting at the front door. The next will review evidence agents shot from helicopters.

BATF Agents Confused, Anxious, and Excited

Obvious flaws in raid planning may have heightened agents' anxiety. According to the Treasury report, there never had been a contingency plan for armed resistance, bad weather, the loss of surprise, or retreat. The commanders of the raid were in a helicopter and a cattle truck where they could not communicate effectively with agents. Two-way radio communications quickly broke down between agents.[46]

During the trial BATF agent Barbara Maxwell testified the contingency plan was to retreat without returning fire if the Davidians began shooting, but that some agents were confused about the contingency plans.[47] Agent Rolland Ballesteros confessed at trial that he was "excited" at the prospect of taking on the Davidians.[48] Doubtless other agents felt the same.

A *Houston Post* reporter wrote, "Unless you have a very disciplined group, you can expect all hell to break loose once any shot is fired; and according to Charles Beckwith, a retired army colonel and founder of the military's anti-terrorist Delta Force, the ATF's raid was 'very amateur.' "[49]

Davidian Allegations

Davidians in the back of the building who saw the helicopters approaching believe agents in helicopters shot first. Those in the front of the building support Koresh's version of events, described to a KRLD radio reporter: "I had the front door open so they could clearly see me. And then what happened was, I told them, I said 'Get back. There's women and children here. Get back. I want to talk.' And all of the sudden 9-millimeter rounds started firing at the front wall. . . . They hit the metal doors which deflected them. I had my face out where they could see me. And then I moved back, and all of a sudden the guy started firing." Koresh told CNN, "They fired on us first. Like I said, they were scared." He blamed BATF's agents' fear on the "rumors going 'round." Koresh was wounded in one arm. His father-in-law Perry Jones was mortally wounded in the abdomen.[50]

Davidian Jaime Castillo, who approached the front door from the west hallway as the firing began, told a Texas Ranger that BATF agents fired first as Koresh closed the door.[51] Brad Branch, who was right behind Koresh claims he saw one agent shoot a dog. Panicked agents then shot at the door. Clive Doyle told reporter James Pate, "The first shots were fired outside."[52] During his grand jury testimony Graeme Craddock also asserted that the first volley of gunfire "appeared to come from outside."[53] Just fifteen minutes after the raid began, Davidian Wayne Martin, an attorney, told 911 Sheriff's Lieutenant Larry Lynch, "I have a right to defend myself. They started firing first." He demanded the BATF agents be arrested.

BATF Agents' Conflicting Testimony

BATF agents told conflicting stories about where the first shots came from and who shot them. Moreover, some agents changed their trial testimony from that which they gave Texas Rangers immediately after the raid. The Treasury report seems to have been written to explain away some inconsistencies, such as agent statements regarding firing at the dogs: "As they left the trailer, the agents heard gunfire. At first, the agents thought it came from the dog teams. During training the agents had been told that they might hear the dog teams firing at the dogs if they were not able to subdue them with fire extinguishers."[54]   However, in trial testimony, while several agents mentioned seeing the fire extinguisher go off, none mentioned seeing the first shots come from agents shooting at the dogs. If Brad Branch's account is correct, agents would be strongly motivated to change their testimony.

The first six BATF agents who exited the back of the cattle trailer closest to the front door were members of the entry team and the dog team. Entry team member agent Rolland Ballesteros, the first to arrive at the front door, gave trial testimony different from his statements to Texas Rangers and Waco police right after the raid. He told Rangers that he thought agents shooting at the Davidians' dogs fired the first shot. At trial he changed his story and testified that the Davidians shot first through the front door, "ambushing" them. Ballesteros claimed he saw wooden splinters coming from the door. When a defense attorney pointed out the doors were metal, Ballesteros replied, "It was something exiting." While he confessed he did alter his story after talking with other agents, he blamed medication for impairing his memory. He also asserted that no one had ever asked him some questions asked at trial.[55]

Agent Kris Mayfield, who was in Ballesteros' team, said he heard the first shots from the northwest end of Mount Carmel, not from the front door.[56] Kevin Richardson, in the same team, also first heard shots from the northwest corner of the building.[57] Their testimony suggests that the first firing might well have come from helicopters, as several Davidians claim.

Two members of the dog team, right behind the first team, also told different stories. Robert Champion claimed that after testing his fire extinguisher, he heard gunfire from the front door. Both he and agent Steven Willis shot back. Clay Alexander first heard gunfire from the second story of Mount Carmel, to the right of the front door.[58]

Some speculate an agent exiting the first cattle trailer truck, which stopped near the tornado shelter, accidently shot the first shot, which entered the second trailer truck behind it. Agent Mike Curtis, who was driving the second truck, reluctantly testified that as he stopped and jumped out of his truck, a bullet came through the front window and straight out the back, as if fired from the cattle trailer in front of him.[59]

Non-Agents' Dubious Testimony

Two non-agents testified they thought shots first came from inside Mount Carmel. *Waco Tribune-Herald* reporter Marc Masferrer, who conceded he had no prior ballistics training, was about three-hundred yards south of Mount Carmel at the time. A defense attorney commented, "At that distance, those people would look like ants."[60] KWTX-TV cameraman Dan Mulloney, who was driving up the driveway at that point, testified that "gunfire originated inside the compound." He admitted under cross-examination that this was merely his opinion.[61]

BATF/FBI Lost Davidians' Front Door

The pro-BATF television movie, "In the Line of Duty: Ambush at Waco," shows a line of eight to ten armed Davidians firing out at BATF agents as they begin their raid on the front of the building. Davidians claim the first shots were fired at David Koresh and entered through the front door. It becomes clear the movie's dramatic image is a BATF-inspired lie when one realizes that the two most significant pieces of evidence that it was BATF who shot first—half the front door and Perry Jones' autopsy report—are missing or falsified.

The *Waco Tribune-Herald* photos taken within twenty to thirty seconds of the first shots show no barrage of larger holes as would be expected if the Davidians had fired out at the agents. There was certainly no indication that "the force of the gunfire was so great that the door bowed outward," as the Treasury report puts it. During the trial attorney Jack Zimmermann, who had an opportunity to examine the hollow metal front doors before the fire, testified that one door had a "spray pattern" of holes made by bullets fired into the house and no bullet holes going out.[62]

Early in the trial Texas Ranger Fred Cummings disclosed that the half of the front door which allegedly had been hit by the most gunfire from the outside was missing. He revealed that he did not start his search of the area where the one door was found until April 22, three days after the fire, and that the door was not found until April 24. When the other half of the double doors was brought into court it was discovered to have four bullets holes directed inward and nine bullet holes directed outward. Attorneys noted that the missing door took more gunfire than the one that was found.[63]

Later in the trial FBI agent R. J. Craig said his tank knocked down the front doors and dragged them *away* from the building. Photos taken during the fire showed that the doors were well away from the building.[64]

Texas Ranger David A. Byrnes acknowledged that there were a "couple of hours" between the fire and the time Texas Rangers took control during which FBI and ATF agents "could have had access." Ranger Cummings confirmed that in the days before he found the door FBI agents loaded "trash" into a giant dumpster. It was hauled off before defense attorneys were allowed to visit the site.[65]

Many suspect BATF and/or FBI agents destroyed this crucial piece of evidence. After the trial one juror told reporters that the missing door was an important issue to jurors. It might not have proved definitively who shot first, but it might have indicated "how much of a barrage was headed in which direction" in the first minutes of the raid.[66]

Questionable Perry Jones Autopsy

Something which has received less publicity than the missing door, but is equally damning, is an inaccurate autopsy report on Koresh's father-in-law Perry Jones. Davidian survivors claim the unarmed Jones, standing next to Koresh when he opened the front door, was hit in the abdomen by the first barrage of

bullets.[67] In the March 8 home movie Davidians sent to
the FBI, Rachel Jones Koresh says: "Thanks a lot for
killing my dad. He was an unarmed man. And you guys
just shot him through the door and killed him."

Clive Doyle describes how, after he heard David
Koresh beg BATF agents to talk, he heard gun shots
and ran down the hall. "I found Perry Jones laying in
the hall crying in great pain, saying he had been shot.
Perry Jones was an older man in his sixties. He
apparently had been standing behind David as David
opened the door. . . . We helped Perry up into the north
end of the building, where the men's quarters were, and
put him on a bunk bed away from the front wall where
the bullets were continuing to fire. Perry was in great
pain."[68]

However, the medical examiner and Treasury
report describes only one wound for Jones—a bullet
through the brain, from one shot to the mouth. The
type of weapon and ammunition used are listed as
"unknown."[69] Kathryn Schroeder testified at trial she
heard the now-deceased Neil Vaega ask David Koresh
for "permission to finish off" Perry Jones, so it is not
clear if Jones committed suicide or died from a mercy
killing. Schroeder testified she believed the government
was about to kill them all; believing the same, Jones
probably decided to die immediately.[70] It is doubtful
Jones would have committed suicide, or Vaega would
have had to resort to a mercy killing, unless Jones *was*
severely wounded.

The official autopsy report by Marc A. Krouse,
M.D., describes a man of Jones' age, height, and hair
color. Jones' body was buried in a shallow grave in the

tornado shelter and was not touched by the fire. Krouse reported "no trauma" nor "evidence of fluid accumulation or hemorrhage within the major body cavities nor is there evidence of occult trauma." The stomach and intestines were "intact." Other evidence that this autopsy was botched is the finding that Jones' body contained 52 percent monoxide saturation in the liver, consistent with smoke inhalation! While some believe the government purposely switched bodies to cover up evidence that the BATF shot first and indiscriminately, fatally wounding the unarmed Perry Jones, others believe the medical examiners simply erred or lied.

Perry Jones' family members delayed in claiming Jones' body while trying to finance an independent autopsy to be done in conjunction with their civil law suit. Perry Jones' body and that of twenty-nine other Davidians were being kept by the Tarrant County Medical Examiner's office in Fort Worth, supposedly in a special refrigeration unit meant to preserve the remains. As late as August, 1993, Davidian survivor Clive Doyle was told that he could not view the remains because it might jeopardize the refrigeration process. However, in October, 1993, Davidians discovered that in the spring of 1993, right after former U.S. Attorney Ramsey Clark took on the Jones' and other family lawsuits, the medical examiner's office "accidently" turned off the refrigeration. The bodies were nearly totally decomposed and consumed by maggots. Pathologist Rodney Crowe described them as being "pieces of sludge."[71]

Suspicions About Unreleased BATF Video Tape

Both Waco television station KWTX-TV and
BATF videotaped the February 28 raid. KWTX-TV had
not yet set up their camera when the first shots were
fired and has no relevant footage. Soon after the raid,
BATF Associate Director Edward Conroy said a video
tape taken from a BATF helicopter during the raid might
clarify the question of who fired the first shots. David
Koresh told negotiators that when he stepped out on to
the front porch to beg BATF agents to call it off, "I saw
the guys right across the street when I was on the front
porch over there taping it." He referred to agents in the
undercover house directly across the street. In April,
1993, Davidian attorneys succeeded in having U.S.
District Court Judge Walter A. Smith, Jr.—who also
presided over the trial—order that all BATF audio and
videotapes be preserved. However, he allowed them to
remain in the BATF's hands.[72]

The BATF never has released any video from
the beginning of the raid, though some taken at the end
from helicopters has been televised. At trial BATF
agents and National Guardsmen revealed there were
two video cameras in the undercover house itself and
three or more video cameras in the helicopters. But
they could provide no credible excuses for the failure
to obtain footage of the beginning of the raid.

A Texas Ranger testified that there was a video
camera in a communications van near the undercover
house; he did not identify its owner. Undercover agent
Robert Rodriguez stated that there were a number of
agents in the undercover house the night before the raid,

including those operating the two video cameras. Their assignment was to photograph the arrival of the agents and the raid. No one from the undercover house was called to the stand to explain why they did not perform their duty. Rodriguez said that he assumed that "when all hell broke out, everybody forgot about the video and camera, nothing was used." However, he could not explain why agents were not filming before the shooting started.[73]

National Guard pilot Doyle Stone testified recording ended in his helicopter because they were scared when Davidians started firing at the helicopters and stopped running their forward-looking infrared camera. (That camera probably was brought to help detect the alleged methamphetamine laboratory.) Pilot Bryan Dickens revealed that he saw several BATF agents with camcorders get into the big Blackhawk helicopter. Yet prosecutors gave little film to defense attorneys, and most of that contained numerous cuts. Pilot Jerry Seagraves claimed that the cuts in the film were explained by the fact that agents did not want to waste film.[74]

Knowing that BATF agents might well have video footage of agents firing at the front door first or firing from helicopters, defense attorneys complained bitterly about this missing video tape and demanded prosecutors provide it. During closing arguments one attorney asserted, "There is absolutely no explanation of why we don't have those video tapes and still photographs of actually [sic] the arrival of the agents at the front door. You know those were taken, ladies and gentlemen, you know they were." Another told jurors,

"If David Koresh didn't walk out that door unarmed, you can be sure that video would be in your face right now."[75] According to jury forewoman Sarah Bain, jurors found it particularly suspicious that the BATF did not produce the video tapes at trial.[76]

EVIDENCE AGENTS SHOT INDISCRIMINATELY

The Treasury report states that BATF agents "returned fire when possible, but conserved their ammunition. They also fired only when they saw an individual engage in a threatening action, such as pointing a weapon."[77] Both BATF Director Higgins at an April 2, 1993, congressional hearing and Treasury Secretary Bentsen during the September, 1993, Treasury Department press conference, denied allegations that agents fired indiscriminately.[78]

Higgins and Bentsen knew that any agent who was shown to have violated guidelines against indiscriminate firing could be disciplined; if it was proved that agents injured or killed someone while violating this policy, even if they shot in self-defense, they could be charged with assault or manslaughter: and if it was proved that they were shooting in revenge for the wounding or death of fellow officers, they could be charged with intentional homicide.[79] Although evidence abounds that many agents fired indiscriminately, none have been disciplined or prosecuted.

Agents Admitted Indiscriminate Fire

Agent Sprague, when asked to define what he termed as "threats" at which he would shoot, described a pair of hands in a window, a pair of arms, and curtains moving—he fired at all of them.[80] Agent Timothy Gabourie confessed that since he was not wearing a helmet and didn't want to raise his head over the side of the truck, he drew his 9-millimeter pistol and fired twenty-five to thirty shots into the building without looking. He described this dangerous technique as "point and shoot" and admitted he had not learned this technique from either the National Guard or the BATF.[81] As we have seen, agent Barbara Maxwell acknowledged agents were firing indiscriminately through walls and windows.

At trial, Texas Rangers testified that BATF agents in the undercover house three-hundred yards south of Mount Carmel were firing at the building. Rangers collected more than seventy used shell casings from in and around the undercover house.[82] Reporter Marc Masferrer testified that he observed firing from the BATF undercover house.[83] Agents firing from such a distance could not have fired with great discrimination and a Texas Ranger reluctantly agreed such "friendly fire" from the undercover house could have struck the driver's door of one of the BATF pickup trucks that pulled cattle trailers on February 28.[84] Since the door was not facing Mount Carmel, there is no other explanation.

KWTX-TV television video tape clearly shows that agents were exercising little control over their firing as they fired over vehicles with little or no view of their targets. At one point, an agent clearly can be heard saying, "Too much wild fire." Again, we do not know how much footage damaging to BATF may have been edited out.

Davidians Described Indiscriminate Fire

During the trial Kathryn Schroeder described indiscriminate fire. She saw a bullet crash through her bedroom window fifteen or twenty seconds after the first shots began; at least "half a dozen" shots smashed into her room.[85] Wayne Martin's wife Sheila recalls crawling along the floor to pull her disabled young son Jamie from his bed near a window, as glass shattered on his body. She argues she would not have left him there if she were expecting a gun battle.[86] In the March 8 home movie, Koresh's eight-year-old son Cyrus and eight-year-old Joseph Martinez describe bullets smashing through the walls and lodging in the floor of their room, just a few feet from where they huddled for safety. At trial Davidian attorney Jack Zimmermann described bullet-hole evidence of such indiscriminate fire throughout the building.[87]

Clive Doyle told an interviewer: "I noticed a line of bullets down the hallway from the kitchen on down through the front door. It was if somebody with a machine gun on the outside blindly sprayed bullets, hoping to hit somebody running down the hall without being able to see them because there were no windows."[88]

Chapter Four: The BATF Initiated Violent Raid

1. Treasury Department report: 82.
2. Trial transcript: 7174–76.
3. Ibid., 1559.
4. Ibid., 2251.
5. Ibid., 1287.
6. Ibid., 2055; John Kolman, "A Selective Analysis of Operation Trojan Horse," Treasury Department report: B-55.
7. Lee Hancock, "Television Photographer Says He Tipped Waco Cult," *Washington Post*, August 28, 1993.
8. Treasury Department report: 85.
9. Ibid.
10. Trial transcript: 1517–18, 3357.
11. Treasury Department Report, 91.
12. Ibid., 195.
13. Diana R. Fuentes, "Case may wrap up at end of February," *San Antonio Express-News*, February 6, 1994: 5B; James L. Pate, July, 1994: 47; my reading of trial transcripts.
14. Trial transcript: 2242.
15. *USA Today*, April 21, 1993: A4.
16. Trial transcript: 1387–99, 2099.
17. Ibid., 2098, 2133, 2170, 2243, 2560, 2585.
18. Ibid., 2095, 2098.
19. Ibid., 1974–77, 2133.
20. Ibid., 3394, 6384.
21. Clare Tuma report, "Court TV," February 3, 1994; trial transcript: 4462–68.
22. June 16, 1994 trial transcript: 143–44.
23. Trial transcript: 2732–33.
24. Teresa Talerico, "More forces needed on raid, agent says," *Waco Tribune-Herald*, January 25, 1994: 8A; trial transcript: 2344.
25. Trial transcript: 1287, 1333–35, 1361, 1380.
26. Trial transcript: 2577.
27. June 9, 1993, House Appropriations Subcommittee hearing transcript: 175.
28. Trial transcript: 2210–11, 2820, 3153, 6837; James L. Pate, private communication, June, 1994.

29.   Jack DeVault, *The Waco Whitewash* (San Antonio, TX: Rescue Press, 1994): 71.

30.   Trial transcript: 1235.

31.   "Fire Power" video produced by National Endowment for Liberty, 1994; trial transcript: 1234; Treasury Department report: 104.

32.   Associated Press wire story, February 28, 1993.

33.   Daniel Wattenberg: 40.

34.   Diana R. Fuentes, "Jury hears about raid, mass suicide plan," *San Antonio Express-News*, February 2, 1994; James L. Pate, "Judgment Day: The Waco Trial, Part II," *Soldier of Fortune*, June, 1994: 35; trial transcript: 4091–5; 4464–5.

35.   Trial transcript: 6808–12.

36.   Ibid., 2567–68.

37.   Ibid., 1949–50.

38.   Ibid., 1995, 2037.

39.   Ibid., 2813–14.

40.   Trial transcript: 4494; Jaime Castillo, private communication, September, 1994.

41.   Trial transcript: 6613.

42.   Ibid., 580, 2139, 2428–29, 2459.

43.   Treasury Department report photograph: 99.

44.   Trial transcript: 1369, 2062, 2542.

45.   Ibid., 1377.

46.   Treasury Department report: 143–156.

47.   Trial transcript: 2280–88.

48.   Ibid., 1359; Renos Avraam, private communication, June, 1994.

49.   *Houston Post*, March 4, 1993: A20.

50.   Jaime Castillo, private communication, January and February, 1995.

51.   Trial transcript: 3053.

52.   James L. Pate, July, 1994: 47; Brad Branch, private communication, July, 1995.

53.   Trial transcript: 6392.

54.   Treasury Department report: 98.

55.   "Witness Says Cult Ambushed Agents but Acknowledges Blunders," *New York Times*, January, 19, 1994; trial transcript: 1291, 1295, 1314, 1319, 1382, 1401, 1461, 1509.

56.   Trial transcript: 1937, 1943, 1981.

57.   Ibid., 1990.

58.   Ibid., 2059, 2064–7, 2069, 2071, 2135.

59.   Ibid., 1833, 1834–35, 1845.

60.   Scott W. Wright, "Agents at Branch Davidian trial describe blitz of bullets at raid," *Austin-American Statesman* January 21, 1994: B3; trial transcript: 1930–31.

61.   "Agent Explains Why Cult Raid Was Moved Up," *New York Times*, January 28, 1994; trial transcript: 3307.

62.   Trial transcript: 6594.

63.   Ibid., 1070–73, 6120.

64.   Ibid., 1073, 5535.

65.   Ibid., 610, 1081.

66.   Teresa Talerico, "Trial was grueling, juror says," *Waco Tribune-Herald*, March 3, 1994.

67.   "3 Waco Cultists Shot Point Blank, Autopsies Show," *Washington Post*, July 15, 1993; *New York Times*, February 6, 1994; James L. Pate, July, 1994: 47.

68.   Gary Null, "Holocaust at Waco," *Penthouse,* April, 1994: 32.

69.   Treasury Department report: 104.

70.   Teresa Talerico, "Cultist says deaths were biblical," *Waco Tribune-Herald*, February 4, 1994; trial transcript: 4476–77.

71.   Sharon Fisher, Dewey Millay, Clive Doyle, and David Thibodeau, private communications, October, 1994; Ramsey Clark lawsuit, February 25, 1995: 48.

72.   Ken Fawcett: 44; Order, April 20, 1993, *U.S. v. Vernon Wayne Howell,* U.S. District Court of the Western District of Texas, Waco Division; "FBI Places Full Blame on Koresh for Tragedy," *Los Angeles Times*, April 21, 1993: A6; Carol Moore, review of section of negotiation tape.

73.   Trial transcript: 688, 3424, 3553–56.

74.   Ibid., 688, 3182, 3213, 3235, 3293.

75.   Ibid., 3248, 3553–56, 7097–98, 7178.

76.   Sarah Bain, private communication, June, 1994.

77.   Treasury Department report: 101.

78.   "Sect's Lawyers Dispute Gunfight Details," *New York Times*, April 5, 1993: A10; transcript of September 30, 1993, Treasury Department press conference.

79.   Kirk Lyons, private communication, June, 1994.

80.   Trial transcript: 2241–42, 2252–53.

81.   Ibid., 2496–98.

82.   Ibid., 1149–52.
83.   Ibid., 1926.
84.   Kathy Fair, January 15, 1994: 36A; trial transcript: 1116–22.
85.   Trial transcript: 4464.
86.   Sheila Martin, private communication, January, 1995.
87.   Ibid., 6597–6602.
88.   Gary Null, April, 1994: 32.

5
The BATF Actions
Led to Ten Deaths

I thought I was going to die that day. I thought I was going to get blown away. . . . Put in that situation where you've got women and children crying and screaming, "Oh, my God, please help us, save us, do something! They're shooting at us!" . . . You do anything, you pick up anything you can, if your life is threatened, to defend yourself.

Kevin Whitecliff before sentencing[1]

BATF's violent attack resulted in the deaths of five Davidians—four may have been killed by shots fired from helicopters. Considering the amount of gunfire directed at the Davidians from the helicopters and from ground fire, it is amazing so few were injured or killed. Koresh did tell KRLD radio on February 28 that his two-year-old daughter had been killed. Jaime Castillo explains that some of Jaydean Wendell's blood fell on the child and in the confusion it was explained to Koresh that the child had died.[2] Other Davidians besides David Koresh not mortally wounded included Judy Schneider, who was sitting in a chair when the firing began. David Jones was wounded in the gluteus maximus and Scott Sonobe in the leg.[3]

Rather than take responsibility for the deaths of the five Davidians who died during or shortly after the raid, the government has labelled them "ambushers." At trial, prosecutors falsely claimed Davidians "not only killed ATF, they killed their own. People who were too wounded to fight were put out of their misery."[4]

While there is no evidence Davidians ambushed the BATF, it is clear they were forced to take up weapons to defend themselves. While they probably killed and injured BATF agents, some agents were hit by friendly fire. Later that afternoon BATF agents killed a possibly unarmed Davidian who was trying to return to Mount Carmel.

EVIDENCE AGENTS SHOT FROM HELICOPTERS

The Treasury report claims that when the National Guard helicopters got within 350 meters of the building, they were fired upon and forced back.[5] At trial, helicopter pilots alleged that the lead helicopter was hit by three shots and the other two by one shot each.[6]

However, Davidians allege that agents in one or more helicopters started unprovoked firing at them as they arrived at the north side of the building and continued to pass back and forth over the building, firing at will, for several minutes. They claim there were over one hundred bullet holes from the agents in helicopters shooting into the walls and roofs. The three largest Davidian lawsuits, filed by the Cause Foundation, Ramsey Clark, and Caddell & Conwell, all charge there was firing from helicopters.[7]

In KPOC-TV's "Incident at Waco," investigator Gordon Novel charged, "In Vietnam, when they would attack a building like this, they would shoot up the ceiling so everyone would get down." Indiscriminate firing into a building from helicopters, especially that which killed unarmed civilians, would open agents to prosecution for negligent or intentional homicide."[8] If Mount Carmel had stood and the public discovered agents' firing indiscriminately from helicopters had killed four Davidians, citizens and politicians would have demanded prosecutions.

When questioned by the author during a May, 1995, televised debate about whether agents should be charged with murder should evidence of lethal firing be revealed, former BATF Director Stephen E. Higgins, who approved the raid, replied, "Absolutely. If they fire at someone who was not firing at them or pointing a weapon at them it would absolutely be murder. The rules of the federal government and other law enforcement officials are that you can only fire when you are trying to save your own life or lives of other innocent people." Higgins did not believe the agents were firing from helicopters. However, if this was his attitude as head of the Bureau, BATF agents would have had much to fear. There is substantial evidence that BATF agents did shoot from at least one helicopter.[9]

Davidian Allegations

Davidians in the back of the building claim first shots came from the helicopters. In the "Day 51" video Catherine Matteson, seventy-seven, states: "I heard three helicopters. The reason I knew there were three was I looked out the window and I could see they were firing on us.... I was in the back of the building. That's where my room was. And they were firing towards David's room. And they turned, and when they turned I fell to the floor 'cause I could see that those bullets could hit me if I was standing. They went to the front of the building. And it seemed like by the time they got to the front, they were firing again.... Definitely. They were the only ones I heard and saw at the time. They were coming in on the helicopters. There was no one else firing."

In the same video another elderly woman, Annetta Richards, recounts: "I was actually getting ready for worship. I heard a noise like a helicopter, and then I heard bullets start firing, bullets start coming in from every direction. And the helicopters were flying over the building. The sound of it was so low that at that time I thought they had landed on the roof. Bullets were coming from all directions."

Marjorie Thomas, a Davidian severely burned in the fire, agreed to testify for the prosecution in exchange for immunity. In her video taped testimony, Thomas said she was in her third floor room overlooking the tornado shelter when she noticed her roommates looking out the window. She looked out and saw three helicopters approaching. The lead one was shining a bright light, as one helicopter pilot admitted at trial. "I could see a person hanging from one side of the helicopter, because it was that close." Since she could see him from "the waist, down," his legs obviously were hanging outside the aircraft.

On the March 8, 1993, video tape sent out to the FBI, Thomas said, "One minute you're looking out of the window seeing three helicopters and the next minute you're on the floor with bullet shells flying all over your head." At trial she said, "As the helicopter drew nearer, I heard a sound. It was a bullet coming, which came through the window and shattered the blinds. We all dived to the floor. We moved from the window and dived to the floor on hearing the bullets flying over our heads." While she could not swear the bullets came from the helicopter, she saw no BATF agents on the ground. At least one bullet went through the third story window closest to the driveway.[10] Agents may have thought the women were armed and purposely fired upon them.

Clive Doyle told interviewer Gary Null why he was convinced Winston Blake, a twenty-eight-year-old black man from England, was shot from a helicopter. Blake's room was next to the three plastic water tanks at the northwest corner of the building. "I could see Winston laying down in a pool of water. The water tank, which was right up against his window, was riddled with bullets. Since the tank was at an angle, I would almost bet my life on it that Winston was shot from a helicopter. That was the only thing out there that could shoot at that angle. There weren't any buildings there. There weren't any ATF people on the ground who would be able to shoot at that angle." Jaime Castillo confirms that bullets came in at that angle.[11]

In late March, 1993, Rita Riddle told reporters there was "no question" agents fired from helicopters. "They say these helicopters were not armed? Bull puck. I heard them spraying the building when they went over."[12] In the March 28, 1993, taped interview with attorney Dick DeGuerin, David Koresh denied that Davidians fired on helicopters before the cattle trailers arrived and challenged the BATF's claim that BATF agents did not fire on Davidians from helicopters.[13] The negotiation audio tapes reveal that both Steve Schneider and David Koresh informed negotiators of the firing.[14]

Psychologist Bruce D. Perry, who interviewed Davidian children who left Mount Carmel after the raid, described a child drawing a picture of a house beneath a rainbow. "When Perry asked, 'Is there anything else?' the child calmly added bullet holes in the roof."[15]

At trial Kathryn Schroeder said she saw bullet holes in the ceiling and walls of the four-story tower.[16] During allocution before sentencing Davidian prisoner Kevin Whitecliff said he was scared when he heard women and children screaming as agents began their raid: "There were three or four helicopters buzzing around shooting at people. I thought I was going to die."[17]

At allocution, Renos Avraam tried to call to the stand BATF investigator Davy Aguilera, who was in one of the helicopters, to prove that helicopter pilots had lied when they denied there was shooting from the helicopters. When Judge Walter Smith would not permit it, Avraam asserted the BATF came "with helicopters blazing. Davy Aguilera, he was firing one of them. He ain't going to deny it. Helicopters blazing." Avraam bitterly complained that National Guard helicopter pilots perjured themselves. He himself saw the firing on February 28.[18]

Fifteen minutes into the raid, in their second phone call to 911, Davidians complain frantically to Lieutenant Lynch about helicopters firing on them as nearly continuous gunfire can be heard in the background.

> *Wayne Martin:* Another chopper with more people; more guns going off. They're firing. That's them, not us.
>
> *Steve Schneider:* There's a chopper with more of them.
>
> *Lt. Lynch:* What!?
>
> *Schneider:* Another chopper with more people and more guns going off. Here they come!
>
> *Lynch:* All right, Wayne, tell . . .
>
> *Schneider:* We're not firing. That's not us, that's them!
>
> *Lynch:* All right. Standby. I'm tryin' to reach 'em. Stand. Don't return fire, okay?

> *Schneider:* We haven't been.
> *Lynch:* What?
> *Schneider:* We haven't been.

Later in the 911 tape Martin demands: "Don't land any more choppers," and "We don't want any more choppers out here."[19] At trial, both Judge Smith and the prosecutors tried to dismiss these statements as "self-serving," implying that panicky civilians would make up such a story for some nefarious purpose.[20]

KWTX-TV Video Shows Shots Fired From Sky

The frequently shown KWTX-TV video of an agent being shot at through the wall of the second-story room displays clear evidence that at least four bullets were fired from above, even as the sounds of helicopters flying overhead can be heard. "Waco, the Big Lie Continues" slows down the video and points out obvious bullet entries from overhead into the roof, eaves, and wall. While BATF agents alleged in court that Davidians were firing at them from the four-story tower,[21] the trajectory of the bullets appears much too steep to have come from the tower.

The holes are shot through the roof right after an agent appears to fire into the arms room, so it is possible Davidians were defending against that agent's attack. However, it also is possible that an agent in a helicopter, seeing the other agent shooting into the room (and not knowing there were already three agents inside) attempted to help him by shooting in as well.

Many suspect KWTX-TV managers, fearful of offending the government and the Federal Communications Commission (FCC), edited out even more damaging evidence of helicopter and other illegal gunfire. At trial KWTX-TV cameraman Dan Mulloney stated that although he was on the scene for more than two hours and brought four hours of video tape, he shot only seventeen minutes of video because he was trying to save tape. He asserted that the video shown by prosecutors "was not edited, it was shot from the camera. The glitches and things were myself turning the camera on and off. But it did come from a raw tape, and I'm not familiar [with] who dubbed in down from the raw master tape." However, he then admitted that prosecutors had not shown some film at the end of the tape, where BATF agents had physically assaulted and knocked him down.[22] It is likely Mulloney does not remember every inch of tape shot and that some could have been edited out without his knowledge. There has been no explanation for why in some of the audio—especially of shots while the agents are on the roof—the sounds of gunfire and aircraft overflying the building cut in and out erratically.

Attorneys' Statements and Testimony

Davidian attorneys Dick DeGuerin and Jack Zimmermann, who visited Mount Carmel during the siege, insist that there was extensive evidence that BATF agents shot indiscriminately through Mount Carmel's front doors, walls, and roof. They were very concerned with preserving this evidence of an out-of-control assault.

In early April, 1993, the *New York Times* reported, "both lawyers clearly believed that helicopters flying over the compound during the raid had fired into upper floors of the main building from above." BATF spokesperson Jerry Singer denied this. "The helicopters did not overfly the compound on Feb. 28, and I have no information that anyone fired from the helicopters." However, Jack Zimmermann stated, and Dick DeGuerin concurred, "an expert will be able to tell from the angle of the trajectory plus the pattern whether there are entry or exit holes. If it's in the ceiling and it's clearly an exit hole, it had to come from above. How else could it have come in?"[23]

At trial, Zimmermann, who is an army colonel and Vietnam veteran, described eight or nine bullet holes coming into the ceiling of David Koresh's bedroom in the top floor of the four-story tower. "You could see the sky through the roof. They appeared to be exit holes, and the wood was splintered downward. My conclusion was that they came from the sky."[24] He held that these holes could not have come from the water tower, which was not as high as the four-story tower. He did acknowledge that bullet holes in the chapel roof could have come from a Davidian shooting from the four-story tower.[25]

Helicopter Pilots Lied about Circling Mount Carmel Before Raid

At trial three National Guard helicopter pilots

testified. Captain Bryan Dickens piloted a small OH-58 helicopter which carried another National Guardsman and raid commander SAC Philip Chojnacki. CWF Doyle L. Stone, Jr. piloted another OH-58 which carried two National Guardsmen.[26] CW4 Jerry Seagraves piloted the large Blackhawk which carried five Guardsmen and eight BATF agents. BATF agents aboard included Ted Royster, commander of many past aggressive raids and an unofficial commander for this one, and lead investigator Davy Aguilera, who had told Marc Breault that David Koresh should be "put away."[27]

At trial two helicopter pilots claimed that they left the staging area at Texas State Technical College at approximately 9:30 A.M. However, Captain Dickens revealed that flight log books had been destroyed ninety days after the raid, so he could not verify the time the helicopters left.[28] Pilot Seagraves made the not-very-credible statement that it took helicopters fifteen to twenty minutes to fly the short six to eight miles to Mount Carmel. While pilot Stone acknowledged the helicopters flew to a "loiter point" while waiting for "ground forces" to make their way to the "target," pilot Seagraves insisted that the helicopters did not circle Mount Carmel.[29]

However, KWTX-TV cameraman Dan Mulloney and reporter John McLemore told a very different story at trial, one that discredited the testimony of the pilots. Mulloney testified that the newsmen parked their white Bronco about two miles from Mount Carmel as they waited for the helicopters they expected would warn them the raid was imminent. When Mulloney saw the helicopters, he checked his watch. It was 9:30 A.M.

During the next ten to fifteen minutes the helicopters "flew behind the compound and made three big loops around the compound." Between the second and third loops they drove their vehicle closer to Mount Carmel. When they were a quarter mile away, Mulloney videotaped the helicopters making their third loop as they came in for the raid. Defense attorneys called John McLemore who repeated the exact same story.[30]

In an interview for Arts and Entertainment television's *American Justice* series, McLemore and Mulloney complained bitterly that their allegation about the helicopters circling Mount Carmel is "something that the BATF and the FBI categorically deny. They tell us we are lying."[31] However, the Treasury report does repeat KWTX-TV cameraman Peeler's statement he also saw the helicopters between 9:15 and 9:30 A.M. from about a mile east of Mount Carmel. And it notes that according to *Waco Tribune-Herald* cellular phone records, at 9:26 A.M. photojournalist Robert Sanchez called his superior to advise him that the helicopters were leaving the staging area.[32] Obviously the helicopters had plenty of time to move to Mount Carmel and circle it several times before the 9:48 A.M. beginning of the raid.

McLemore and Mulloney have no reason to lie about seeing the helicopter make the three big loops. However, National Guardsmen might have lied as part of the coverup of their witnessing illegal and deadly firing from their helicopters. Their lies also cast doubt on their assertions that it was Davidians who fired the bullets found in their aircraft.

Did Helicopter Pilots Lie About Overflying Mount Carmel?

National Guard pilots testified that they approached Mount Carmel flying southwest at approximately 500 feet; however, when they got within 350 to 400 feet, Davidians shot at them so they immediately broke off in a northeast direction. While one pilot admitted the helicopters were as low as fifty feet off the ground, all denied an overfly.[33]

KWTX-TV video clearly shows the helicopters low on the horizon west of Mount Carmel several minutes into the raid, after agents are in place behind parked vehicles. In later KWTX-TV footage the cameraman or reporter can clearly be heard to say, "Two of them right over our heads," evidently a reference to aircraft which can be heard noisily flying above them.[34]

At trial, cameraman Mulloney stated that after the shooting started, the helicopters were at approximately the same height as Mount Carmel. He then lost sight of them. While defense attorneys did not specifically question him about the statement "two of them right over our heads," they did question him about the engine noises evident on the video tape. Mulloney stated that there was a single-engined aircraft overhead.[35] The Treasury report reveals that the surveillance aircraft started at 2,500 feet and then circled at 1,500 feet in order to "spot shooters."[36] It is possible that on February 28 military spy satellites were taking photographs which could reveal just how many times helicopters circled and whether or not they overflew Mount Carmel.

Did Helicopter Pilots Lie About Shooting from Helicopters?

Defense attorneys questioned all three helicopter pilots about whether National Guardsmen or BATF agents in the helicopters were armed, whether the doors or windows were open, and whether there was any firing from the helicopters. Pilots Dickens and Stone in the two small helicopters (one of which held BATF raid commander Philip Chojnacki), both asserted that the doors to their crafts were closed, no one held a loaded weapon or was armed, and that no one fired from the helicopters.[37]

Defense attorneys concentrated their questions on Jerry Seagraves who was the pilot of the Blackhawk helicopter which carried eight BATF agents, including the belligerent Royster and Aguilera. Seagraves recited the rules—"you cannot have any chambered rounds in the weapon while in the aircraft and no weapon will be discharged from the aircraft." However, he disclosed that the agents on board were armed.[38]

Seagraves asserted the cargo doors were closed during the whole flight but revealed that the "door gunners window" was opened because a BATF agent was shooting video from it. (He said the purpose of that window was to carry an M-60 machine gun but there was no such machine gun.) Pilot Dickens testified that he saw one agent's head and shoulders hanging out of the window as he shot his video camera.[39]

Seagraves insisted he knew no one fired from the helicopter because he had been in helicopters overseas in Vietnam and would have recognized the sound of such gunfire. He asserted that no helmet, radios, or other gear would have stifled the sound. One defense attorney, in an attempt to suggest a reason Seagraves might lie about whether there was firing from the helicopters, made Seagraves confess that his National Guard pilot job was one of several odd jobs on which he survived. As a former serviceman, Seagraves also may have put loyalty to the National Guard and his comrades above the Constitutional rights of those living in what pilot Stone called the "target."[40]

No Real Investigation of Firing from Helicopters

The investigation of the helicopters' actions after the raid was cursory and concerned with gathering evidence that Davidians fired at and damaged the helicopters, and not the other way round. Captain Bryan Dickens, the leader of the helicopter squad, debriefed Stone and Seagraves and wrote the only report on the helicopters' activities. He did not forward his report to the U.S. Attorney or the Texas Rangers. The March, 1993, Texas Rangers' interview of Seagraves and June, 1993, Treasury agent interview of Stone certainly revealed no new evidence.[41] At trial, defense attorneys could not question BATF agents who had been in the helicopters about whether there was firing from the aircraft because Judge Smith effectively prevented the defense from calling Chojnacki, Royster, Aguilera, and other agents from the helicopters as witnesses.

If these BATF agents finally are put under oath and admit their crimes, it will be important that they

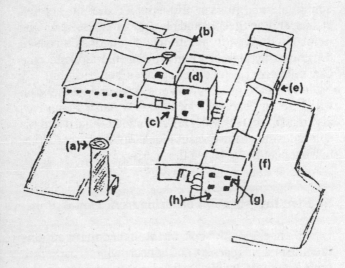

Where Helicopter and Indiscriminate Fire Killed Davidians

(a)   Peter Gent killed on water tower from shot from helicopter
(b)   KWTX-TV footage shows bullets entering second-story roof from sky.
(c)   Peter Hipsman mortally wounded on fourth-story from shot from helicopter.
(d)   Davidian attorneys saw bullet holes in roof of four-story tower.
(e)   Perry Jones mortally wounded at front door by agents on the ground.
(f)   Jaydean Wendell killed on second-floor by shot from helicopter.
(g)   Marjorie Thomas saw bullet from helicopter enter third-floor window.
(h)   Winston Blake killed in first-floor room by shot from helicopter that passed through water tanks.

not be allowed to seek protection by claiming of self-defense. For their justifiable fear of prosecution is a primary motivation for the vicious treatment of the Davidians by federal agents during the fifty-one days that followed.

DAVIDIANS CLAIM HELICOPTER
FIRE KILLED FOUR

If indiscriminate fire from helicopters, which easily could have escaped a dangerous situation, did kill four people, as Davidians claim, some BATF agents surely would have been prosecuted. During the siege, Davidians refused to tell the FBI how the following Davidians died, fearful that it would prompt the kind of assault the FBI eventually launched.

Peter Hipsman

Kathryn Schroeder and Jaime Castillo reveal Peter Hipsman, 28, was shot on the fourth floor. He may have been shot from a helicopter, since the medical examiner revealed that the shots traveled from left to right.[42] The Treasury report states Hipsman received two allegedly nonfatal wounds from "more than four feet," one to the chest and one through an arm. It claims he was "later killed by a cult member who shot him at close range in the back of his skull—an apparent mercy killing."[43] Kathryn Schroeder claimed that she overheard Neal Vaega say it took "two shots to finish

him off."[44] Like Perry Jones, Hipsman probably chose
to be killed by friends, rather than by "the beast."

Winston Blake

Davidians claim Englishman Winston Blake, 28,
was sitting on his bed, eating French toast, when a shot
from a helicopter came through the north wall and hit
him in the head, killing him instantly.[45] As stated
previously, Clive Doyle alleges that the bullet passed
through a water storage tank outside the room. (The
government claims these water tanks were destroyed
by the fire.) Jaime Castillo saw Blake's body in the room
just minutes after the shooting began.[46]

Prosecutors alleged Davidians killed Blake
because he would not fight. However, at trial Kathryn
Schroeder, who claimed Jones and Hipsman were put
out of their misery by Neal Vaega, did not claim Blake
was similarly shot.[47]

The Treasury report alleges Blake died of
"craniocerebral trauma," and was shot from a distance
of "two to three feet" by a "cult member" using a ".223"
bullet. The Tarrant County medical examiners' official
autopsy report on Winston Blake describes powder
burns around the wound, as if Blake had been shot from
a few feet away. However, an English pathologist
conducted a second autopsy on Blake and concluded
that Blake had died from a long-range, high-velocity
gunshot wound and that the bullet had penetrated a wall
before hitting him. This disturbing finding led to a full-

fledged, if inconclusive, investigation by Manchester, England, police in 1994 and 1995.[48]

Peter Gent

Davidians assert an unarmed Peter Gent, 24, was cleaning the inside of the water tower, heard the commotion, stuck his head out to see what was going on, and was shot through the heart by an agent in a helicopter.[49] The Treasury report states he died from a "distant" 9-millimeter hydroshock "perforation of aorta gunshot to upper left chest."[50] The government denies he was shot from a helicopter.[51]

At trial, agent Lowell Sprague said he saw two men armed with long rifles on the water tower and shot at them. Agent Roger Gutherie, stationed northwest of Mount Carmel, near the hay barn, claimed he actually did shoot an armed man on the water tower.[52] However, the government has never alleged Davidians retrieved Gent's weapon when they buried his body. And Texas Rangers found only a pistol in the tower and "rifle arms for AR-15 or M-16" near the concrete room.[53]

Jaydean Wendell

Davidians claim Jaydean Wendell, 34, had just finished nursing her baby and was asleep when a bullet shot from a helicopter came through the ceiling and penetrated her skull, killing her.[54] At trial, attorney Jack Zimmermann, who visited Mount Carmel during the siege, said he saw bullet holes by the "upper bunk wall" going in the direction of a pool of blood on the bed. This suggests Wendell was shot from above as she lay in bed.[55] The Treasury report offers no explanation for Jaydean Wendell's death from "craniocerebral trauma" caused by a distant shot from a 9-millimeter hydroshock bullet.[56]

At trial, Davidian prosecution witness Victorine Hollingsworth testified she saw Wendell come out from her room looking for a gun and return to it with one. Kathryn Schroeder asserted she saw Wendell's body on the bunk and held her bloody gun.[57] Given the government's desperate efforts to prove that agents were not firing from helicopters, we must wonder if they pressured the women to give this testimony.

The bodies of Perry Jones, Jaydean Wendell, Winston Blake, and Peter Hipsman were buried in the tornado shelter. The FBI waited a week before they allowed Davidians to bury Peter Gent's body in the yard. Davidians were furious that FBI tanks ran back and forth over the grave for the next five weeks.[58]

NO EVIDENCE BRANCH DAVIDIANS AMBUSHED BATF

The BATF has alleged all along that dozens of Davidians "ambushed" agents on February 28, 1993. In June, 1993, BATF Intelligence Chief David Troy told Congress: "This issue was unprecedented in the history of American law enforcement, when you had forty or more persons open fire indiscriminately with automatic weapons at law enforcement, be they state, or local, or federal. It never happened before."[59] Such BATF ambush allegations were repeatedly disproved at trial. There is ample evidence Davidians did not ambush BATF.

Koresh Warned Undercover Agent "They're Coming"

By definition, the Davidians could not have ambushed the BATF because BATF commanders and agents knew the Davidians were expecting them. Both undercover BATF agent Robert Rodriguez, at trial, and Davidian Graeme Craddock, before the grand jury, testified about what happened on Sunday morning, February 28, 1993. During a Bible study with Rodriguez, Koresh was called away from the room, supposedly to take a long distance phone call from England. When he returned, he was visibly shaken. He told Rodriguez that he knew law enforcement was coming. Graeme Craddock recalls Koresh saying, "Robert, they're coming. Whether BATF or FBI or whatever, they're coming." Craddock believes Koresh was trying to warn Rodriguez that some kind of raid was imminent.[60]

At trial, Rodriguez said Koresh "told me the ATF and National Guard were coming. 'They got me once. They'll never get me again.'" (Since neither the BATF or the National Guard had ever arrested or "gotten" Koresh before, Craddock believes this was another warning.) Rodriguez grew alarmed as five or six Davidians joined the three already in the room.

Convinced they were going to take him hostage, he considered diving through the window or even taking David Koresh hostage. However, Davidians made no threatening moves. When Rodriguez left, Koresh shook his hand as he bid him farewell.[61]

Cautious Koresh Warned Few Davidians

Agent Ballesteros testified that the BATF was ambushed because the Davidians did not shoot at them until they were close to the building.[62] Doubtless, David Koresh prudently waited to discover if approaching agents really intended to engage in a shootout or if their intentions were peaceful. Ballesteros admitted that an unarmed David Koresh came to the front door.[63] This is something no one planning an ambush would attempt.

Graeme Craddock told the grand jury that he was one of just a few who were given secret information that there might be a raid. Koresh told Craddock not to fire unless Koresh told him to. Koresh never did and Craddock never fired.[64] At trial Kathryn Schroeder testified that before the raid Koresh told women in the chapel to "get back to your rooms and watch," something he would not have told them if he expected shooting from building windows. She was dressing her children when the shots began.[65] Sheila Martin argues she would not have left her disabled son near a window if she were expecting a gun battle.[66]

At trial prosecutors mocked the Davidians for not using non-violent action when they heard the BATF was coming. They suggested they could have called 911, gone out in the yard and sung peace songs, quoted the Bible, waved protest signs, or lay down in front of the front gate.[67] Prosecutors did not note the irony of their lecturing citizens on the necessity of using nonviolence to defend themselves against brutal government attacks.

Davidians Had to "Hustle" to Find Guns

Davidians claim that Paul Fatta had taken many of their guns to a gun show and that most of the rest were boxed to retain their value.[68] Survivors contend few Davidians were even armed at first to return the BATF's gunfire. One who confessed some Davidians returned fire said: "People were running around everywhere, asking if anybody had any guns. Nobody had any handy. Most of what we had was new, still in the box."[69]

After the trial one juror, reacting to the testimony, stated: "They had forty-five minutes to get their people positioned, to get the guns all passed out. It seems to be quite apparent that there was no such plan because of the hustle-bustle to get the guns, even after the ATF drove up."[70]

Photographs and Video Show Little Fire from Davidians

Waco Tribune-Herald photographs, which reporter Marc Masferrer testified were all taken within the first twenty to thirty seconds of the raid, show windows intact with screens still in place, and no one in the windows, even as the agents are firing at the home. During the trial one defense attorney asked if it would not have made sense for persons planning an ambush to remove screens. Agent Ballesteros acknowledged the photographs showed agents firing at the building, but no people or guns visible in the windows. Reporter John McLemore said he never saw any Davidians in the windows firing back. And agent Barbara Maxwell testified she saw Davidian gunfire coming from only two second- floor windows during the whole shootout.[71]

One Waco Tribune-Herald photograph shows two agents only a dozen feet from Mount Carmel's front door kneeling and firing. These agents are not hiding behind cars or fences, as one would expect were they taking heavy gunfire. Agent Dan Curtis conceded at trial that he could not explain why, if these agents were under such intense gunfire from Davidians, they were not injured or killed.[72] Similarly, KWTX-TV video of agents firing at the front of the building shows no evidence of Davidian gunfire ripping up the ground or striking vehicles.

Two Agents Killed Late in the Raid

BATF Chief of Intelligence David Troy told the press that "in the first two minutes, sixteen agents were injured and four were killed," which allegedly supported the BATF's contention agents were "ambushed."[73] The Treasury report agrees: "Special Agents Steven D. Willis and Robert J. Williams were killed during the ambush."[74]

However, at trial BATF agent Dan Curtis stated Willis ran to the porch area, then retreated behind a green and white Chevy van and participated in firing at the building for fifteen to twenty minutes before being shot. Agent Sprague confirms this account.[75]

Robert Williams was shot while firing at the building from behind an outside safe on the east side of the building. Agent Kevin Richardson at trial claimed he was shot from the arms' room. However, KWTX-TV video shows no evidence Davidians were firing from the arms' room in the first minute or so as agents climbed the ladder—something agent Buford was forced to concede under cross-examination. And it is unlikely Davidians gained complete control of that area, and the ability to fire out of its windows, until agents had left it several minutes into the raid. This indicates Williams, who a defense attorney claimed was firing at Mount Carmel, also was shot late in the raid.[76]

Davidians Did Not Use Tactical Advantage

Perched as they were in a large building on a hill with a superior view of all oncoming vehicles, the

Davidians had an excellent opportunity to shoot at oncoming vehicles and kill dozens of agents, had they chosen to do so. They did not.

Justice Department outside expert Alan A. Stone, M.D., commented: "The BATF investigation reports that the so-called 'dynamic entry' turned into what is described as being 'ambushed.' As I tried to get a sense of the state of mind and behavior of the people in the compound the idea that the Davidians' actions were considered an 'ambush' troubled me. If they were militants determined to ambush and kill as many ATF agents as possible, it seemed to me that given their firepower, the devastation would have been even worse. ... The ATF agents brought to the compound in cattle cars could have been cattle going to slaughter if the Davidians had taken full advantage of their tactical superiority."[77]

During the trial Kathryn Schroeder testified that none of the exterior walls had been fortified with hay or barricaded until after the initial ATF attack. Davidians then did so because everyone was frightened.[78]

Davidians Called 911

One minute after BATF agents charged out of their cattle trucks, Davidian Wayne Martin, a Harvard-educated attorney, did what most Americans do when they are under criminal attack—he called 911. His desperate cries become etched in the minds of those who hear them: "There are about seventy-five men around our building shooting at us in Mount Carmel. Tell them there are children and women in here and to call if off! Call it off!"

McLennan County Sheriff's Lieutenant Lynch, who the BATF had assigned to the "minor" role of fielding any calls about the raid that might come from neighbors or motorists, ended up playing a critical role. However, because his only contact, Sheriff's Lieutenant Barber, had turned off his radio, it took Lynch nearly forty minutes to establish even indirect contact between the Davidians and BATF.[79]

On the 911 tapes Martin and other Davidians plead with Lieutenant Lynch to stop the BATF's shooting, even as Lynch desperately tries to contact the BATF. The BATF continues shooting even after contact is established, Martin skillfully arranges a cease-fire, and Davidians have passed the word on cease-fire. Played for the jury, an hour of the 911 tape was the most compelling evidence that the Davidians had not ambushed BATF agents but were fighting back in self-defense.

DAVIDIANS HAD LEGAL RIGHT TO SELF-DEFENSE

A few Davidians fought back against what they considered to be a murderous assault by unknown attackers. David Koresh told his attorney Dick DeGuerin in their March 28 audio-taped telephone conversation: "I don't care who they are, nobody is going to come to my home, with my babies around, shaking guns around, without a gun back in their face. That's just the American way."[80]

Davidian Stan Sylvia, who was in California the day of the raid, expressed his feelings on national television: "These people were on their own property. That didn't give the government right to come in shooting. . . . For once in people's lives they stood up for God and what they believed."[81]

The BATF's excessive force in attempting to deliver search and arrest warrants—warrants they did not even have with them—gave Davidians the right to use armed force in self-defense, even if it resulted in the deaths of some attacking agents. The Firearm Owners Protection Act of 1986 recognizes the Common Law rule of self-defense, which is that the defender must have reasonable belief that the circumstances of immediate danger warrant self-defense. And Section 9.31 of the Texas Penal Codes states: "The use of force to resist an arrest or search is justified: (1) If, before the actor offers any resistance, the peace officer (or persons acting at his direction) uses or attempts to use greater force than necessary to make the arrest or search; and (2) When and to the degree the actor reasonably believes the force is immediately necessary to protect himself against the peace officer's (or other person's) use or attempted use of greater force than necessary."[82]

Dick DeGuerin, who believed he would have obtained an acquittal of David Koresh had he lived, explained, "if a warrant is being unlawfully executed by the use of excessive force, you, or I, or anybody else has a right to resist that unlawful force. If someone's trying to kill you, even under the excuse that they have a warrant, you have a right to defend yourself with deadly force, and to kill that person."[83]

One of the Justice Department's handpicked outside experts, Dr. Robert Cancro, suggested Davidians were within their rights to defend themselves. "Certainly an armed assault by 100 agents had to be seen as an attack *independent* of who fired the first shot. If an armed individual enters your home by force and you have reason to believe that person represents a mortal threat, you are allowed to fire a weapon in self-defense in most states. The law does not usually allow the potential attacker to fire first before a response can be called self-defense."[84]

Davidian survivor Clive Doyle, who was acquitted at trial, told an interviewer: "I believe there were a few people who grabbed some weapons. I believe they retaliated because Perry and David had both been shot at the front door without being armed. I guess some people took the stand that they were defending the women, the children, and their teacher. You might say it was in self-defense, or a reaction to seeing people gunned down for no reason."[85]

Imprisoned Davidian Livingstone Fagan has written: "Our use of these guns were with restraint and strictly defensive. It is tragic that people were harmed, but were our intentions anything but defensive, the death toll would have been much higher."[86]

QUESTIONABLE EVIDENCE DAVIDIANS
USED MACHINE GUNS OR GRENADES

The Treasury report alleges "unrelenting automatic and semiautomatic weapons fire" from the Branch Davidians.[87] At trial agents Dan Curtis, Kris Mayfield, Robert Champion, Lowell Sprague, Clay Alexander, Larry Shriver, Gerald Petrilli, Samuel Cohen, and Bill Buford all testified they heard machine-gun fire coming from the Davidians.[88] However, BATF's MP-5s, which fire two shots per trigger pull, also are, and sound like, machine guns.

FBI weapons expert James Cadigan acknowledged there was no way to tell if the few bullet holes found in cars facing Mount Carmel were made with automatic or regular weapons.[89] A defense attorney pointed out that if fifty Davidians used fully automatic weapons "we wouldn't have four [agents] dead, we'd have seventy dead."[90] Another attorney said that if the Davidians had ambushed the BATF, "Those trailers would have looked like Bonnie and Clyde's car, but they didn't."[91]

After the raid BATF spokespersons continually claimed there was .50-caliber machine-gun fire—it was their primary excuse for keeping the press far from Mount Carmel. However, while agents Dan Curtis, Kris Mayfield, Kevin Richardson, Gerald Petrilli, and Timothy Gabourie all alleged they heard .50-caliber gunfire, only agents Curtis and Petrilli alleged they heard .50-caliber machine-gun fire. After the fire Texas Rangers found only two legal .50-caliber rifles. At trial FBI weapons expert James Cadigan was forced to admit that he did not find any .50-caliber cartridge cases with firing pin impressions, indicating that no .50-caliber weapon was fired during the fifty-one days.[92]

In early March, 1993, BATF officials alleged that "two of the wounded agents were hit by fragments of hand grenades lobbed from the compound."[93] Only one of those agents, Gerald Petrilli, testified. But he was unsure what had hit him, describing it as, "a shotgun round, explosive device or something."[94]

EVIDENCE FRIENDLY FIRE
INJURED OR KILLED SOME AGENTS

It is obvious that frightened, excited, and angry agents were firing wildly from the undercover house, from behind vehicles and structures surrounding the building and, very probably, from helicopters. With all that gunfire, it is inevitable that BATF agents injured, and even killed, some of their own. In fact, the April 5, 1993, *Newsweek* reported that a "federal source" in Waco stated "there is evidence that supports the theory of friendly fire," and that during the assault "there was a huge amount of cross fire."[95] Another highly placed federal source told James Pate, "about half of ATF casualties in the raid apparently resulted from 'friendly fire.' "[96] After these statements were made to the press, BATF placed a gag order on its agents.

BATF Agents Admitted Friendly Fire on Roof

There is one known case—and several suspected ones—of friendly fire on agents who climbed to the second-story roof over the chapel and tried to enter what had been, months before, Koresh's second floor living quarters—a bedroom on the west side and an arms' room on the east side. The Treasury report and trial versions of two agents killed on the roof, near the bedroom, is substantially different from the version the BATF originally released, which held that three agents were killed in the arms' room.[97] The Treasury report concedes, "Contrary to some publicly disseminated reports, none of the agents that entered the armory were killed."[98] Some are convinced that the original BATF report is true and the government is trying to cover up extensive friendly fire on the roof. The fact that both BATF helicopter and KWTX-TV video seems to have been cut at crucial moments only reinforces this suspicion.

At trial agent Kenneth King testified that on the west side of the roof, away from the KWTX-TV camera, agent Conway LeBleu's gunfire "covered" himself, David Millen, and Todd McKeehan as they tried to break into what they thought was David Koresh's bedroom on the west side of the roof. However, as soon as the agents—who never yelled "police" or "search warrant"—broke the window, someone in the back of the room shot at them. They did not even get a chance to throw their flash-bang in the room to disorient the shooter. King was shot. McKeehan and LeBleu were killed.[99] The government claims all were shot by Davidians; others speculate some could have been shot by BATF wildfire, including that from helicopters.

Agents Bill Buford, Glen Jordan, and Keith Constantino threw a flash-bang into and entered the old arms' room on the east side. They admitted great confusion in the room as they and unseen Davidians exchanged gunfire. They claim to have shot two Davidians inside. Buford estimated he fired a total of forty to fifty shots and that Constantino fired twenty to thirty.[100] (Davidian David Thibodeau confirmed deceased Davidian Scott Sonobe participated in an exchange of gunfire with agents. Jaime Castillo heard that David Koresh was the second Davidian shot there.[101])

Constantino testified that he had heard that a portion of the bullet removed from Agent Jordan was a 9-millimeter hydroshock bullet like his own and acknowledged "it's possible" he may have shot Jordan.[102] (FBI agent Cadigan confirmed that the Q-87 bullet found in Jordan came from a Sig-Saur, the gun carried by Constantino.) Under cross-examination Constantino at first asserted that Jordan did not go into his line of fire and might have been hit by a ricochet. Later he conceded that he had been behind Jordan at one point, so he could have shot him directly.[103]

There is some evidence of a cover-up in this incident, as in so many others. Prosecutors never called Jordan, the man most likely to know whether agents or Davidians shot him, to the stand. And Constantino revealed that he shared a room with Buford for several days before Texas Rangers interviewed them, giving them a chance to compare notes and alter their stories.[104]

Video evidence of apparent friendly fire of agent Millen on the roof comes from KWTX-TV video. After the three agents in his team were shot, Millen ran back to the east side of the roof, to the arms' room window where Buford, Constantino, and Jordan had entered. The Treasury report merely notes that he "stood guard."[105] However, video clearly shows Millen pull back the curtain of the armory and either try to or actually shoot into the room. (Both "Waco, the Big Lie" videos claim Millen threw something into the room; however, that does not appear to be true and neither Davidians nor Jack Zimmermann claimed to have seen evidence of a second grenade. Similarly, many doubt the agent climbing the ladder shot himself in the leg, as the video claims.) After Millen raised the curtain, there was a barrage of return gunfire through the wall out toward him. At trial, defense attorneys asked Buford whether Constantino had shot at Millen, but he denied it.[106]

It was right after Millen shot in the window that bullets began to fly down into the roof of the second-story arms' room—bullets possibly fired by BATF agents in helicopters. Millen rolled onto the roof and then slid down the ladder.

If Millen did shoot into the room, he might have injured the other agents. And if it were agents shooting back at him, he barely may have escaped being a victim of friendly fire. The Treasury report's list of injured agents did not include Millen.

Deaths of BATF Agents

Official autopsy reports on the two agents who died on the roof show that most of the bullets that killed them passed through their bodies, mostly from above and in a downward direction. Conway LeBleu, who two agents testified had been firing at Davidians in the tower, had four entry wounds, including one to the head. Medical examiner Nizaam Peerwani, M.D., testified that LeBleu also might have shot himself in the face while falling. Found in his body were "a flattened fragment of projective jacket with adherent core material" and "a distorted small-caliber full-jacketed projectile."[107] Todd McKeehan, who was helping King smash into Koresh's old bedroom, had one bullet wound to the chest in which Peerwani found "a deformed fully jacketed bullet . . . (consistent with a .223)."[108]

At trial, defense attorneys inferred that the two agents on the ground who were killed could have been shot by friendly fire.[109] As we have seen, there is definitive evidence that agent Steven Willis was killed approximately twenty minutes into the raid, after firing numerous shots at Mount Carmel. At trial Nizaam Peerwani, M.D., identified the bullet that hit Willis' left temple as a 7.62 round.

Robert Williams, who was shooting from behind a safe on the east side of the building, died from a gunshot wound to the head. Marc A. Krouse's autopsy reported no bullets or fragments found in Williams' body. Had he been killed by friendly fire, it is possible medical examiners would have turned the incriminating bullets over to BATF agents before the Texas Rangers were assigned to lead the investigation.

No Attempt to Determine Source of Bullets

The BATF formed a "shooting review team" to get details of agents' actions on February 28 but the U.S. Attorney's office ordered them to shut it down because it was duplicating their investigations.[110] However, at trial, agents claimed that this job really was given to the Texas Rangers because they were more independent.[111] Nevertheless, FBI weapons expert James J. Cadigan acknowledged that all Texas Rangers' evidence actually was turned over to FBI laboratories.

The FBI could not compare bullets and fragments from injured and dead BATF agents to bullets fired from Davidian guns, which were burned in the fire. FBI Agent Cadigan's testimony suggests the FBI did not bother to test BATF guns to compare them to bullets which wounded agents, though pathologists noted in their autopsy reports that bullets and fragments had been forwarded to the crime laboratory.[112] The Treasury report notes that besides the four agents killed by gunshot, twenty agents were wounded, seven by shrapnel and thirteen by gunshot.[113] Therefore there should have been a number of bullets available for testing by the FBI.

BATF SNIPERS KILLED RETURNING MICHAEL SCHROEDER

Woodrow Kendrick, Norman Allison, and Michael Schroeder were at the Davidians' rented garage, the Mag Bag, three miles from Mount Carmel Center, when they heard about the raid. Around 5:00 P.M. the three approached Mount Carmel on foot from the northwest in an effort to re-enter the property and check on their families and friends. They came upon BATF agents moving away from the hay barn and toward the evacuation point. According to the Treasury report, "When the agents identified themselves as federal agents, the cult members opened fire. After a prolonged exchange of gunfire, one of the three cult members surrendered."[114] (The Justice Department report claims the three ambushed BATF agents and were attempting to "shoot their way into the compound."[115])

However, at trial agents alleged that only Schroeder had shot at them. It was revealed that while Norman Allison was carrying a gun zipped inside his clothes, he never took it out or fired it. And sniper Roger Gutherie testified that while he had Woodrow Kendrick in his gun sight, he did not fire because he could not see if Kendrick had a gun.[116]

BATF agents testified that after Schroeder fired at the fourteen agents, they returned fire. The Treasury report notes Schroeder died of six gunshot wounds, two of them to the head and three to the back.[117] Allison surrendered and Kendrick left the area. BATF agents did not pursue him but did label him an escapee.

Neither Allison nor Kendrick, who were acquitted at trial, have been outspoken about the day's events. Yet troubling evidence suggests that angry BATF agents may have shot an unarmed Schroeder, assassinated the wounded man, planted a gun and shells around his body, and impeded the Texas Rangers' investigation in order to cover up their crime.

Did BATF Agents Shoot First?

At trial BATF agent Wayne Appelt disclosed that after the morning gun battle, the agents in the barn area, most of whom were out of sight of Mount Carmel, had heard radio traffic about wounded agents, seen the wounded being removed, and discussed what had happened among themselves.[118] Agent Guthrie, who claimed to have shot Davidian Peter Gent already, stated that when agents left the barn they were looking for "hostiles."[119]

After the shooting, agents were so convinced that Schroeder, Allison, and Kendrick were perpetrators trying to leave Mount Carmel that they refused to believe Allison's assertion the Davidians were trying to enter the property.[120] BATF even released the story that Davidians were trying to shoot their way out of Mount Carmel.[121]

Given their certainty that they had perpetrators in sight, it is quite possible that after yelling "police" at the three men—who were over forty yards away and might not have been able to hear them clearly—they began shooting. BATF agent Wayne Appelt claimed he saw a man—Michael Schroeder—in the ravine shooting at them; agent Jimmy Brigance admitted that he could not tell if Schroeder had a gun—nevertheless he asserted Schroeder shot several shots; agent Jeffrey Pearce testified he heard shots coming from Schroeder's direction.[122] At trial, defense attorneys brought out that these agents had from three to ten days between the incident and their interviews by Texas Rangers to concoct such a story.[123]

Did Agents Assassinate the Wounded Schroeder?

Neither the Treasury report nor agents at trial mentioned any attempt to see if Schroeder was injured, dying, or dead immediately after the shooting. It is possible that after most agents left the area with their captive, Norman Allison, two or three agents did in fact find Schroeder—and kill the wounded man.

Four agents—Wayne Appelt, Jeffrey Pearce, Charles Myers, and Roger Guthrie—testified they heard gunshots in the distance as they left the area; two mentioned hearing *two* gunshots. Prosecutors tried to blame the gunfire on the fleeing Woodrow Kendrick— a slow-moving old man with a heart condition.[124]

Defense attorney questioning pointed to the theory that agents approached the wounded Schroeder, shot him twice in the head, and then removed his blue stocking cap, which would have contained powder burns had he been shot at close range. Schroeder's autopsy report shows two close-space bullet wounds at and below the right ear. A photograph of Mike Schroeder's body at the site of his death showed him wearing what looked like the blue stocking cap which agents Appelt and Pearce described. However, the medical examiner revealed he always looks for powder marks in shooting cases. He testified that he never received the blue cap, and that had Schroeder been shot at close range wearing the cap, it could have absorbed the evidence of such powder marks.[125]

Did Schroeder Have a Gun?

On March 3, 1993, the FBI sent a helicopter to find Michael Schroeder's body. BATF agent Roger Guthrie testified that he went with them to find the body "left there." Gutherie claims the helicopter set down by Schroeder's body, he jumped out, grabbed a Glock 17 semiautomatic pistol and magazine laying next to the body, and then flew off in the helicopter.[126] Prosecutors proved that Schroeder had bought two Glock 17s, but they did not establish that either was the gun allegedly found near Schroeder's body.[127]

While the Justice Department report claims that Schroeder's body was "retrieved" that day, March 3, David Byrnes, head of the Texas Rangers Investigation Team testified that it was not until March 5 or 6 that the FBI could arrange transport in a Bradley vehicle to actually retrieve the body. (The autopsy was conducted on March 5, 1993.)[128] Ranger Thomas Almond testified that when he got to the body he found a stun gun next to it. Almond did not explain why a man supposedly carrying a pistol also would be armed with, and evidently holding, a stun gun.

Almond also testified that on the hillside where the agents were shooting, he found seventy-two shell casings, one live shotgun shell, and two shotgun casings. He found only four projectiles between the body and agents, and he did not know if these were from agents or Schroeder.[129] Evidently the FBI did not test these bullets, either.

Why Did FBI Impede Texas Rangers' Investigation?

According to the Justice report, for ten days after Michael Schroeder's body was recovered, FBI siege commander SAC Jeff Jamar refused to allow the Texas Rangers to finish investigating the area where Schroeder was killed, something which greatly angered Texas Rangers.[130] This permitted wind and weather to eliminate footprints which might indicate whether Schroeder had turned toward or fired in the direction of BATF agents, or whether several agents had approached Schroeder as he lay wounded.

The lies that the BATF and the Treasury Department have told about Schroeder's death, retrieval of a gun by the BATF agents who left the body at the scene, the missing stocking cap, and the FBI's interfering with the investigation all suggest that BATF and the FBI are covering up the intentional homicide of Michael Schroeder. The fact that the government prosecuted Allison and Kendrick, both of whom were acquitted, on such little evidence, suggests the two men were charged as part of the cover-up of the crime.

DESTRUCTION OF THE MAG BAG

On March 3, 1993, BATF agents served a search warrant on the Mag Bag. In heavy-handed fashion, BATF used Bradley fighting vehicles. Agent Danny Dwight testified that vehicles "gently" nudged open the Mag Bag's doors. However, defense attorneys confronted Dwight with photos showing crumpled metal and gaping holes and he confessed that the vehicles "pushed in the front of the building."

During the search the building owner, who was not a Davidian, pleaded with BATF agents to use the key and not to damage the structure. He was later arrested for creating a disturbance.[131] After the BATF broke into the garage, thousands of dollars in specialty tools and three $600 air compressors disappeared, possibly looted by BATF agents.[132]

Chapter Five: BATF Actions Led to Ten Deaths

1.   Trial transcript: 144–45.
2.   Jaime Castillo, private communication, January, 1994.
3.   Judy Schneider, March 8, 1993, "home movie"; Treasury Department report: 104.
4.   Trial transcript: 511
5.   Treasury Department report: 95.
6.   Trial transcript: 3170, 3228, 3277.
7.   David Thibodeau, private communication, December, 1994; Cause Foundation lawsuit (February 24, 1994): 26; Ramsey Clark lawsuit (February 25, 1995): 28; Caddell & Conwell lawsuit (July 26, 1994): 19.
8.   Kirk Lyons, Cause Foundation, private communication, June, 1994.
9.   "Mitchells in the Morning Show," National Empowerment Television, May 31, 1995.
10.   Marjorie Thomas Testimony, November 17–18, 1993: 27–29, 144, 181, 197, 200; trial transcript: 3292.
11.   Gary Null, 33; Jaime Castillo, private communication, May, 1995.
12.   J. Michael Kennedy and Louis Sahagun, March 30, 1993: A17.
13.   "Koresh defends actions in tape of interview," *Dallas Morning News*, May 28, 1993: 36A.
14.   Dr. Phillip Arnold, private communication, June, 1995.
15.   Sue Anne Pressley, May 5, 1993: A17.
16.   Trial transcript: 4616, 4618.
17.   June 16, 1994, trial transcript: 147.
18.   Ibid., 137–38; David Thibodeau, private communication, July, 1995.
19.   Jack DeVault, transcript of 911 tape: 223.
20.   Trial transcript: 6481–82, 6504.
21.   Trial transcript: 2545, 2727.
22.   Ibid., 3327–28.
23.   *New York Times*, April 5, 1993, A10.
24.   "Defense Rests Without Calling Cultists," *New York Times*, February 18, 1994.
25.   Trial transcript: 6646, 6795–96.
26.   Ibid., 3230, 3255.

27.   Clifford L. Linedecker: 27; Kirk Lyons, private communication, June, 1994; James L. Pate, June, 1994: 33; trial transcript: 3192.

28.   Trial transcript: 3162, 3230, 3284.

29.   Ibid., 3212, 3231, 3256.

30.   Ibid., 3314–17, 6547–54.

31.   "American Justice" program, "Attack at Waco," August 3, 1994.

32.   Treasury report: 92.

33.   Trial transcript: 3162, 3178, 3184, 3202–03, 3226, 3256, 3297.

34.   The first video shot can be seen in "Waco, the Big Lie." It is referred to in the trial transcript: 3179. The second is in "Waco, the Big Lie Continues."

35.   Trial transcript: 3322, 3334, 3346.

36.   Treasury report: 172.

37.   Trial transcript: 3225, 3266, 3275.

38.   Ibid., 3161, 3185.

39.   Ibid., 3164–65, 3295.

40.   Ibid., 3164–65, 3209, 3231.

41.   Ibid., 3199, 3234, 3246, 3281–82.

42.   Trial transcript: 4477, 5992; Jaime Castillo, private communication, March, 1994.

43.   Treasury Department report: 101.

44.   *New York Times*, February 6, 1994.

45.   David Thibodeau, private communication, January, 1995.

46.   Trial transcript: 3058–59.

47.   Ibid., 7312.

48.   Treasury report: 104; "British Police Slam Davidian Siege," *The Balance*, newsletter of the Cause Foundation, March–April, 1995: 2.

49.   Ron Cole, *Sinister Twilight* (Portland, OR: Augie Enriquez, 1993): 48.

50.   Treasury report: 104.

51.   Brad Bailey and Bob Darden: 172–73.

52.   Trial transcript: 2212–13, 3828.

53.   Ibid., 6053, 6057.

54.   James L. Pate, "What the Feds Don't Want You to Know about Waco," *Soldier of Fortune,* October, 1993: 101–02; *New York Times*, April 5, 1993: A10.

55.   Trial transcript: 6603.

56.   Treasury Department report: 104.

57. Trial transcript: 4093–94, 4490.
58. David Thibodeau, private communication, July, 1994.
59. House Appropriations Subcommittee hearing, June 9, 1993: 173.
60. Trial transcript: 6384.
61. Ibid., 3394–95, 3407–10; Graeme Craddock, private communication, August, 1995.
62. Ibid., 1382.
63. Ibid., 1377, 1381.
64. Ibid., 6386–90.
65. Ibid., 4459–62.
66. "Day 51" video; Dan McGraw, "One True Believer's Trials and Tribulations," *U.S. News & World Report*, January 17, 1994.
67. Trial transcript: 7074, 7313, 7345; June 16–17, 1995 trial transcript: 191.
68. Ron Cole, 32.
69. James L. Pate, October, 1993: 102.
70. Teresa Talerico, March 3, 1994.
71. Trial transcript: 1480–88, 1850-51, 1858, 1929, 2270, 6554.
72. Trial transcript: 1850–51, 1858.
73. Roy Bragg, "Ill-fated ATF raid: the beginning of the end," *Houston Chronicle*, April 20, 1993: 17A.
74. Treasury report: 100.
75. Trial transcript: 2069, 2216–17.
76. Ibid., 2006, 2242, 2691, 2704, 2728, 7165.
77. Alan A. Stone, M.D. report to Justice Department in *Report and Recommendations Concerning the Handling of Incidents Such As the Branch Davidian Standoff in Waco, Texas*, November 8, 1993: 18–19.
78. Ken Fawcett: 26.
79. Treasury report: 105.
80. *The Houston Chronicle*, May 28, 1993.
81. "The Maury Povich Show," November 8, 1993.
82. Larry Pratt report: 6.
83. *Houston Press,* July 22, 1993.
84. Robert Cancro report to the Justice Department, 1993: 3.
85. Gary Null, April, 1994: 33.
86. Livingstone Fagan paper, August, 1994: 15.
87. Treasury report: 101.

88. Trial transcript: 1744, 1957, 1966, 2064–67, 2077, 2091, 2142, 2222, 2331, 2405, 2523, 2689, 2706.

89. Ibid., 1223.

90. Ibid., 7269.

91. Teresa Talerico, "Attorneys give closing arguments," *Waco Tribune-Herald,* February 21, 1994: 10A.

92. Trial transcript: 1251, 1558, 1744–46, 2000, 2331, 2463.

93. Mary Jordan and Sue Anne Pressley, "Cult Leader Wants to Die a Martyr in 'All-Out Firefight'," *Washington Post,* March 9, 1993.

94. Trial transcript: 2363.

95. "Was It Friendly Fire?" *Newsweek,* April 5, 1993: 50.

96. James L. Pate, July, 1993: 53.

97. Jennifer Nagorka, "Agents seen on roof in video were among ATF casualties," *Dallas Morning News,* March 3, 1993; *Newsweek,* March 15, 1993: 54.

98. Treasury Department report: 100.

99. Trial transcript: 2545–2550.

100. Ibid., 2840–50.

101. David Thibodeau on "A Current Affair" television program, May 3, 1993; Jaime Castillo, private communication, January and February, 1995.

102. Trial transcript: 2582–83.

103. Ibid., 2852–53, 2874–75, 6125.

104. Ibid., 2854–55.

105. Treasury report: 98; trial transcript: 2737.

106. Trial transcript: 2740.

107. Ibid., 2545, 3154, 5998, 6002–37; Marc A. Krouse, M.D., autopsy report.

108. Trial transcript: 5998; Nizaam Peerwani, M.D. autopsy report.

109. "Much evidence and conflict in Branch Davidians' trial," *New York Times,* January 17, 1994; trial transcript: 116–22.

110. Treasury report: 197.

111. Trial transcript: 2384–86, 3658.

112. Ibid., 1247, 1257–58.

113. Treasury report: 102.

114. Ibid., 111.

115. Justice Department report: 25.

116. Trial transcript: 3842; "Ranger Says FBI Moved Evidence at Davidian Site," *San Antonio Express-News,* January 13, 1994.

117. Treasury Department report: 104; trial transcript: 3835.

118. Trial transcript: 3524–25.

119. Ibid., 3844.

120. Ibid., 3631, 3729.

121. Ibid., 3631; "The Seven Week Siege," *Washington Post*, April 20, 1993: A8.

122. Trial transcript: 3620, 3666, 3699, 3746.

123. Ibid., 685, 698.

124. Ibid., 3623, 3666, 3795, 3795, 3833.

125. Ibid., 3618, 3668, 6011–13, 6047; Nizaam Peerwani, M.D., autopsy report.

126. Ibid., 3822–23.

127. Ibid., 1105, 4037.

128. Justice Department report: 38; trial transcript: 642.

129. Trial transcript: 3863–64.

130. Justice Department report: 229.

131. Scott W. Wright, "Agent Says Armored Vehicles Used on Shop to Ensure 'Safety'," *Austin American Statesman*, February 1, 1994.

132. James L. Pate, July, 1994: 49.

6

The BATF and
Treasury Department Cover-ups

*I didn't even know there was such a thing as
the ATF. I had heard of Eliot Ness and the
Untouchables. . . . I didn't know they still
existed. . . . I don't have any animosity toward
them, then or now, especially the line agents,
the street guys. I figure they were just doing
what they were told.*

Clive Doyle[1]

BATF agents and officials have a strong motivation
for covering up agent crimes: the fear of disciplinary actions,
firing, lawsuits, and even prosecution for negligent or even
intentional homicide in the deaths of Branch Davidians.
Treasury Department officials' motivation is more
bureaucratic: preventing dissolution of BATF and transfer of
its functions and personnel to the FBI. While the Treasury
Department did find fault with actions of raid commanders

and high BATF officials, it staunchly denies that any crimes were committed against the Davidians.

Throughout the preceding chapters indications of BATF and Treasury Department cover-ups have been noted. Additional evidence follows.

THE BATF COVER-UP

The Treasury Department report admits only that BATF commanders tried to cover up their decision to go ahead with the raid despite the loss of surprise, and that several officials disregarded evidence of this cover-up. Some believe that the "loss of surprise" accusation is just a smoke screen for BATF's real crime: using illegal military tactics on civilians, leading to ten deaths.

The BATF Intimidated the Press

In the hours before the raid, law enforcement made no attempt to stop reporters from approaching Mount Carmel, including the television camera crew that drove up Mount Carmel's driveway right behind BATF cattle trucks. However, once the raid became a debacle, captured on film, the BATF turned against the press.

On February 28 BATF agents verbally and physically assaulted KWTX-TV cameraman Dan Mulloney as he filmed dead BATF agents. Mulloney captured the assault on video tape. In trial testimony Mulloney denied he had impeded BATF in any way.[2]

BATF planners and agents blamed the *Waco Tribune-Herald* for not delaying publication of "The Sinful Messiah" series until after the BATF raid. The BATF later accused KWTX-TV's Dan Mulloney and John McLemore of making a deal with Davidians that they would warn them of the impending raid if they were allowed to hide in a tree and tape the raid.[3]

Some BATF agents and families accused the publisher of the *Waco Tribune-Herald* of being a "murderer" for running his series on the Branch Davidians before the raid. In March, 1993, wounded BATF agent John T. Risenhoover filed a lawsuit claiming that an unnamed *Waco Tribune-Herald* employee warned David Koresh about the impending raid. Risenhoover's lawsuit claimed the newspaper reneged on an agreement to withhold its series on David Koresh and the Branch Davidians until BATF completed its investigation. Assumedly, Risenhoover could have found out about this alleged agreement only from higher-up agents and officials who mistakenly thought they had such an agreement with the newspaper.[4] In early 1994 the families of deceased agents sued the *Waco Tribune-Herald* and KWTX-TV for tipping off the Davidians about the raid.[5]

The BATF immediately distanced itself from Risenhoover's lawsuit. "This is strictly between the agent and the newspaper," said BATF spokeswoman Sharon Wheeler.[6] However, many suspect that this was just part of a broader government effort to intimidate the media. In March, 1993, the BATF and FBI "gagged" their agents, forbidding them to speak to the press, a policy which continues to this day. Both agencies warned that "loose and often uninformed comments to the press" might jeopardize the investigation and undermine public confidence in the agencies.[7] Such warnings, of course, are backed by the threat of disciplinary action and even firing.

The BATF Spread Disinformation

Examples of disinformation have been mentioned in previous chapters—especially the dubious allegation the Davidians ambushed the BATF agents and used grenades and machine guns. The press widely quoted BATF spokeswoman Sharon Wheeler's statement the day after the raid, "Everything would have been fine, except their guns were bigger than ours." Other examples are BATF officials harping on the most lurid accusations of child abuse, religious fanaticism, and arms buildups.

BATF spokesman Jack Killorin claimed, "The warrant is for an imminent threat to the life and safety of everybody in that compound. The warrant is for the illicit manufacture of explosives and explosive devices which right away is an immediate threat to the life and safety of every person in there."[8] However, the Treasury report never mentions this "for-their-own-good" rationale.

The greatest disinformation related to cover-ups of BATF agent errors and crimes—the shooting from helicopters that killed four Davidians, the shooting of Perry Jones, friendly fire, and the death of Michael Schroeder. Other BATF disinformation was disseminated as part of additional cover-ups described in the following section.

The BATF Raid Commanders Covered Up Loss of Surprise

When the BATF finally informed the Treasury's Office of Law Enforcement of the planned raid on Friday, February 26, 1993, Acting Assistant Secretary of the Treasury John P. Simpson decided the action was too dangerous and "directed that the operation not go forward." Also expressing reservations was Ronald K. Noble, the designated, but unconfirmed, Assistant Secretary of the Treasury for Law Enforcement, who was acting as a consultant.

In a Friday night conference call, BATF Director Stephen Higgins told Simpson and Noble that he had obtained reassurance from raid co-commander Phillip Chojnacki that the "raid could be executed safely" and that "the raid would be aborted . . . if things did not look right," i.e., if there was any evidence of a "change in routine." Noble told a House Appropriations Subcommittee that Higgins had told him, "if for any reason they lose the element of surprise . . . express orders or directives to call off the operation."[9]

Simpson allowed the raid to go forward, "after these assurances were given." Deputy Treasury Secretary Roger Altman was informed of the upcoming raid, but Treasury Secretary Lloyd Bentsen, who was in Europe, was not.[10]

However, even after Chojnacki learned from his co-commander Chuck Sarabyn that the Davidians knew the BATF was coming, and after consulting briefly with SAC Ted Royster, he allowed the raid to go forward. (Royster did not have a "raid-specific" title, but he had the power to abort the raid because of his position as Special Agent-in-Charge of the Dallas BATF.) Chojnacki even called the National Command Center in Washington and reported that the raid was commencing. He did not report that the Davidians knew about the raid. When undercover agent Rodriguez learned that the raid was underway he was "distraught."[11]

It would be more than two months before this account of what really happened that morning would be related to the press and the public. From the start, BATF officials denied reports like one in the *Los Angeles Times* that an agent was heard shouting, "We've gotta move. He's been tipped off."[12] Undercover agent Robert Rodriguez and three other agents who overheard the conversation told BATF investigators that Rodriguez had told Sarabyn that Koresh knew a raid was imminent.

However, commander Chuck Sarabyn claimed that Rodriguez "was not real descriptive as to the ATF-National Guard statement" and commander Phillip Chojnacki claimed that Sarabyn had not told him anything about Koresh's prior foreknowledge. Chojnacki and Sarabyn also tried to cover up their lack of professionalism and errors by altering the written plan of the raid, which they had not issued before it took place. They did not tell the Texas Rangers or the Treasury review team that it had been altered. They then tried to blame the alterations on a lower-ranking agent who had assisted them. Finally, they confessed the truth to the Treasury review team.[13]

The BATF Officials Covered Up Loss of Surprise

Associate Director Daniel Hartnett and Intelligence Division Chief David Troy gave less credence to Rodriguez and other low-ranking agents' accounts than to those of their superiors Sarabyn and Chojnacki. So Troy continued to deny to the press that the commanders knew that Koresh had been alerted.[14] Rodriguez testified during the trial that he wondered if there was some strategy behind this continued disinformation; however, just in case, he hired himself an attorney. (In February, 1995, Rodriguez filed suit against the BATF, raid commanders, and officials, alleging they had violated his privacy and civil rights, defamed him and conspired to make him a scapegoat.)[15]

During March, 1993, the Texas Rangers were gathering even more evidence, including from sixty BATF agents, that raid commanders Sarabyn and Chojnacki knew that they had lost the element of surprise. They passed this along to Hartnett and Conroy. However, "Hartnett and Conroy failed to keep [BATF Director] Higgins informed about the mounting weight of evidence that Sarabyn and Chojnacki's account was false," so Higgins continued to mislead the press and the public. In late March Director Higgins wrote a memo to BATF agents denying there was a cover-up of "mistakes in planning, leadership, or both" after he discovered some agents were planning to make cover-up allegations to the media.[16]

Finally, in early April, after a number of agents contacted Higgins directly to complain about these misstatements, Higgins asked for a copy of Rodriguez' statement. Yet for another month Higgins allowed Hartnett and Conroy to instruct Troy to keep denying that raid commanders had definitive knowledge about the loss of surprise. And only under pressure from the Treasury review team did Sarabyn, Chojnacki, Hartnett, and Conroy finally admit to their roles in the cover-up.[17] Ted Royster also participated in the cover-up, claiming he did not know that surprise had been lost. When Noble threatened him with disciplinary action, "Royster then sent agents a three-page letter outlining personal pressures and career problems that caused his memory lapse."[18]

The BATF Involved with Texas Rangers' Investigation

As we have seen, the U.S. Attorney's office in Waco deputized the Texas Rangers as U.S. marshals for the criminal investigation. Nevertheless, the BATF continued to interfere with the investigations, including after the fire. The Justice report reveals, "a memorandum of understanding between the FBI and ATF gave the ATF jurisdiction in cases involving the injury or death of their own agents."[19] It was BATF agents Aguilera and Dunagan who continued to issue search and arrest warrants during the siege.

Texas Ranger David Byrnes testified that on April 19, 1993, Texas Rangers did not start taking over the scene until 3:00 P.M., two hours after the fire had burned the building to the ground. Thirty-two Texas Rangers supervised sixty or more federal agents.[20]

News footage clearly shows dozens of agents walking through the smoldering ruins in the hours immediately following the fire. Clearly, they considered themselves to be in complete control of the crime scene—local news video tape taken a few hours after the fire shows a federal agent urinating against the side of a tank sitting amidst the ruins.[21]

Byrnes revealed that one or more BATF explosives experts did the "initial explosive sweep." He claimed that BATF agents were excluded from within the police tape so that no one could claim BATF had "salted" the scene. Ranger Fred Cummings revealed the BATF bomb squad was there on April 20 as well as on the 19.[22]

Byrnes also disclosed that Texas Rangers had run the BATF flag up Mount Carmel's flag post on request of BATF agents. During closing arguments defense attorney Dan Cogdell said angrily, "What kind of people stuck a flag like they've won a war, like some overgrown G.I. Joes?"[23] Again, many believe that deputizing Texas state investigators as U.S. marshals prevented them from fully investigating the BATF and FBI crimes.

BATF Took Koresh's Gun Dealer Into "Protective Custody"

March 1, 1993, the day after the failed raid, BATF agents took custody of gun dealer Henry McMahon and his woman friend, Karen Kilpatrick. In September, 1993, Dick DeGuerin revealed: "They told these two people they were in danger from Branch Davidians who were not inside Mount Carmel who might try to kill them and convinced them to ask for protective custody."[24] The BATF obviously was afraid the public and politicians would be sympathetic with the Davidians if it learned David Koresh had cooperated fully with BATF agents. For four weeks BATF agents also tried to keep McMahon and Kilpatrick away from the press and the FBI.

When the couple finally rebelled against BATF's confinement, the BATF flew them to Waco. BATF agents Davy Aguilera and Dale Littleton grilled them for hours seeking evidence of criminal conduct by the Davidians. Aguilera threatened to arrest them for conspiracy to commit murder of federal agents. In a lawsuit, Kilpatrick accuses Littleton of physically assaulting her by knocking her against a wall when she would not answer his questions. They later were interviewed by a U.S. staff attorney, but the government never charged either with a crime. BATF agents made it clear they would never allow McMahon to work as a gun dealer again and he let his license lapse due to fears of harassment.[25]

Given the damaging testimony that McMahon could have provided against agent Aguilera and the BATF agents who took him into custody, it is not surprising that prosecutors claimed that McMahon told "Elvis" stories about BATF's mistreatment of him after the raid. Smith agreed to the prosecution's demand that McMahon not be allowed to testify in person during the trial and that his written testimony be restricted.[26]

Davidian Paul Fatta Charged After Press Interviews

Another individual who could attest to David Koresh's legal gun business was Paul Fatta, who ran the business. He was in Austin with his son selling weapons and equipment at a gun show on the morning of February 28. Fatta offered his assistance to the FBI to bring about a peaceful end to the standoff. However, they refused his help and were abusive toward him. Fatta began to give interviews to reporters, asserting that the Davidians were not violent or paramilitary and that Davidians had a gun business. His comments received national attention.[27]

The fact that Fatta was drumming up sympathy for the Davidians in the press doubtless motivated BATF to bring charges against Fatta, something his attorney brought up at trial. When Fatta heard these charges had been brought, he contacted an attorney—but BATF would not tell him what the charges against Fatta were. Fearful for his life, and wanting to get his son to safety, Fatta left Texas for Oregon.[28]

BATF issued a warrant for Fatta's arrest and declared that he was "armed and dangerous." This action further frightened Fatta into believing that the BATF would murder him if he surrendered to them. Fatta finally surrendered to Texas Rangers in Houston on April 26. Fatta's attorney Mike DeGeurin told reporters Fatta did not surrender earlier because of his "mistrust of federal agents."[29]

Government Kept Warrants Sealed After Koresh Saw Them

Immediately after the failed February 28 raid, the BATF had the magistrate seal the contents of the affidavit and search and arrest warrants supposedly "to ensure the integrity of an ongoing criminal investigation." The Associated Press noted, "One problem with either criticism or support for the government is that the reasons for the raid remain largely secret. The original search and arrest warrants remain sealed, and the ATF won't say exactly what it was looking for, or what information it has."[30]

However, on March 19 the FBI delivered to David Koresh "copies of legal documents concerning the ATF warrants."[31] Despite the fact that Koresh now knew the contents of the February and later March affidavits and warrants, the government refused to release these to the press and public until April 20, 1993, the day after Koresh's death.[32]

TREASURY DEPARTMENT COVER-UP

The Treasury Department's official report on BATF actions does expose inept planning and execution of the BATF raid. However, it defends the probable cause basis for the search and arrest warrants, excuses the decision to go forward with a paramilitary raid, and ignores evidence that agents committed crimes like firing from helicopters and killing Michael Schroeder. Throughout these chapters documentation shows where the Treasury report has failed to provide information or has provided questionable information.

Questions about Oversight of the Review

In late April, 1993, Treasury Secretary Lloyd Bentsen selected Assistant Secretary of the Treasury for Law Enforcement Ronald K. Noble to head the investigation. As we know, Noble approved the decision to go ahead with the raid. Since he had not been confirmed at that point, Noble had no formal authority. However, he still retains moral responsibility. Therefore, Noble would have little interest in issuing a report that either would challenge significantly BATF's investigation or operations modus operandi or would admit these led to crimes against the Davidians.

The Treasury Department named three individuals to be "independent reviewers" of BATF's actions in Waco. There have been questions about two of them. Henry S. Ruth, Jr., a former Watergate prosecutor, served on the Special Investigative Commission that examined law enforcement actions in connection with the police assault on the MOVE group which resulted in a devastating fire that destroyed two city blocks and killed eleven MOVE members. Another reviewer, Willie L. Williams, had been a high-ranking Philadelphia police official during the MOVE incident and became police commissioner in 1988.[33] Because Ruth's investigation never recommended any prosecutions, despite the Philadelphia police's dropping a fire bomb on a building that killed eleven MOVE members, many doubt either man was likely to criticize the BATF's actions.

No Testimony Taken Under Oath

There is no indication that any individuals gave testimony under oath to those who conducted the review. In fact, the Treasury's review team seems to have been hampered in getting at the whole truth by "employment contracts," the "Privacy Act" and the "Federal Advisory Committee Act."[34] Also, some BATF officials who testified before congressional committees were not sworn in, and they still could be prosecuted were it proved they had lied to a congressional committee—as some of those who were eventually dismissed may have done.

It is likely that some BATF agents who met with the Treasury Department's review teams later changed their stories at trial to conform to the "official line" that agents had been ambushed and that Davidians shot first. So not only did review teams not take testimony under oath, they may have encouraged those interviewed to lie under oath.

Treasury Department Attempted to Seal Investigation Records

In mid-August 1993, the Treasury Department proposed exempting the Treasury Department's report from public scrutiny. The Treasury Department gave the public a month to comment. Because radio talk show hosts encouraged protest, the Treasury received 5,150 telegrams and letters, an unusually large number. David Kopel, director of the Firearms Research Project in Denver said, "I think it is a scandalous attempt to cover up the facts surrounding one of the greatest governmental disasters in the 20th century."[35]

Treasury Department Report Demonizes Davidians

The Treasury report demonizes David Koresh and the Branch Davidians in an obvious attempt to excuse the BATF's shoddy investigation and aggressive raid. The Treasury report makes allegations against Koresh which were not made either in Davy Aguilera's original affidavit *or* during the trial, including the Bunds' family accusations about Koresh's preparing a "hit list" of former members, the finding of an alleged machine-gun conversion kit, and Donald Bunds' alleged comments that he himself would resist authorities if they tried to arrest him.[36]

The report claims Mount Carmel Center had been renamed "Ranch Apocalypse." The only evidence I found of this is Clifford L. Linedecker and a *Washington Post* reporter's repeating two different stories that Perry Jones had made this claim when paying bills in late 1992. Judge Smith would not allow mention of such a name change during the trial because of the lack of evidence.[37]

The Treasury report also refers to Kathryn Schroeder's allegation—which they discovered well after the raid—that Koresh "told his followers that soon they would go out into the world, turn their weapons on individual members of the public, and kill those who did not say they were believers. As he explained to his followers, 'you can't die for God if you can't kill for God.' Koresh later canceled the planned action, telling his followers that it had been a test of their loyalty to him." However, even prosecutors admitted this description of a conversation Koresh had with a few Davidians after the 1991 massacre at Luby's restaurant in Killeen, Texas, was a prejudicial accusation of questionable value and did not ask Schroeder to repeat it during the trial. And Schroeder at trial did not link the statement about "killing for God" to any specific event.[38]

The Treasury report also made much of social worker Joyce Sparks' allegation that during one of her conversations with him he said: "My time is coming. When I reveal myself as the messenger and my time comes, what happens will make the riots in L.A. pale in comparison."[39] However, even the anti-Davidian trial judge would not allow this obvious reference to biblical prophecy to be mentioned in court, because, even if Koresh said it, he did not do so in furtherance of any conspiracy.[40] American political activists of both the right and left often use aggressive rhetoric and joke about violence. If these are the only examples of aggressive rhetoric that Koresh's critics could find, Koresh appears to have been a relatively non-aggressive individual.

No Prosecutions of Agents or Officials

Immediately after the September, 1993, release of the Treasury report, Treasury Secretary Bentsen put Hartnett, Conroy, Troy, Chojnacki, and Sarabyn on administrative leave. Hartnett and Conroy immediately resigned. Bentsen also removed BATF Director Higgins, who had another month to go before retirement.

In February, 1994, BATF recommended that Phil Chojnacki and Chuck Sarabyn be fired for improperly supervising the 1993 raid on the Davidians. They challenged the recommendation.[41] It was not until late October, 1994, that BATF finally fired Sarabyn and Chojnacki, and even then they were asserting they had been wronged. They asserted they ignored Koresh's statement about "ATF coming" because he "often said such things." They did not explain why they alerted most BATF agents to the fact Koresh had said this.[42]

After their case went before the Federal Merit Systems Protections Board, Chojnacki and Sarabyn were rehired by BATF in December, 1994. Sarabyn was moved to Washington, D.C., and named chief of the BATF's Visual Information Branch which aids in criminal trial preparation. Chojnacki remained in Houston and was named liaison between the BATF and the U.S. Customs Service. Sarabyn's attorney Steve Gardner told reporters, "Our position all along was that the Treasury review had been a jerry-rigged, cooked-up piece of work that had been cooked up at the getgo so they could blame Chuck and Phil. When [the raid] backfired and didn't go the way they thought it should go, Treasury started looking for scapegoats."[43] Many believe Chojnacki and Sarabyn threatened to reveal BATF crimes if they were not rehired.

National Association of Treasury Agents deputy director Jim Jorgensen denounced the Treasury Department for reinstating Chojnacki and Sarabyn. "It defiles the memory of the brave ATF agents who gave their lives doing their duty. ... It sends a message to these living agents that their lives aren't worth a plugged nickel."[44]

Dallas BATF Chief Ted Royster was not disciplined, but instead he was made director of Project Alliance, a multi-agency drug task force on the Mexican border. "I was cleared of any wrongdoing. If I had done anything wrong, it would have come out in the report," Royster told a reporter.[45]

The U.S. government has conspired successfully to hide from the public that the BATF actually drove the Branch Davidians to self-defense. The Justice Department and FBI, instead of taking pity on the persecuted Davidians, merely continued the persecution, ultimately killing most members of the group.

Chapter Six: The BATF and
Treasury Department Cover-ups

1. James L. Pate, July, 1994: 47.

2. Trial transcript: 3325.

3. From audiotape of John O. Lumpkin, Texas Bureau Chief of the Associated Press, speaking at September 10, 1993, Freedom of Information Foundation panel on "Mt. Carmel: What Should the Public Know"; John McLemore and Dan Mulloney statement on "The Maury Povich Show," November 9, 1993.

4. John Lumpkin comments; Treasury Department report: 59, 71.

5. Tommy Witherspoon, "Wife of slain ATF agent sues Trib, KWTX," *Waco Tribune-Herald*, March 23, 1994; Tommy Witherspoon, "ATF agent's family sues media, ambulance service," *Waco Tribune-Herald*, March 31, 1994.

6. Associated Press wire story, March 13, 1993, 02:57 EST.

7. Reporters Committee for Freedom of the Press report, "The Clinton Administration and the News Media," 1994; Jacque Crouse, "ATF agents fume beneath Waco gag order," *Washington Times*, April 5, 1994.

8. Daniel Wattenberg: 38.

9. June 9, 1993, House Appropriations Subcommittee hearing transcripts: 18, 60.

10. Treasury Department report: 75–76, 178.

11. Ibid., 89–91, 165.

12. *Newsweek*, March 15, 1993: 55.

13. Treasury Department report: 196–199, 208–10.

14. Ibid., 196–99.

15. Associated Press, "ATF brass lied, agent testifies in Waco trial," *Washington Times*, January 29, 1994; Lee Hancock, "Agent sues ATF officials, Bureau in Koresh cult raid, He says agency made him scapegoat to hide its errors," *The Dallas Morning News*, Saturday, February 25, 1995: 28A.

16. Jerry Seper, "ATF chief denies Waco cover-up," *Washington Times*, April 19, 1993: A3.

17. Treasury Department report: 199–206.

18. Kathy Fair, "Report on Waco cult raid likely to be scathing," *Houston Chronicle*, September 26, 1993: 9A.

19. Justice Department report: 23.

20. Trial transcript: 603, 1162.

21. Video footage included in "Waco, the Big Lie Continues."

22. Trial transcript: 614, 1087–88.

23. Ibid., 643, 7256.

24. From audiotape of September 10, 1993, Freedom of Information Foundation media panel on "Mount Carmel: What Should the Public Know?" in Austin, Texas.

25. "Gun Couple Sues Feds," *The Balance*, newsletter of the Cause Foundation, March–April, 1995: 6, 8.

26. Trial transcript: 6841–43.

27. Michael deCourcy Hinds, March 6, 1993: A1.

28. Trial transcript: 527, 4375–76.

29. Ron Engelman, "Ron's Waco Update," *The Freedom Report*, September, 1993; Ron Cole: 53; Hugh Aynesworth, "Koresh followers set fires," *Washington Times*, April 27, 1993.

30. Associated Press wire story, March 11, 1993, 16:23 EST.

31. Justice Department report: 74.

32. Sam Howe Verhovek, "FBI Cites Fresh Evidence That Cult Set Fatal Fire," *New York Times*, April 21, 1994: A20.

33. Treasury Department report: 3.

34. Ibid., 6.

35. Lee Hancock, "Thousands protest proposal to limit access to cult data," *Dallas Morning News*, September 23, 1993; Jerry Seper, "Treasury wants to hide reports on Waco raid," *Washington Times*, September 2, 1993.

36. Treasury Department report: 28.

37. Ibid., 127; Clifford L. Lindecker: 17–18; Mary Jordan and Sue Anne Pressley, "Freed Cult Members Depict Horror Scene," *Washington Post*, March 4, 1993: A11; trial transcript: 446–47.

38. Treasury Department report: 127; Clare Tuma report, "Court TV," February 3, 1994; trial transcript: 4415–18.

39. Treasury Department report: 30.

40. Trial transcript: 456.

41.   Pierre Thomas, "ATF Officials Ousted Over Raid," *Washington Post*, October 1, 1993; "ATF recommends firing Davidian raid leaders," *Washington Times*, February 12, 1994.

42.   "Agents Dismissed in Raid on Sect Say They Were Blamed Unfairly," *New York Times*, November 13, 1994: A38.

43.   Lee Hancock, "ATF rehires two agents fired after raid on cultists," *Dallas Morning News*, December 22, 1994: 26A.

44.   Theresa Talerico, "A Time for Tears," *Waco Tribune-Herald*, March 1, 1995.

45.   Associated Press, "Top ATF official transferred," *Waco Tribune-Herald*, October 27, 1993: 3C.

7

The FBI Imposed
Militaristic Siege

*None of us could have gone through this whole
experience without faith. The truth that we
believe is what kept me going this whole time.
We weren't really following David Koresh. We
were following truth.*

Jaime Castillo[1]

On the evening of Sunday, February 28, 1993,
the Treasury Department and the BATF agreed to turn
over control of what had become a siege to the Justice
Department and the FBI. However, this was hardly
enough to convince the Branch Davidians to surrender,
for they believed the BATF attack was God's way of
warning America and humanity that the time to save
souls was very short and that Davidians had been
anointed to spread that word—even if it meant they
would be killed by the FBI.

The government of the United States, from President Clinton on down to FBI snipers hunkered down in the barns, believed it was dealing with a gang of "Bible-babbling" criminals. It determined to make these people bow to federal authority—even if it meant the Davidians' deaths.

The two groups were definitely on a tragically conflicting course. The pro-Davidian video "Day 51: The True Story of Waco" later described the standoff as being, "A surreal cosmic struggle between good and evil, freedom and slavery, free will and tyranny."

SIEGE CHRONOLOGY

This chronology was assembled from the Justice Department report, Dr. James Tabor's chronological log, a Waco Tribune-Herald chronology,[2] and sources referenced in the following pages.

March 1—FBI Special Agent-in-Charge Jeff Jamar arrives at command post. BATF Associate Director of Enforcement Daniel Hartnett and FBI Hostage Rescue Team arrive. FBI takes charge. Acting Attorney General Stuart Gerson tells President Clinton the strategy is negotiation. The FBI cuts off Davidian phones except to FBI. Armored vehicles move into inner perimeter, upsetting Davidians. Total of ten children leave. Deputy Treasury Secretary Roger Altman goes to Waco, meets with BATF agent Bill Buford. Koresh promises to come out after a taped message is played on nationwide radio in prime time.

March 2—Two elderly women, Catherine Matteson and Margaret Lawson, and four children leave. Some Davidians allege there were discussions of a suicide plan for that day. At 1:30 P.M. Koresh's message is played over only two radio stations in Waco and Dallas, not nationwide at prime time, as the FBI promised. Koresh reports God has told him to await instructions before exiting.

March 3—Davidians upset when the two elderly women are charged with attempted murder, and the FBI has charges dropped. One child exits. BATF agent in helicopter claims to retrieve gun from Michael Schroeder's body but leaves body at scene.

March 4—One child exits. Koresh admits most remaining children are his. FBI reads Koresh the rules of engagement. Koresh makes a variety of threats against the FBI should they attack Mount Carmel. He reveals his desire for "one honest Bible study in this great nation of America."

March 5—(or March 6) Texas Rangers and the FBI retrieve Michael Schroeder's body with an armored vehicle. Talk show host Ron Engelman suggests Davidians move satellite dish to communicate with outside world.

March 6—Steve Schneider, Koresh's second-in-command, asserts the FBI wants to burn the building to destroy the evidence from February 28. Koresh agrees to send out Melissa Morrison if he can talk to Robert Rodriguez. The FBI refuses, and she does not leave Mount Carmel.

March 7—Dr. Phillip Arnold offers services as a religious consultant to FBI agent Bob Ricks.

March 8—The FBI allows Davidians to bury Peter Gent's body. Davidians send out video tape where many adults state why they refuse to exit.

March 9—Davidians send out second similar video tape. Davidians unfold banner that reads: "God Help Us We Want the Press." Unnamed FBI officials pressure behavioral analysts Smerick and Young into issuing memorandum to support increased harassment of Davidians.

March 11—The FBI turns Koresh's mother Bonnie Haldeman and attorney Dick DeGuerin away from road block. Judge Walter Smith refuses Haldeman's request to allow Koresh to meet with DeGuerin.

March 12—Janet Reno sworn in as Attorney General. Attorneys complain about secrecy of weapons charges. Kathryn Schroeder and Oliver Gyrfas exit Mount Carmel. Nevertheless, FBI siege commander Jamar cuts off electricity permanently, angering Schneider and Koresh.

March 13—Schneider charges again that the government wants to kill them all and burn the building. FBI receives letters from attorneys DeGuerin and Zimmermann but will not let them speak with Koresh and Schneider.

March 14—Koresh rebukes Kathryn Schroeder for not being an adequate spokesperson. Davidians hang banner that reads, "FBI broke negotiations, we want press," and flash S.O.S. signals. The FBI begins illuminating Mount Carmel with bright stadium lights at night.

March 15 —FBI negotiators insist they will not listen to any more "Bible babble." The FBI allows Schneider and Martin to meet outside with FBI chief negotiator Byron Sage and Sheriff Jack Harwell.

March 16 —Schneider repeatedly requests that Dr. Phillip Arnold, who they had heard on KRLD, be allowed to discuss the Seven Seals with Koresh, but FBI refuses permission. The FBI calls Dr. Arnold about getting audiotapes of his radio program, their last contact with Arnold.

March 19 —FBI delivers Arnold audiotapes and letters from attorneys to Koresh. After assurances from FBI that Mount Carmel will not be destroyed and Davidians eventually can return, Koresh promises they will all come out soon. Brad Branch and Kevin Whitecliff exit Mount Carmel and are jailed.

March 21 —Possible beginning of mass exit: Victorine Hollingsworth, Annetta Richards, Rita Riddle, Gladys Ottman, Sheila Martin, James Lawton, and Ophelia Santoya leave Mount Carmel. The FBI begins blasting loud music and angry Schneider and Koresh say because of this, no one else will exit.

March 22 —Agent Jamar calls strategy session and discusses "stress escalation" and using tear gas. Jamar sends in letter promising Koresh live media coverage of exit, freedom to preach in jail, and worldwide radio broadcast. Angry at past FBI lies, Koresh destroys the letter.

March 23 —Livingstone Fagan exits.

March 24 —The FBI insults Koresh at news conference. Christian sympathizer Louis Alaniz sneaks into Mount Carmel.

March 25 —The FBI demands people exit, and when they do not, tanks destroy go-carts and vehicles.

March 26 —The FBI demands people exit and removes more vehicles. Christian sympathizer Jesse Amen sneaks into Mount Carmel.

March 27 —Angry Schneider asserts they will not come out, no matter what the FBI does.

March 28 —The FBI demands people exit and then moves away more cars, fences, trees, and other obstructions. The FBI finally allows DeGuerin to talk to Koresh. A third video tape of Koresh interviewing children is sent out.

March 29 —Koresh and DeGuerin meet.

March 30 —Koresh and DeGuerin meet twice. Schneider speaks with attorney Jack Zimmermann by phone.

March 31 —Koresh has two long meetings with DeGuerin. *Los Angeles Times* reports Rita Riddle claimed BATF shot from helicopters.

April 1 —Attorney General Reno appoints Ray Jahn as lead prosecutor. Dr. Arnold and Dr. Tabor broadcast message on Ron Engelman show encouraging Koresh to write a "little book" and leave Mount Carmel. DeGuerin and Zimmermann spend day at Mount Carmel. They report Koresh will exit after Passover.

April 2 —Schneider reports they will come out sometime after Passover.

April 3 —In a press conference the FBI says if Davidians do not exit after Passover, they will step up their actions. During this week FBI Director approves the gassing plan. Several dozen libertarian, patriot, gun-rights activists protest. Linda Thompson's armed "unorganized militia" protests near Mount Carmel.

April 4 —Attorneys bring in Arnold and Tabor audiotape. Jesse Amen exits. DeGuerin and Zimmermann claim that the BATF shot from helicopters and that they can see such evidence in the roof. *New York Times* carries the story the next day. BATF denies claims.

April 6 —Steve Schneider complains about music and lights disturbing Passover, but the FBI continues harassment.

April 8 —Schneider confirms everyone will come out after Passover. Davidians hang out more banners, including one that says: "Rodney King, We Understand."

April 9 —Koresh sends out first defiant letter filled with biblical allusions. The FBI completes plans for gassing Mount Carmel. Schneider gives the FBI names of those killed on February 28.

April 10 —Koresh sends out two more defiant letters. The FBI tells Davidian attorneys they will not be allowed back in unless there is an immediate surrender.

April 11 —Koresh sends out fourth defiant letter.

April 12 —Attorney General Reno first briefed on gassing plan.

April 13 —Koresh repeats he will not exit until God tells him to. Passover ends. At White House meeting Webster Hubbell informs White House counsel Bernard Nussbaum and Deputy Counsel Vince Foster about the plan; Nussbaum informs President Clinton.

April 14 —Koresh writes Dick DeGuerin saying God has spoken to him and he promises to exit as soon as he finishes a short book about the Seven Seals. Reno briefed again on gassing plan.

April 15 —FBI negotiator Sage tells Assistant Attorney General Webster Hubbell that negotiations are going nowhere.

April 16 —Koresh tells the FBI he has completed work on the First Seal. After private conversation with FBI Director William Sessions, Reno requests that the FBI prepare documentation about gassing plan.

April 17 —Louis Alaniz exits Mount Carmel. Attorney General Reno approves gassing plan for April 19.

April 18 —Attorney General informs President Clinton about gassing plan. Armored vehicles remove remaining vehicles from around the building.

WHY DAVIDIANS STAYED
INSIDE MOUNT CARMEL

Koresh and other Davidians had reasons both spiritual and practical for staying inside Mount Carmel Center. Few of these reasons ever were communicated accurately to the public.

Desire to Spread God's Word

Less than an hour into the raid, David Koresh can be heard on the 911 tape trying to arrange to get his story out to the media.[3] That night he did two Dallas KRLD radio interviews and a nationally broadcast phone interview on CNN television. He told the CNN interviewer: "If the scholars of this world, if anybody, ministers that claim that God talks to them, will contact me, and I hope it's soon, if they'll call me and show the world what the Seven Seals are and where they're at in the prophecies, then I'll be satisfied. And then we'll all come out to you." He told the KRLD interviewer, "All that is happening here is the fulfillment of prophecy!"

Koresh and other Davidians were convinced that the BATF's attack was the opening of the Fifth Seal of the Book of Revelation and that they were living the events predicted in that seal. They believed the six Davidians killed February 28 were slaughtered for "preaching God's word" and the surviving Davidians would only have to "rest a little longer" until the "remainder" also were put to death. Thus would begin the countdown to the Apocalypse and the Second Coming of Christ.

Davidians believed that the siege was a God-given opportunity to spread Koresh's message to the world and that humanity was being given its last opportunity to hear God's word and repent. It was only through repentance that America and the world could save itself from destruction. Rita Riddle, who left Mount Carmel during the siege, told reporters in late March, 1993, that Koresh's goal was not merely publicity. "All he is trying to get out of this is people knowing about these Seven Seals. . . . He is interested in lost souls."[4]

In his fifty-eight-minute March 2, 1993, audiotape, Koresh states that while he was concerned about the lives of his friends at Mount Carmel, "I am really concerned even greater about the lives of all those in this world. Without Christ, without Jesus, we have no hope." Koresh told negotiators, "It would be so awesome if everyone could just sit down and have one honest Bible study in this great nation of America. . . . America does not have to be humiliated or destroyed." The Justice report admits, "The FBI has questioned whether its negotiations with David Koresh could even be characterized as 'negotiations' at all, but rather as Koresh's attempt to convert the agents before it was too late and God destroyed them."[5]

Koresh was angry that the FBI immediately cut off their phone lines to the outside world and even angrier when the FBI broke its promise to play Koresh's fifty-eight-minute March 2 sermon nationwide at prime time. Livingstone Fagan, who left Mount Carmel and became the Davidians' spokesperson, complained in a March 26, 1993, CNN interview that the FBI was preventing Koresh from spreading his message, which would facilitate a resolution. "The whole thing has a divine hand guiding the process. God is really just demonstrating that He can do what He wants."

Koresh's demand would have been reprehensible had he made it as a result of some aggressive action. However, because the Davidians were attacked unjustly, many see the demand as a call for understanding from a people wronged, as well as an act of faith. All Davidians were committed to staying inside Mount Carmel until Koresh was satisfied that their stand made a spiritual impression upon the world.

In June, 1993, Ruth Riddle, sister-in-law to Rita, told a television interviewer, "We felt that this would provide us, David, an opportunity to get the message out, in great detail. . . . We were all well aware of what was going on, to the extent that we were backing what

David wanted to do, and turn a bad situation around
into a good one. . . . Companionship was closer. Our
commitment was stronger. Our desire to study was
more. The more we studied, the more we could see
plainly what David had taught."[6] Koresh and the
Davidians said they were willing to come out under only
two conditions: God instructed Koresh that it was time
to leave, or some theologian convinced Koresh he was
misinterpreting the word of God.

Angry at/Frightened of Federal Agents

Given David Koresh's past efforts to cooperate,
the fact that the arrest warrant had been for Koresh
only, and the fact that agents had come in shooting when
they could have simply knocked on the door if they
wanted to search Mount Carmel, Davidians were angry
at the injustice of the BATF attack. Davidians also were
afraid of the government. Audiotapes of a 911 call reveal
that just hours into the siege Wayne Martin complained
to negotiators that the radio was reporting the BATF or
the FBI intended to attack them again. In "The Waco
Incident: The True Story" video, Sheila Martin revealed,
"Those first few days we still worried they were going
to come. They would come and get us in the middle of
the night. . . . It was the scariest time. We knew that
they were angry and we knew that they could come."

Some Davidians, convinced that Koresh was
about to die from a gunshot wound and convinced the
government intended to kill them when they exited, did
discuss various "mass suicide" scenarios for their

planned exit on Tuesday, March 2. However, not all agree that David Koresh knew of or approved of the plan. According to Kathryn Schroeder and Victorine Hollingsworth, deceased Davidian Neal Vaega was the prime instigator of this plan. When Koresh began to feel better and told them God had canceled their exit plans, such discussions ceased.[7]

Davidians were suspicious of the government's intentions, especially after federal agents broke promises about getting them medical help, keeping armored vehicles off their property, allowing them to retrieve Peter Gent's body, and sending their children to relatives instead of foster homes.

The FBI also claimed they simply gave the Davidians milk for the children; when in truth they sent it in only after Davidians paid $1,000 for it.[8] Federal agents also disconnected their phone lines to the outside world and, probably illegally, cut off their "ham" radio communications and jammed their radio and television reception.[9] And while the FBI claimed that those who left Mount Carmel would be treated fairly, when two old women did so on March 2, they were immediately charged with attempted murder.[10] Even though the charges quickly were dropped, Davidians then knew that all would be arrested upon leaving Mount Carmel.

Koresh revealed his distrust of the FBI's motives during the March 8 home movie when he says, "It's like a fight with the neighbors. Little brother comes over to beat you up and then big brother comes over to investigate."

Desire to Preserve Evidence

Davidians were convinced that once they exited Mount Carmel BATF and FBI agents would tamper with or destroy evidence of the BATF attack, such as entry bullet holes in the walls and ceilings and damage from the flash-bang grenades. Koresh told his attorney they also feared the BATF would plant evidence of illegal weapons on their property. (While the FBI told the press they were fearful of Davidians destroying evidence, they never mentioned the Davidians' fears.[11])

On March 12 Davidians attempted to convince negotiators to allow Ron Engelman or a national news team to come in with television cameras and film the evidence. The FBI refused this request.[12] The Justice Department report does not acknowledge Davidians wanted the press to document these crimes and prevent destruction of evidence.[13] It was not until the Davidians' first meeting with attorneys in April that they received their first credible assurance that Texas Rangers and not federal authorities would be in charge of the investigation.[14]

Believing that authorities would want to investigate BATF crimes against the Davidians, Koresh suggested they write down "raid statements" of what happened to them and why they fired. Unfortunately for three Davidians later prosecuted, the person taking their statements was Kathryn Schroeder who prosecutors bullied into becoming a prosecution witness.[15]

Fear of Losing Their Church and Home

Davidians were afraid that their church and property would be confiscated permanently if everyone was forced to leave Mount Carmel Center. Dozens of old and poor people would have been rendered homeless. The community they had worked so hard to create would be destroyed. In the video "Day 51" Sheila Martin explained the Davidians' fear that they would lose Mount Carmel Center if they all left before March 22, which was the five-year deadline specified by the court when Koresh took over in 1988. Their fears heightened as they watched FBI agents loot jewelry, cash, and other possessions from a house trailer and other buildings on the property and run tanks into and over the Davidians' bus, house trailer, cars, and childrens' bicycles and go-carts.

Koresh's attorney Dick DeGuerin stated: "It was their home. They felt persecuted. They felt there was no justification in asking them to give up their home. . . . The search warrant doesn't say, 'You are hereby dispossessed of your home and all your worldly belongings 'til we decide you can have them back.' It simply says that the agents are allowed to go inside to seek evidence of wrongdoing."[16] One of the documents which DeGuerin brought in to Koresh was a "trespass to try title lawsuit" to preserve their title when they all came out so that no one could say they abandoned the property.[17]

Davidians have been criticized for not sending all the children out of Mount Carmel. However, in the March 8 home movie several parents who did so complained about the childrens' unruly behavior, something which deterred others from letting their children leave. Davidian David Thibodeau's mother Balenda Gamen explained another reason children stayed with their parents: "Because we're a very arrogant, proud nation of people. . . . The bottom line is, if you truly believe in what you are doing that passionately, you don't send your children out to the enemy."[18] And Livingstone Fagan notes that in keeping their children with them, "The residents of Mount Carmel are fully persuaded of God's approval of their actions."[19] And, despite their fears, Davidians simply could not believe the government would launch another murderous assault, so they felt their children were safe.[20]

While Davidians were willing to defend themselves against federal agents should they try to enter Mount Carmel, David Koresh was looking for a way to come out that would be consistent with their religious views and protect evidence and property. It was for all these reasons that most adults, and even some teenagers, volunteered to take up arms and stand guard during the siege.[21]

FBI'S UNPROFESSIONAL MOTIVATIONS

FBI Special Agent-in-Charge Jeff Jamar of the San Antonio office automatically assumed control of the operation under FBI guidelines. Jamar's chief contact and immediate superior at FBI headquarters was then-Assistant Director of the Criminal Investigation Division

Larry A. Potts. Potts also was the supervising FBI official in the siege of Randy Weaver's family. Potts and his assistants, Danny Coulson and Michael Kahoe, regularly briefed their superiors, FBI Director William S. Sessions, Deputy Director Floyd Clarke, and Associate Deputy Director for Investigations Doug Gow.[22]

The FBI Hostage Rescue Team (HRT) under the command of Richard Rogers and several Special Weapons and Tactics Teams (SWAT) also began arriving that day. HRT commander Dick Rogers soon brought in a .50-caliber rifle, a machine gun and grenade launchers.[23]

In the coming weeks law enforcement agencies would deploy the following numbers of personnel: FBI–668, ATF–136, U.S. Customs–6, U.S. Army–15, Texas National Guard–13, Texas Rangers–31, Texas Dept. of Public Safety Patrol–131, McLennan County Sheriff's Office–17, and Waco Police–18. While the main headquarters for these agencies was at Texas State Technical College several miles away, Texas Rangers, the BATF, and the FBI had vans and other offices close to Mount Carmel. FBI tactical agents also were stationed nearby, while negotiators were stationed at the college.[24]

Despite its reputation for "professionalism," agents and officials of the lead agency in charge, the FBI, were driven by base and unprofessional emotions: anger, revenge, protection of fellow agents, and bigotry.

WHITE HOUSE, JUSTICE DEPARTMENT, AND FBI CHAINS OF COMMAND
FEBRUARY 28–APRIL 19, 1993

WHITE HOUSE

Bill Clinton - President

Thomas McLarty - Chief of Staff

Bernard Nussbaum - White House Counsel

Vince Foster - Deputy White House Counsel

Bruce Lindsey - Presidential Advisor

George Stephanopolous - Communications Director

JUSTICE DEPARTMENT

Stuart M. Gerson - Acting Attorney General (February 28–March 12)

Webster Hubbell - Assistant to Acting Attorney General Gerson, liaison between Clinton and Justice Department

Janet Reno- Attorney General (From March 12)

Richard Scruggs - Assistant to the Attorney General

Webster Hubbell - Assistant to Attorney General (later confirmed as Associate Attorney General)

Carl Stern - Director of the Office of Public Affairs

Mark Richard - Deputy Assistant Attorney General

John C. Keeney - Acting Assistant Attorney General for the Criminal Division

Ronald Ederer - U.S. Attorney

Bill Johnston - Assistant U.S. Attorney in Waco

John Phinizy - Assistant United States Attorney in Waco

LeRoy Jahn - Assistant United States Attorney in Waco, lead Prosecutor of Branch Davidians

FEDERAL BUREAU OF INVESTIGATION

Officials in Washington

William S. Sessions - Director

Floyd Clarke - Deputy Director

Doug Gow - Associate Deputy Director for Investigations

Larry Potts - Assistant Director of the Criminal Investigative Division

Danny Coulson - Deputy Assistant Director of Criminal Investigative Division

E. Michael Kahoe - Section Chief of Criminal Investigative Division Violent Crimes

Agents in Waco

Jeff Jamar - Special Agent-in-Charge ("SAC") of the Waco Operation

SAC Robert Ricks, SAC Richard Schwein, SAC Richard Swensen, aides to Jamar

Richard M. Rogers - Assistant Special Agent-in-Charge and commander of Hostage Rescue Team

Byron Sage - Supervisory Special Resident Agent, Chief negotiator, in charge of 24 negotiators.

Anger and Revenge Against Davidians

That all this law enforcement could not "tame" a small group of defiant "religious fanatics" aggravated agents and officials. According to the Justice report, they regarded Davidian resistance as "a direct challenge to lawful federal warrants and to duly authorized law enforcement officials. The report admits one primary goal was to "demonstrate the authority of law enforcement."[25]

Scholar Nancy Ammerman, one of the outside experts who reviewed the FBI's handling of the siege for the Justice Department, commented in her report on the FBI's desire for revenge on those they blamed for the deaths of federal agents. "There was an understandable desire among many agents in Waco to make Koresh and the Davidians pay for the harm they had caused. Arguments for patience or unconventional tactics fell on deaf ears."[26]

Davidians further angered FBI agents because David Koresh, Steve Schneider, and Wayne Martin subjected negotiators to constant sermons, and Koresh issued several threats that either Davidians or God himself would repel any FBI attack. Davidians committed small acts of defiance like hanging out signs for the media to read and putting their amplifiers up to the windows and playing loud rock music and walking outside the building. One commentator opined that the FBI doubtless regarded the whole situation as an "embarrassing daily soap opera starring the FBI and its public enemy number one."[27] Davidian prisoner Livingstone Fagan wrote, "It was evident that these

agents were angry; they had just received a major blow
to their pride and arrogance."[28]

Desire to Spare BATF Agents from Prosecution

Like the BATF, FBI officials and agents had
little sympathy with either the Davidians' religious
beliefs or their complaints about BATF's use of excessive
force. And FBI agents in Waco befriended and
sympathized with BATF agents who were intent on
revenge against the "cultists" who had killed their
comrades.

David Koresh's self-assurance in the March 8
home movie when he asserts the BATF killing of the
unarmed Perry Jones will be "taken care of in the
investigations" must have infuriated them further. Steve
Schneider—Koresh's second-in-command and an
ordained minister—was so certain that the evidence was
incriminating that on March 6 he told negotiators, "It
wouldn't surprise me if they wouldn't want to get rid of
the evidence. Because if this building is still standing,
you will see the evidences of what took place."[29] On
March 13 he again claimed that "the government wanted
to kill all of them and burn down the building."[30]

News stories about evidence BATF agents had
shot from helicopters began circulating at the end of
March. A March 30 *Los Angeles Times* article, "Sect
member says helicopters shot at compound in gun
battle," repeated such an allegation by Rita Riddle, who
had left Mount Carmel a week before. On April 5, 1993,
the *New York Times* published attorneys Jack

Zimmermann and Dick DeGuerin's allegations that they had seen definite evidence that helicopters had been shooting into the upper floors of Mount Carmel Center.[31]

The Davidians' cocky assurance that evidence in the building would prove BATF crimes, and even lead to acquittals, plus the increasing public revelations, must have hardened the BATF's and the FBI's determination to destroy that evidence, even if it meant many deaths. Leading agents Rogers and Jamar, spokesperson Bob Ricks, chief negotiator Byron Sage, and other agents may have adopted a likely BATF agenda: creation of an incident that would give them an excuse to destroy the building and its incriminating evidence.

Religious Hostility

Scholar Nancy Ammerman believes FBI agents had a negative view of Koresh's religious views for three reasons: some agents did not understand religion, others were antagonistic toward religion in general, and others were antagonistic toward Koresh's specific views, which differed from their own.[32]

In her report to the Justice Department, she notes FBI officials and agents' "tendency to discount the influence of religious beliefs and to evaluate situations largely in terms of a leader's individual criminal/psychological motives." Their consensus was that "when they encountered people with religious beliefs, those beliefs were usually a convenient cover for criminal activity."[33] Siege commander Jeff Jamar expressed his contempt for Koresh when he declared

at the April 28, 1993, House Judiciary Committee
hearing that Koresh had "corrupted people" and
"corrupted religion to his own ends" and that there was
"no way to convince Koresh that he was not the
Messiah." He also declared that having theologians,
especially renowned ones, negotiate with Koresh would
just make him more egomaniacal.

Possible FBI Racism, Anti-Semitism, Sexual Unease

More than half of those who remained inside
Mount Carmel were of African, Asian, or Hispanic
descent. The sight of more than a dozen people of color
explaining to the FBI on the March 8 home movies why
they considered the word of Koresh to be more
compelling than that of the FBI and the United States
government may have raised the hackles of the more
racist agents.

Moreover, that Koresh compared himself to the
Jewish King David and flew a big blue and white Star of
David flag over Mount Carmel for the duration of the
siege may have annoyed any anti-semites among them.
Finally, Koresh used the home movies to freely and
boldly introduce in person and in photos some of his
wives and all of his natural and adopted children,
claiming that the children were "biblical." This may have
prompted sexual jealousy or disgust among some FBI
agents.

FBI'S VIOLENT ATTITUDE

Given that FBI agents and officials were motivated by the desire for control, revenge, cover-up, and religious and personal animosity, it is not surprising that their "rules of engagement" led to a predicted violent ending.

Rules of Engagement

On March 1, 1993, then-Assistant FBI Director Larry Potts and siege commander Jeff Jamar decided upon the FBI rules of engagement. According to the Justice Department report: "the FBI should avoid any exchange of gunfire with those in the compound, if at all possible. Only if there was a threat of imminent bodily harm or death would the FBI return fire."[34] The report does not reveal if these rules were communicated to the Davidians.

On March 4, after Davidians did not surrender on March 2 as planned, the FBI finally conveyed to Davidians their rules of engagement. The FBI drafted a "statement regarding safety" because of "concern that the movement of Branch Davidians in and around the compound might trigger a gunfight." It read as follows: "Rules for your safety: No one will be allowed to exit the building with a weapon. We tell you this for your own protection—for if our agents perceive that their lives or the life of someone else is at risk they will take appropriate action to ensure their own safety. No one will be allowed to aim a weapon from a window as this may also be perceived by our agents as a threat to their lives to the life of others [sic] and compel them to act accordingly. Any time you exit the building and are approaching our agents, you must fully comply with any verbal instruction to avoid exposing yourself to potential risk."[35]

These rules of engagement, at least as they were communicated to Davidians, seem to be closer to those approved against Randy Weaver—if you are seen with a gun, you will be shot. However, since few people believe the FBI shot any Davidians, this has not been an issue as it has been in the Weaver case.

Early in the siege Danny Coulson, Deputy Assistant Director of Criminal Investigative Division, and Hostage Rescue Team commander Richard Rogers concluded that a "direct assault would lead to tremendous loss of life on both sides." Evidently the FBI gave agents no specific plan for any large-scale action, since FBI agents complained there was no specific plan for a "large scale breakout"—i.e., armed Davidians breaking out of Mount Carmel.[36] Whether the FBI was merely confused about its various plans and options and their rules of engagement, or "bungling" its way toward allowing the harshest possible treatment of Davidians, is not clear.

FBI Predicted Violent Ending

During the April 19 afternoon FBI conference, Bob Ricks did make one true statement: "I have repeated it often, David wanted as many people killed as possible."

The FBI seemed intent on doing everything possible to make sure something happened that they could label another Jonestown. (For this reason many consider it obscene that Ricks, the head of the FBI's Oklahoma office, was later put in charge of the Oklahoma City bombing investigation.[37])

The day after the BATF raid, former McLennan County District Attorney Vic Feazell, who had unsuccessfully prosecuted the Davidians for the shootout with George Roden, criticized federal agents for "storm trooper" tactics in laying siege to Mount Carmel and predicted a grim end to the standoff. "The feds are preparing to kill them," he said, noting the mobilization of military equipment. "That way they can bury their mistakes. And they won't have attorneys looking over what they did later at a trial."[38]

FBI's Purposeful Bungling

Many have accused the FBI of bungling its handling of negotiations and its April 19 attack on Mount Carmel. Others believe agents and officials purposely bungled their way to exactly the conclusion they preferred—a mass murder they could label as "mass suicide."

Susan J. Palmer, an expert on new religious movements, wrote: "The line between manslaughter and murder begins to attenuate when we consider that some of this 'bungling' might have been deliberate. It is impossible for an outsider to understand the process of decision-making in the ATF and FBI, and the complexities of the power relationship between these two agencies; but if one considers that four ATF agents had been killed, one might presume that there is an unwritten code among police officers which would automatically rule out decisions which decreased the opportunity to avenge the death of their comrades. Decisions which endangered lives of Branch Davidians would therefore tend to be favored."[39]

James Ridgeway of the *Village Voice* agreed: "All in all, it's hard to believe that after the first shootout the government had not determined to kill the Branch Davidians. In that sense, the incident leaves the impression of having been a calculated massacre."[40]

ABUSE OF THE *POSSE COMITATUS* LAW

American tanks equipped with bulldozer blades buried alive tens of thousands of Iraqi soldiers during the 1991 war against Iraq.[41] It is possible some of these very same army tanks, shipped from Fort Hood, Texas, also killed dozens of Americans in Waco and then plowed evidence of government crimes into the burning rubble.

The Justice report is not as forthcoming as the Treasury report regarding the FBI's obtaining military tanks despite *posse comitatus* prohibitions on the use of the military for civilian law enforcement. First, the report does not reveal whether the FBI used the allegation of a "drug nexus" at Mount Carmel to obtain the tanks from the military on a no-charge, "nonreimbursable" basis. However, a *Legal Times* reporter wrote, "Much of the equipment used at Waco was provided by the Army, under an agreement that all costs would be reimbursed."[42]

The report states: "the FBI requested Bradley fighting vehicles from the U.S. Army. Nine of these— without barrels, pursuant to an agreement between the FBI and the Army to avoid *posse comitatus* prohibitions— were ultimately provided." However, when David Koresh (falsely) claimed he had weapons that could blow these vehicles into the air, the FBI "sought and obtained from the Army two Abrams (M1A1) tanks and five M728 Combat Engineering Vehicles (CEVs)."[43]

At trial, tank driver and FBI agent R. J. Craig revealed the tanks did have barrels but insisted they had no ammunition. He acknowledged that he did not know if the Davidians knew these guns were not loaded. However, survivor Jaime Castillo asserts that every time a Davidian would look through a hole in the wall the tank driver would turn its barrel straight at them, convincing them the guns were in fact loaded.[44]

These "Combat Engineering Vehicles" (CEVs) are converted M-60A1 tanks. The tanks are thirty feet long and weigh fifty tons, the weight of twenty-five mid-sized automobiles. Each one has a bulldozer blade on the front and a thirty-foot boom on back which can be swung forward to be used as a battering ram.[45]

Upon learning that tanks had been brought to Waco, "the President called [Acting Attorney General Stuart] Gerson, requesting an explanation for the deployment of military vehicles. Gerson assured the President that no assault was planned . . . [and] that it was legal for the FBI to use the military vehicles for safety purposes."[46] Evidently, this means that it was illegal to use the tanks for actions like the April 19 assault.

The U.S. government consulted not only with American military, but with British and Russian military advisors and scientists. *Sunday Times of London* in a March 21, 1993, article "FBI Brings Out Secret Electronic Weapons as Waco Siege Drags On," alleged that members of the British elite paratroop strike force, the Special Air Service Regiment, were involved in Waco as "observers." One columnist reported the FBI consulted with Russian military scientists about a "mind control" device which supposedly could send subliminal messages over the telephone wires.[47]

FBI CONTROLLED THE PRESS

According to *Mad Man in Waco* authors Brad Bailey and Bob Darden, the FBI used its daily press briefings as a way of "controlling" the media and the public perceptions of David Koresh so that everyone would consider him an unpredictable psychopath. They assert another FBI goal was "inflaming the already beleaguered cult leader."[48] Reporter Charles Jaco confirmed that the FBI used "jamming devices" in Waco and that around 10:30 in the morning the jamming was lifted specifically so Davidians could listen to FBI press briefings.[49] The press and media barely protested these controls. And for the most part reporters did little investigative reporting and merely regurgitated FBI and Justice Department propaganda.

FBI Restricted the Press

The FBI imposed a number of harsh restrictions on the press. It prohibited reporters from getting closer than two to three miles to Mount Carmel Center, claiming the Branch Davidians' .50-caliber "machine guns" could hit anyone closer than three thousand yards, almost two miles. The day before the fire the FBI moved television cameras back another mile from Mount Carmel and away from the northern sides of the building, restricting television cameras to the south front.[50] A Dallas Channel 8 reporter in a helicopter reported the FAA prohibited them from getting closer than five miles to Mount Carmel on April 19.

The FBI strictly controlled its daily press briefings, limiting the number of questions and punishing reporters who displeased them by refusing to call on them. The FBI also prevented agents and officials from granting media interviews. Federal prosecutors closed magistrate hearings of Davidians who surrendered during the siege and moved hearings from the courthouse to the jail to thwart media coverage.[51]

Speaking at the September 10, 1993, Freedom of Information Foundation panel on "Mt. Carmel: What Should the Public Know?" John O. Lumpkin of the Associated Press commented, "it is my personal opinion . . . the argument could be made the situation could have turned out differently, and certainly not tragically, if there had been much more open access instead." Lumpkin asserted that because of FBI control of information, the public still does not know the truth about what happened in Waco. Panelist Shelly Katz, a *Time Magazine* photographer stationed in Waco, said this was the worst suppression of the press he had seen in twenty-seven years of journalism.[52] And reporter Charles Jaco told another newsman the FBI's control of the press reminded him of his experience reporting during the war against Iraq in "Operation Desert Storm."[53]

FBI Intimidated the Press

Federal agents assaulted and arrested a reporter who had merely asked about a Davidian apprehended right after the BATF raid and illegally confiscated his film. When journalist Louis Beam, who had valid press credentials for the right-wing publication *Jubilee*, asked whether the country was "witnessing a fascist takeover," he was whisked out of the press room. When he tried to return, he was arrested on charges of criminal trespass.[54] The Society for Professional Journalists' report on Waco stated that SAC Jeff Jamar felt it necessary to remind radio station KRLD that the FCC licenses radio stations.[55]

After state troopers arrested two news photographers and confiscated their film near the ruins of Mount Carmel on April 22, 1993, Tony Pederson, managing editor of the *Houston Chronicle*, protested: "In a situation already marred by tragic loss of life and questionable actions, this seems to be a rather sorry follow-up. One has to wonder seriously if the Bill of Rights has been suspended in McLennan County."[56] During the Freedom of Information Foundation media panel, Dick DeGuerin asserted that during the siege the press should have committed civil disobedience and continued getting arrested until they were allowed to get closer to the scene of the action.

FBI Lied to the Press

Louis Alaniz, a Christian sympathizer who sneaked into Mount Carmel in late March and left just before the fire, said the Branch Davidians listened to the FBI press conferences. "What really got them is they constantly heard the story changing—another lie, another lie, another lie. These people were saying, 'Why are they saying all this about us?' I didn't see anything that [the FBI] was telling the press that was true."[57] Dick Reavis, who has compared the full contents of the 20,000 pages of negotiation tapes to the FBI transcripts of its news conferences, confirms that FBI spokesperson Bob Ricks constantly lied to the press about what was happening in negotiations.[58] In the March 8 home movie Judy Schneider and Kathryn Schroeder complained bitterly about the lies the FBI was telling.

The FBI told the press the Davidians had created tunnels and booby traps in back of the property to keep people off it, but reporters who slipped back there did not find any.[59] The FBI made the false claim that Davidians were using illegal drugs.[60] They asserted most of those inside were white, although half were of

African, Asian, or Hispanic descent. (In early March African-American columnist William Raspberry naively wondered what the government would have done to the Davidians if they were black instead of white.[61])

The FBI claimed Davidians had several years worth of food stored, when they had less than six months. They frothed over descriptions of Mount Carmel's rickety buildings as a bunkered "fortress" built for war. The FBI claimed that Davidians were placing their children in windows as shields when they were merely holding them up to watch the tanks.[62] Bob Ricks claimed that operations were costing two million dollars a day, but it was revealed in June, 1993, congressional hearings that the total was $6,792,000, an average of $130,000 a day.[63] The disinformation ended in a crescendo of falsehoods immediately after the April 19 fire.

The FBI would not let the press or public see video tapes sent out of Mount Carmel. Even the Justice Department report admits Davidians spoke in "calm, assured tones of their desire to remain inside," and that "the abiding impression is not of a bunch of 'lunatics,' but rather of a group of people who, for whatever reason, believed so strongly in Koresh that the notion of leaving the squalid compound was unthinkable."[64]

Former Black Panther Eldridge Cleaver said of the disinformation campaign: "I recognized early on that the government was systematically poisoning and prejudicing public opinion with a blitz of inflammatory disinformation to stir up hatred against David Koresh and to foment a thirst for his blood. . . . Sifting through the tons of verbiage dished out by the government and spewed forth by the genuflecting mass media, I am yet unable to discern any justification for the government's initial, tactically stupid raid on the compound. There's only the arrogant, abusive, fascist exercise of state power."[65]

Press Repeated FBI Propoganda

During the Freedom of Information Foundation media panel, Dick DeGuerin condemned journalists for engaging in "pack journalism" and for regurgitating BATF and FBI propaganda and repeating charged words like "cult," "compound," "fortified bunkers," "Ranch Apocalypse," etc. He also criticized journalists for merely waiting for the Treasury and Justice Department reports as if they would be a final "Warren Commission Report" and not doing any investigative reporting to find out the truth. Few members of the press examined their own prejudices against deeply committed religious groups.

Some reporters even lied to the public. At trial KWTX-TV's John McLemore confessed he had lied in his news reports when he reported that he himself had heard automatic gunfire from the Davidians and that he had heard BATF agents announce "search warrant."[66]

The media repeated Cult Awareness Network propaganda and gave CAN spokespersons ample "cult busting" forums. NBC's May, 1993, television movie "In the Line of Duty: Ambush at Waco" presented the law-enforcement perspective and repeated dubious government assertions, including that Davidians ambushed the BATF and used machine guns and grenades.

After the trial Davidian Livingstone Fagan bitterly criticized the media's role: "And all you media people, what did you do to us during the period between February 28 and April 19? We were dehumanized and demonized. We were a cult! We were portrayed as criminals."[67]

Press Practiced Self-Censorship

The media also engaged in self-censorship and suppressed criticism of the government. In his media panel comments, Dick DeGuerin chastised the national press for ignoring two important stories: (1) the BATF's refusing Koresh's invitation to view his guns before the raid, and (2) the BATF's taking Koresh's gun dealer and business partner Henry McMahon into "protective custody" after the raid and forbidding him to speak to the press or the FBI. Even reporters at that event, which I attended, reported only the first story and not the second.

The producers of Pensacola's television show "Lawline" sent copies of their April 21, 1993, interview with McMahon, titled "Fiasco in Waco," to television stations all over the country. However, stations ignored McMahon's allegations.[68]

After the April 19 fire there was more self-censorship. Despite excellent network video footage of the havoc wreaked by tanks on April 19, no network has dared to compile and show to the American people the most controversial footage of tanks destroying the gymnasium, ramming the building early in the fire, and later pushing burning debris into the fire. And despite the Davidians' and their attorneys' repeated claims that BATF agents were firing from helicopters, few news reports ever have mentioned this one fact that best explains the FBI's actions on April 19, 1993.

Dallas talk show host Ron Engelman was forced to quit his job because of his Davidian advocacy on his radio show. Davidians listened to his show and on March 5, after Ken Fawcett called in and suggested Engelman ask the Davidians to move a satellite dish if they needed help, he did so, angering the FBI.[69] The Davidians even requested that Engelman be made a negotiator.[70] After the fire, Engelman's callers remained obsessed with the destruction of the Branch Davidians. Management demanded Engelman move his show to 6 A.M., take a co-host, and make the show "light and fluffy." Engelman refused and resigned.[71]

NBC originally planned to do a sequel to the television movie "Ambush at Waco" about the ending of the siege. However, it canceled the sequel, claiming it would be "too violent." Perhaps NBC network executives did not want to offend government officials with vivid portrayals of tanks gassing Davidians, tanks ramming away at the building, and Davidian men, women, and children dying grisly deaths by fire.

While some newspapers like the *New York Times* and the *Washington Times* denounced the Justice report as a "whitewash," others applauded it. An October 12, 1993, *Washington Post* editorial declared:

"[I]t is difficult to cast blame after reviewing the evidence. . . . [A]n earnest effort was being made to talk the group's members out of the buildings. . . . The finding of mass suicide and/or murder is a reasonable one."

January, 1993: BATF photograph of Mount Carmel Center, taken from Texas National Guard aircraft.

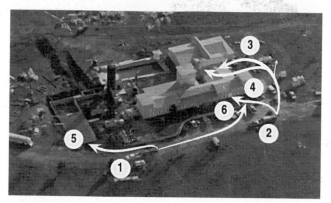

March, 1993: BATF photograph taken after failed BATF raid shows the original entry plans for four "Special Response Teams" in BATF's first test of its "National Response Plan".

1. ATF Trailer
2. ATF Trailer
3. New Orleans SRT – to roof
4. Dallas SRT – to second floor; Houston SRT to first floor
5. Portion of Houston SRT/ Arrest Team – secure pit
6. Dallas SRT – to second floor; Houston SRT to first floor

February 28, 1993: Waco Tribune-Herald photograph taken within the first minute of the raid shows that agents are kneeling in front of the front door, with no protection — something that they would not do if they were being "ambushed" by heavy Davidian gunfire.

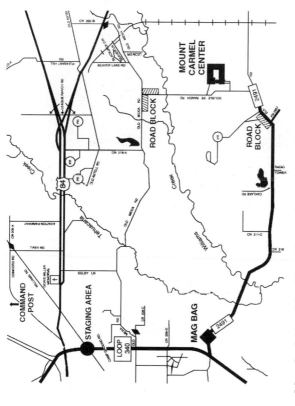

Map depicting Mag Bag, Mount Carmel, road blocks and staging area.
(Note graphic of Mount Carmel is incorrectly positioned.) *From Treasury Department report*

Trailer and bus destroyed by FBI tank early in the siege at Mount Carmel. *Photo by Paul Watson*

March 15, 1993: McLennan County Sheriff Jack Harwell and FBI chief negotiator Byron Sage meet with Davidians Wayne Martin and Steve Schneider outside Mount Carmel. *FBI photo*

April 8, 1993: Davidians hang banner for world to see. Habakkuk 3:14 refers to "wretched victims devoured in secret." *FBI photo*

April 19, 1993: Tank begins demolition of Mount Carmel's gymnasium. *FBI photo*

April 19, 1993: Tank at front attacks Mount Carmel's kitchen/concrete room area. Tank at rear continues demolition of gymnasium. *FBI photo*

April 19, 1993: As a result of the tank action, hundreds of pounds of concrete fell from the ceiling of the concrete room, killing three women and six children before the fire. *FBI photo*

April 19, 1995: Remains of concrete room at Mount Carmel. *Photo by Paul Watson*

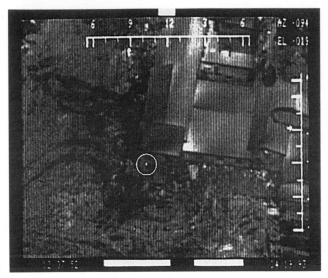

April 19, 1993: Aerial infrared photograph shows exact point of origin of second floor fire, right above the corner of the building ripped out by a tank 1 1/2 minutes before the fire. *FBI photo*

April 19, 1993: In the first minutes of the fire, second floor fire quickly spreads to dining room and chapel. *FBI photo*

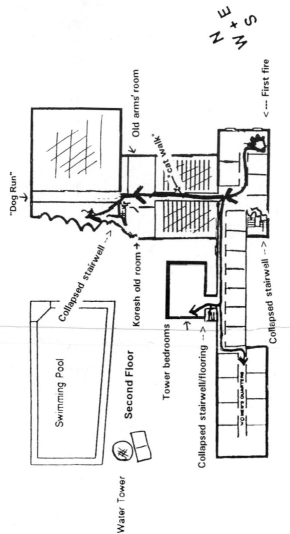

"Flue Effect" as Smoke and Flame Shoot Through Mount Carmel

April 19, 1993: Overhead shot of Mount Carmel less than 10 minutes into the fire. *FBI photo*

April 19, 1993: Fire trucks arrive after the building is destroyed. *FBI photo*

April 19, 1993: An unidentified federal agent poses for posterity in front of the burning Mount Carmel Center. At trial, defense attorneys presented a similar "trophy photo" of FBI chief negotiator Byron Sage. The photo cast severe doubt about the sincerity of his negotiations. *FBI photo*

April 19, 1995: At memorial at Mount Carmel, survivors and family members gather by crepe myrtle trees planted in memory of the 82 Branch Davidian victims. *Photo by Paul Watson*

April 19, 1995: Survivors David Thibodeau and Clive Doyle during the memorial at Mount Carmel. *Photo by Paul Watson*

April 19, 1995: Daniel Martin, who lost his father, Wayne, and one brother and three sisters, prays over granite memorial placed at Mount Carmel. *Photo by Paul Watson*

April 19, 1994: Carol Moore and Committee for Waco Justice protest near White House. *Photo by Ian Goddard*

April 19, 1995: Carol Moore and Committee for Waco Justice at FBI Headquarters in Washington D.C. *Photo by Dick Sanford*

1995 House Waco Hearings. (**A**) Author Carol Moore and former BATF Director Stephen Higgins agree BATF agents should be prosecuted for murder if they fired from helicopters and killed Davidians. (**B**) Bill Johnston chats with David Jewell who paraded his allegedly abused daughter before millions of television viewers. Undercover agent Robert Rodriquez (**C**) and BATF investigator Davy Aguilera (**D**).

Photos by Phil Ottman and Carol Moore

1995 House Waco Hearings. FBI siege commander Jeff Jamar (**E**) and chief negotiator Byron Sage (**F**). (FBI agents blocked Carol Moore from taking a picture of Hostage Rescue Team commander Dick Rogers.) (**G**) Former FBI Director William Sessions. (**H**) Former FBI Deputy Director Larry Potts who was removed because of questions regarding the FBI killing of Vicki Weaver. (**I**) Former Associate Attorney General Webster Hubbell, imprisoned in Fall, 1995 for fraud. (**J**) Former Deputy Treasury Secretary Robert Altman who resigned because of his actions regarding the "Whitewater" affair.

Photos by Carol Moore

1995 House Waco Hearings. (**K**) Davidian survivors Gladys Ottman, Annetta Richards, Myrtle Riddle and Sheila Martin were not called as witnesses but hoped to inspire the conscience of Congress. Theologians Phillip Arnold (**L**) and James Tabor (**M**) testified about the Davidians' belief the BATF attack was a sign from God and Davidians' determination to follow God's Word. (**N**) David Koresh's attorney Dick DeGuerin and Steve Schneider's attorney Jack Zimmerman testified about the Davidians' intention to exit Mount Carmel.

Photos by Carol Moore

Chapter Seven: The FBI Imposed Militaristic Siege

1.   Ronda Templeton, "3 sect members speak from jail of convictions, Koresh's return," *San Antonio Express-News*, February 27, 1994: 3A.

2.   "How the Siege Unfolded," *Waco Tribune-Herald*, April 20, 1994: 7A.

3.   Jack DeVault, transcript of 911 tape transcript: 233.

4.   Dr. Phillip Arnold and Dr. James Tabor, "Comments and Clarifications" section of "The Decoded Message of the Seven Seals of the Book of Revelation" by David Koresh; Carmen Stair and Glenn Fawcett, "Breaking the Long Silence: Davidian member paints a different picture of the standoff," *The East Texan*, April 1, 1993: 3.

5.   Justice Department report: 17, 45–46.

6.   Ruth Riddle interview, NBC's "Dateline" June 15, 1993.

7.   Diana R. Fuentes, February 2, 1994; Jack DeVault: 104, 130; Dick Reavis, private communication, December, 1994; trial transcript: 4117, 4480; Marjorie Thomas Testimony, November 17–18, 1994: 59–64, 112, 114.

8.   Statement from Mount Carmel Survivors, "The Branch Davidian Response," April 17, 1994.

9.   George Zimmerlee, in "Waco: Truth and Warning; How Truth Was Suppressed by Technology and Terror," *Full Disclosure* #30, 1993, alleges these actions violate the 1934 Communications Act (47 USC 305, 326, 333). He states Section 326 refers to the FCC, but holds the FBI is a co-conspirator. He alleges the FBI's actions violated the International Radio Regulations (ITU 1947, Sec. 44) and the International Covenant on Civil and Political Rights (Art. 19).

10.   Treasury Department report: 37.

11.   William Claiborne, "Officials in Waco Fear Destruction of Evidence," *Washington Post*, April 7, 1993: A3.

12.   David Thibodeau, private communication, December, 1994; Justice Department report, appendix on Davidians' demands.

13.   Justice Department report: 65 and Appendix C: 3.

14.   Trial transcript: 6608–09.

15.   Ibid., 4514–17.

16.   Steve McVicker, July 22, 1993.

17.   Trial transcript: 6634.

18.   "The Maury Povich Show," November 8, 1993.

19.   Livingstone Fagan paper, August, 1994: 16.

20.   Renos Avraam, private communication, October, 1994.

21.   Trial transcript: 4723.

22.   Justice Department report: 120–21.

23.   Ibid., 9, 27; trial transcript: 5027.

24.   Justice Department report: 10, 117.

25.   Ibid., 12, 135.

26.   Nancy Ammerman report in Justice Department report: 4.

27.   ABC television program "Turning Point," August 8, 1994.

28.   Livingstone Fagan paper, August, 1994: 14.

29.   Justice Department report: 53.

30.   Ibid., 68.

31.   *New York Times*, April 5, 1993: A10.

32.   Nancy Ammerman presentation at November 22, 1993, American Academy of Religion panel on Branch Davidians.

33.   Nancy Ammerman report to Justice Department, 1993: 5.

34.   Justice Department report: 28, 120.

35.   Ibid., 42–43.

36.   Ibid., 147, 149, 258.

37.   All quotes from April 19, 1993, afternoon FBI press conference and April 20, 1993, FBI press conference from CNN broadcast of conference; quotes from April 19, 1993, morning FBI press briefing, from transcript and from CNN broadcast; Susan Schmidt, "FBI's Point Man at Waco Leads Probe," *Washington Post*, April 28, 1995.

38.   "Ex-prosecutor laments agents' 'storm trooper' tactics," *Houston Chronicle*, March 2, 1993.

39.   Susan J. Palmer article, "Excavating Waco," James R. Lewis, editor, *From the Ashes: Making Sense of Waco:* 106.

40.   James Ridgeway, "Armies of God," *Village Voice*, May 4, 1993: 26.

41.   Ramsey Clark, *The Fire This Time* (New York: Thundermouth Press): 1991.

42.   Naftali Bendavid, "The Costs of Cult Standoff: Were Estimates Too High?" *Legal Times*, May 3, 1993: 18.

43.   Justice Department report: 123–124.

44.   Trial transcript: 5500; Jaime Castillo, private communication, February, 1995.

45.   "A countdown to disaster," *USA Today*, April 20, 1993: 3A.

46. Justice Department report: 239.

47. Rowland Nethaway, " 'Mind control' machine," *Waco Tribune-Herald*, March 4, 1994: 8A.

48. Brad Bailey and Bob Darden: 206–07.

49. Doug Ireland, "Operation Waco Storm," *Village Voice*, May 4, 1993.

50. Ron Cole: 69.

51. Reporters Committee for Freedom of the Press report, "The Clinton Administration and the News Media," 1994.

52. Audiotape of the September 10, 1993, Freedom of Information Foundation media panel on Waco.

53. Doug Ireland, *Village Voice*, May 4, 1993.

54. Brad Bailey and Bob Darden: 232.

55. "Day 51: The True Story of Waco" video.

56. Paul McKay, "Photographers for *Chronicle*, AP arrested," *Houston Chronicle*, April 22, 1993.

57. Brad Bailey and Bob Darden: 206.

58. Dick Reavis, private communication, December, 1994.

59. James L. Pate, private communication, June, 1994.

60. Tim Sullivan report, "Court TV," February 2, 1994.

61. William Raspberry, "What if they were the Black Davidians?" *Washington Post*, March 10, 1993: A19.

62. Brad Darden and Bob Bailey: 246.

63. Mary Jordan and Sue Anne Pressley, May 9, 1993, A1; April 22, 1993; Senate Committee on Appropriations hearing: 122.

64. Justice Department report: 205.

65. Eldridge Cleaver, "Waco: Bill Clinton's Bay of Pigs," James R. Lewis, editor, *From the Ashes: Making Sense of Waco:* 235–36.

66. Trial transcript: 6561, 6569.

67. James L. Pate, July, 1994: 76.

68. Paul H. Blackman report: 56.

69. Ken Fawcett commentary on Ron Cole's *Sinister Twilight*, May 11, 1994; "Day 51: The True Story of Waco" video.

70. Justice Department report, Appendix C: 3.

71. Libertarian Party of Dallas, Texas 1993 promotional materials on Ron Engelman talk video tape.

8

The FBI Sabotaged
Negotiations

*The truth is, the Branch Davidians were for
peace, but the government was for war.*
Paul Fatta before sentencing[1]

The federal government has successfully
negotiated past sieges, like the 1973 siege of Native
Americans at Wounded Knee that lasted seventy days,
and the 1985 siege of the white supremacist group the
Covenant, the Sword and the Arm of the Lord. And
despite the deaths of son Samuel and wife Vicki Weaver,
after Bo Gritz became a third-party negotiator, Randy
Weaver did surrender without further bloodshed.
Toward the end of the siege at Mount Carmel, there
was a prison uprising in Louisville, Ohio, which

negotiators also ended peacefully, despite the deaths of several prisoners and death threats against guards held hostage. The FBI's failures raise questions not only about the FBI agents and officials' motives and expertise, but about those of President Clinton, who may have played a much greater role in siege decisions than he has acknowledged.

QUESTIONS ABOUT PRESIDENT CLINTON'S MOTIVES AND ROLE

President Bill Clinton had been in office little more than a month when terrorists blew up a garage below the World Trade Center, killing six people. Two days later, Branch Davidians fought off a BATF assault, and four agents died. As fate would have it, three of them had served as Clinton's bodyguards during the presidential campaign. In a March 18, 1993, speech before employees of the Treasury Department Clinton said: "My prayers and I'm sure yours are still with the families of all four of the Alcohol, Tobacco, and Firearms agents who were killed in Waco—Todd McKeehan and Conway LeBleu of New Orleans, Steve Willis of Houston, and Robert Williams from my hometown of Little Rock. Three of those four were assigned to my security during the course of the primary or general election." David Koresh would remain a thorn in Bill Clinton's side for the next fifty-one days.

Clinton, Altman, and Buford

The Justice report devotes a section to describing President Clinton and his staff's involvement in the siege and the FBI decision to assault Mount Carmel. Clinton spoke with Treasury Secretary Lloyd Bentsen the evening of February 28. Both agreed "there shouldn't again be a dangerous frontal assault on the Waco compound, and that the Bradley fighting vehicles dispatched there should be kept out of sight, for fear of inciting more violence."[2] Nevertheless, Davidians report the vehicles began moving all over the property almost immediately. Clinton also requested that Acting Attorney General Stuart Gerson's Justice Department "apprise" him if the FBI was considering any tactical moves against the Davidians.[3]

The evening of February 28 Clinton also spoke with Deputy Treasury Secretary Roger Altman.[4] Altman had been informed about the raid beforehand and did not attempt to stop it. Roger Altman, a long-time "friend-of-Bill," was a top Clinton campaign advisor, fundraiser, and contributor who would later be forced to resign his position because of the "Whitewater" affair.[5]

According to the *Wall Street Journal*, the day after the raid, Clinton told his Chief of Staff Thomas McLarty that he wanted "to know the condition of one particular ATF agent who was wounded at Waco: Jay William Buford, an acquaintance of his from Arkansas."[6] Resident Agent-in-Charge Buford was a lead investigator and planner in the botched February 28 raid on Mount Carmel. Doubtless acting under Clinton's instructions, Altman immediately made a trip to Waco and reported the results to Clinton. According to the Justice report, Altman returned from Waco and briefed White House Counsel Bernard Nussbaum and Presidential Advisor Bruce Lindsey about the trip.[7]

The *Wall Street Journal* reports what the Justice report omits—that on March 3 Altman also spoke to Clinton about it. The reporter, who was doing a "day in the life story" about Clinton, wrote: "Altman reports on his visit with the president's friend, Mr. Buford, who was nicked in the nose by a bullet. The president wants to know if there will be any permanent scarring. Mr. Altman says he doesn't think so." (Buford's injuries were actually more serious, as he received gunshot wounds to both legs.)[8] Considering Clinton's sometimes perverse relationships with Arkansas law enforcement, it is possible that Buford, through Altman, nefariously influenced Clinton to acquiesce to BATF's "revenge" against the Davidians.

Clinton and Hubbell

Webster Hubbell, a former law partner of Hillary Clinton, has been called by Arkansas Senator Dale Bumpers "the best friend of the President of the United States."[9] Many believe Hubbell, who some claim was the de facto attorney general during his year at the Justice Department, in secret consultation with Clinton, had a much greater influence on Waco decision-making than admitted.

During the siege of the Davidians, Hubbell first reported to Acting Attorney General Stuart Gerson.[10]

After Janet Reno was confirmed as attorney general he became her "assistant." He was confirmed as Associate Attorney General, third in command, after the April 19 fire.

According to the Justice Department report, "In preparation for the arrival of Attorney General Reno on March 12, Gerson decided to pass his responsibility for Waco to Hubbell."[11] The report never does describe Hubbell's full powers under this "responsibility" and whether Hubbell remained effectively in charge until the end of the siege.

During the April 28, 1993, House Judiciary Committee hearing, Representative Sensenbrenner expressed concern that Hubbell had been having "out-of-the-loop" discussions with Clinton about the standoff. He asked FBI Director William Sessions whether the FBI had briefed Hubbell outside Washington, D.C. Sessions admitted he did not know. During Hubbell's May 19, 1993, confirmation hearing, Senator Arlen Specter (R-PA) specifically asked Hubbell if, besides his purely personal contacts with Bill Clinton, he had had any direct contact with Clinton regarding any issues before the Department of Justice. Hubbell answered he had only spoken to President Clinton directly about appointment of a Supreme Court justice.[12] Considering that in December, 1994, Hubbell pled guilty to mail fraud, including against two government agencies, it would not be surprising if he was similarly dishonest in his statement to the Senate Judiciary Committee.

Evidence that Hubbell actually was de facto head of the Justice Department and capable of just such actions surfaced in February, 1994. Immediately after resigning in early 1994, former Deputy Attorney General Phillip B. Heymann, who had been in charge of the investigation into FBI actions at Waco, charged that Hubbell had become "the one person" in the Justice Department to deal with the White House. One reporter wrote in a Hubbell exposé: "Foes painted him as a shadowy figure pulling strings from behind the scene at the Justice Department and taking orders directly from the Oval Office." Hubbell, not Reno, is said to have held the real power in the Justice Department.[13] Hubbell resigned his position in early 1994 because of accusations of improprieties by former law partners.

It is clear that the Justice Department exercised more control than usual over the FBI during the siege at Waco. An hour and a half after the beginning of the April 19 fire, Wolfe Blitzer reported on CNN that White House sources, while denying that the White House had been "micromanaging" Waco decision-making, conceded that the Justice Department had been doing so. At the time FBI Director William Sessions was facing possible dismissal as a result of various ethics violations. As we shall see, he was a rather weak and confused leader and his ideas were sometimes overruled by Justice Department officials. FBI agents in the field had little respect for him and he evidently had little control over them.

When Attorney General Janet Reno fired Sessions on July 19, 1993, Sessions complained bitterly that he "would not be part of politicizing the FBI, from within or without." He referred specifically to the FBI's "compromised role" in the investigations of "Travelgate" and White House Counsel Vince Foster's death.[14]

However, White House interference and politicizing of
the FBI started much earlier during the siege in Waco.

SMERICK AND YOUNG ADVISED
AGAINST TACTICAL PRESSURE

The FBI consulted its own behavioral scientists,
whose specialty was applying psychology to law
enforcement situations, but ignored their
recommendations. Pete Smerick and Mark Young
recommended in several March 5 to 9 memorandums
that this was not a typical hostage situation since the
Davidians insisted on staying with their leader. They
wrote that "tactical presence . . . if carried to excess,
could eventually be counter-productive and could result
in loss of life."[15]

Smerick and Young recommended that the FBI
"establish some trust with Koresh" and even suggested
"moving back from the compound, not to show law-
enforcement weakness, but to sap from Koresh the
source of his powerful hold over his followers—his
prediction that the government was about to start a war
against them." They concluded by saying that the FBI
could "always resort to tactical pressure, but it should
be the absolute last option we should consider."[16]

In their last memorandum Smerick and Young
did recommend mild pressures, like sporadic cutting
off power, sudden movements of equipment and
manpower, but only if exercised with "extreme caution."
However, in April, 1995, Peter Smerick revealed to a
reporter that unnamed senior FBI officials complained

the earlier memorandums were "tying their hands." Smerick said, "The whole point of our assessment was to provide unbiased intelligence [to FBI decision-makers]. If I couldn't analyze it as I saw it on site, the process was jeopardized." The FBI officials pressured the behavioral analysts to endorse the more aggressive approach. Smerick revealed he then left Waco in disgust. He later resigned from the FBI.[17]

TACTICAL AGENTS OVERRULED NEGOTIATORS

Justice Department outside expert Dr. Alan A. Stone notes that "pushed by the tactical leader [Rogers] the commander on the ground [Jamar] began to allow tactical pressures."[18] Civil suit attorneys have evidence that former Dallas FBI chief Oliver Buck Revell also was involved in that effort and have included him as a defendant in their civil suits.[19]

Dr. Stone criticized these actions: "I have concluded that the FBI command failed to give adequate consideration to their own behavioral science and negotiation experts. They also failed to make use of the Agency's own prior successful experience in similar circumstances. They embarked on a misguided and punishing law-enforcement strategy that contributed to the tragic ending at Waco."[20]

The Justice report acknowledges that negotiators criticized the tactical commanders for undercutting negotiations: "the negotiators felt that the efforts of the tactical personnel were directed toward

intimidation and harassment."[21] Davidian David
Thibodeau charges that tactical agents would find out
from negotiators what kind of harassment most
bothered the Davidians so that they could do more of
it.[22]

The Justice report alleges that negotiators did
not believe negotiations alone could have avoided the
April 19 fire.[23] However, Dr. Stone conducted his own
interviews and found, "FBI's behavioral scientists and
negotiators . . . share my belief that mistakes were
made." He wrote they "expressed their determination
to have the truth come out, regardless of the
consequences."[24] Another outside expert, Nancy
Ammerman, agreed that the FBI did have negotiators
and experts giving them good advice—advice not
heeded because these individuals were "outranked and
outnumbered by the tactical types."[25] FBI negotiators
could not maintain the respect of the Davidians who
quickly realized they had little power to protect them
against the aggressive tactical agents.

FBI REJECTED FAMILY AND
THIRD-PARTY INTERVENTION

FBI commanders rejected two important
negotiation tactics: allowing direct communication
between families and Davidians, and allowing third
parties to negotiate a surrender. While the FBI would
send in video and audiotapes from families, in order to
"drive a wedge" between Koresh and his followers, they
did not allow them to speak directly to family members.

Months after the massacre, Balenda Gamen, mother of fire survivor David Thibodeau, recalled: "I originally came to Waco because I was challenged by the FBI when they said to me, 'There is no room for family in this operation. Perhaps we'll do it in the future.' When I heard those words I knew that the writing was on the wall for this community."[26]

Gamen and other family members repeatedly sent the FBI and Janet Reno faxes and registered letters requesting that they be allowed to negotiate directly with relatives inside Mount Carmel. During the April 28, 1993, House Judiciary Committee hearings Reno revealed that she had never heard about the families' attempts to reach her.

During the April 20, 1993, final FBI press conference SAC Jeff Jamar explained they did not allow family intervention because, "Who would you choose to talk to them?" Obviously, they could have started with David Koresh's mother. Yet when Bonnie Haldeman and Dick DeGuerin drove up to a roadblock early in the siege, the FBI turned them away.[27]

A number of third-party negotiators were considered and rejected. On March 6, FBI Director William Sessions had discussions with Koresh's former attorney Gary Coker—who happens to be a personal friend of Sessions from his days in Waco[28]—about negotiating with Koresh. However, FBI commanders rejected him because they thought he merely was looking for a client. Sessions himself offered to negotiate, but Acting Attorney General Gerson forbade it.[29]

All through the month of March, Davidians requested outside negotiators including any theologian who could convince him his interpretation of the Seven Seals was incorrect, theologian Dr. Phillip Arnold, the Texas Constitutional Foundation Association, government critic Don Stewart, talk show host Ron Engelman, and McLennan County Sheriff Jack Harwell.[30] The FBI did allow Wayne Martin and Steve Schneider to meet face to face with Sheriff Harwell on March 15, but it would not allow him a free hand as a third-party negotiator.[31] On March 16 frustrated Davidians used flashlights to send a Morse code to reporters reading, "SOS, SOS. FBI broke negotiations. Want negotiations from the press."[32] The FBI soon started flashing bright lights at the compound at night, perhaps in part to end such communications. On March 27 Steve Schneider again requested a "neutral negotiator." Only after the Davidians were in Mount Carmel for a full month did the FBI allow David Koresh and Steve Schneider to meet with their attorneys.

FBI DESTROYED "CRIME SCENE" DESPITE COMPLAINTS

One form of harassment which had important legal implications was the FBI's moving and destroying Davidian vehicles. This enraged the Davidians because they believed the vans and automobiles would prove that they had done relatively little firing at the agents hiding behind them and that the BATF was responsible for most of the shooting, including of its own agents.

The vehicles might also provide evidence that helicopters had shot from the air. At trial defense attorneys contended that the real reason a Davidian's red camino was crushed by a tank was to destroy evidence of just such holes. Davidians also complained that FBI tanks moved and destroyed shell casings lying about the ground which would prove the volume and direction of BATF firing.[33]

Davidians were convinced that the BATF and the FBI would destroy evidence once they entered Mount Carmel. In early March, Steve Schneider expressed fear that the government wanted to destroy Mount Carmel because the building itself was evidence of BATF crimes. Schneider's attorney Jack Zimmermann said, "There is no question that the FBI is destroying evidence. If nothing else they've moved the location of physical objects from a crime scene before they had been photographed." Dick DeGuerin agreed. "They're destroying evidence with the bulldozers."[34]

The FBI even annoyed prosecutors when it began the removal of the vehicles from in front of the building. On March 23 Assistant U.S. Attorney William Johnston wrote Attorney General Janet Reno to complain. The FBI then agreed to "photograph, graph and grid" the areas from which vehicles were moved in order to preserve evidence.[35] However, the Justice report does not mention if the FBI told the Davidians about this new policy.

FBI RELIED ON EXPERTS AND CULT BUSTERS URGING TACTICAL PRESSURE

Despite Koresh's preoccupation with the Seven Seals, the FBI never allowed anyone who was an expert on the subject to have direct contact with him. The only theologian the Justice report took seriously was one from Baylor University which the report notes "has one of the largest 'cult' reference and research facilities in the country."[36] Instead the FBI relied primarily on the advice of psychologists, psychiatrists, and—though they deny it—"cult busters" who only confirmed the FBI's negative view of the Davidians.

FBI Relied on Psychologists and Psychiatrists

The FBI was particularly attentive to the advice of psychologists and psychiatrists who supported the belief that David Koresh was mentally unbalanced and would not surrender voluntarily. Dr. Park Dietz asserted, "continuing to negotiate in good faith would not resolve the situation, because Koresh would not come out." Dr. Anthony J. Pinizotto said, "Koresh displayed psychopathic behavior, that he was a 'con-artist' type, and he had narcissistic tendencies." Dr. Mike Webster opined, "Koresh appeared to be manifesting anti-social traits." Dr. Bruce Perry and social worker Joyce Sparks, who interviewed children from Mount Carmel, agreed that "Koresh was stalling for time, to prepare for his 'final battle' with authorities."

Dr. Joseph L. Krofcheck (with FBI psychological profiler Clinton R. Van Zandt) held that Koresh appeared to be a "functional, paranoid-type psychotic," and that he was unlikely to "give up the power and omnipotence he enjoyed inside the compound," except through "some form of tactical intervention."[37]

FBI Relied on Three Cult Busters

There is evidence that the Justice Department tried to cover up the FBI's association with professional or amateur "cult busters" in response to three events: the New Alliance Party's May, 1993, suit against the FBI for classifying the group as a "cult"; deprogrammer Rick Ross' summer, 1993, indictment for "unlawful imprisonment"; and Nancy Ammerman's sharp criticisms of the FBI's association with Ross. The Justice report asserts the FBI "did not solicit advice from any 'cult experts' or 'cult deprogrammers.' "[38]

During the siege Ross went to Waco and continued his propaganda campaign. He told the *Houston Chronicle* that Koresh was "your stock cult leader. They're all the same. Meet one and you've met them all. They're deeply disturbed, have a borderline personality, and lack any type of conscience."[39] During one television appearance Ross declared he hoped Koresh would be a coward and surrender rather than end up a corpse.[40] (On April 8, 1993, former Cult Awareness President Patricia Ryan told the *Houston*

Chronicle, "Officials should use whatever means necessary to arrest Koresh, including lethal force."[41])

Rick Ross' contention that he was in close contact with the BATF and the FBI is backed up by Nancy Ammerman's September 10, 1993, one-page addendum to her report (which the Justice Department did not bother to include in its report). In it she wrote, "The interview transcripts document that Mr. Rick Ross was, in fact, closely involved with both the ATF and the FBI. . . . He clearly had the most extensive access to both agencies of any person on the 'cult expert' list, and he was apparently listened to more attentively." Nevertheless, the Justice report states: "The FBI did not 'rely' on Ross for advice whatsoever during the standoff."[42]

The Justice report claims that the FBI determined Marc Breault was talking to the media and therefore only accepted affidavits and electronic mail from him but decided "not to contact him." However, Breault in his book asserts: "as soon as the siege began . . . the FBI tried for hours to contact us. . . . They almost sent the police to drag us to police headquarters. Just before they took that drastic action, the negotiators broke through." Breault asserts he gave them detailed information about Koresh and his followers and declares: "The FBI contacted us throughout the siege. They showed us Koresh's [April, 1993] letters." Breault further claims he and his wife "told the FBI that Koresh was starting to lose his grip and that he would probably end the siege violently."[43] Clearly, either Breault is lying or the FBI and Justice Department are trying to cover up their reliance on him.

Most disturbing of all, the FBI either did not know—or did not admit—that long-time FBI consultant Dr. Murray S. Miron, a professor of psycholinguistics at Syracuse University, is an outspoken cult critic. During the 1970s he had been involved with the Citizens Freedom Foundation, the anti-cult group which evolved into the Cult Awareness Network. The week of April 14, even while he was consulting with the FBI, Miron published an article called "The Mark of the Cult" in the *Syracuse New Times*. The article contains stereotypical anti-cult propaganda: "The totalitarianism of the cult banishes dissent and fosters dependence upon fallible, power-mad leaders. It is the system of every dictator, whether benign or benevolent."[44]

After reading the first and third letters Koresh sent out of Mount Carmel, Miron concluded that they bore: "all the hallmarks of rampant, morbidly virulent paranoia. . . . In my judgment, we are facing a determined, hardened adversary who has no intention of delivering himself or his followers into the hands of his adversaries."[45]

In typically media-savvy cult-buster fashion, Miron managed to make himself almost the only FBI consultant quoted in major media right after the fire—thus using his FBI connections to promote his anti-cult propaganda. On April 21 and 22 his insulting anti-Davidian comments appeared in the *Los Angeles Times*, the *Washington Post,* and the *New York Times.*[46]

On April 21 Miron appeared on NBC's "Today" program and dismissed Koresh as a "diseased megalomaniac" who had been "stalling." He then spewed forth ferocious anti-cult rhetoric: "This particular cult was particularly destructive, particularly aggressive, being led by a man who was a paranoid, mentally ill and psychopathic and manipulative." With Murray Miron on their side, the FBI had all the expert sanction they needed to gas and demolish the Davidians' home.

During the April 28, 1993, House Judiciary Committee hearing, FBI siege commander Jeff Jamar admitted, "we had a white paper on cults that was very, very useful to us." The white paper outlined the traits of cults with one "dynamic, manipulative, egomaniacal, psychopathic leader." It also had repeated references to the Jonestown massacre. Jamar asserted that the traits fit Koresh "to a T." Jamar did not tell the committee what individual or organization gave him the white paper. It is evident there was a definite cult-buster influence on—and justification for—decisions to replace negotiations with harassment and to launch the gas and tank attack.

FBI'S ESCALATING SABOTAGE

Dr. Alan A. Stone writes: "By March 21st, the FBI was concentrating on tactical pressure alone. . . . This changing strategy at the compound from (1) conciliatory negotiation to (2) negotiation and tactical pressure and then to (3) tactical pressure alone."[47] A description of these escalating tactical pressures and the Davidians' response to them, grouped into Dr. Stone's three phases follows.

March 1–6: FBI Relatively Conciliatory

During this period twenty-three of the thirty-five individuals to leave Mount Carmel did so. Koresh promised that Davidians all would exit on March 2 if the FBI played a fifty-eight-minute audiotape on prime time radio all over the country. The FBI agreed to this demand. However, they played the tape only on local stations in the mid-afternoon. Why would the FBI lie, effectively sabotaging the exit?

Nevertheless, the FBI did not punish Koresh's change of mind, which he explained by saying that God had spoken to him and told him to wait. When the U.S. Attorney's office enraged the Branch Davidians by charging the two elderly women who left Mount Carmel on March 2, negotiators quickly convinced them to drop the charges. However, the FBI did read to them their very strict rules of engagement, effectively threatening that FBI agents were free to shoot anyone they perceived to be carrying a gun. And much to the Davidians' dismay, the FBI cut off their phone contact to everyone except authorities, sent armored vehicles onto the Mount Carmel property, broke promises about getting medical help, sent their children to foster homes, and refused to let them retrieve Peter Gent's body.[48]

The FBI also "bugged" Mount Carmel, sending in recording devices with deliveries of milk, a typewriter, and other requested items. At the trial an FBI agent testified that the FBI had planted eleven listening devices in or around Mount Carmel during the siege. Many of them were discovered and destroyed by the Davidians.[49]

A *Sunday Times of London* article claimed that the FBI even used aircraft to pick up conversations, infrared devices to pinpoint individual's positions, and tiny fiber-optic microphones and cameras inserted in walls to relay audio and visual images back to the command center.[50] CNN reporter Bonnie Anderson revealed on April 19, 1993, that the FBI used a robot with a fiber optic camera to look into the windows. No such video evidence was presented at trial.

March 7–21: FBI Increased Harassment

During this period eleven more people left Mount Carmel. Negotiators began trying to drive a wedge between Koresh and his followers. FBI spokespersons ridiculed Steve Schneider because his wife Judy had borne Koresh's child. They played family tapes over loudspeakers, using the tapes for harassment instead of persuasion, as well as tapes of Koresh's more aggressive statements to negotiators, hoping to undermine Davidians' faith in him. The FBI turned the electricity on and off as a pressure tactic. On March 12, despite the exit of one Davidian and the promise three would exit the next day, the FBI turned off the power for good.[51]

These punishments, despite the Davidians' cooperation, made them more distrustful. Koresh and Schneider called this "bad faith" by the government. On March 15 negotiators made it clear they would refuse to listen to any more "Bible babble." However, they did allow the face-to-face meeting with Sheriff Harwell.[52]

On March 19, after the FBI sent in attorneys' letters and an audiotape from theologian Phillip Arnold—and the FBI finally reassured Davidians their home would not be confiscated and those not prosecuted could return—Koresh told the FBI that "he was ready to come out and face whatever might happen to him." He even joked, "When they give me the lethal injection, give me the cheap stuff."[53] Between just March 19 and 21 alone ten people left Mount Carmel. The fact that in just a few more days the Davidians legally would gain control of Mount Carmel may have figured into Koresh's willingness to discuss surrender. Nevertheless, the FBI began exposing the "negative part of [Koresh's] personality"—including his alleged threats—during Davidian-monitored press conferences explaining, "it is important for the American people to know what we are dealing with."[54]

March 22–April 19: FBI Escalated Harassment Despite Cooperation

Despite these successes, the FBI siege commander Jeff Jamar, influenced by Hostage Rescue Team commander Richard Rogers, decided it was time to increase tactical pressure and "demonstrate the authority of law enforcement."[55] On March 21 seven people left Mount Carmel, evidently the beginning of a mass exodus, as promised by David Koresh just a few days before. Nevertheless, that very night the FBI started blaring music over its loudspeaker system. They continued despite Davidian complaints. At 11:45 P.M.

Koresh sent out the message, "Because of the loud music, nobody is coming out." The next day Schneider asserted that the "music had been counterproductive." The FBI did not tell the public that Koresh had been on the verge of surrender, only that those who left had been kicked out for disobedience, drinking, or being a "drain" on their resources.[56] Nevertheless, according to Davidian Brad Branch, Koresh gave those exiting Mount Carmel Bible studies instructing them on the biblical purpose of their exit.[57]

On March 22 the FBI promised Koresh that if he surrendered immediately he could communicate with his followers in jail, hold religious services, and make a worldwide religious broadcast. Probably reacting to past FBI lies, Koresh angrily threw their letter away.[58] The last Davidian to leave Mount Carmel before the fire, Livingstone Fagan, exited on March 23.

During the March 24 press briefing, as the Davidians listened, "the FBI increased its 'verbal assault' against Koresh, calling Koresh a liar and coward, and accusing him of hiding behind his children."[59] They even allowed BATF spokesperson David Troy to get in on the slugfest; Troy declared that Koresh was just a "cheap thug who interprets the Bible through the barrel of a gun."[60]

The FBI harassed the Davidians by blaring loud music night and day and playing back audiotapes of negotiation and family members' and released members' greetings. The FBI shined bright lights in the Davidians' windows all night long while loudspeakers blared sounds of screeching rabbits being slaughtered, dentist drills, Tibetan monk chants, telephone busy signals, clocks ticking, cows mooing, and airplanes taking off. The FBI also "tightened the perimeter" by stringing razor wire all around the building.

Some of the harassment was quite violent. The FBI declared deadlines by which Davidians were to exit on March 23, 24, 27, and 28. When these were not met, the FBI removed and often crushed and destroyed automobiles, vans, go-carts, and motorcycles. Also, according to Edward S. G. Dennis, Jr., the chief reviewer of the Justice Department report, "Bradleys [tanks] were run up and down in front of the compound in what negotiators believed was a show of force." Davidian Graeme Craddock charges that late in the siege a tank actually rammed the room two rooms west of the front door where he was sleeping, slamming into the head of his bed. He claims that at trial he saw photographs in which damage to the room clearly is visible.[61]

Helicopters brazenly buzzed the building, reminding Davidians of the fatal attacks of February 28. And if any individuals tried to leave the building without permission, agents would hurl dangerous flash-bangs at them until they returned inside. The FBI played over and over again the song "These Boots are Made for Walking," which contains the line, "and if you play with matches you know you're gonna get burned."[62]

Despite the FBI's violent harassment, Davidians never retaliated or fired a shot during the siege, even to ward off threatening tanks or helicopters, to silence annoying loudspeakers, or to put out bright lights. Nevertheless the FBI continued to assert Davidians posed an immediate threat to anyone within two miles.

Louis Alaniz, who sneaked into Mount Carmel for several days, described "these Bradley's running around and the guys in them shooting the finger at these kids, and one incident where they actually mooned some of the girls. These people were scared." Graeme Craddock, who witnessed this, said in a June 20, 1995, interview on National Public Radio: "If that was their attitude toward us, we didn't particularly want to go out and surrender to these people. We didn't particularly want to send our kids out to these sort of people."[63]

Outside expert Dr. Robert Cancro told reporters: "the threats implicit in the use of armored vehicles, razor wire, and a tightening perimeter tend to negate the positive and friendly tone attempted by negotiators.... Even a person who isn't paranoid would interpret that as lack of consistency and good faith in negotiations. A paranoid individual needs more reassurance, not less."[64]

Edward Dennis wrote, "Some negotiators believe that as a result of these actions the Davidians concluded that the negotiators had no influence over the decision makers and that the FBI was not trustworthy."[65] In early April Dick DeGuerin told reporters, "They're still intimidated by the FBI. We're not coming out until we know the media are going to be there."[66]

On March 28 Davidians sent out another home movie to assure federal officials the children were healthy and to give members another opportunity to reiterate their commitment to staying inside.[67] In fact, according to Louis Alaniz, Koresh actually kept members "in line" by threatening to make them leave Mount Carmel.[68]

To show his lack of concern about the government's harassment, at one point Steve Schneider declared "you can burn us down, kill us, whatever."[69] Koresh told the FBI, "If they want blood, then our blood is here for them to shed. . . . We are not afraid of the government. If we have to die for what we stand for, we're going to. I don't mind if I die."[70] Dick DeGuerin said, "There was a collective feeling that the harassment was making them more stubborn."[71]

During the 1993 House Judiciary Committee hearing, Representative William Hughes asked SAC Jamar which experts had recommended they use pressure tactics like blasting loud noises all night long. Jamar did not answer the Congressman's question but merely repeated his claim that the purpose of the noise was sleep deprivation. Outside expert Nancy Ammerman also could not get a straight answer about who had recommended these pressure tactics.[72] The Justice Department report infers it was Richard Rogers, commander of the Hostage Rescue Team, who decided to use these tactics, with the consent of Deputy Assistant Director of the Criminal Investigative Division Danny Coulson.[73]

Throughout the siege, Davidians attempted to communicate with the outside world, by putting out banners that read: "Rodney King We Understand," "FBI, God Sees Your Lies," and "Habakkuk 3:14," a biblical reference to wretched victims devoured in secret.

FBI REFUSED TO HONOR KORESH'S
PROMISE TO SURRENDER

Despite all this harassment, third-party intervention by attorneys and theologians did convince David Koresh to make a credible promise to surrender on April 14. There is solid evidence that, as a result of these contacts, David Koresh did indeed receive his "message from God" and that he and all Davidians would have left Mount Carmel had the FBI waited only a few more days.

DeGuerin and Zimmermann Visited Mount Carmel

Attorney Dick DeGuerin was well known for clients he had defended in highly publicized homicides. Steve Schneider's family retained another respected criminal attorney, Jack Zimmermann. Attorneys DeGuerin, Gary Coker, Vic Feazell, Gary Richardson, and Kirk Lyons signed on to a temporary restraining order to prevent the FBI from further assaulting the Davidians. DeGuerin filed a writ of habeas corpus on behalf of Koresh.[74]

However, the FBI initially refused to allow the Davidians to consult with attorneys. In mid-March U.S. District Judge Walter S. Smith, Jr., wrote, "One simply cannot point a gun, literally or figuratively, at constitutional authority and at the same time complain that constitutional rights are being denied."[75] Eventually the FBI relented and on March 28 DeGuerin met with Koresh for two hours. DeGuerin met four more times with Koresh. Zimmermann met twice with Steve Schneider. The last meeting was April 4. After that point, the FBI told the attorneys they could not re-enter Mount Carmel unless they could assure them of an immediate surrender.[76]

During DeGuerin's and Zimmermann's visits to Mount Carmel, they inspected the damage done by BATF gunfire, saw the blood spots where Davidians had died, and told Davidians to photograph or video tape the damage. They reassured Davidians that Texas Rangers, not federal agents, would investigate the crime scene.[77]

Both assured Davidians they had very "triable" cases and could be acquitted by juries on the grounds of self-defense. DeGuerin told a reporter, "I don't think there would have been any evidence that David Koresh held or fired a weapon during that entire stand-off."[78] Koresh also had a will and documents prepared to protect the property and even allowed DeGuerin to meet with New York attorneys to discuss film and book rights to his story.[79]

Zimmermann testified at trial that he had no doubt Davidians would have exited. He described the plan Davidians had accepted that reassured them that federal agents would not shoot Koresh as he left the building: Koresh would exit first with DeGuerin. Other Davidians would exit one at a time.[80]

Drs. Arnold and Tabor Suggested Koresh Write a "Little Book"

Dr. Phillip Arnold, executive director of Houston's Reunion Institute and an expert in apocalyptic studies and the Seven Seals, read a newspaper transcript of David Koresh's February 28 sermon on KRLD and immediately resolved to be of assistance.[81] He drove to Waco several days later and explained his expertise to SAC Bob Ricks, Chief Aide to SAC Jeff Jamar. However, Ricks put Arnold off several times saying, "You could never talk Book of Revelation with him. You've never heard anything like this."

An FBI agent did take Arnold's number and contacted him a few days later, but he did not ask for his assistance. Dr. Arnold has lamented that the FBI considered the Seven Seals "to be a big joke," but noted, "The Seven Seals was [Koresh's] language, and if you didn't speak that language, there was no way of showing him what he had to do."[82]

On February 28 David Koresh told a KRLD interviewer that he believed the attack was the fulfillment of prophecy and an opportunity for him to spread his message—but he conceded even then he was willing to have a minister prove him "wrong." On March 17 Davidians happened by chance to hear Dr. Arnold's five-minute radio show during which he discussed the Book of Revelation. The negotiation audiotapes reveal that Steve Schneider told negotiators that Dr. Arnold's comments were the "best things" they had heard so far and that allowing Koresh to speak with Arnold "positively" could resolve the situation. The FBI "denied the request."[83] Edward Dennis notes that Steve Schneider specifically mentioned Phillip Arnold as possibly being a "theologian [who] could convince the people Koresh was wrong" about their being in the deadly Fifth Seal.[84] The FBI's only concession was to contact Dr. Arnold for a copy of the tape—their last contact with Arnold—and send in the tape of Arnold's radio show.[85]

Dr. Arnold reveals that after a telephone conversation with a reporter on March 29, 1993, it became apparent to him the government was planning some more forceful action—he rightly guessed a gas attack. He hurriedly contacted talk show host Ron Engelman and arranged a radio interview between himself and Dr. James Tabor to try to convince the Davidians to exit Mount Carmel.[86] Tabor, a professor of religious studies at the University of North Carolina who also specializes in apocalyptic studies, had been consulting with Arnold on the Davidians.

During the radio program they explained to Koresh that the "little season" mentioned in the Fifth Seal, the time that the Davidians needed to wait before the rest of them died, was not merely a couple of months but might be a much longer time. They stressed that the Book of Revelation referred to a "little book" which would be given to the world. They reminded Koresh that although he had achieved worldwide publicity, no one knew what his message was. And they mentioned that great prophets like Jeremiah, John, and Paul had gone to prison, and produced great literature there.[87]

Dr. Arnold gave this tape to Dick DeGuerin who took it to Koresh on April 4. On this date Koresh said everyone would come out "after Passover." The FBI would later claim that Koresh had broken his "promise" to come out after Passover. However, the Justice report reveals that on April 9 Steve Schneider "repeated that Koresh would not come out until told to do so by God."[88]

On April 9 Koresh delivered to the FBI the first of several defiant letters explaining God's anger at the FBI's mistreatment of his people and warning of God's coming wrath. The FBI would use these letters to excuse their assault on Mount Carmel. The FBI released information about the April 9 letter to the press, emphasizing that it "was threatening in tone." SAC Bob Ricks said the letter would not be made public.[89] However, the *Washington Post* obtained excerpts from this letter in which Koresh wrote God might destroy a local dam and revealed nervous authorities were monitoring the dam.[90] On April 10 and 11 Koresh sent out nearly identical letters.

However, on April 14, Koresh sent out to Dick DeGuerin a very different letter. It reads, in part:

> As far as our progress is concerned, here is where we stand: . . . I am presently being permitted to document, in structured form, the decoded messages of the Seven Seals. Upon the completion of this task, I will be freed of my "waiting period." I hope to finish this as soon as possible and to stand before man to answer any and all questions regarding my actions.
>
> I have been praying so long for this opportunity; to put the Seals in written form. Speaking the truth seems to have very little effect on man.
>
> I was shown that as soon as I am given over into the hands of man, I will be made a spectacle of, and people will not be concerned about the truth of God, but just the bizarrity of me—the flesh (person).

> *I want the people of this generation to be saved. I am working night and day to complete my final work of the writing out of "these Seals."*
>
> *I will demand the first manuscript of the Seals be given to you. Many scholars and religious leaders will wish to have copies for examination. I will keep a copy with me. As soon as I can see that people, like Jim Tabor and Phil Arnold have a copy I will come out and then you can do your thing with this Beast.*
>
> *We are standing on the threshold of Great events! The Seven Seals, in written form are the most sacred information ever!*
>
> *David Koresh*

Dick DeGuerin immediately gave a copy of the letter to the FBI and released excerpts to the press. Jack Zimmermann revealed on the April 20, 1993, "Larry King Live" show that Steve Schneider read him the letter on April 14 "in the most excited tone I had every heard him in the fifteen hours of our conversation. . . . They said they were working day and night. David was dictating it. . . and Steve was editing. . . . The FBI only waited four days."

On April 16, Koresh told the FBI he had finished the First Seal and "asked for a word processor and batteries to speed production of the other six chapters."[91] At an October 15, 1993, congressional briefing, Dr. Tabor said that Koresh and Ruth Riddle, who was typing the manuscript for him, worked until 9 P.M. Sunday, April 18, putting the final touches on the First Seal. It would have been the longest of the seven. That meant the Davidians could have been leaving Mount Carmel in just a few more days. Tabor said, "they were so happy that night, shades of the last supper." Riddle escaped the April 19 fire carrying Koresh's First Seal on a computer disk.

Drs. Arnold and Tabor severely criticized the FBI. "I think they were convinced from the start that he was evil, horrible, and wicked. . . .They didn't take his religion seriously enough. They needed to have input from people who are trained in biblical symbols."[92]

FBI Lied to DeGuerin and Zimmermann

After receiving Koresh's April 14 promise-to-surrender letter, Dick DeGuerin had a face-to-face meeting with FBI siege commander Jeff Jamar and his second in command, Bob Ricks. In reply to DeGuerin's asserting Koresh would come out when he finished his book, probably within two weeks, Ricks blurted, "And then what's next? He's going to write his memoirs?" But Jamar interrupted, looked directly at DeGuerin and said, "No, we've got all the time it takes." DeGuerin told interviewer Peter Maas: "I figured I had the two weeks. In my world, you don't always have time for contracts. You have to operate on a person's word."[93] Jack Zimmermann testified at trial that the FBI had reneged on the agreement: "They said they wanted to resolve it peacefully and had all the time in the world to resolve it peacefully."[94] On April 18, the FBI assured Davidians they would help Koresh finish his book, even as it cleared automobiles away from the building in preparation for the next day's attack.[95]

FBI Ridiculed Koresh's Promise to Surrender

FBI spokesperson Bob Ricks mocked Koresh's efforts: "It's like the Peanuts cartoon—is Lucy going to pull that football out one more time? We get the impression that's probably what's going to happen." Ricks alleged that there were three other times in the siege when Koresh promised to surrender.[96] However, FBI lies about playing Koresh's sermon on March 2, and FBI harassment despite the apparent beginning of a mass exit on March 21, caused Koresh to break his first two promises to exit. This last promise doubtless would have been the fulfillment of Koresh's promise to come out after Passover.

The April 26, 1993, *Time* devoted a whole article to David Koresh's promise to write the book and described the FBI's frustration that it had taken Koresh four days to write thirty pages. "No one at our place is holding his breath," said FBI special agent Dick Swensen. An anonymous FBI official told the *Washington Post*, "Were we going to sit there and wait for this guy to finish his treatises on the Seven Seals?"[97] Bob Ricks' statement on April 16 sums up the FBI attitude: "We are going to get them . . . to bring them before the bar of justice for the murder of our agents. They're going to answer for their crimes."[98]

FBI Lied After the Fire

After the April 19 fire, the FBI claimed that it had evidence that David Koresh's contacts with his attorneys were just stalling techniques. During his April 20, 1993, press conference SAC Jamar claimed that listening devices picked up Davidians joking about DeGuerin's involvement being a ruse, a claim the Justice report repeats. However, while prosecutors threatened to play this alleged tape during the trial, they never did so.[99]

At the April 20 FBI press conference, Jamar also asserted, "This latest business with the Seven Seals, we have intelligence that it was just one more such stalling technique." (He said this twenty-four hours after Texas Rangers confiscated the computer disk from fire survivor Ruth Riddle.) When a reporter pressed him for "hard evidence" that "writing of the biblical manuscript was just another stall," Jamar replied his evidence was "intelligence information we're not prepared to disclose now." However, the FBI never has provided such intelligence information, including at trial.

Justice Report Misrepresented Koresh's Letter

The Justice report does include the April 14 letter after the April 9 and 10 letters in an appendix. However, only Koresh's April 14 phone call is mentioned in the chronology for that date, while the April 9 letter is quoted extensively and the April 10 letter analyzed. When the report finally mentions the letter, it inaccurately describes it as "Koresh's request that the FBI give him time to finish his manuscript about the Seven Seals." It then dismisses the letter, noting, "Dr. Miron noted that the letter appeared to be a ploy designed to buy more time for Koresh." This statement by a de facto cult buster is the only evidence the report presents that Koresh's writing his book on the Seven Seals was a stalling technique.[100] The negotiation tapes reveal that on April 15, 1993, an FBI negotiator claimed that Koresh's writing his book was mere "stalling." Steve Schneider replied, "If I was stalling, I'd pull out the phone cord. If you think we are stalling, run ten tanks through the building. If you think we're stalling, do what you want. You'll see what these people are made of." Schneider made the FBI aware that Davidians would not be pushed out of Mount Carmel by a tank attack.[101]

Dr. Ronald Theman, dean of the Harvard Divinity School, told ABC news the day after that fire, "If there had been better understanding of the worldview out of which he was operating, there would have been an opportunity to give him a way out." What is clear is that those who understood Koresh's worldview actually had convinced him to come out. However, FBI agents in Waco, and their BATF cronies, were more concerned with punishing the defiant Davidians and destroying evidence of BATF crimes than convincing them to exit the building.[102]

Chapter Eight: The FBI Sabotaged Negotiations

1.   June 16, 1994 trial transcript: 154.
2.   Jeffrey H. Birnbaum, "A Week in the Life: The Presidential Style Is Exuberant, Informal and Totally in Control," *Wall Street Journal*, Tuesday, March 9, 1993: 30.
3.   Justice Department report: 241.
4.   Ibid., 241.
5.   Susan Schmidt, "Altman Testimony Disputed," *Washington Post*, July 24, 1994: A1.
6.   Jeffrey H. Birnbaum, March 9, 1993.
7.   Justice Department report: 242.
8.   Treasury Department report: 102.
9.   Transcript of Confirmation Hearing for Webster Hubbell, U.S. Senate Committee on the Judiciary, May 19, 1993.
10.   Justice Department report: 235.
11.   Ibid., 239–40.
12.   Transcript of Confirmation Hearing for Webster Hubbell, U.S. Senate Committee on the Judiciary, May 19, 1993.
13.   Carleton R. Bryant, "Heymann decries Hubbell's Justice-White House link," *Washington Times*, February 19, 1994: A4; Julia Malone, "Does 'first buddy' really run Justice?" *Washington Times*, February 21, 1994; Jerry Seper, "Now that Hubbell's out, who's minding the store at Justice?" *Washington Times*, March 16, 1994.
14.   Michael Hedges, "Sessions says White House 'compromised' Foster probe," *Washington Times*, February 4, 1994: A1.
15.   Justice Department report: 180–81.
16.   Ibid.,182.
17.   Ibid., 180; Dan Freedman, "FBI analyst says he was ignored on Waco," *Washington Times*, May 1, 1995: A1, A20.
18.   Alan A. Stone, M.D., report to the Justice Department, 1993: 9.
19.   Kirk Lyons, Cause Foundation lawsuit (February 26, 1995); Caddell and Conwell lawsuit (February 27, 1995).
20.   Alan A. Stone, M.D., report to the Justice Department, 1993: 1.
21.   Justice Department report: 139–40.
22.   David Thibodeau, private communication, July, 1994.
23.   Justice Department report: 142.

24.   Alan A. Stone, M.D., report to the Justice Departn

25.   Nancy Ammerman presentation at November 22, 1993,
American Academy of Religion panel on Branch Davidians.

26.   "The Maury Povich Show," November 8, 1993.

27.   "American Justice" program, "Attack at Waco," August 3, 1994.

28.   James L. Pate, October, 1993: 73.

29.   Justice Department report: 131, 239–40.

30.   Ibid., 58.

31.   Ibid., 133–34.

32.   Associated Press wire story, March 16, 1993, 4:42 EST.

33.   David Thibodeau and Dick Reavis, private communications,
December, 1994; trial transcript: 1125.

34.   *New York Times*, April 5, 1993: A10.

35.   Justice Department report: 81, 229, 255.

36.   Ibid., 186–87, 190–93.

37.   Ibid., 168–74, 176–79.

38.   Ibid., 190.

39.   Steven R. Reed, "Would-be Messiah gave death, not life,"
Houston Chronicle, April 20, 1993: 18A.

40.   Justice Department report: 167.

41.   Ross S. Green report: 13.

42.   Justice Department report: 192.

43.   Ibid., 192; Marc Breault and Martin King: 335–337.

44.   Information from Dr. Gordon Melton presentation November
22, 1993; private communication with Dr. Melton, January, 1993.

45.   Justice Department report: 174–76.

46.   Louis Sahagun and J. Michael Kennedy, "FBI Places Full
Blame on Koresh for Tragedy," *Los Angeles Times*, April 21, 1993;
Michael Isikoff and Pierre Thomas, "Reno, FBI Took Fatal
Gamble," *Washington Post*, April 21, 1993: A15; Sam Howe
Verhovek, "F.B.I. Saw the Ego in Koresh But Missed Willingness to
Die," *New York Times*, April 22, 1993: B13.

47.   Alan A. Stone, M.D., report to the Justice Department, 1993: 10.

48.   Justice Department report: 21–57.

49.   Sam Howe Verhovek, April 21, 1993: A20; Paul McKay,
"Compound fire set and spread by cultists, tapes indicate," *Houston
Chronicle*, February 15, 1994; trial transcript: 6210.

50. "FBI brings out secret electronic weapons as Waco siege drags on," *Sunday Times of London*, March 21, 1993.

51. Justice Department report: 66–68.

52. Ibid., 70.

53. Ibid., 74–75; Sheila Martin, private communication, May, 1995.

54. Mary Jordan and Sue Anne Pressley, March 8, 1993.

55. Justice Department report: 135.

56. *Waco Tribune-Herald*, April 20, 1993: 7A.

57. James Scott Trim in his paper, "The Place of Fire in Branch Davidian Theology," 1994, reveals this private communication with Brad Branch.

58. Justice Department report: 78–80.

59. Ibid., 83.

60. "Primetime Live" television special on Waco, January 13, 1994.

61. Edward S. G. Dennis, Jr., report to Justice Department, 1993: 44; Graeme Craddock, private communication, May, 1995.

62. Justice Department report: 79–109.

63. Brad Bailey and Bob Darden: 246.

64. Dan Friedman, "Wealth of advice seen as costly to FBI at Waco," *Washington Times*, October 8, 1993.

65. Edward S. G. Dennis, Jr., report to Justice Department, 1993: 45.

66. *New York Times*, April 5, 1993: A10.

67. Howard Schneider, "Waco cultists send out home movies," *Washington Post*, March 30, 1993: A5; Justice Department report: 201.

68. JoAnn Zuniga, "Outcome shocks compound visitor," *Houston Chronicle*, April 20, 1993: 16A.

69. Justice Department report: 87.

70. Associated Press wire story, March 25, 1993, 03:53 EST.

71. Dirk Johnson, "Inside the Cult: Fire and Terror on the Final Day," *New York Times*, April 26, 1993: B10.

72. Nancy Ammerman report to Justice Department, September, 1993: 2.

73. Justice Department report: 147.

74. Clifford L. Linedecker: 215; Kirk Lyons, private communication, June, 1994.

75. Associated Press wire story, March 16, 1993, 04:25 EST.

76. *Waco Tribune-Herald*, April 20, 1993: 7A.

77. Trial transcript: 6605–09.

78. Steve McVicker, July 22, 1993.

79. Brad Bailey and Bob Darden: 236.

80. Trial transcript: 6636–37.

81. Dr. Phillip Arnold and Dr. James Tabor, private communication, November, 1993; Dr. Arnold article "The Davidian Dilemma—To Obey God or Man?" and Dr. Tabor article "The Waco Tragedy: An Autobiographical Account of One Attempt to Avert Disaster," printed in *From the Ashes: Making Sense of Waco*; audio tape of Drs. Arnold and Tabor radio interview on Ron Engelman show, April 1, 1993.

82. *Time*, May 3, 1993: 43.

83. Justice Department report, Appendix C: 3; Carol Moore review of section of negotiation audio tape.

84. Edward S. G. Dennis, Jr. report to Justice Department, 1993: 15.

85. Paper compiled by Dr. James Tabor, "Chronological Interpretative Log/Major Events," 1993; Justice Department report: 186.

86. Dr. James Tabor, paper, 1993; Dr. Phillip Arnold, private communication, April, 1995.

87. Drs. Arnold and Tabor radio interview on Ron Engelman show, April 1, 1993.

88. Justice Department report: 95–99.

89. "Cult leader gives 'letter from God'," *New York Times*, April 11, 1993: A18.

90. Pierre Thomas, "Koresh appears defiant in letters, officials say," *Washington Post*, April 13, 1993: A3.

91. Justice Department report, 107; Michael Isikoff and Pierre Thomas, "Reno Says, 'I Made the Decision'," *Washington Post*, April 20, 1993: A9.

92. Associated Press wire story, April 21, 1993, 18:24 EDT.

93. Peter Maas, "What Might Have Been," *Parade*, February 27, 1994.

94. Paul McKay, "Jury hears tape of Davidian plea for a 'cease-fire'," *Houston Chronicle*, February 17, 1994; trial transcript: 6660.

95. Justice Department report: 284.

96. Drew Parma, "FBI likens Howell's latest offer to cartoon," *Waco Tribune-Herald*, April 17, 1993: A1; James Tabor, speech, November 22, 1993.

97. Michael Isikoff and Pierre Thomas, April 20, 1993: A9.
98. Brad Bailey and Bob Darden: 205.
99. Justice Department report: 143–44; trial transcript: 6627.
100. Ibid., 99–100, 102, 105, 175–77.
101. Carol Moore review of section of negotiation tape.
102. ABC news special, "Waco: The Decision to Die," April 20, 1993.

9

The FBI Tricked Attorney General into Approving Gas and Tank Assault

I want the people of this generation to be saved. I am working night and day to complete my final work of the writing out of "these Seals" . . . As soon as I can see that people, like Jim Tabor and Phil Arnold have a copy I will come out and then you can do your thing with this Beast.

David Koresh in promise-to-surrender letter

The FBI Hostage Negotiation Training Manual asserts, "Time is always in our favor," and urges negotiators and agents not to grow impatient in hostage situations.[1] *London Times* bureau chief James Adams, author of a number of books on covert warfare, wrote about the government's handling of the standoff with the Branch Davidians: "Every professional in the hostage rescue business knows that the best chance of survival for all the innocents held captive is to play out a waiting game. The theory, which has been proved again and again, is that the longer you wait, the better the chances of a peaceful resolution."[2]

RICHARD ROGERS GAINED
SUPPORT FOR HIS PLAN

In late March, FBI Hostage Rescue Team commander Richard Rogers, who was continuing to push for more aggressive action, gave visiting FBI officials "a briefing on the use of CS gas and suggested an operation plan for such use." FBI Director Sessions approved it the first week of April.[3] Sessions' own plan to use a water cannon to drive the Davidians out already had been shot down as unrealistic.[4] Rogers' plan had two steps, with the second step even more vicious than the first. The first was to "introduce the liquid CS into the compound in stages"; the second, "eventually walls would be torn down to increase the exposure of those remaining inside." The Justice report notes, "While it was conceivable that tanks and other armored vehicles could be used to demolish the compound, the FBI considered that such a plan would risk harming the children inside."[5]

Nevertheless, Rogers' plan clearly included de facto demolition of Mount Carmel. "If all subjects failed to exit the structure after 48 hours of tear gas, then a modified CEV [tank] would proceed to open up and begin disassembling the structure at the location that was least exposed to the gas. The CEV would continue until all the Branch Davidians were located."[6] On April 28, 1993, FBI Deputy Director Floyd Clarke told the House Judiciary Committee that the FBI thought two days of gassing would drive out most everyone but the hard core. "At that point, we would systematically take away parts of the building to reduce it down to a section where we could control it." In fact, the FBI would proceed with this plan only five hours into the assault.

Justice Department outside expert Robert Cancro writes of the plan: "A decision was made to utilize gas to drive out the occupants of the compound with the full knowledge that infants and children were in the compound. . . . The rationale appeared to be that the parents would leave the compound in order to protect the children from the potential noxious effects of the gas."[7] In effect, the children would be tortured in order to force the parents to surrender.

Cancro notes the limitations of this de facto torture strategy: "If a significant percentage of a group are willing to die for their beliefs, the death of their children may not have the same meaning as it would to other people."[8] The gas never reached such a level of consistent concentration to prompt any parents to leave with their children.

Rogers' plan first was introduced to Attorney General Janet Reno and Associate Attorney General Webster Hubbell on April 12, with a suggested implementation date of April 14. Reno asked, "Why now? Why not wait?" and refused to approve the plan.[9]

On April 13 (though the Justice report claims none of the participants could recall the exact date), Hubbell explained the gassing plan to White House

Counsel Bernard Nussbaum, Deputy Counsel Vince Foster, and presidential advisor Bruce Lindsey. No one objected to it. Doubtless they regarded it as a convenient way to end a politically embarrassing situation. Nussbaum then met with President Clinton about the plan and told him that the "handling of the standoff was 'a Department of Justice call, not a White House call.'" Clinton responded that he had great confidence in the Attorney General and the FBI.[10]

Whether Hubbell and Clinton had any private conversations about the matter remains a subject of conjecture. Reno, Hubbell, and FBI officials attended further meetings to discuss the effects of the gas on April 14. Richard Rogers himself traveled to Washington to promote the plan. However, Reno was not ready to act.[11]

ATTORNEY GENERAL APPROVED PLAN AFTER "CURSORY REVIEW"

FBI officials and agents, with Webster Hubbell as an intermediary, continued to "work on" Reno for the next three days. On April 16 she still disapproved the plan—until a telephone conversation with FBI Director William Sessions which even the Justice report admits swayed her to the point that she asked for a documented statement of why the plan should go forward.[12] This may be the conversation in which the most inflammatory accusations of child abuse were made.

On April 17 Reno received the documents. According to the Justice report, "She read only a chronology, gave the rest of the materials a cursory review, and satisfied herself that 'the documentation was there.' " In contrast, Reno assured the House Judiciary Committee she had been *thorough*, saying, "I'm not a law enforcement expert, but I was asking every question I knew to ask."[13] After this cursory review, Reno approved the gassing plan.[14] The known arguments the FBI used to break down Janet Reno's resistance to the plan follow. Despite Reno's assertions to the contrary, we can see that the FBI clearly did mislead and even bully her into approving their plan.

FBI MISINFORMED RENO ABOUT PROGRESS OF NEGOTIATIONS

Outside expert Alan A. Stone writes: "It is unclear from the reports whether the FBI even explained to the AG [Reno] that the agency had rejected the advice of their own experts in behavioral science and negotiation, or whether the AG was told that FBI negotiators believed that they could get more people out of the compound by negotiation. By the time the AG made her decision, the noose was closed and, as one agent told me, the FBI believed they had 'three options—gas, gas, and gas.' "[15]

Rogers Met with Reno

HRT commander Richard Rogers himself met with Reno. "Rogers and others offered the following additional reasons [for the assault]: Koresh had broken every promise he had made; negotiations had broken down; no one had been released since March 23; and it appeared that no one else would surrender."[16] In effect, HRT commander Rogers, who had pushed SAC Jamar to use the tactical harassment that had so disrupted negotiations, now informed Attorney Janet Reno that negotiations were not working.

It is possible Rogers' impatience to end the standoff in part was related to his fear the upcoming Weaver trial would bring out facts about Rogers' criminal misconduct in that case—something the Waco spotlight would only exaggerate. In case Rogers needed reminding, on April 10 an article, "Trial to view actions of marshals in Idaho," appeared in the *Waco Tribune-Herald* which explicitly compared the siege of the Branch Davidians to that of Randy Weaver.[17]

On April 28, 1993, Janet Reno told the House Judiciary Committee: "Throughout this fifty-one-day process, Koresh continued to assert that he and the others inside would at some point surrender. However, the FBI advised that at no point did he keep his word on any of these promises."[18] On this point, the FBI had thoroughly "brainwashed" Janet Reno.

Hubbell Conveyed FBI Disinformation

On April 15 Webster Hubbell, Deputy Assistant Attorney General Mark Richard, Acting Assistant Attorney General for the Criminal Division John C. Keeney, and two unidentified FBI officials had a two-hour conversation with chief FBI negotiator Byron Sage. "Hubbell recalls that Sage said further negotiations with the subjects in the compound would be fruitless. . . . Sage further advised Hubbell that Koresh had been disingenuous in his discussions with Sage about the 'Seven Seals.' . . . Hubbell recalls Sage saying he believed there was nothing more he or the negotiators could do to persuade Koresh to release anyone else, or to come out himself. . . . Hubbell advised the Attorney General about this conversation."[19] Whether Hubbell uncritically accepted the FBI's disinformation or was part and parcel of creating it is unknown. Many more questions should be asked about Hubbell's involvement in convincing Reno that negotiations were not working.

FBI Withheld Koresh's Promise-to-surrender Letter

There is no evidence that the FBI showed David Koresh's April 14, 1993, letter—what Dick DeGuerin called "an absolute agreement signed that they would come out peacefully"—to Attorney General Reno. The Justice report states only, "The FBI provided the Attorney General with copies of the memoranda prepared by Dr. Miron and Dr. Krofcheck and SSA Van Zandt analyzing Koresh's April 9 letter, both in the April 12 briefing book and in the briefing book prepared over the weekend of April 17–18."[20] There is no mention of providing her with the April 14 letter.

During both her April 19 post-fire press conference and the House Judiciary Committee hearing,

Reno was asked direct questions about Koresh's writing his book. At the press conference she asserted, "negotiators had told them that they wouldn't negotiate and weren't coming out." During the hearing she said, "The FBI felt he had lied to them." Her answers were sufficiently vague to indicate that she had bought the FBI line, without either receiving or bothering to read Koresh's letter.

At the 1993 House Judiciary Committee hearing, FBI Director Sessions insisted that the last Koresh letter was related to Passover, i.e., one of Koresh's earlier letters. And when Representative Schiff asked a question regarding the fact David Koresh had "inferred" to his attorneys he would come out after he finished his book, no one bothered to inform him it was more than a mere inference.

If the letter was withheld from Reno, it would have been especially important to withhold it from the press—which the FBI and Justice Department proceeded to do. Two days after the fire senior FBI officials held a background briefing for reporters to explain their decision to gas Mount Carmel. They included Koresh's April 9 and 10 letters as examples of "his irrational and 'insane' behavior during negotiations."[21] However, there is no indication they showed reporters the April 14 letter or reminded them of its existence. While the May 3, 1993, issue of *Time* mentions the letter, it displays color photographs of only the April 10 and 11 letters under the heading of "Last Letters from David."

FBI MISINFORMED RENO
ABOUT CS GAS SAFETY

CS gas is a white crystalline powder that causes involuntary closure of eyes, burning of the skin, severe respiratory problems, and vomiting. The United States is one of 100 countries that signed an agreement banning the use of CS gas in war during the Chemical Weapons Convention in Paris in January of 1993. FBI officials claimed they did not know this when they recommended it.[22] The FBI withheld from Janet Reno evidence about CS gas dangers to health and its flammability. It probably downplayed the dangers of the delivery system.

Dangers to Health

The goal of the gassing was to drive Davidians out of the building. However, the U.S. Department of the Army manual on Civil Disturbances (October, 1975, FM19–15) notes: "Generally, persons reacting to CS are incapable of executing organized and concerted actions and excessive exposure to CS may make them incapable of vacating the area."

Dr. Alan A. Stone was particularly critical of the FBI's decision to use CS gas against the Davidians, especially the children: "I can testify from personal experience to the power of C.S. gas to quickly inflame eyes, nose, and throat, to produce choking, chest pain, gagging, and nausea in healthy adult males. It is difficult to believe that the U.S. government would deliberately plan to expose twenty-five children, most of them infants and toddlers, to C.S. gas for forty-eight hours. . . . The official reports are silent about these issues and do not reveal what the FBI told the AG [Attorney General] about this matter. . . . Based on my own medical knowledge and review of scientific literature, the information supplied to the AG seems to minimize the potential harmful consequences for infants and children."[23]

Dr. Stone quotes a case of an unprotected child's two to three hour exposure to CS gas which resulted in first degree facial burns, severe respiratory distress typical of chemical pneumonia, and an enlarged liver. "The infant's reactions reported in this case history were of a vastly different dimension than the information given the AG suggested. . . . Whatever the actual effects may have been, I find it hard to accept a deliberate plan to insert C.S. gas for forty-eight hours in a building with so many children. It certainly makes it more difficult to believe that the health and safety of the children was our primary concern."[24]

Attorney General Reno met with Dr. Harry Salem, an army toxicologist, who assured her that CS gas "powder," which would be delivered only through "compressed air," would simply cause temporary discomfort and that it posed no danger of fire or explosion.[25] What the Justice Department experts never told Reno, and Stone evidently did not know, is that in a June 1, 1988, report Amnesty International claimed that CS (and CN) gas had contributed to or caused the deaths of more than forty Palestinians—including eighteen babies under six months of age—who had been exposed to tear-gas in enclosed spaces. The Israeli government never acknowledged the gas had caused the deaths, but the American manufacturers of CS gas halted the export of the gas to Israel because of its misuse.

Flammability of Gas and Solvent

The CS gas particulate was mixed with a solvent, methylene chloride, something army toxicologist Harry Salem did not tell Janet Reno. One manufacturer of CS gas told a reporter that "he was not certain if the chemical—when spread as a fine powder throughout buildings and exposed to fire—would act as a catalyst for flames." Chemical consultant Dr. Jay Young said that a mixture of CS gas and air could be ignited, but only if the ratio of the gas and air was within a very narrow range.[26] Attorney Jack Zimmermann, who spoke with military experts, asserted, "All three types of C.S. can spontaneously ignite if occurring in a high-enough concentration in a confined space that is exposed to open flame."[27] Rick Sherrow, a former army and BATF explosives expert and fire investigator consulting for Davidian civil suits, confirms this, though he doubts the CS gas ever became dry enough inside Mount Carmel to explode. He asserts that once a fire starts, CS gas sustains the combustion.[28] Nevertheless, "the FBI informed [Reno] that the tear gas would not cause a fire."[29]

The FBI evidently did not inform Reno that manufacturers like Aldrich Chemical Company of Milwaukee, Wisconsin, clearly warn that when burned,

CS gas emits toxic fumes, including hydrogen cyanide and hydrogen chloride. Aldrich also warns that when water is poured on a CS gas fire it can release a lethal cloud of hydrogen cyanide gas.[30]

At trial, two fire investigators, Andrew Armstrong and James Quintiere, conceded that there was "ambiguity" in the literature about the flammability of methylene chloride, in both its vapor and liquid states. Rick Sherrow reveals that when burned the solvent gives off toxic phosgene gas.[31]

Dangers of Delivery Systems

Both methods of delivering the CS gas which the FBI used also are dangerous. One was the Mark-V system, "a liquid tear gas dispenser that shoots a stream of liquid tear gas (propelled by noncombustible carbon dioxide) approximately 50 feet for a duration of approximately 15 seconds."[32] The highly irritating gas, which was sprayed out the thirty-foot booms, could suffocate a child or person with respiratory problems if sprayed directly into their face.

The second method of delivery—"40mm ferret liquid tear gas rounds" delivered by a M79 grenade launcher—was even more lethal. According to the Justice report, more than 400 of these "gas grenades" were used to deliver the twenty-five grams of CS gas on impact. The report notes: "when fired from 20 yards or less the rounds are capable of penetrating a hollow core door."[33] According to Dick DeGuerin, survivors claim that during the gas attack the grenades did in fact penetrate multiple walls before exploding.[34]

What the FBI and Justice Department have denied repeatedly is that these ferret liquid tear gas rounds or gas grenades are "pyrotechnic," i.e., burn and give off sparks upon impact. What they cannot deny is that FBI agents used the same M79 grenade launchers used to deliver flash-bangs and other pyrotechnic grenades to deliver the gas grenades.[35] This leads some to suspect agents could have substituted the pyrotechnic flash-bang for a non-pyrotechnic gas grenade.

FBI PUSHED RENO'S
CHILD ABUSE "HOT BUTTON"

The one bit of possible FBI trickery which the mainstream press has noted is Janet Reno's original assertion that she had been told children were being beaten in Mount Carmel. She withdrew her assertion as soon as the FBI denied making such claims, yet it appears the FBI did indeed trick her.

Child Abuse Information Available to Reno

The Justice Department summarizes some, but not all, of the evidence of alleged child abuse and sex with minors presented to Janet Reno. Reno would have read the social worker's report on Kiri Jewell's allegation Koresh "got on top of her" in a hotel room; she also would have read that the girl refused to press charges.

She doubtless was not told that David Jewell seemed as committed to the destruction of the Davidians as was Marc Breault.

The Justice Department report quotes just two 1990 affidavits by former members. Ian and Allison Manning alleged that Koresh insisted disobedient children be spanked with a wooden paddle and that such beatings sometimes severely bruised the children's bottoms. Michelle Tom alleged that in 1988 Howell [Koresh] once threatened to kill a child if her mother gave her a pacifier, and he spanked her eight-month-old daughter for forty minutes because she would not sit on his lap.[36]

It is unknown how much information was presented to Reno about the 1992 Texas Department of Human Services investigation by social worker Joyce Sparks. On three occasions she visited Mount Carmel with two other Human Services employees and two McLennan County Sheriff's deputies. Koresh allowed the visit to be videotaped.[37] Koresh also visited her office. The case was closed on April 30, 1992. The Department offered this summary of the nine-week investigation: "None of the allegations could be verified. The children denied being abused in any way by adults in the compound. They denied any knowledge of other children being abused. The adults consistently denied participation in or knowledge of any abuse to children. Examinations of the children produced no indication of current or previous injuries."[38]

Dr. Bruce Perry, who interviewed children released from Mount Carmel during the siege, told the FBI on March 26, "these children had a number of strict behavioral and verbal prohibitions. Violations of these resulted in punishment, sometimes severe. The children, for example, expected to be hit when they spilled. The style of discipline often involved being beaten with what these children labeled 'the Helper'... some variation on a wooden spoon. Other forms of discipline included restrictions of food, sometimes for a day."[39]

However, after the fire, at a May, 1993, press conference Dr. Perry confessed: "We can't say, 'Aha, physical abuse,' that's the crux of the issue. President Clinton and Janet Reno say 'child abuse.' Child protective services say, 'Well, we didn't see any.' . . . It's very complicated. It is an ongoing dilemma for what is the threshold for saying what is abuse."[40]

BATF agent Davy Aguilera's February 25, 1993, affidavit, which was used to secure search and arrest warrants, states: "Mrs. [Jeannine] Bunds also told me that Howell had fathered at least fifteen (15) children from various women and young girls at the compound. Some of the girls who had babies fathered by Howell were as young as twelve years old. . . . He also, according to Mrs. Bunds, has regular sexual relations with young girls there. The girls' ages are from eleven (11) years old to adulthood."

However, only six of Koresh's children had been born by the time Bunds left Mount Carmel. And a review of the ages of living and deceased mothers of Koresh's children shows only one was fourteen years old when she had her first child; the rest were seventeen or over.

In the *Waco Tribune-Herald* "The Sinful Messiah" series former Davidians Marc Breault, Bruce Gent, Robyn Bunds, and Joel Jones allege that in 1989 Koresh talked about having had sex with Michelle Jones when she was twelve. They allege Koresh admitted that she had fought him off on the first occasion.[41] They charge Aisha Gyarfas had sex with Koresh when she was fourteen. However, even Marc Breault admitted that Aisha Gyarfas was "completely captivated by Vernon. She was like his little puppy dog tied to his leash. Aisha would do anything for Vernon."[42] Michelle later married David Thibodeau, and Aisha married Greg Summers. Both young women, then ages seventeen and eighteen, chose to stay with Koresh inside Mount Carmel and died with their five children by him in the April 19 fire.

Dr. Park Dietz wrote in a memorandum, "Koresh may continue to make sexual use of any female children who remain inside."[43] FBI Director William Sessions went on at length during the April 28, 1993, House Judiciary Committee hearings about Victorine Hollingsworth leaving her thirteen- or fourteen-year-old daughter inside Mount Carmel where she was one of David Koresh's "child brides." Deputy Director Floyd Clarke, sitting next to Sessions, confirmed the information to him. However, the fifty-nine-year-old Hollingsworth, a single woman, did not leave a teenage daughter inside Mount Carmel. We must wonder if this is one of the things Sessions told Reno during the private conversation that evidently convinced her to approve the gassing plan.

Child Abuse "Misunderstanding"

The Justice report states: "During the week of April 12, someone had made a comment in one of the meetings that Koresh was beating babies. When Reno inquired further, she had the clear impression that, at some point, since the FBI had assumed command and control of the situation they had learned that the Davidians were beating babies. She had no doubt that the children were living in intolerable conditions."[44] On April 19 Janet Reno pronounced with confidence: "We had information that babies were being beaten. I specifically asked, 'You really mean babies?' 'Yes, that he's slapping babies around.' "[45]

After the FBI denied that they had emphasized child abuse, Reno retracted her allegation. On April 28, 1993, she admitted to Congress, "I can't tell you that a child was being beaten after the 28 [of February]." The Justice report relates that in retrospect Reno "did not believe that anyone at the FBI deliberately played up the issue of child abuse."[46]

Did The FBI Lie About Davidian Water Shortage?

If Davidians had run out of water they would have had to exit immediately or their children would have died quickly of dehydration. Janet Reno has admitted that "exhausting their water supply" was one of the options at which she looked. The Justice Department report appendix "Intelligence on Water

Supply" notes that Louis Alaniz, a sympathizer who sneaked into Mount Carmel and left on April 17, said each individual was receiving two eight-ounce glasses of water a day. Davidian survivor Clive Doyle reveals that at the end Davidians were praying for rain and knew they would have to leave soon for that reason.

Did the FBI tell Janet Reno this? Did she fail to note it in her cursory review of information the FBI gave her? The possibility they did not is suggested by the fact that the appendix blacks out the April 13 and 15 water intelligence entries. These entries may contain evidence—such as Davidian comments in negotiations or those caught on surveillance audio tape—that the FBI knew Davidians were almost out of water and would soon exit because of this.[47]

FBI THREATENED TO WITHDRAW HOSTAGE RESCUE TEAM

On April 14 HRT commander Richard Rogers "advised that his team had received sufficient breaks during the standoff that they were not too fatigued to perform at top capacity in any tactical operation at the time. He added, however, that if the standoff continued for an extended length of time, he would propose that the HRT stand down for rest and retraining."[48]

When Reno asked about using SWAT teams to take the place of the HRT, "she was told that the HRT's expertise in dealing with the powerful weapons inside the compound, driving the armored vehicles, and maintaining the security of the perimeter was essential."

She also was discouraged from using the Army's "Delta Force" or other forces because of *posse comitatus* restrictions. The FBI put further pressure on Reno warning her that "Koresh might actually mount an offensive attack against the perimeter security, with Branch Davidians using children as shields. This would have required the best trained forces available to the FBI." They also expressed concerns about the "possible incursion of fringe groups."[49]

On April 15, FBI chief negotiator Byron Sage told Associate Attorney General Webster Hubbell that "law enforcement personnel at Waco were getting tired and their tempers were fraying." Hubbell passed this information on to Reno. Upon hearing on April 16 that Reno had turned down the gassing plan, Deputy Assistant Attorney General Mark Richard told Hubbell "that the FBI would not be pleased, that they would nonetheless accept the decision, and that they may then talk in terms of withdrawal." Despite these threats to withdraw the FBI Hostage Rescue Team, the Justice report asserts Reno believes, "The FBI did not try to 'railroad' her."[50]

FBI SUDDENLY DE-EMPASIZED MASS SUICIDE

The BATF had used rumors that the Davidians might commit suicide to excuse the paramilitary raid. And the FBI had alluded to the possibility of mass suicide, as when SAC Bob Ricks told the press in March, "We're very concerned that part of Koresh's grand

scheme is he would like to see a large number of his
people die, which would be justification for his
pronouncements of the fulfillment of the Scriptures."[51]
However, when it came to promoting their gassing plan,
the possibility of mass suicide suddenly became a minor
issue. "[T]he FBI told the Attorney General they
regarded the possibility of mass suicide as remote."[52]

Given the other information withheld from
Reno, one wonders if the FBI revealed to her the facts
about former and still-affiliated Davidians' disturbing
allegations of potential mass suicide listed in the Justice
report: March 2 suicide discussions by a few Davidians
convinced Koresh was dying; Dana Okimoto's allegation
that if Koresh died, all his followers would commit
suicide; Marguerita Vaega's note sent out with her
released daughter telling relatives the mother might
soon be dead;[53] or Kiri Jewell's allegation she had been
"taught" to commit suicide.[54] (The seriousness of these
incidents probably have been blown out of proportion.)

Janet Reno's response to a Larry King question
during his April 19, 1993, broadcast on which she
appeared suggests she had not been well briefed on
these possibilities. King asked her, "Didn't Koresh say
it would end in fire?" Reno snapped back, "I forget
exactly now what his particular description of it was."

Reno asserted during the October 8, 1993,
Justice Department press conference on federal actions
in Waco, "I don't think there were any misleading
statements about suicide because we talked about it."[55]
During the 1993 House Judiciary Committee hearing,
she repeated essentially what FBI spokesperson Bob
Ricks told the press after the fire: "We went through

the world and interviewed former cult members, associates of cult members, the number that I last checked was sixty-one people. The vast bulk, the substantial majority of those believed that they would not commit suicide."[56]

Given even the remote possibility that the allegations were true, the FBI's plan to gas and demolish the building was as irresponsible as yelling "jump" to a person threatening to leap from a ledge. Dr. Stone, who believes Davidians did commit mass suicide, wrote he is "convinced that the FBI's noose-tightening tactics may well have precipitated Koresh's decision to commit suicide and his followers to this course of mass suicide. The official reports have shied away from directly confronting the possible causal relationship."[57] Much as the FBI denied to Reno that the Davidians would commit suicide, within minutes of the fire's beginning both the FBI and the Justice Department declared that the Davidians had set the fire in an act of mass suicide.

FBI ASSURED RENO "THIS IS NOT D-DAY"

The Justice report states: "The action was viewed as a gradual, step-by-step process. It was not law enforcement's intent that this was to be 'D-Day.' Both the Attorney General and Director Sessions voiced concern for achieving the end result with maximum safety. [FBI Deputy Director Floyd] Clarke made it clear that the goal of the plan was to introduce the tear gas one step at a time to avoid confusing the Branch Davidians and thereby maintain the impression that they were not trapped."[58]

Reno asserted at her April 19 press conference, "Today was not meant to be D-Day. We were prepared to carry it out tomorrow and the next day, and do everything we could to effect a peaceful resolution of this matter."[59] In her April 18 telephone briefing of President Clinton, Reno "emphasized that the operation was intended to proceed incrementally, and that it might take two or three days before the Davidians surrendered. The Attorney General told the President that Monday, April 19 was not 'D-Day.' "[60]

FBI WITHHELD EVIDENCE OF
SELF-DEFENSE DISCUSSION

While both Attorney General Janet Reno and the Justice Department have gone into detail about their consideration of the suicide issue, neither has addressed evidence that Davidians discussed fighting off any tank attack against Mount Carmel. This is probably because the FBI withheld such alarming last-minute evidence from Reno.

It is unknown whether the FBI told Reno—or she bothered to read in their briefing papers—about Koresh's early threats to "blow the tanks to pieces" if agents attacked Mount Carmel again.[61] In the March 8, 1993, home movie sent out of Mount Carmel, Koresh said to the FBI, "Being an American first, I'm the type of guy, I'll stand in front of the tank. You can run over me, but I'll be biting one of the tracks. No one is going to hurt me or my family, that's American policy here."

There is evidence the FBI misled Reno about Koresh's reaction to their moving obstructions, including his favorite black camaro automobile, away from the building on April 18. During the April 28, 1993, House Judiciary Committee hearing, Reno declared that Koresh was not alarmed when the FBI moved his car on April 18, and that the FBI thought that was a good sign. Yet a week before FBI Director William Sessions said during an April 20, 1993, ABC special, "Koresh had great distress over moving of the camaro." The Justice report alleges Koresh was extremely angry and that FBI agents reported seeing a sign in the window reading, "Flames await."[62] (Davidian Graeme Craddock claims that he witnessed this conversation and Koresh actually was not angry and threatening, as the FBI has alleged.[63]) So his actual reaction remains unclear.

On April 18 FBI surveillance devices picked up a conversation in which several Davidians discuss the possibility God would "take us up like flames of fire." Some consider these discussions suspicious. (Jack Zimmermann testified at trial Graeme Craddock said Wayne Martin had suggested "if a tank penetrated the building and was actually in there attacking them, to throw one of those coleman lantern storage cans on the tank and light it up.")[64]

At trial tank driver R. J. Craig revealed that "a tanker's biggest fear is fire, and I had been concerned all along, getting to close to the building, of a burning object coming out of there, a bottle of gasoline that's a fire and landing on top of the tank, then you're trapped inside."[65] (The Davidians' relatively non-violent behavior is illustrated that they did not use "Molotov cocktails" against the tanks, as rioters and revolutionaries have done for decades, while tanks were still outside the building.)

During the trial prosecutors objected to the jury's hearing April 18 taped statements and Judge Smith upheld their objection.[66] Prosecutors did not want the jury to hear clear evidence that the FBI went ahead with the attack despite their knowledge the night before that Davidians had discussed fire. Nevertheless, prosecutor Jahn later used Zimmermann's testimony to allege to the jury that setting tanks on fire was part of the "conspiracy."[67]

On April 19, after the fire, Janet Reno appeared on "Larry King Live" and inadvertently revealed that the FBI withheld from her these last minute facts when she said: "We heard nothing that would indicate that he would do something like this, so we stepped up the pressure." However, in an August, 1993, speech SAC Bob Ricks said, "What we think was in his mind was that he expected us to come in and mount a frontal tactical assault against the compound. Once we were inside, he would light it up and burn us up with his own people."[68] Would Janet Reno have approved the gas and tank assault had she heard about this speculative Davidian discussion about fire the day before the attack?

DID THE FBI TRICK RENO REGARDING "RULES OF ENGAGEMENT"?

Despite Janet Reno's stated concern for the safety of the Davidians and their children, and her desire to "effect a peaceful resolution of this matter," she approved rules of engagement which ensured the resolution would be violent. And there is evidence that the FBI tricked Reno regarding the true rules of engagement—assuming she bothered to read them at all.

Did Reno Know Agents Might Fire on Davidians?

As described in the Justice report, the "rules of engagement that the Attorney General and the FBI had agreed to observe" for April 19, which were communicated to siege commander Jeff Jamar and HRT commander Rogers on April 17, were: "(1) If during the insertion of the CS gas, the Davidians told the FBI to back off or they would harm the children, then the FBI should back off and continue to negotiate; (2) If a Davidian threatened a child, the FBI snipers were to shoot the threatening subject only if they had a clear shot; otherwise, the FBI was to back off and continue to negotiate; (3) Ensure that all those who leave the compound following the insertion of the CS gas were interviewed regarding the condition and location of the children and the other subjects still inside; (4) The mere presence of a child in plain view in a door or other opening would not require the FBI to cease the gas insertions. Instead, the gas should be injected at an alternative point, away from the child; (5) If mass suicides were indicated, then the FBI was to proceed with the emergency rescue plan."[69]

These rules of engagement make no reference to FBI agents' permitted response to Davidians firing on the tanks or agents in sniper positions. On April 28, 1993, Janet Reno told the House Judiciary Committee that if the Davidians fired at the tanks or agents—something she said she knew was a likely contingency—the FBI would be permitted "to return fire." Or, as the Justice Department report states: "Under the operations plan, approved by the Attorney General, 'If during <u>any</u> tear gas delivery operations, subjects open fire with a weapon, then the FBI rules of engagement will apply and appropriate deadly force will be used. Additionally, tear gas will immediately be inserted into all windows of the compound utilizing the four BV's as well as the CEVs.' "[70] Still, it is not clear that Janet Reno knew agents might resort to deadly force on April 19.

One possible evidence that Reno did not understand the rules of engagement is President Clinton's statements during his April 20 press conference: "The plan included a decision to withhold the use of ammunition, even in the face of fire, and instead to use tear gas that would not cause permanent harm to health, but would, it was hoped, force the people in the compound to come outside and to surrender." Later, he repeats this assertion, "I was further told that under no circumstance would our people fire any shots at them even if fired upon." Yet on April 19 negotiators were telling Davidians over loud speakers, "Do not fire your weapons. If you fire your weapons, fire will be returned."[71]

Were Janet Reno and Davidians Given Different Rules?

FBI snipers and tank drivers assigned to carry out HRT commander Rogers' plan may have been confused by the rules. Tank driver R. J. Craig revealed at trial that in their three briefings, Rogers gave them no written plan or rules of engagement for the dangerous and unprecedented gas and tank attack. Drivers were never even told they might be expected to demolish the building.[72]

The April 19 rules of engagement the FBI communicated to the Davidians sounded much more aggressive than the April 17 rules approved by Janet Reno. While Rogers had told Reno that if Davidians went into the tower the FBI would simply inject gas grenades to drive them out, negotiators announced repeatedly over loudspeakers, "Anyone observed to be in the tower will be considered to be an act of aggression [sic] and will be dealt with accordingly."[73] This implies anyone merely looking out a window of the four-story tower would become a target of FBI snipers.

Did Reno Know FBI Might Speed up Demolition?

Attorney General Reno told the House Judiciary Committee that she would leave tactical decisions up to the FBI because she was not "an expert in tactical law enforcement." The Justice report states: "It was also agreed that once she approved the overall plan, decisions would be made on the scene. Although she had the specific authority to stop the action and tell the FBI to leave, tactical decisions were to be made by law enforcement officers in Waco."[74] Did the FBI ever tell Reno that if Davidians fired they would speed up demolition of the building, as they did in fact do?

The Justice report asserts Reno made it clear that if children were endangered, to "get the hell out of there. Don't take any risks with the children."[75] Janet Reno obviously did not make it clear that the FBI should be equally careful not to do anything themselves to harm the children. In fact, FBI agents in Waco were certain the outcome would be violent. According to one news report the day after the fire, Bob Ricks told the *Dallas Morning News*, "We knew that the chances were great that the adults would not come out unharmed. So we felt that if we got any of them out safely, that would be a great bonus."[76] However, anything that threatened the adults inevitably would threaten the children. Once FBI agents killed all Davidians, Attorney General Janet Reno stood solidly behind the perpetrators.

Chapter Nine: The FBI Tricked Attorney General into Approving Gas and Tank Assault

1. Paul Craig Roberts, "Unsettling questions in probe of Waco," *Washington Times,* June 1, 1993: E3.

2. James Adams, "They Could Have Waited: A Lesson in How Not to Play the Hostage Game," *Washington Post,* April 25, 1993: C3.

3. Justice Department report: 256–58.

4. *Time,* May 3, 1993: 36.

5. Justice Department report: 260–63.

6. Ibid., 277–278.

7. Robert Cancro report to the Justice Department, 1993: 4.

8. Ibid., 4.

9. Justice Department report: 264–66.

10. Ibid., 264–66.

11. Ibid., 262–70.

12. Justice Department report: 271.

13. Associated Press wire story, April 28, 1993, 16:15 EDT.

14. Justice Department report: 271–72.

15. Alan A. Stone, M.D., report to the Justice Department, 1993: 10–11.

16. Justice Department report: 269.

17. Christopher Hall, "Trial to view actions of marshals in Idaho," *Waco Tribune-Herald,* April 10, 1993: 4A.

18. Associated Press wire story, April 28, 1993, 16:15 EDT.

19. Justice Department report: 270–71.

20. Ibid., 274.

21. Michael Isikoff and Pierre Thomas, "FBI Negotiators Detail Koresh's Threats to Avoid Being Captured," *Washington Post,* April 22, 1993: A14.

22. Jerry Seper, "FBI used chemical banned for war," *Washington Times,* April 22, 1993.

23. Alan A. Stone, M.D., report to Justice Department, 1993: 29–30.

24. Ibid., 35.

25. Paul Anderson, *Janet Reno: Doing the Right Thing* (New York: John Wiky and Sons, 1993) 187.

26. Malcolm W. Browne, "Chemical Isn't Meant to Cause Fire," *New York Times,* April 20, 1993.

27.   James L. Pate, October, 1993: 102.

28.   Rick Sherrow, private communication, May, 1995.

29.   Justice Department report: 266.

30.   Aldrich Chemical Company information on CS gas; "Waco Suits Continue," *The Balance*, newsletter of the Cause Foundation, July, 1994: 5.

31.   Trial transcript: 5735, 5756, 5916, 5921.

32.   Justice Department report: 278.

33.   Ibid., 277.

34.   Dick DeGuerin interview, ABC's "Primetime Live," April 22, 1993.

35.   Trial transcript: 5162.

36.   Justice Department report: 224–26.

37.   Trial transcript: 5600.

38.   Gustav Nieguhr and Pierre Thomas, April 25, 1993: A20.

39.   Justice Department report: 224.

40.   Sue Anne Pressley, "Waco Cult's Children Describe Beatings, Lectures, War Games: Experts Fail to Confirm Abuse of Cult's Children," *Washington Post*, May 5, 1993: A17.

41.   Mark England and Darlene McCormick, "The Sinful Messiah," *Waco Tribune-Herald*, March 1, 1993: 7A; Davy Aguilera, April 12, 1993, affidavit in support of search warrant.

42.   Marc Breault and Martin King: 92.

43.   Justice Department report: 223.

44.   Ibid., Appendix H, "Sanitary Conditions in the Compound."

45.   Sam Howe Verhovek, "Scores Die as Cult Compound is Set Afire," *New York Times*, April 20, 1993: A20.

46.   Justice Department report: 268–69.

47.   Janet Reno interview, "60 Minutes," May 14, 1995; Clive Doyle, private communication, April, 1995; Justice Department report, Appendix I, "Intelligence on Water Supply."

48.   Justice Department report: 268.

49.   Ibid., 268–69.

50.   Ibid., 271, 275–76.

51.   Associated Press wire story, March 18, 1993, 21:40 EST.

52.   Justice Department report: 274.

53.   Ibid., 210–11.

54.   Edward S. G. Dennis, Jr. report to Justice Department, 1993: 37.

55.   Michael Isikoff, "FBI Clashed Over Waco, Report Says," *Washington Post*, October 9, 1993: A10.

56.   Michael deCourcy Hinds, "Texas Cult Membership," *New York Times,* April 20, 1993: A20.

57.   Alan A. Stone, M.D. report to the Justice Department, 1993: 15.

58.   Justice Department report: 267.

59.   Michael Isikoff and Pierre Thomas, "Reno Says, 'I Made the Decision'," *Washington Post,* April 20, 1993: A9.

60.   Justice Department report: 280.

61.   Ibid., 45.

62.   Ibid., 273.

63.   Graeme Craddock, private communication, August, 1994.

64.   Dick Reavis, *Ashes of Waco* (New York: Simon and Schuster, 1995), 272; trial transcript: 6770.

65.   Trial transcript, 5514.

66.   "Tape Transcripts from Agents' Bug Indicate Fire Plans," *San Antonio Express-News*, February 15, 1994.

67.   Trial transcript: 6161–62.

68.   Associated Press wire story, August 26, 1993, 05:29 EDT.

69.   Justice Department report: 281–82.

70.   Ibid., 288.

71.   Ibid., 286.

72.   Trial transcript: 5652–53.

73.   Justice Department report: 286.

74.   Ibid., 273.

75.   Ibid., 273.

76.   Dirk Johnson, April 26, 1993: B10.

10

The FBI's April 19, 1993 Gas and Tank Attack

Who ever heard of Americans using tanks against Americans on American soil?

Ruth Riddle[1]

Attorney General Janet Reno claims she directed that the operation was to proceed incrementally, negotiations were to remain an option, and the FBI should pull back if the children were endangered. While Reno permitted the FBI to make tactical decisions, the attorney general, or anyone to whom she delegated that power, could still call off the assault at any time. However, whoever was in charge did not call it off, despite the Davidians' pleadings for negotiations, despite their stubborn refusal to surrender to what they regarded as unjust authority, and despite mounting evidence the attack would lead to massive loss of life.

APRIL 19 CHRONOLOGY

During the morning of April 19, 1993, five tanks,[2] some flying American flags, began the attack on Mount Carmel Center. Ironically, the Branch Davidians were flying the Star of David on this day, the fiftieth anniversary of the Nazi attack on the Jewish Warsaw ghetto—and the 218th anniversary of the first battles of the American Revolution at Lexington and Concord. Cause Foundation's Kirk Lyons alleges that driving one of those tanks was Lon Horiuchi, the sniper who killed Vicki Weaver. R. J. Craig, another tank driver at the Weaver siege, drove the tank that probably started one or more of the fires at Mount Carmel.[3] Commander of the Hostage Rescue Team, of course, was Richard Rogers, who also commanded the murderous siege against the Weavers.

The chronology that follows was assembled from the relevant Justice report text and FBI forward looking infrared ("infrared" or "FLIR") photographs which show heat spots as light, FBI overhead photographs, trial testimony, news video, newspaper accounts, and survivors' reports, which are referenced in this and the following chapters. I also referred to Michael J. McNulty's analysis of the full infrared video tape.[4] I have viewed only the short sections played on ABC's "Nightline," May 5, 1995. Because eyewitnesses' watches were not synchronized, some times below are

> *approximate. The infrared camera was set to what one government witness called "National Standard Time."* [5]

(Note: All times are Central Time.)

5:55 A.M.—Tanks go to front, east, and west of building and back of the gymnasium.

5:59—The FBI tells a Davidian the gas attack is about to begin. The FBI alleges Davidian throws the phone out the window. Davidians deny this.

6:00—FBI loudspeakers begin demanding surrender, continue through the morning. Bradley vehicle begins delivering "liquid ferret tear gas rounds," i.e., gas grenades, into the underground tornado shelter.

6:04—Agents allege Davidians are firing on the tanks. FBI opts to speed up delivery of gas, begins launching first of four–hundred gas grenades into the building.[6]

6:07–6:31—Tanks poke holes in building and insert gas at front east and west sides of building. Four Bradleys deploy gas grenades through the windows.

6:24—FBI tells Davidians to hang out a white flag if the phone is not working. Davidians place dark blanket in the front door.

6:45-7:04—Tanks deliver more gas grenade rounds to every part of the building.

7:30—Tank rips hole in front east first floor of building and inserts gas.

7:58—Tank breaches a hole in the second floor back east corner of building. Tank rips into second floor womens' quarters.[7]

9:10—Davidians hang out banner that reads, "We want our phones fixed."

9:17—Tank breaks through the front door, wedging doors against barrier.

9:28—Tank enlarges the opening in middle front of building and may have collapsed stairway near kitchen at this time. CEV2 breaks down and a new CEV2, which is not equipped with tear gas, replaces it.

9:49–9:54—The FBI says phone will be connected only if there is a clear signal it is for surrender purposes. Graeme Craddock exits, discovers the phone line has been severed, and signals that. The FBI does not reconnect phone.

10:00—(11:00 Eastern Time) Attorney General Janet Reno leaves the Justice Department for a speech in Baltimore. She calls President Clinton at this time.[8]

10:30—Bob Ricks holds FBI press briefing and announces, "We're not negotiating," and mentions plans for dismantling building if necessary.

10:41:58—Infrared video camera begins taping.

10:47:16–10:52:57—Period of missing infrared video tape.

10:00–11:00—Bradleys continue delivering gas grenades through various openings.

11:19–26—Tank begins demolition and enters fully into the gymnasium.

11:30–35—Tanks continue demolition of gymnasium. Tanks smash into both the front door and the middle front of the building. Agents try to call into compound. The FBI steps up operations. Tank smashes through gymnasium wall and roof collapses.

11:40—FBI claims last gas grenades delivered.

11:42—Tank rams middle front of building and building debris that looks like flame is seen on front of tank.

Unknown time —Tank boom rams through window and wall of the second-floor old arms' room.

11:52—Tank smashes into front door again. Both front doors have pulled away from the building.

11:55–11:59 —Gymnasium "dog run" collapses; tank smashes around inside gymnasium.

11:56—The FBI claims tank through front door destroys surveillance device.

11:56 A.M.–12:02 P.M. Approx.—Largest tank smashes through front door, finishes collapsing stairway. It probably collapses part of concrete room's ceiling, killing women and children. Tank knocks over several gallon containers of lantern fuel in south end of chapel.

12:01—A loudspeaker message mocks Koresh: "David, we are facilitating you leaving the compound by enlarging the door. David, you have had your fifteen minutes of fame. . . . Vernon is no longer the Messiah. Leave the building now."[9]

12:06—Tank rips away part of the east front corner of exterior wall, ground floor level; boom smashes into second floor. "A few minutes later, from the section of the building, a flicker of orange could be seen."[10] Survivor Renos Avraam claims tank knocked down lamp in second floor room above where tank ripped away wall and started fire.

12:07:41 —Infrared photo indicates first fire on second floor, east front.

12:08:11 —Infrared photo shows large fire already developed on dining room wall and tank sitting north of collapsed gymnasium roof. News video shows tank west of dining room from which smoke is seen billowing.

12:08:17–22 —Infrared video shows two large flashes in end of dog run.

12:09:25 —Infrared photo shows second floor front fire is well developed. Tank sits outside church area throughout fire.

12:09:45 —Chapel fire first visible on infrared. Approximate time Graeme Craddock escapes from the west side of chapel and makes way to concrete building next to water tower. He hears gun shots fired from within building and "elsewhere."

12:10—One FBI agent three hundred yards south of building claims he sees a man start fire near the piano, in the area where front doors had been. News video shows no fire in this area for at least another five minutes. Another FBI agent north of building notes collapse of gymnasium.

12:10:40 —Infrared photo shows room between chapel and collapsed gymnasium on fire and dining room wall fully inflamed. Gymnasium fire meets chapel fire. After this point fire burns too brightly for infrared video to be of use.

12:12—An FBI agent notes fire in gymnasium.

12:13—The FBI calls fire department.

12:20–12:25 approx.—Four-story tower collapses. News videos show tank smashing into front of building as it burns, possibly preventing Davidians from escaping. Chief negotiator Byron Sage has a trophy photograph taken of himself with the burning Mount Carmel in the background. Huge fire ball explodes near concrete room.

12:25 and/or 12:30— Agents report sounds of gunfire inside Mount Carmel Center. About same time SWAT team video footage indicates gunfire which might be coming from outside building.

12:34—Fire vehicles arrive, but are held back by the FBI.

12:30–12:45 Approx.—Tanks with bulldozer blades push burning walls and debris into burning rubble of Mount Carmel.

12:41—Fire vehicles approach burning remains of building and begin showering the ruins with water.

LACK OF SAFETY AND FIRE PRECAUTIONS

Despite their undertaking a large-scale operation with great potential for loss of innocent life, the FBI had minimal safety and fire precautions on April 19, 1993. The Treasury report emphasized that the BATF requires their agents to have a written plan for the kind of dynamic entry it attempted against the Davidians. Yet FBI agent R. J. Craig revealed at trial that the supposedly more professional FBI prepared no written plans or instructions for agents for the assault. Nor was there a post-assault written report of the day or a log of moment-by-moment battlefield decisions.[11]

Reckless Tank Drivers Took No Precautions

According to the Justice report, "Members of the HRT were assigned to be tank drivers, tank commanders, Bradley vehicle crew, snipers, and sniper's support.... An orbiting helicopter with SWAT personnel aboard would apprehend and arrest subjects attempting to flee from the crisis site."[12]

Well before April 19 FBI agents had been criticized for their sloppy tank driving techniques, especially after a Bradley driver trying to move a *Waco Tribune-Herald* vehicle stranded on the property, ran over and crushed it.[13] The FBI gave no consideration to whether tanks ramming Mount Carmel would injure or kill the people inside. At the April 19 10:30 A.M. press briefing a reporter asked if the FBI warned those inside each time a tank was about to smash into the building. Ricks answered, "We are not advising them ahead of time. We are continuing to advise them to please exit the compound."[14] At trial FBI Agent Mike Toulouse acknowledged that in his three briefings of tank drivers FBI HRT commander Richard Rogers did not discuss "contingency plans" if the ceilings or stairways collapsed or if tanks injured people inside. And agent R. J. Craig testified that although he had had about fifteen briefings on the gassing plan, the demolition plan was never described to him, even though it was part of Richard Rogers' plan since its first formulation.[15] Obviously, the FBI had no fire marshals on the scene who could advise the FBI as to whether its ramming and breaching actions could start a fire—or prevent Davidians from escaping one.

Justice Department Deemed Fire Precautions Useless

Fire precautions were equally lacking. According to the Justice report, one assistant U.S. attorney raised the possibility of fire and suggested fire fighting equipment be placed on standby. Deputy Assistant Director Danny Coulson explained that "due to the range of the Branch Davidians' weapons," fire fighting equipment could not be brought in because it would pose "an unacceptable risk to the fire fighters."[16] Of course, threat of gunfire has not stopped inner-city fire departments from doing their jobs. And CNN and network news footage before and during the fire shows FBI agents, obviously with little fear of being shot, leaving their tanks on a number of occasions.

If the FBI had been serious about saving lives, it did have other options. One raised by defense attorneys at trial, and possibly considered and dismissed by FBI agents, was the use of "flamex," a fire retardant material which can be used before or during a fire. According to James Pate, Flamecheck Corporation of Santa Paula, California, offered the FBI the use of an armored, remote-controlled fire fighting tank made in the Czech Republic. The tank has a rotating water/foam canon that can deliver 600 gallons of foam or water per minute. The FBI declined the offer.[17] The U.S. military also has access to such heavy-duty fire extinguishing tanks.

Janet Reno admits she gave little thought to the possibility of fire and worried more about an explosion.[18] Reno asserted at the April 28, 1993, House Judiciary

Committee hearing, "I was concerned about intentional or accidental explosions and ordered that additional resources be provided to ensure that there was an adequate emergency response." Evidently, her orders were not followed.

One precaution the FBI may have taken was to create a "fire break" around the building, to prevent any fire from spreading to the tall grass nearby. At trial one FBI agent rejected an attorney's suggestion he was trying to scrape away such grassy top soil.[19] Yet widely broadcast FBI photographs taken just before the fire indicate such a cleared area.

Social Worker Not Informed About Assault

Texas Department of Social Services social worker Joyce Sparks told a particularly damning story about the FBI's lack of preparation to Oklahoma KPOC-TV producers of "The Waco Incident." An FBI agent had told Sparks about their plans to gas Mount Carmel. The agent told her that since there were no gas masks for the children, there would be only light gassing and that Davidians would be brought to the showers afterwards and given new clothes. She was told social workers would be called to the scene the morning of the gassing to help at the showers.

However, Sparks was not notified by the FBI and learned about the attack only at 9:30 in the morning when the governor's office called to ask why she and her staff were not there. An angry Sparks immediately called FBI siege commander Jeff Jamar. When asked if she should come to the site, she was told the FBI "doesn't know if anyone is coming out." She then told her husband, "They intend to kill them all."[20]

Parkland Burn Unit Alerted to Fire Possibility

Many speculate that the FBI did in fact expect a fire at Mount Carmel because of reports that the FBI had called Parkland Memorial Hospital in Dallas about its burn unit the morning of April 19. These were confirmed in November, 1993, when Parkland announced it was planning to sue the federal government for refusal to pay $370,000 in medical bills of three Davidians in the hospital's burn unit. According to the *Dallas Morning News*, Tom Cox, Parkland's legal director told reporters, "a call was made to the hospital about 6 A.M. that day, but it was unclear if it was during that call or a later call that day that the burn unit was mentioned." The hospital demanded the government pay because the Davidians were in federal custody when brought to Parkland. The government eventually did pay the bill.[21]

A less publicized but equally suspicious fact is that less than an hour after the start of the fire, BATF's Special Agent-in-Charge in Dallas, Ted Royster, met the emergency helicopters at Parkland's burn unit. And he had a full contingent of BATF agents mobilized to guard them around the clock.[22]

Fire Trucks Were Not on Standby

During her April 19 press conference, Reno said she thought that the fire department "had been" given advance notice of the assault. However, the department denied this.[23] As the fire raged, CNN reporters asked R. G. Wilson of the Waco Fire Department if the Department was "on standby." He answered, "We have been in the past but we weren't today. We had been in contact with ATF and FBI, and they were to use normal procedures and use 911 to get a hold of us."

Fire trucks were not called until 12:13 P.M., eight minutes after the fire broke out, and did not arrive until 12:34 P.M. The FBI then held the trucks up for seven minutes before allowing them to approach the burning ruins.[24] CNN video tapes show that thirty-one minutes after the fire was first reported, the building was entirely gone. Representative James Traficant commented on the FBI's lack of precautions. "When you have 100 TV crews but not one fire truck, that's not a well-thought-out plan, that's box office."[25]

However, the FBI's failure to call fire trucks may have been a secret precaution since the FBI probably knew that spraying thousands of gallons of water on burning CS gas might produce a hydrogen cyanide cloud that could kill nearby federal agents. The Cause Foundation claims news video footage shows several federal agents wearing Scott Air Packs (breathing apparatus) outside the burning Mount Carmel, a possible precaution against hydrogen cyanide fumes.[26]

FBI SURVEILLANCE AND COMMUNICATIONS

The FBI had several operational surveillance and communication systems on April 19. However, when it came to trial, defense attorneys discovered that crucial FBI tapes, photographs, and logs were missing or never kept.

Surveillance Devices Inside Mount Carmel

At trial FBI agent Matthew Gravel revealed that the FBI had sent eleven surveillance devices into Mount Carmel, all but one of which had been discovered or had failed. The devices had a pickup range of ten to twenty feet. The last two devices were delivered on April 18 with typewriter supplies. Davidians checked for, but could not find, any devices in the supplies. Davidian Graeme Craddock, an engineer who was in charge of the Davidians' telephone and other electrical equipment, believes that the devices were inside the corrugated cardboard of the boxes in which the FBI delivered the supplies.

Gravel estimated that the device delivered April 18 ended up approximately ten feet inside the front door, near the communications room. Craddock saw one cardboard box inside the communications room on April 19. Agent Gravel revealed that the other device somehow ended up outside the building, perhaps in another cardboard box thrown out the door.[27]

Gravel testified that three FBI monitors in an airplane hangar at the FBI command post several miles from Mount Carmel took notes from conversations caught by the devices, even as they watched the action on television screens. Sounds also were audiotaped. FBI siege commander Jeff Jamar was right down the hall and visited several times during the day.[28]

Did FBI in Washington Have Live Feed of Surveillance?

The Justice report reveals that on the morning of April 19, "the Attorney General and several senior Justice Department representatives gathered with senior FBI officials in the FBI SIOC [Strategic Information Operations Center], where they monitored events throughout the morning via CNN footage and a live audio feed directly from the FBI forward command post in Waco." Officials also remained in phone contact with FBI commanders in Waco throughout the gas and tank attack.[29] Reno's biographer Paul Anderson notes that a live audio feed came from "the FBI's operations center, a specially outfitted recreational vehicle parked beside Route 7." (It was nearby Mount Carmel.) He writes that the FBI operations center was filled with "specialized electronic monitoring equipment."[30]

What neither account specifies is whether the "live audio feed" included conversations from the FBI surveillance devices hidden inside Mount Carmel Center. A *New York Times* article suggests it did. The article describes the scene in the Washington Operations Center as Reno and the officials listened to unfolding events inside the building.

In Washington, Ms. Reno and the other officials
watched and listened. An agent in Waco said
gunfire was coming from the tower of the
compound.... Attorney General Reno and the
other Federal officials, watching from
Washington, were assuming that gas would
compel the Davidians to evacuate. Over the
eavesdropping device, someone inside the
compound was heard saying, "Don't shoot until
the very last minute." Hearing that, a Federal
official in Washington wondered aloud if the cult
was expecting a fierce "banzai" raid. Another
voice, believed to be that of David Koresh, was
heard on the eavesdropping device saying,
"Stay low, stay ready and loaded." Moments
later, another voice was picked up inside the
compound: "Have you been gassed yet?"[31]

The story gives no further details about what
else was heard over the eavesdropping equipment. (And
it should be noted that this alleged Davidian
conversation was never presented as evidence of
Davidians firing at tanks during the trial.) Nevertheless,
the story indicates that high ranking officials could hear
whatever the surveillance devices picked up, even as it
happened. Considering that the FBI supposedly uses
the most sophisticated and advanced technology, it
would be surprising if they did not have such a simple
live audio feed.

Defense attorneys described some of these
sounds, ones the jury was not allowed to hear: people
praying as tanks bashed through the walls, children

crying and calling for their parents, Davidians discussing whether the government meant to kill them and begging the FBI for negotiations, and, in the background, the FBI loudspeaker droning on "this is not an attack."[32]

The critical question of what officials and agents could or could not hear as it happened should be investigated and its moral and legal implications explored. A related question is, did the FBI make audiotapes of conversations between decision-makers inside the Washington FBI Operations Center on April 19? If so, these were not made available to defense attorneys at trial.

Aerial Infrared Video and Other Photography

Forward looking infrared photography and video shows heat as light. It is used increasingly by law enforcement for night surveillance and tracking suspects fleeing at night. Infrared also can be used to detect "hot spots" inside a building, be they from heaters, cooking, manufacturing processes (as in illegal drugs), and fires. However, this technology is not perfectly sensitive, even in detecting very hot spots like incipient fires. A fire deep within a building might not be detected as soon as one on a higher floor or closer to a window.

The infrared camera the FBI used on April 19 contained a small viewer that identified and placed a box around new areas of heat or fire that showed up on the developed film. Many wonder why the FBI used infrared video on April 19. Was it expecting a fire? At trial defense attorneys got no satisfactory answers from fire investigators. And when the chief fire investigator, Paul Gray, appeared on ABC's May 5, 1993, "Nightline," he admitted he did not know the reason and speculated it was to see Davidians exiting the building, something which would have been impossible on that warm day.[33]

FBI agents started the infrared camera at 10:41:58 A.M. However, there is a four-and-a-half minute gap between 10:47 and 10:52 A.M. In a June 14, 1994, letter to Davidian defense attorney John F. Carroll, who had requested an explanation for the missing minutes, prosecutor Ray Jahn explained: "the gap apparently occurred when the CEVs were at the T intersection refilling their tear-gas tanks." Jahn notes he asked the FBI to "ascertain if any tape exists or if the equipment was simply not operating while the CEVs were away from the scene."

There have been press reports that the FBI's infrared cameras could tell where people were in the building from the heat radiated from their bodies and rammed those areas. Also, some have reported they ran fiber optic cameras cables through the walls.[34] If the FBI used such sophisticated technology, prosecutors withheld that fact from defense attorneys at trial.

The FBI also took color photographs from aircraft. Rick Sherrow reports that he has documentation that over 3,000 such photographs were taken. However, in discovery the government gave civil suit attorneys only a few hundred.[35] It is likely that on April 19 military spy satellites were taking photographs as well. If these could be obtained, they might reveal important details about when the fire started and acts by FBI agents and tanks not otherwise caught on camera or video.

Communications with Agents in the Field

Prosecutors were required to turn over to defense attorneys all recorded audio communications and logs of communications between FBI commander Rogers and other commanders and agents at observation posts, in tanks, or in aircraft.

However, two agents whose testimony was particularly important did not have any recorded radio transmissions. Agent John Morrison claimed he had seen a Davidian start a fire and had informed other agents of that fact over his radio. He stated he "definitely didn't know of any recording of radio traffic."[36] Agent R. J. Craig drove the tank that smashed in the middle front and front door of Mount Carmel and probably started one or more fires in the building. He claimed that he "had a problem" with his "intercom" around 10:00 A.M. and could not talk on his radio. When asked about missing logs of radio communications, Craig stated that normally a log of radio communications is kept but he did not know if one was kept on April 19.[37]

FBI AGENTS HOSTILE TOWARD DAVIDIANS

The "Waco, the Big Lie Continues" video contains credible FBI SWAT team video with various scenes of Mount Carmel Center, evidently taken by friends of FBI agents in the footage. In one scene middle-aged FBI agents jump into their helicopters enthusiastically yelling, "Good morning, Vietnam." One of these agents later brags that he is ready for action and that he is "honed to a fine edge, honed to kill." The June, 1994, issue of *Soldier of Fortune* included a full-color "trophy" photograph, shown at trial, of an unidentified, gun-toting, bulletproof vest-clad federal agent proudly posing as Mount Carmel burns 300 yards away.[38]

More disturbingly, during the trial a similar trophy photograph of the FBI's chief negotiator Byron Sage with the burning building was revealed and shown to the jury.[39] This photo was taken within ten minutes of the time Sage, after urging Davidians to come out over a loudspeaker, betrayed his true feelings when he inadvertently left the microphone on and was heard to say: "I've been in the FBI for twenty-seven years and I've never seen anything like these people. They think they can get away with murder. Well, they'll have another thing coming as soon as they come out of there."[40]

Davidians allege that FBI agents treated harshly those who escaped the fire. One grabbed Ruth Riddle by the hair and shook her when she would not answer his questions. He only stopped when another agent warned him, "You better stop that, you're on camera." Another put handcuffs on Clive Doyle despite the painful burns on his arms and wrists.[41] When attorney Dan Cogdell visited Doyle in the hospital shortly after the fire, he was shocked to find his feet also were still shackled, despite burns on his lower body.[42] One must remember this hostility when considering the many questions about FBI agents' actions described in the following pages.

FBI ALLEGED DAVIDIANS SHOT AT TANKS

During his April 19 morning press briefing, FBI spokesperson Bob Ricks claimed that Davidians had shot at FBI tanks. At his press conference the next day, siege commander Jeff Jamar claimed they fired "hundreds of rounds." However, evidence presented at trial did not support this claim.

Agents' Testimony

The Justice report alleges FBI agents reported automatic and semiautomatic gunfire shortly after the gassing began.[43] FBI sniper Kenneth Vincent, who was stationed three hundred yards south of Mount Carmel, testified that shortly after the first tank assaults at 6:00 A.M. he saw rounds ricochet off the tank, heard "sounds consistent with gunfire," and saw fabric moving. Tank driver James McGee testified he "observed rounds penetrate a screen," but admitted he did not hear any gunfire.[44]

Tank driver Tom Rowan said he saw "muzzle flashes" from a shoulder weapon held by a Davidian in one of the three-story towers and he returned several gas grenade rounds at the man; he claims they exchanged fire for thirty to forty seconds until the man stopped shooting. (Rowan said he did not choose to use the M-16 machine gun he carried in his tank.)[45]

Mike Toulouse, an observer stationed in the barn north of Mount Carmel, testified that he heard periodic gunfire during the day—including just once from an automatic weapon—and that shots flew over his head after the fire started. Toulouse conceded that although he saw a man standing near what looked like a .50-caliber gun, he did not hear any .50-caliber gunfire.[46]

At trial, the government never provided evidence that the tanks had suffered gunshot damage. Nor did it provide evidence of the sounds of gunfire from the surveillance device placed inside the building. Agents' paltry evidence of gunfire provided the excuse for the massacre that followed.

Agents Not Afraid to Leave Tanks

According to *Newsweek*, "HRT was under orders not to leave its tanks or enter the compound on foot. . . . HRT agents did have authority to leave their tanks but only in the rarest circumstances, such as children being killed or held hostage."[47] During the 10:30 A.M. press briefing SAC Bob Ricks stated, "We are not exposing any of our agents individually to firearms." However, news footage contained in "Waco, the Big Lie" clearly shows agents jumping in and out of the open back hatch of a tank early that morning.

One particularly troubling piece of news video, contained in KPOC-TV's video "The Waco Incident," seems to show an agent walking beside a tank as it pulls out of the front door. This may be a cut of Davidian Graeme Craddock exiting. CNN news video shows agents, even early in the fire, jumping out of their tanks to apprehend Davidians fleeing the building. If there really had been "hundreds of rounds" of gunfire coming from Mount Carmel, it is doubtful agents would have left their tanks so freely.

Davidians Deny Firing at Tanks

Defense attorneys asserted that surveillance audio recorded inside Mount Carmel on April 19 contains evidence that Davidians did not fire on tanks. They claim Davidians can be heard making statements like, "I want no firing around the back or anywhere else," and "I don't know why they say that cause we haven't been firing."[48]

When fire survivor David Thibodeau heard on the radio that the FBI alleged Davidians had fired on the tanks, Thibodeau's reaction was: "I knew it was over. I didn't hear any shots from my side of the building. . . . I could see they were setting up the American people for a disaster. I was prepared to die at that point."[49]

On April 21, 1993, fire survivor Jaime Castillo's attorney Jeff Kearney told NBC "Today" that Castillo said Davidians were instructed not to fire on the tanks. Graeme Craddock asserts he heard no such firing. Craddock and Thibodeau both concede it is possible some Davidians shot in self-defense, but they did not hear it over the sounds of rampaging tanks and grenades.[50] However, it also remains possible that some or all agents fabricated their stories of hearing or seeing firing in order to excuse actions which still conceivably could lead to serious charges against FBI agents.

FBI APPLIED NEW RULES OF ENGAGEMENT

The Justice report states that upon hearing there was return fire, the "FBI"—what individuals actually made the decision is not revealed—immediately moved to apply the attorney general-approved "rules of engagement," i.e., "appropriate deadly force will be used," and "opted to escalate the gassing operation." The report states that, "In fact, <u>the FBI did not fire a shot during the entire operation</u>."[51] (Their emphasis.)

The FBI obviously does not consider the more than four hundred ferret tear gas rounds—or gas grenades—that M79 grenade launchers shot into the building to be artillery, even though they are capable of penetrating a hollow core door and killing human beings. As we have seen, FBI tank driver Tom Rowan revealed he shot gas grenades at a man allegedly shooting a gun at him.

The Justice report justifies its speed up of operations, mentioning the attorney general's prior approval, danger to tank drivers from rounds penetrating tank openings, and the claim that the FBI had "exercised remarkable restraint" during the fifty-one days.[52] FBI agents used their gas grenades and their tanks as deadly weapons—ones that succeeded in killing most Davidians.

THE GAS ATTACK

Because of the FBI's concern Davidians might escape into the large underground tornado shelter, they gassed it early in the morning. (Contrary to assertions in "Waco, the Big Lie," no Davidians were burned to death in what the video calls the "underground bunker.") Agent Rowan's tank delivered gas grenades into the back window of the "dog run" over the gymnasium, where allegedly there was a .50-caliber weapon, and into the four-story tower.[53] Agent Craig's tank then gassed the hallway leading to the buried bus that was a tunnel to the shelter to prevent people from escaping into the buried bus. At trial Craig denied ever driving over the bus because he didn't want to crush it.[54] However, in news video, including that in both "Waco, the Big Lie" videos, it does appear that FBI tanks both smash into the building next to the bus and actually run over the bus.

The gassing had relatively little effect on Davidians because they wore gas masks and because stiff winds rushing through the large holes created by tanks quickly dispersed the gas. Some childrens' masks were made to fit with the help of wet towels; other children had wet blankets placed over their heads to protect them from the gas. Attorney Jack Zimmermann revealed that Davidians donned gas masks and went about their normal routines. "They thought they were going to spray some tear gas and retreat." Survivors said they still believed the FBI's promise it would allow Koresh to finish his book about the Seven Seals.[55]

The tank attacks and gas grenades drove most Davidians into the concrete room or to the second-floor hallways or third floor bedrooms to escape injury. When asked by a defense attorney about the dangers of gas grenades to children, FBI agent Rowan answered, "I'm sure everyone was concerned about the children's safety. That's why we used a nonlethal means to get them out of there."[56] One wonders if there had been no children there whether Rowan and the FBI would have considered it proper to use lethal gas—or even to bomb Mount Carmel to smithereens.

FBI REFUSED TO NEGOTIATE

On April 28, 1993, Attorney General Janet Reno told the House Judiciary Committee she directed that, "if it appeared that, as a result of the initial use of tear gas, Koresh was prepared to negotiate in good faith for his ultimate surrender, the FBI was to cease the operation." Defense attorney Mike DeGeurin, who had heard the surveillance tapes, said that Davidians were pleading for negotiations.[57] However, at 10:30 A.M. central time, one half hour after Reno had left the FBI's Washington Operations Center, FBI spokesperson Bob Ricks stated: "We're not negotiating. We're saying come out. Come out with your hands up. This matter is over."[58]

Davidians Did Not Throw Out Phone

During his 10:30 A.M. press briefing FBI spokesperson Bob Ricks claimed that Steve Schneider threw the phone out the window at 6:00 A.M., right after the FBI told him that they were about to begin the gas attack. The Justice report does not specify Schneider, one of the Davidians' chief negotiators.[59]   However, engineer Graeme Craddock, who was in charge of Davidian equipment, asserts that as soon as he heard this report on the radio, he went to the communications room and found all the phones in their usual positions. None had been thrown out the window.

Tank Broke the Phone Line

At 6:24 A.M. FBI loudspeakers instructed the Davidians to fly a white flag to signal "their phone was not working and they wanted to reestablish phone contact." They did so, but quickly replaced it with a non-surrender dark blanket hung outside the front door. Chief negotiator Sage then gave them two minutes to surrender. They did not. At 9:10 the Davidians hung out a white banner reading, "We want our phones fixed."[60]

According to the Justice report, at 9:49 A.M. FBI negotiators announced over loudspeakers that "the phone would be reconnected only if the Davidians clearly indicated they intended to use the phone to make surrender arrangements." At this time "Craddock went outside to retrieve the phone, holding it up to indicate the line had been severed."[61] However, Graeme Craddock denies that he found a phone outside the building. Instead he says he pulled at the phone line until he discovered that it had been severed by a tank and then, using a scissor motion, indicated the line had been cut. He believes he saw further confirmation the line had been severed by tanks in FBI photographs presented at trial. They clearly showed the line intact on April 18 and severed on April 19.[62]

Neither the FBI nor Justice Department have admitted tanks broke the wire. At trial FBI tank driver R. J. Craig did concede that tanks could have cut the line.[63] And the Justice report conveniently "redacts" the sentence after that which describes Craddock's action—a sentence which probably reveals that the tank cut the line. Texas Ranger Fred Cummings, whose job it was to find evidence on the ground in front of Mount Carmel, testified that he found neither a phone nor a phone wire during his search.[64] That Rangers found no phone line suggests FBI agents destroyed that evidence.

FBI Excuses for Not Negotiating

Craddock's gesture that the line had been severed did not motivate the FBI to action. "The FBI was unwilling to expose its agents such a risk [sic] absent a clear signal from the Davidians that they would use the reconnected phone to make surrender agents [sic] with the FBI. The Davidians never provided such a signal."[65] The two syntax errors in the Justice report smack of desperate and hasty rewrites as Justice employees tried to excuse the FBI's failure to do the minimum necessary to facilitate any surrender.

After the fire, FBI commander Jeff Jamar told reporters that although the Davidians seemed willing to talk, "We tried to figure out a way to get a line, but we couldn't figure out a way to do it safely."[66] Obviously, it never occurred to Jamar—or to Janet Reno, Webster Hubbell, or William Sessions—that a "safe" way to do so would be to stop the gas attack and pull back the tanks.

We must wonder if Janet Reno lied to Congress when she asserted that she told the FBI that if Koresh was prepared to negotiate in good faith, the FBI was to desist. Surely she could hear evidence the Davidians wanted to negotiate, including from any live audio feed, before she left the FBI Operations Center at 10:00 A.M. Central Time. And she probably saw on television the banner requesting the phones be "fixed." Why didn't she direct the FBI to do so at that time?

WHO WAS IN CONTROL AFTER RENO LEFT FBI OPERATIONS CENTER?

The Justice report does not mention which officials besides Attorney General Janet Reno gathered in the Washington FBI Operations Center—nor did news reports. However, former FBI Director William Sessions revealed during the April 28, 1993, House Judiciary Committee hearing that Associate Attorney General Webster Hubbell and Assistant Deputy Attorney General Mark Richard also were there. Sessions revealed they "probably" were there when the fire started. Given Hubbell's alleged penchant for control, we must assume he was.

FBI Deputy Director Floyd Clarke disclosed during the April 28 hearing that he also was in the Operations Center. Other FBI officials in attendance probably included Associate Deputy Director for Investigations Doug Gow and Assistant Director of the Criminal Investigative Division Larry Potts.

The report notes that Janet Reno left the FBI Operations Center at 10:00 A.M. Central Time (11:00 A.M. Eastern Time) because "The Attorney General believed it was not necessary to remain in the SIOC because it appeared that the operation would continue for many more hours."[67] She mentioned in the House Judiciary Committee hearing that she called President Clinton at this time before leaving to speak at a judicial conference in Baltimore. She did not reveal the content of that conversation.

After Reno departed, Webster Hubbell would have been the highest ranking official in the FBI Operations Center. However, it has never been revealed if Reno put him in charge. When quizzed by Representative Lamar Smith during the April 28, 1993, House Judiciary Committee hearing, Reno answered that after she left she communicated with the President through the intermediary of Webster Hubbell who spoke with the White House counsel. (Reno did confess that, while she had claimed on television the evening of April 19 that Hubbell had spoken directly to Clinton on April 19, she really did not know whether he had. The Justice report later stated Hubbell had actually spoken to White House Chief of Staff Thomas McLarty and not to Clinton.[68])

FATAL DECISION TO ESCALATE TO DEMOLITION

FBI tank attacks became more and more vicious as the morning progressed. At least three times a tank smashed into the middle front of the building, toward the concrete room under the tower, collapsing hallway walls and the interior stairwell by the kitchen. A tank rammed into the double front doors—which contained important evidence of BATF crimes—and damaged the stairwell near them. Other tanks ripped away at the old arms' room and the gymnasium. At some point some yet unidentified official in Washington or agent in Waco gave the order to begin demolition of the building.

FBI Expected Demolition Would Be Necessary

The FBI did not expect gassing alone to work. One reporter wrote that SAC Bob Ricks at the 10:30 A.M. press briefing revealed the FBI "did not expect cult members to begin leaving the complex, despite the power of the tear gas."[69] He stated, "The pounding of the compound that you see is really a necessary function of the insertion of the gas.... So, it's not necessarily, at this point, one of destruction to the compound." However, he did point out that the tanks could destroy the building within an hour if they so chose.

The "Apparent Deviation" from the Plan

Edward S. G. Dennis, who oversaw the Justice Department's review of the FBI's action in Waco, wrote in his report that at sometime after 11:00 A.M. "an apparent deviation from the approved plan began. The plan had contemplated that the building would only be dismantled if after forty-eight hours not all the people had come out." However, the FBI did not wait forty-eight hours.[70]

At trial, Judge Walter Smith would not allow defense attorneys to call FBI siege commander Jeff Jamar or HRT commander Richard Rogers to question them under oath about whether there was a specific decision to demolish the building. Some evidence must be gleaned from the testimony of R. J. Craig, the tank driver who made the entries into the middle front and the front doors. (Prosecutors did not call to the stand the tank driver who brought down the gymnasium, whom Craig identified as Garry Harris.)[71]

Craig testified that Rogers first told him to go as far as possible inside the middle section of the building toward the tower to gas the area. Craig went in cautiously at first, afraid of falling into a cellar or collapsing the roof onto the tank. He eventually drove fifteen feet inside the building. News video shows substantial damage to the roof area where the tank went in. Craig's tank also entered the front door area several times, dragging the doors completely away from the building.[72]

At noon Richard Rogers ordered Craig to enter the front door to gas the interior and told him that a second tank at the back of the building would be advancing toward the tower and the concrete room below it at the same time, in a coordinated attack. However, the swimming pool to the north and storage tanks to the north west of the building blocked the second tank's approach to the concrete room. This second tank, which at 9:30 A.M. had replaced another which threw a track that morning, did not have a gas delivery system as had the one it replaced. It was used purely to smash away at the gymnasium, and its goal was to smash in the concrete room which held more than thirty people, mostly women and children. It never reached that room.[73]

Craig denied that he was given any instructions to begin the "collapse" of the building. However, since there is no log or tape of his communications with Rogers, his denial remains suspect.[74]

Why Did FBI Speed Up Demolition?

At 8:01 A.M. the FBI asked the National Guard to make arrangements to refuel the tanks at 2:00 P.M., "indicating that even after the FBI had escalated the pace of the gas insertions it expected the standoff to last many more hours."[75] Why did FBI agents in Waco or FBI and Justice Department officials in Washington decide to speed up the operation and proceed to demolition, instead of waiting forty-eight hours? One explanation is that agents gave up on gassing, realizing that the stiff winds and large holes in the building were rendering the CS gas ineffective as a means of persuading the

Davidians to surrender. Another is that they calculated agents had put on enough of a "show" of gassing and that it was now time to advance to the true agenda— forcing the defiant Davidians out and destroying a building filled with incriminating evidence of the brutal BATF attack.

Justice Department and FBI Deny Demolition Decision

While Edward Dennis acknowledges that the tanks began demolition of Mount Carmel, Justice Department and FBI agents and officials refused to admit it. At the April 19 afternoon FBI press conference following the fire, Bob Ricks explained that the FBI was just trying to insert gas into the concrete room where they assumed Koresh and the other leaders were hiding, and "that's why the CEV went in so far." During an April 21, 1993, press briefing in Washington, unnamed senior Justice Department officials also told reporters that agents began battering the walls so tanks could inject the CS gas deeper into the building to counteract high winds.[76]

However, on April 19 FBI Director William Sessions told CNN's Bernard Shaw that the tank punched the hole in the front door to help people escape. On April 28, 1993, FBI Deputy Director Floyd Clarke explained to the House Judiciary Committee the reason the FBI simultaneously drove the tanks through the front door, side, and back of the building was "to give these people ways to exit the building, which some later used." These explanations remain dubious.

When reporters asked Justice spokesperson Carl Stern if Reno thought agents in Waco had exceeded the plan that she approved, Stern claimed she had said, "I don't think so."[77] The only relevant comment Reno herself has made is her oft-repeated statement, "I made the decision. The buck stops here."

DEMOLITION TRAPPED AND KILLED DAVIDIANS INSIDE THE BUILDING

The fact that debris trapped Davidians inside Mount Carmel was reported immediately. What was not reported, and was barely mentioned ten months later during the trial of eleven Branch Davidians, was that at least three women and six children were killed before the fire by ceilings and floors that were collapsed by the tank that smashed into the front of the building.

Tanks Collapsed Stairwells, Smashed Exits

The tank attacks destroyed the three stairways—one near the front door, one in front of the four-story tower, and one near the back of the gymnasium—and smashed in the front door and several side and back doors. Attorney Jack Zimmermann described the bedlam: "People were trapped; the building was falling down, the damn tanks had just destroyed the structure, and nobody knew where they were because the ceiling had fallen in."[78] He also said the big tank's "concussion tipped everything over on the second floor, collapsed the walls and stairwells."[79]

Fire survivor Jaime Castillo "tried to move around the building, but the repeated pounding on the exterior had piled rubble everywhere. The central stairway between the first and second floors was littered with plasterboard and wood and had partially collapsed."[80] Ruth Riddle explained, "I believe that they couldn't get out. Where the buildings were rammed is where the staircases were."[81] David Thibodeau agreed: "I could see people being trapped, 'cause when the tanks did go in there, there were hallways, there were places that were cut off."[82]

Tank Attack Killed Davidians in Concrete Room

FBI tank assaults killed at least three women and six children before the fire started. An Associated Press story describes the tank that smashed through the front door at noon: "Then the FBI sent in its biggest weapon—a massive armored vehicle larger than the others and headed for a chamber lined with cinder blocks where authorities hoped to find Mr. Koresh and Mr. Schneider and fire the chemical irritant directly at them. When the tank rumbled in, it produced such trembling it felt like an earthquake. The tank took out everything in its path."[83]

The concrete room contained two rooms, a walk-in refrigerator and a gun room. And it supported three more stories of the tower. Tanks repeatedly knocking the front roof, tower walls, and wooden struts supporting the tower doubtless loosened the concrete ceiling and roof. The noontime tank attack may have provided the final stress that collapsed several hundred pounds of concrete from the room's ceiling onto women and children. Partitions between the two rooms, shelving in the rooms, or stacked boxes of foodstuffs and ammunition also may have fallen on them.[84] FBI photographs clearly show a thick layer of fallen concrete debris on the inside floor of the room after the fire.

Tarrant County medical examiner Nizaam Peerwani testified at trial that the three women and six children who died in that room had no smoke in their lungs, indicating they died before the fire. He speculated that five children suffocated when the debris fell on blankets protecting them from the CS gas.[85] (It also is possible some were suffocated by the CS gas.) David Koresh's wife, Rachel, and Steve Schneider's wife, Judy, as well as another woman and a child, were "buried alive." The official autopsy report notes they died of "suffocation due to overlay and burial in structural collapse."[86] (Peerwani's autopsy list also indicates a teenage girl and a one-year-old girl died of blunt force trauma and that a male child had been "stabbed"— however, this could have been a wound from a sharp object in the falling debris.) Because most of these people died as a result of the tank attack, before the fire, government agents and officials could and should be held accountable for their deaths.

In November, 1993, pathologist Dr. Rodney Crowe told "The Maury Povich Show" audience that he was incensed that these deaths, which clearly were caused by the tanks, later were blamed on the Davidians.

"In our local Fort Worth paper on the front page it said, 'Cultist Children Executed'. . . and mentioned that children were shot, stabbed, beaten to death. . . . Nowhere did we say execution. Nowhere did we say beaten to death. It was blunt force trauma. Three children had blunt-force trauma. But it was from the falling concrete in the bunker that fell on them."

Color overhead shots of the ruins in the May 3, 1993, editions of both *Time* and *Newsweek* show a two-foot hole near the middle of the roof. A two-page photo spread of the concrete room in *Time* magazine shows the corner of the concrete room left of the door smashed and crumbling and at least two good sized dents in a wall which might have been caused by debris smashed against the wall by a tank.

At trial Texas Ranger Ray Coffman alleged that an "explosion" of some kind knocked the hole in the roof, which was made of six-inch rebar concrete. He testified that hundreds of pieces of exploded grenades were found on top of the concrete room, inferring these might have created the hole. However, there is no evidence any explosion occurred before the fire. The hole kept getting bigger as the roof sagged.[87] A large propane tank near the concrete room exploded at approximately 12:20, after the collapse of the four-story tower, creating the huge fireball so often shown in news reports. Its shockwaves also could have caused or enlarged the hole.

The Ramsey Clark lawsuit contains Gordon Novel's controversial assertion that around noon "FBI defendants proceed to the second floor and placed an explosive material on the top of the concrete Church vault at the second floor level," a device which later caused the explosion killing those inside the room ten minutes into the fire.[88] This theory is questionable because it relies on agents somehow making their way to the second floor, despite collapsed staircases, and encountering no living Davidians. (Several surviving Davidians saw others on the second floor right before the fire.)

At trial medical examiner Peerwani also testified that a woman (later identified as Diane Martin, 41), died from a fall before the fire because she had no smoke in her lungs. She died of multiple fractures of the cervical spine, caused by blunt-force trauma. Because Martin's body was found in front of the concrete room, it is possible that she fell down into the collapsed stairwell. There have been no assertions by medical examiners or civil suit attorneys that any Davidians were injured or killed by the collapse of the large gymnasium roof.[89]

Tank Debris Blocked Entrance to Buried Bus

During the April 20 FBI press conference SAC Jeff Jamar alleged, "Mr. Koresh obviously intended for the children to die or he would have put them in a safe place—such as the buried bus beneath the compound .... Had Koresh wished those children to survive, that was one place they could have been put safely when he had the fire started." President Clinton also mentioned this "fact" during his April 20 press conference.

However, Jamar should have known that during the morning a fifty ton tank had pulled down debris on top of the trap door leading to the bus. The Fire Report admits that "a significant amount of structural debris was found in this area indicating that the breaching operations could have caused this route to be blocked."[90] Medical examiner Peerwani testified that six women found a few feet from the trap-door leading to the buried bus may have been blocked from reaching it by rubble.[91]

Jurors Shocked by Evidence of Demolition

A defense attorney commented to reporters on photos presented to the jury: "They clearly show that the damage to Mount Carmel center was far, far greater than either the jury or the public was previously led to believe. It's obvious that the tanks smashed huge portions of that place to smithereens."[92]

After the trial, one juror told reporters: "I couldn't imagine anybody being in a home with that many women and children and having a big tank coming through the front door. And they penetrated a room's length or more. . . . This is America. This isn't a police state. I don't care what they did. I can't see that. And I wasn't predetermined. I didn't realize the tanks had done that until I was shown by the government."[93]

Government Denied Davidians Were Trapped

Despite all this evidence, the Justice report refuses to concede the possibility that the tanks ramming the building trapped Davidians. "While the fire was burning the negotiators repeatedly broadcast repeated [sic] messages to the compound, pleading with the residents to leave. Only a few of the Davidians heeded those pleas."[94]

The government claims that twenty-two bodies, including that of David Koresh, were found in the first floor communications room, kitchen/serving area or in front of the bunker, rooms which caught fire later than other rooms. However, Davidian Graeme Craddock testified he stuck his head up through the chapel ceiling tiles and looked down the second floor hallway just minutes before the fire broke out. He saw David Koresh and a number of people in the hallway.[95] Fire survivor David Thibodeau claimed in a television interview that Koresh was on the second floor earlier that day.[96] Clive Doyle says Renos Avraam told him he was in a second floor bedroom with David Koresh and Steve Schneider when the smoke engulfed them, making it impossible to see. He managed to jump through a window.[97]

It is likely the government, with the help of investigators and medical examiners, is covering up the fact that most of these people were trapped by tanks on the second, third, and fourth floors. The government claims David Koresh and Steve Schneider committed suicide in the first floor communications room just a few feet from the wide open hole in what had been the front door. However, they, like perhaps two dozen other

Davidians, were trapped on the upper floors of the building where they fled to escape the tanks.

During the April 28, 1993, House Judiciary Committee hearing, Representative James Sensenbrenner, who himself had barely escaped a disastrous house fire, questioned why so many bodies were found near the first floor middle front of the building, which caught fire later than the back and the side. Assistant Director for the Criminal Investigative Division Larry Potts answered that the FBI had "statements from people in there who chose to come out" that others had "chosen not to come out." However, no such statements were included in the Justice report or alleged at trial. This is just one more example of FBI officials and agents lying to Congress and the public.

Chapter Ten: The FBI's April 19, 1993 Gas and Tank Attack

1.   Ruth Riddle interview, NBC's "Dateline," June 15, 1993.
2.   Sue Anne Pressley, "Davidians Set Blaze, Officials Say," *Washington Post*, April 20, 1993: A20.
3.   Kirk Lyons, August 14, 1994 speech at Lincoln Memorial Gun Rights Rally; trial transcript: 5498.
4.   Justice Department report: 285–300, 331; Michael J. McNulty and Michael Salmen, Citizens Organization for Public Safety, "Infrared Government Video Analysis, June 1, 1994": 1–2; Michael McNulty, private communication, April, 1995.
5.   Trial transcript: 5892, 5943–44.
6.   Dirk Johnson, April 26, 1993: B10.
7.   Ibid.
8.   Reno statement at April 28, 1993, House Judiciary Committee hearing.
9.   Justice Department report: 294.
10.   Ross E. Milloy, "An Angry Telephone Calls Signals the End of the World for Cult Members," *New York Times*, April 20, 1993: A21.
11.   Trial transcript: 5498, 5648–52.
12.   Treasury Department report: 279.
13.   Brad Bailey and Bob Darden: 211.
14.   All references from e-mail transcript of the April 19, 1993 FBI 10:30 A.M. press briefing.
15.   Trial transcripts: 5067, 5608–09, 5648–52.
16.   Justice Department report: 302–303.
17.   Trial transcript: 5477; James Pate, "Wacogate," *Soldier of Fortune*, June, 1995: 49.
18.   Justice Department report: 274.
19.   Trial transcript: 5573.
20.   Confirmed by Joyce Sparks' husband, Frank Leahy, private communication, March, 1995.
21.   Laura Bell, "Parkland to Sue Over Davidians' Medical Bills," *Dallas Morning News*, November 4, 1993; "Feds to repay Texas hospital for Branch Davidians' medical care," *NurseWeek*, California Edition, June 2, 1994: 4.

22.   Hugh Aynesworth, "Fire kills Koresh, most of his flock,"
Washington Times, April 20, 1994.

23.   Stephen Labaton, "Reno Says Suicides Seemed Unlikely," *New York Times*, April 20, 1993: A21.

24.   Justice Department report: 303.

25.   Louis Sahagun and J. Michael Kennedy, April 21, 1993.

26.   "Waco Suits Continue," *The Balance*, newsletter of the Cause Foundation, July, 1994: 5; Michael McNulty, private communication, April, 1995.

27.   Trial transcript: 6119, 6206–07, 6241; Graeme Craddock, private communication, January, 1995.

28.   Trial transcript: 6228, 6237.

29.   Justice Department report: 285.

30.   Paul Anderson, 186, 192–193.

31.   Dirk Johnson, April 26, 1993: B10.

32.   "Prosecution Completes Case Against 11 Koresh Followers," *New York Times*, February 16, 1994; James L. Pate, June, 1994: 34.

33.   Trial transcript: 5946, 5957.

34.   "FBI brings out secret electronic weapons as Waco siege drags on," *Sunday Times of London*, March 21, 1993; Bonnie Anderson, CNN News, April 19, 1993.

35.   Rick Sherrow, private communication, May, 1995.

36.   Trial transcript: 5278–79; Justice Department report: 296–97.

37.   Ibid., 5583, 5585.

38.   James L. Pate, June, 1994: 32.

39.   Trial transcript: 6415–17, 6418.

40.   "Bad Attitude Turns Fatal," *The Balance*, newsletter of the Cause Foundation, August, 1993; Cause Foundation lawsuit (February 14, 1994).

41.   "The Waco Incident: The True Story" video, September, 1994.

42.   Arts & Entertainment "American Justice" program "Attack at Waco," August 3, 1994.

43.   Justice Department report: 288–289.

44.   Trial transcript: 5373–74, 5399, 5470–71.

45.   Ibid., 5142, 5149, 5151.

46.   Ibid., 5017, 5021.

47.   *Newsweek*, May 3, 1993: 28.

48.   Trial transcript: 6308, 6311.

49.   David Thibodeau comments at Reunion Institute Dinner, November 22, 1993.
50.   David Thibodeau and Graeme Craddock, private communications, January, 1995.
51.   Justice Department report: 288–289.
52.   Ibid., 289.
53.   Trial transcript: 5144, 5147.
54.   Ibid., 5518, 5538.
55.   Sue Anne Pressley and Mary Jordan, "Cult survivors offer glimpse inside Waco inferno," *Washington Post*, April 24, 1993: A7.
56.   Trial transcript: 5165.
57.   Sam Howe Verhovek, *New York Times*, February 24, 1994; trial transcript: 6303–04.
58.   James L. Pate, "A Blundering Inferno," *Soldier of Fortune*, July, 1993: 40.
59.   Sue Ann Pressley, "Davidians set blaze, officials say," *Washington Post*, April 20, 1993: A8; Justice Department report: 286.
60.   Justice Department report: 292–293.
61.   Ibid., 293.
62.   Graeme Craddock, private communication, January, 1995.
63.   Trial transcript: 5659.
64.   Ibid., 1083.
65.   Graeme Craddock, private communication, January, 1995; Justice Department report: 293.
66.   Dirk Johnson, April 26, 1993: B10.
67.   Justice Department report: 293.
68.   Ibid., 245.
69.   Sue Anne Pressley, April 20, 1993: A20.
70.   Edward S. G. Dennis, Jr. report to Justice Department, 1993: 59.
71.   Trial transcript: 5595, 5652–53.
72.   Ibid., 5526–28, 5548, 5588, 5592.
73.   Justice Department report: 292; trial transcript: 5641–42.
74.   Trial transcript: 5608–09, 5640–41.
75.   Justice Department report: 291.
76.   Michael Isikoff and Pierre Thomas, April 22, 1993: A14.
77.   Ross Milloy, April 20, 1993: A21.
78.   Associated Press wire story, April 22, 1993, 08:26 EDT.
79.   James L. Pate, October, 1993: 75.
80.   *Newsweek*, May 3, 1993: 26.

81.   Ruth Riddle interview, NBC's "Dateline," June 15, 1993.

82.   David Thibodeau interview, "Good Morning America," May 15, 1993.

83.   Associated Press story, "Tanks, chemicals couldn't break resolve of cultists," *Washington Times*, April 23, 1993.

84.   Kirk Lyons, private communication, June, 1995.

85.   Trial transcript: 5979, 6029.

86.   Paul McKay, "Witness claims Davidian bragged about shooting," *Houston Chronicle*, February 12, 1994.

87.   Trial transcript: 900, 904, 916, 937, 938–39.

88.   Ramsey Clark lawsuit: 43–44.

89.   Mark England, "27 more cultists identified," *Waco Tribune-Herald*, February 16, 1994: 3C; trial transcript: 5973, 6026–27.

90.   Justice Department report, Fire report: 10.

91.   "Davidian's Fiery Escape Ill-Fated," *San Antonio Express-News*, February 12, 1994.

92.   *New York Times*, "Jury in Sect's Trial Views Photo of F.B.I. Assault," February 8, 1994.

93.   Associated Press wire story, "Cult Trial Jurors Rip Government's Actions," *Austin American-Statesman*, March 1, 1994: B3.

94.   Justice Department report: 299–300.

95.   Trial transcript: 6373–76.

96.   David Thibodeau interview, "Current Affair," May 3, 1993.

97.   Clive Doyle, private communication, May, 1995.

11

FBI Tank Attacks
Led to Fire and Death

*I do believe the Government was responsible. I
don't care what the Government says, how much
they try to whitewash it. I have evidence that the
CS gas was flammable, even self-combustible. I
don't believe it was right for them to use tanks to
go straight into the building where women and
children are.*

Renos Avraam before sentencing[1]

Surveillance audio tapes indicate that on April 19
Davidians argued about whether the government was trying
to kill them. Some believed the FBI would gas for a while and
then retreat. However, Davidians refused to be bullied into
surrendering to those they believed had brutalized them and
would bow only to the word of God.

Fire survivors insist that it was FBI tank attacks which caused the fire that consumed Mount Carmel and killed seventy-six people. Many believe that the FBI systematically turned Mount Carmel into an inescapable fire trap and kept smashing away at it until they "accidently" started a lethal fire. Some believe the FBI gave that fire a "boost" by shooting pyrotechnic devices into the building. The government claims that a few Branch Davidians spread fuel and lit fires in an act of mass suicide or mass murder. Evidence suggest that the least likely scenario is that Davidians started any of the fires.

TANKS RENDERED BUILDING A WELL-VENTILATED TINDER BOX

Mount Carmel Center was constructed of old wood from the Davidian homes which had been torn down; walls and roofs were made of plasterboard and tar paper. After BATF shot out the windows, black curtains and bales of hay were placed against them to protect against the cold. There were also large quantities of flammable paper, furniture, clothing, and bedding throughout the building. Dozens of gallons of paint, paint thinner, and other flammables were stored in the gymnasium.[2]

FBI Forced Davidians to Use Flammable Fuel

After the FBI cut off the building's electricity, the Davidians became totally dependent on flammable fuel for light and heating. Attorney Jack Zimmermann noted that "almost every room had a coleman lantern." Survivor Clive

Doyle reveals that for an entire month the eighty-five inhabitants were reliant on flammable fuel which was spilled and splattered by individuals filling lanterns or carrying them through the building.[3] At trial Jack Zimmermann testified that he saw a number of gallon coleman fuel containers stored in the kitchen area and in the nearby hallway.[4]

One defense attorney noted that on April 19, "As they awoke, kerosene lamps hanging on the outside walls were lit." Because of the black curtains hung on the windows to protect them from any sniper attacks, lamps needed to be lit even during the daytime. Some rooms contained butane gas heaters and propane gas tanks.[5]

Gas Grenades and Tanks Dispersed Fuel

Surviving Davidians claim that rocketing gas grenades knocked over unlit coleman lamps and tanks knocked over other fuel containers. Graeme Craddock and Clive Doyle claim that there were a dozen gallon lantern-fuel containers near the front door which they had to move when the tank came in the front door. Some of that fuel spilled on the floor.[6] David Thibodeau told interviewers that after tanks smashed up the gymnasium, "I know kerosene was all over that room."[7] Even the pro-government Fire Report, written without benefit of survivor interviews, admits that due to "structural damage . . . it is possible that some flammables were spilled inside the building as a result." [8]

Flammable Gas and Solvents Saturated the Building

As we have seen, the CS gas and methylene chloride, the solvent with which the FBI claims it was mixed, both are flammable and will sustain and accelerate a fire. Dozens of gallons of these materials were sprayed into the building through the Mark-V liquid tear gas dispenser system—liquid CS gas sprayed out the front of the boom—and through the liquid CS gas in the gas grenades. The floors, walls, ceilings, and furnishings would have been saturated. During his April 19 afternoon press conference, SAC Bob Ricks mentioned that the FBI "put massive gas" into the building at noon, minutes before the fire.

Tank Damage Increased the "Flue" Effect

Most fires begin small, heat up an ever-increasing area as they consume more fuel, and then, when a certain critical mass of heat is reached within the room, they "flashover" or explode into full room engulfment.[9] Fire also can spread rapidly through the "flue" effect—wind rushes the flame through a long, enclosed space like air rushing smoke through a chimney flue. Mount Carmel was filled with natural flues—its long, unobstructed first-and-second floor hallways in the south front of the building, the "cat walk" over the chapel that joined the second-floor hallway, David Koresh's old quarters, and the the "dog run" on top the gymnasium that also joined those quarters. The tanks' destruction of the whole back of the gymnasium increased the flow of air.

The thirty mile-an-hour winds blowing through the tank-created holes would spread any fire quickly—especially if that fire was acting upon floors soaked by weeks of dribbled lantern fuel and upon flammable CS gas and methylene chloride-sodden walls, floors, and furnishings. At trial, fire investigator Quintiere conceded that within five minutes of the first fire, the entire building was engulfed.[10]

EVIDENCE TANK ATTACKS STARTED FIRES

The Justice Department report states that fires started first in the second floor east front, next in the dining room, and finally in the east side of the chapel and claims that such an illogically disconnected pattern only could be the result of arson by the Davidians.[11] However, the government refuses to admit how quickly one fire could spread to separated areas. Nor will it concede that tank attacks also could cause such a disconnected pattern of fires. The Justice report does not include a very clear description of the last tank assaults before the fire and never mentions the collapse of half the large gymnasium.[12] Nevertheless, news footage and infrared video tape and photographs released to attorneys and revealed during the trial provide strong evidence that the fires that devoured Mount Carmel were started by one or more FBI tanks and not by Davidians.

Tank-caused Second Floor Fire Flashed Through Building

News video shows a tank ripping away at first floor corner of the building, rattling and perhaps ramming the room above it at 12:06 P.M. Smoke pours from that area within ninety seconds. At 12:07:41 P.M. infrared video first detected fire. At trial, fire investigator James Quintiere conceded that this tank pulled away from the east front corner of the building shortly before smoke started coming from a second-story window above the location.[13]

Two infrared photographs in the Justice Department report, taken at 12:07:52 and 12:07:56 P.M., circle a bright light indicating fire in the east window of the room directly above the area ripped out by that tank. The official Fire Report describes this first fire as being at "southeast corner, second floor."[14]

Yet, on the May 5, 1995, episode of ABC-TV's "Nightline," Paul Gray, the government's chief fire investigator and author of that report, denied that the fire started in that corner. Showing a portion of the government's infrared video tape, pre-edited for "Nightline," Gray points to the front window about ten feet west of the corner and asserts: "As we can see, there's fire here, in the front of the compound." Commentator Ted Koppel asks, "Was that the area that was punched in by the tank?" Gray answers, "The corner. Downstairs, right of where you see fire there. There was no penetration by the tank into the second floor."

However, the window is in the same room rammed from below by the tank—the same room whose east window is shown in the 12:07:52 and 12:07:56 P.M. photographs. And as the camera pans around toward that window from the second window it is clear to see that the whole room is fully aflame. This was but one more inept attempt by a government representative to deny what the public can plainly see—that the fire started in the same room rammed and/or rattled from below by the tank.

Attorney Dick Kettler reported that Renos Avraam "was with a number of people squeezed into a hallway on the second floor when the fire started. He heard a tank crashing against the wall in a room near them. Then that room caught fire. He said it was terrifying. The tanks were crashing into the walls, and the whole building was shaking. He thought he would get crushed between the walls. Others in the hallway didn't have time to escape. The fire went too fast." The attorney noted that Avraam did not see the lantern turn over, but knew there was one in the room that caught fire.[15] April 20, 1993, CNN news footage shows Avraam, as he is being led into a police van, call out, "I heard someone say that a fire started when a tank backed into a room."

Survivor Jaime Castillo also is convinced the first fire started in this second floor area before whipping through the rest of the building.[16] This fire, located at a pivotal point in the building and driven by thirty mile-an-hour winds, could quickly have spread not only down the second floor hallway to the tower, but down the collapsed stairwell into the dining room, where many gallon containers of fuel oil were stored. Fire survivor David Thibodeau reveals that he was in the cat walk over the chapel right after the fire began and actually saw the fireball from the corner room fire flash down the hallway toward the four-story tower. He then jumped down from the cat walk.[17] Sparks from the fire only had to fall through the opening to the cat walk and down into the fuel-filled chapel to spread the fire there.[18]

Independent fire investigator Rick Sherrow confirms that a fire in the second floor could have spread down the hall, down the collapsed stairwell, and into the dining room area in as little as three seconds.[19] Even Paul Gray, on the May 5, 1995, episode of "Nightline," admitted, "One thing about fire is, it's dynamic, it's kinetic, it moves, it changes, it grows." The first fire could have spread down into the nearby chapel, along the cat walk on top of the chapel, through the old arms' room and down into the gymnasium, effectively destroying the whole building.

Tank Through Front Door May Have Started Fires

Television news footage shows the tank that smashed through the front door at noon plowing in and out of the building for almost two minutes, until approximately 12:02. The Justice report does not even mention this entry in its section on the final tank attacks.[20] Because this tank went in so far, shook the building so, and did so much structural damage, it could have started separate interior fires in the kitchen and dining room, in the chapel, or on the second floor front. Because each area would have a different "fire load" of flammable materials, fires started within this two-minute period might show up several minutes apart.

Graeme Craddock and Clive Doyle, both of whom were in the chapel when the tank entered the front door, have described how Davidians, concerned that tanks would knock over the gallon fuel containers near the front door, began moving them. Some fuel was spilled during this process. Craddock left the room briefly, and when he returned he saw the cans afire. He then escaped the building.[21]

It is possible that the tank through the front door so rattled the kitchen and dining room area that it knocked over a lantern lighting that dark interior area and ignited the fuel containers stored there. A smoldering fire could suddenly have "flashed-over" and engulfed the kitchen and concrete room area. James Quintiere did in fact describe the dining room fire as a "flash-over" fire.[22]

Evidence Tank Started Gymnasium Fire

It is probable that a fireball from the second floor fire zapped through the catwalk, through Koresh's old second floor quarters and down into the gymnasium. CNN and other video footage early in the fire shows little smoke. Then suddenly, within seconds, huge amounts of black smoke pour from the gymnasium as it explodes into fire. However, the actions of the tanks remain suspect.

Tanks repeatedly smashed into the gymnasium starting at around 11:20 A.M. FBI overhead photographs show the progressive destruction of the gymnasium in the half hour before the fires began. The 11:59:16 A.M. infrared photograph shows a tank in the midst of the gymnasium, something clearly seen in the FBI overhead photographs.

The government, television networks, and other news media have withheld from the public the fact that the gymnasium collapsed. CBS-TV has never shown to the public its before and after footage of the collapsed gymnasium.[23] Even when this information was revealed during the trial, few newspapers reported it. And when the infrared video was finally shown to the public on ABC's "Nightline," neither fire investigator Paul Gray nor commentator Ted Koppel mentioned this fact obvious in the video.

At trial, defense attorneys showed FBI infrared video in which major flashes of light, indicating heat, occur at 12:08:17 and 12:08:22 P.M. in the window at the end of the dog run at the back of the gymnasium. Smoke follows shortly after. While the Justice Department report's 12:08:48 P.M. photograph does not show these flashes, at trial attorneys insisted the small viewer box on the film, which automatically goes to a new source of heat, indicated fire there. Attorney Mike DeGeurin asserted the collapse of the gymnasium caused the flash and fire there.[24] Because the roofing had collapsed, and because a tank was inside or near the area throughout this period, it is unlikely a Davidian could have started the fire in the dog run. Defense attorneys grilled fire investigator James Quintiere about whether a fire started in the gymnasium could have joined with the chapel fire. However, Quintiere stubbornly denied that possibility, as well as the possibility that anything but purposely poured flammable fluid could have spread the fire.[25]

FBI agent Mike Toulouse, who was north of the gymnasium, testified at trial that he first saw smoke near the four-story tower and then saw "naked flames" in the gymnasium "dog run."[26] Defense attorneys entered the log of FBI agent "Height" who noted that at "12:10" the gymnasium collapsed and at "12:12" the first fire was seen. (Height's watch evidently was not synchronized with the infrared camera timer.)

Paul Gray concealed the existence of this flash, as well as the logs and other information, from other investigators. Not surprisingly, the edited infrared video that chief fire investigator Paul Gray presented on an episode of

"Nightline" did not show the part of the infrared film where the flash in the dog run occurs. Prosecutors did not call as a witness FBI Agent Garry Harris, who drove the tank, so he could not testify about what happened after the collapse. Nor did prosecutors call Agent Height.[27] This deliberate coverup may be the best evidence that the tank started the gymnasium fire.

Stonewalling as usual, Justice Department spokesperson Carl Stern dismissed the survivors' allegations tanks started the fire. "That stuff is preposterous," he told reporters. And, "You can't knock over a lantern in three parts of a building at once."[28]

THEORIES FBI INTENTIONALLY STARTED FIRES

Given that Mount Carmel burned so quickly and thoroughly, many suspect deliberate arson by the government. At trial, Mike DeGeurin repeatedly questioned an FBI agent about whether Louis Alaniz, the Davidian sympathizer who sneaked into Mount Carmel and left the day before the fire, was a government agent who had been told to leave because the government knew there was going to be a fire. And Joe Turner wondered if the government brought infrared cameras because it expected a fire.[29]

The most infamous accusation that FBI agents started the fire is contained in the video "Waco, the Big Lie," which shows what looks like flame coming out of the barrel of a tank. However, "Waco, the Big Lie Continues" contains a full shot of the tank pulling several yards back from the building. Light that at first looks like flame pouring out the front of the tank's barrel quickly positions itself as a bright blob sitting on the side of the tank; as the tank pulls further back, the bright blob dissolves into what obviously is building debris stuck in the plow of the tank.

Theory: The FBI Systematically Created a Fire Trap

Some believe that Hostage Rescue Team commander Richard Rogers who created the plan, trained the field agents, and commanded his troops on April 19, had a systematic plan to render Mount Carmel a lethal and inescapable fire trap. They believe the fire at Mount Carmel was a carefully planned accident.

Many find it incredible that the FBI would order tanks to smash away at a building filled with flammable fuel and lighted lanterns. Some wonder if knocking large holes in the building and collapsing the gymnasium was not a conscious attempt to maximize the "flue effect." Others wonder if the injection of flammable CS gas and methylene chloride solvent—both of which produce toxic gases when burned—was part of a plan to accelerate the fire, and even disable Davidians so they could not escape.

In "The Waco Incident" investigator Gordon Novel charges that the FBI "didn't need to have separate fires started. It just raced around the building. . . . One can only deduce that their intentions were murderous."

Tanks drove thirty-six Davidians into the concrete room, where they died, and most of the rest to the second floor. Many suspect tanks purposely destroyed all three staircases, preventing easy exit from the second floor. There is no doubt that Mount Carmel was systematically turned into a fire trap. The only question is, was it done through criminal negligence or with intention to commit mass murder?

Theory: FBI Pyrotechnic Devices Started Fires

Many believe the FBI used pyrotechnic devices to start or feed one or more fires inside Mount Carmel. After the fire, the FBI and Justice Department repeatedly denied their ferret liquid tear gas rounds were "pyrotechnic," i.e., that they burn and give off sparks on impact. And the Justice report makes a point of noting that "the last ferret round had been delivered at approximately 11:40 A.M.[30]

However, both Caddell and Conwell's 1994 and Ramsey Clark's 1995 civil lawsuits allege that the FBI shot flash-bangs into the building on April 19. Even fire investigator Rick Sherrow, who worked for the BATF for six years, believes the FBI shot pyrotechnic devices into the building. At trial, Texas Rangers mentioned finding a "NICO" brand flash-bang after the fire, in the gymnasium area.[31]

"The Waco Incident" video compares the small amount of dust non-pyrotechnic grenades give off to the fire and smoke emitted by pyrotechnic devices. It shows that just such smoke rises from the underground tornado shelter after it is gassed the morning of April 19. Agents used the same grenade launchers to fire the tear gas rounds as they did to fire the pyrotechnic flash-bangs.[32] Ambiguous trial testimony by agents Toulouse and Rowan leaves open the possibility that flash-bangs were used at some point on April 19 to keep Davidians from leaving Mount Carmel.[33] A careless or homicidal agent easily could have substituted a flash-bang or even a concussion grenade for a ferret round and shot it into the building, starting a fire.

Some believe that the 12:08:17 P.M. flash in the window of the dog run indeed was caused by FBI agents shooting a flash-bang from a tank. The 12:08:11 and 12:08:48 P.M. infrared photographs in the Justice report show a tank north of the gymnasium, pointing toward the dog run.[34]

Theory: FBI Purposely Injected Flammable Solvents

Some suspect that FBI agents mixed the CS gas particulate with a flammable solvent such as benzene, ethanol, or even jet fuel. At trial, tank driver R. J. Craig testified that he got the pre-packaged liquid tear gas canisters that he attached to his tank from FBI agent Monte Jett who dispensed them from the back of a blue rental van.[35] Ramsey Clark's lawsuit alleges that the FBI used ethanol as a solvent, based on the presence of high levels of ethanol in the bodies of a number of deceased Davidians.[36] The government has not released the exact number of gallons of CS gas and solvent dispensed. Because this fire resembled many unexplained and devastating arson fires created for insurance purposes, some theorize a "High Temperature Accelerant" like jet fuel might have been used.[37]

FBI ALLEGATIONS DAVIDIANS STARTED FIRES

During the FBI's April 19 afternoon press conference, SAC Bob Ricks, who earlier in the day had assured reporters the FBI was confidant there would be no mass suicide, said that on seeing the fire his reaction was, "Oh, my God, they're killing themselves!"—as if only a Davidian mass suicide could explain the fire. What follows is evidence the government presents that the Branch Davidians started the fire, plus comments on that evidence. Discussion of the supposedly independent Fire Report follows in the next chapter.

Testimony of FBI Agent

In the April 19 afternoon press conference, SAC Bob Ricks asserted, "Someone appeared on the second floor of the compound wearing a gas mask and made a throwing motion. Flames erupted, and the person signaled to agents he did not want to be rescued."[38] On April 20 SAC Jeff Jamar alleged, "At least three people observed a [cult member] spreading something . . . with a cupped hand and then there was a flash of fire."[39] However, trial testimony proved Jamar and Ricks lied.

The Justice report states only that "at 12:10 P.M. another HRT agent, who was 300 yards away from the compound" reported seeing a man in the front door area near the piano making suspicious motions, "immediately after that [he] noticed that a fire started in that position." The agent then reported what he had seen over the radio.[40]

At trial, this agent, John Morrison, said he watched through binoculars from across the street as the man who was near the pushed-in front doors made "a motion like he was washing his hands. Then I see a fire come up right from where his hands are. Then the fire gets bigger." He couldn't identify the man.[41]

Defense attorneys first showed photographs proving that Morrison's claim that the front doors were still in the building when the fire was lit was false. The tank had already pulled them away from the building. Morrison then admitted photographs showed that area free of fire even after most of the building was aflame. An attorney asked Morrison if the individual he saw could have been trying to extinguish a fire. Morrison confessed, "I don't know what he was doing."[42]

Alleged and Actual Statements of Fire Survivors

During the April 19 press conference Bob Ricks lied when he claimed that three Davidians had confessed to spreading lantern fuel throughout Mount Carmel. During an April 22, 1993, ABC "Good Morning America" morning news interview Bob Ricks lied when he claimed that survivors told the FBI "that the people inside were directed to light the fire; we have direct statements to that effect."

According to the Justice report, FBI agents interviewed surviving Davidians as they escaped the burning building. "During those interviews three of the survivors made statements about the cause of the fire. Renos Avraam told the agents that he had heard someone inside the compound say, 'The fire has been lit, the fire has been lit.'"[43] However, on April 20 Renos Avraam called to the press as he was led into court, "The fire was not started by us. There were no plans for mass suicide."[44] At trial FBI Agent David Johnson testified that Renos Avraam heard voices from downstairs saying, "The fire's been lit. The fire's been lit." Johnson said it was not his job to interrogate Avraam and that he had not written down the statement until some time later.

Avraam's attorney objected that because it was a group trial, Avraam could not testify to deny that he made a statement which might implicate other defendants.[45]

Similarly, the Justice report alleges that Clive Doyle told the Texas Rangers that the "fire was started inside the compound with coleman fuel. Doyle said the fuel had been distributed throughout the compound in specific, designated locations."[46] However, during the trial prosecutors presented no evidence Doyle made any such incriminating statement. Doyle himself asserts that the only thing Davidians did with fuel that day was to move containers so they would not be crushed by tanks.[47]

The report alleges: "Craddock also said that he had heard someone say, 'Light the fire,' and that he had also heard someone else say, 'Don't light the fire.'" However, he told Texas Rangers, "if there was a suicide pact, he knew nothing about it. He said that he knew nothing about a plan to burn the building until he heard someone pass the word to start the fire."[48]

Craddock, who was committed to telling the truth about what he heard and saw, told the grand jury: "I saw where the fire started, but I did not see how the fires started or who lit them.... I did hear some confusing calls that were made in regards to lighting a fire. [From] within the compound. Someone said the building was on fire. It sounded like to me someone said, 'Light the fire.' There was a call back, 'What fire, where?' And the next call I think I heard was, 'Don't light the fire.'" Returning to the chapel, Craddock saw the fire and fled the room.[49] Craddock's disturbing statements probably are a misunderstanding of more general cries that a fire had started. During her trial testimony, Marjorie Thomas said she knew of no discussions of burning Mount Carmel.[50]

Discussions of Fiery Self-Defense

As we have seen, there is evidence that on April 19 Davidians discussed lighting tanks on fire if they came through the walls of the building. At trial prosecutors played an April 19 conversation where Davidians evidently refer to the tanks, saying either, "So we only light 'em as they come in," or "So we only light 'em as soon as they tell me it's the last chance, right?" (The audio expert had conflicting interpretations.)[51]

Attorney Jack Zimmermann criticized the FBI for not taking evidence of such a defense plan seriously in an April 20, 1993, CNN interview: "The FBI knew that David Koresh viewed those tanks out there, for example, as chariots of fire. They know about the prophecies." (Nahum 2:13 states: "See, I am against you, says the Lord of hosts, and I will burn your chariots in the smoke.") Zimmermann emphasized, however, "We don't know what happened inside."

Some theologians and others also have speculated that Davidians lit the fires to replicate the mass suicide of Jews under siege of Masada by Romans in A.D. 66 or to create a wall of fire to drive off the infidels. However, since none of the fires started near the first floor areas being attacked by tanks, this theory remains dubious.

Indistinct Surveillance Audio

At trial, prosecutors presented a small and very prejudicial sampling of the six hours of surveillance audio tape recorded by the surveillance device approximately ten feet inside Mount Carmel. Prosecutors called only two relevant witnesses, FBI transcriber Matthew Gravel, who took notes from the surveillance audio on April 19, and outside audio expert Paul Ginsburg.

A partial transcript taken from news reports of conversations recorded by surveillance devices follows.[52] The trial transcript did not include the full transcript of the tape. (Note: "DK" is David Koresh; "SS" is Steve Schneider; "UM" is Unknown Male; "Pablo" is Pablo Cohen.) Davidian prosecution witness Kathryn Schroeder helped identify voices on tapes.[53]

(Note: All times are Central Time.)

6 A.M.

UM:	Pablo, have you poured it yet?
UM:	Huh?
UM:	Have you poured it yet?
UM:	In the hallway.
UM:	Things are poured, right?

6:10 A.M.

UM:	Don't pour it all out, we might need some later.
UM:	Throw the tear gas back out.
FBI:	(Over loudspeaker) We have received reports that although we have not initiated fire toward you, there has been fire initiated toward the ...
UM:	No Way.

6:12 A.M.

UM:	You got to get the fuel ready.
UM:	I already poured it. It's already poured.
UM:	They're gonna kill us.
UM:	They don't want to kill us.

7:23 A.M.

UM: The fuel has to go all around to get started.

UM: Well, there are two cans here. If that's poured
           soon...

UM: Is there a way to spread fuel in there?

UM: I don't know. I know that one (unintelligible).

UM: (Unintelligible.)

UM: So we only light 'em as they come in
           (unintelligible) right? Not if they
           (unintelligible). (Earlier interpretation
           was: So we only light 'em as soon as they
           tell me it's the last chance, right?)

UM: Well, that's the fuel. We should have got more
           hay in here.

9:08 A.M.

UM: Hey, man, if anything happens, we go to heavier
           things, it doesn't matter man.

9:16 A.M.

DK: They got two cans of coleman fuel down there?
           Huh?

SS: Empty.

DK: All of it?

SS: Nothing left.

DK: Out of both cans?

SS: I got some mineral oil here.

UM: (Unintelligible)

DK: Hey! Come back here! Hold on here! You're
           not supposed to steal those masks, by the way!

UM: Hey!

UM: What?

UM: You shouldn't go stealing that.

DK: *Okay, I'll give you one. Want it?*
10:00 A.M. (11:00 A.M. *Eastern Time*)
                 (Janet Reno leaves FBI Operations Center.)
11:40 A.M.
UM: *I want a fire around the back. (or "There's a fire*
                 round the back.")
Time unknown
UM: *Let's keep that fire going.*
11:56 A.M.
                 (Tank destroys surveillance equipment.)
12:07:52 P.M.
                 (First fire seen on second floor.)

　　　　When these tapes were played in court, few people
heard what audio expert Paul Ginsburg claimed to hear.
Reporter Diana Fuentes wrote that the tapes "were filled with
noise, and voices only occasionally were discernible.... The
words were faint; some courtroom observers said they heard
it, some didn't."[54] Court observers Ken Fawcett, Jack DeVault,
and James Pate assert they could not hear most of what the
audio expert stated he heard. Voices often were inaudible
and words and phrases open to a number of interpretations.
Jury forewoman Sarah Bain said the jury did not find the
tapes or transcripts very credible.[55]

　　　　On the stand Paul Ginsburg admitted he had to
play the poor quality, second generation tape over and over
until the conversations began to make some sense.
Prosecutors provided his first draft to defense attorneys. Only
on February 13, 1994, did Ginsburg get together with FBI
agent Matthew Gravel to make up a new transcript with the
original, clearer copies of the audio tapes. These, of course,
were different from what was originally given to the attorneys.

The judge thwarted attorneys' attempts to let the jury see the transcripts made by FBI transcribers on April 19.[56]

Prosecutors never explained why they failed to enter into evidence one conversation that they made so much of in their opening arguments. In it, one Davidian asks, "What's the plan?" A second laughs and answers: "Haven't you always wanted to be a charcoal briquette?"[57]

Prejudicial Transcripts of Surveillance Audio

Defense lawyers challenged the accuracy of transcripts of the tapes. They pointed to several inconsistencies between the jury's copy of the transcript and earlier versions given to the defense. As we have seen, the 7:23 A.M. line described above as, "So we only light 'em as they come in," had been transcribed earlier as, "So we only light 'em as soon as they tell me it's the last chance, right?"[58] Of course, neither interpretation may reflect what was actually said—nor do speculative statements prove such action was taken.

Defense attorneys were convinced prosecutors had demanded audio expert Ginsburg change the line to take out the inference of self-defense in the original. Under cross-examination Ginsburg stated he did not know what the government was "looking for" in the tapes and denied that after meeting with prosecutor Ray Jahn he changed the statement into one more incriminating to the Davidians.[59] Ginsburg did admit that he had been paid $20,000 for 160 hours of transcripts and that in the previous year the government had paid him $120,000 for such transcriptions. Defense attorneys implied he would be eager to please his FBI employer.[60]

On August 3, 1994, the ABC television program "Turning Point" played the only segments of the recordings of April 19 recordings then released to the public. The line which the government claims is, "I want a fire around the back," sounds to me like an individual shouting, "There's a fire round the back!" Yet at trial attorneys claimed the same person was shouting, "I want no firing around the back."[61]

Prosecutors interpreted some phrases which were clearly audible but ambiguous in the most negative light. As heard on "Turning Point," the phrases "Is there a way to spread fuel in there?" and "Well, that's the fuel. We should have got more hay in here," appear to be accurate. However, since eighty-five Davidians were dependent upon lanterns using liquid fuel, it is not surprising a surveillance device might have picked up discussions of using or pouring fuel.

Davidians also explain that "spreading" fuel might refer to their attempts to move fuel tanks away from rampaging tanks.[62] The phrase "more hay" could have been a reference to pushing hay bales against the windows to stop gas grenades from entering through them.

Prosecutors also left out of the tape presented to the jury a number of "exculpatory" conversations which could have indicated Davidians' innocence of lighting any fire. These included discussions of negotiations and surrender and clear and repeated claims Davidians had not been firing on tanks. For example, Ginsburg transcribes one conversation as, "I don't know why they say that cause (unintelligible)." A defense attorney said that what Ginsburg considered unintelligible was clearly a Davidian saying, "cause we haven't been firing."[63] All in all, while the tapes do reveal some questionable conversations, they hardly prove that any Davidian started any fire.

Suspicions FBI Tampered With Surveillance Audio

Many believe that the FBI actually tampered with and/or destroyed some of this surveillance audiotape. With modern audio technology, FBI audio experts easily could have spliced together innocuous conversations to create incriminating sounding ones.

Also, the FBI claims the surveillance devices failed eleven minutes before the fires started, leaving no definitive audio evidence of how the fires really started. (For example, yells of "A tank knocked over a lantern! A fire's been lit!" or even "A flash-bang started a fire!" are not available.) At trial FBI agent Matthew Gravel, who on April 19 was taking notes from the tapes even as he watched the action on television, testified there was an "abrupt cessation" of transmission at 11:56 A.M. when the tank entered the front door.[64]

FBI CONTINUED ATTACK
DESPITE KNOWN DANGERS

It seems evident that FBI commanders Jeff Jamar and Dick Rogers withheld from Attorney General Janet Reno and other officials the fact that Davidians may have discussed a fiery defense against tanks on April 18. It is possible that on April 19, FBI transcribers told FBI commander Jamar and spokesperson Ricks that they heard what they considered to be suspicious conversations between Davidians. It also is possible FBI and Justice officials in the FBI Operations Center in Washington could hear via a live audio feed such suspicious conversations. Even if these conversations were innocent remarks or speculative defense plans, they should have been enough to prompt anyone concerned with human life to call off the attack.

At trial, FBI transcriber Matthew Gravel stated that during the April 19 attack he was down the hall from FBI siege commander Jeff Jamar. (A Texas Ranger testified Bob Ricks was also at that command center.) However, when defense attorneys asked whether Gravel had talked to Jamar about what he heard on the surveillance tapes, he answered, "I would say I probably did, but nothing sticks in my mind," and, "I don't recall the exact nature of the conversation." He also admitted that in an emergency, he could have passed a note to Jamar.[65] It is possible that the other two FBI transcribers did in fact have very explicit conversations with Jamar about what they heard on the tapes. Prosecutors did not call either to the stand.

It is suspicious that during his April 19 afternoon press conference, Bob Ricks asserted that Graeme Craddock "said that he heard discussions of using lantern fuel to spread it throughout the compound." However, if Craddock only referred to "moving" fuel in his statement to the FBI, Ricks' use of the word "spread" suggests he heard, or heard about, conversations caught by surveillance devices as they occurred.

When a reporter asked if FBI "intelligence" told agents that Koresh's response to the tank attacks was to set the fire, Ricks refused to answer, just as both SAC Jeff Jamar and FBI Director William Sessions refused to do over the next two days.[66] One reporter commented that after Ricks and Jamar's initial remarks, "federal officials have not explained how they came to believe that Koresh issued the order for a mass immolation."[67] However, by the time prosecutors played these surveillance tapes at trial, ten months after the fatal fire, few reporters bothered to question what the FBI heard from inside Mount Carmel in the days, hours, and minutes before the fire. Nor did the press repeat defense attorney Joe Turner's question, "Why didn't they bring you the tapes of the bug on April 18th, the night before? Do you think it's just a coincidence that they had a FLIR tape up there the morning of April the 19th, that they had a heat sensitive camera up in the air that morning, an infrared camera that morning?"[68]

It would seem that the FBI, and perhaps Justice Department officials, had a pre-planned explanation for any catastrophe: mass suicide. As seen on CNN coverage, little more than an hour into the fire a CNN reporter told viewers that the "White House" had stated that "Justice people" had told them the Branch Davidians had started the fire. As we know, such a statement would have come from Webster Hubbell reporting to Clinton Chief of Staff Thomas McLarty (or, despite White House denials, to Clinton himself). Was Hubbell's evidence Davidian conversations which he himself had heard from the FBI's live audio feed of conversations caught by surveillance devices? Or did Hubbell merely accept FBI SACs Jamar's or Rick's lies that more than one agent alleged seeing Davidians start fires and that Davidians had confessed to doing so?

SMOKE, FIRE, SNIPERS, AND TANKS TRAPPED DAVIDIANS

We have seen how the tanks destroyed staircases, collapsed walls and ceilings, and blocked exits with debris. Once the fire started Davidians were further trapped not only by smoke, gaseous fumes, and fire, but by their fear of snipers and of tanks standing outside the building—tanks which continued to ram the building as it burned. The bodies of five Davidians were found in the first floor stage and gymnasium area. Thirty-six were found inside, and seven were found on top of the concrete room. While the government claimed the remaining twenty-eight died on the first floor, it is more likely most died on the second floor.

Smoke, Fumes, and Fire

According to a reporter who spoke with outside fire experts who viewed video tape of the fire, Davidians "may have had less than five minutes to escape after the fire began. ... The fire produces an enormous amount of toxic gases that cause confusion."[69] One reporter wrote survivors "said the smoke was so black, that one of them said within seconds he couldn't see where he was .... The building erupted." Another article notes, "escape attempts were hampered because gas masks clouded up in the smoke and heat."[70]

Marjorie Thomas testified at trial she was on the second floor when, "all of a sudden, we all felt a warm glow. The whole, entire building felt warm all at once, and after the warmth, then thick, black smoke, and the place became dark. I couldn't see anything." She could hear people yelling and screaming, lost a friend who was just a few feet away, and was severely burned over half her body as she fought her way to a window and jumped.[71]

According to Renos Avraam's attorney, Avraam, who escaped from the second floor, stated that "others in the hallway didn't have time to escape. The fire went too fast. It was total blackness and confusion. In seconds, everybody was disoriented."[72] David Thibodeau saw a fireball shoot down the hallway toward the four-story tower.[73] And Clive Doyle and Jaime Castillo, who were in the stage area back of the chapel, have described how the room suddenly exploded into fire. Those in that area found themselves on fire. Doyle was severely burned before he managed to jump through a hole the tank had knocked in the wall.[74]

As noted, manufacturers warn that burning CS gas can emit lethal hydrogen cyanide fumes, and fire investigator Rick Sherrow claims methylene chloride emits toxic phosgene gas. Attorney Ramsey Clark's investigator Gordon Novel, working on the civil lawsuits, obtained forty-eight Branch Davidian death certificates indicating possibly lethal blood levels of cyanide, a byproduct of burning CS gas. In June of 1994, Novel and other civil suit investigators were permitted to enter Mount Carmel to retrieve soil samples to test for just such cyanide. The results were not available as of publication.[75]

Fear of FBI Snipers

The FBI had at least three sniper nests: in the barn, in a dug-out, and south of Mount Carmel in the undercover house.[76] Davidians were fearful of FBI sniper fire. In "The Waco Incident," Clive Doyle describes the reaction of several people in the chapel near a hole in the building when the fire began. "We were just standing there looking out the hole.

People were saying, 'What are we going to do?' There was concern there were sniper positions, at least two of them, at the south side that we knew of. There probably were more. But there were two that were fairly close. We didn't know if we would be shot when we came out." When the room suddenly exploded into flames Doyle managed to jump through a hole to safety, but others did not.

Tanks Rammed Building, Blocked Escape

Perhaps the most shocking news video footage contained in "Waco, the Big Lie Continues" is of a tank continuing to smash into the building early in the fire. The tank rams the middle front of the building, which is not burning. (It does pull fiery material out of the roof, which leads to the video's dubious claim this is more proof the FBI used "flamethrower tanks.") If six women were indeed trying to escape down the first floor hallway as the medical examiner claimed, the tank would have been smashing that hallway at about that time. A full review of all video footage of tank activity during the fire might well disclose other instances of tanks ramming the building early in the fire, even as Davidians may have been trying to escape.

At least one tank stays near the buried bus and dining room as the room goes up in smoke. CNN footage shows a tank standing outside the chapel throughout the fire. Infrared photos in the Justice report show one tank stationed behind the building, near the swimming pool. Some Davidians may have been intimidated by tanks or even forced back into the burning building by them.

Davidian Survivors Barely Escaped

Jaime Castillo, Clive Doyle, Derek Lovelock, David Thibodeau, and Graeme Craddock were all in the chapel area at the beginning of the fire. All but Craddock escaped out the east side near the stage as fire raged around them. Craddock hopped through a west window of the chapel and made his way to the concrete building next to the water tower and hid there until his arrest several hours later.[77]

Renos Avraam made it through thick black smoke to a second floor window and slid down the front roof where he remained for several minutes. He waved off a tank that offered to rescue him, and then, as the flames grew nearer, finally jumped off the roof and walked away from the building—a scene shown over and over again in news stories about the tragedy. (Both "Waco, the Big Lie" videos claim the man on the roof was a government agent. However, study of the full video shows that only one individual jumps from the roof. Avraam asserts it was himself. He even insisted during his allocution at sentencing that he had told Linda Thompson this, but she ignored his assertion.[78])

Marjorie Thomas made her way out the front of the building. CNN news footage shows an agent jump out of his tank and spray the burning Thomas with a fire extinguisher. Misty Ferguson, hands and arms ablaze, also managed to escape from the west front. Ruth Riddle remained inside the far west corner room on the second floor until it was surrounded by fire. News video shows her jumping to the ground through a hole a tank had punched in the room's wall. ("Waco, the Big Lie Continues" inaccurately claims she too is an escaping government agent.) FBI agents claim they saved her as she ran back into the burning building but she denies that she intended suicide. "I knew the building was on fire. I wouldn't want to burn up. That's why I jumped." At trial, Riddle's attorney revealed that she ran back into the building because she was frightened of the federal agents pursuing her.[79]

FIRE DROVE SOME TO SUICIDE

In late September, 1994, McLennan County Justice of the Peace David Pareya announced that twenty-eight Davidians had bullet wounds.[80] Autopsy results below indicate that eighteen of those proved fatal. The day after the fire, FBI siege commander Jeff Jamar repeatedly speculated that because gunshots were heard during the fire, those trying to escape might have been shot by other Davidians; he considered this to be the logical explanation for the fact so few escaped.[81] However, given the fact that most exit routes were blocked by debris, collapsed staircases, and smashed hallways, and Davidians were lost and confused in the black smoke and toxic fumes, many of those trapped doubtless chose suicide over asphyxiation or burning to death.

Davidian survivors deny there was a suicide pact. David Thibodeau said, "No, there was not a suicide pact.... I know that if I were trapped in a fire and there was a fire next to me, and I was ... it was very probable that I was going to burn, that I may, I may just taken the easy way out." When the interviewer asked why people didn't try to get out, Thibodeau answered, "I believe some people did try to get out or else I wouldn't be sitting here."[82]

Fire survivor Ruth Riddle said, "Given the fact that they may have been trapped, they may have opted for that rather than burning to death, that's a terrible way to die."[83] Jaime Castillo told a reporter, "If I was in that situation, where I couldn't get out and the fire was coming my way, I'd probably take myself out."[84] Derek Lovelock said Koresh "didn't want to commit suicide and he didn't want to be killed. . . . We knew the end was coming, but we honestly thought it would all pass peacefully, David included."[85]

Pathologist Dr. Rodney Crowe told "The Maury Povich Show" audience, "I think they did what you would have done, what I would have done, and I've put myself in that position. If I was on fire, if my child was on fire, if the heat was so unbearable, I'd shoot my child. I would hope I'd have the strength to shoot myself. As we were examining these people we hoped that we would find gunshot wounds because we knew that they went out quickly that way rather than suffer the horrible death that we knew some of them did." A few Davidians, hearing their friends and families dying around them, may have chosen death rather than escape.

SPECULATION FBI AGENTS SHOT DAVIDIANS

At the start of the Davidian trial, Darren Borst, son of Mary Jean Borst who died from gunshot wounds to the back, told the press that an "FBI hit team" killed his mother and other Davidians found with gunshot wounds.[86] What follows is evidence that prompts Borst and others to make the damning allegation that FBI agents shot Davidians escaping the building and/or entered Mount Carmel to shoot some of those trapped inside.

FBI Rules of Engagement Permitted Shooting Davidians

On April 15, 1993, the *Dallas Morning News* reported that FBI officials had considered having snipers assassinate David Koresh, who was sometimes seen near windows. Officials decided that this would raise "serious legal questions."[87]

While the Justice Department claims FBI agents never fired a shot, agent Tom Rowan revealed he fired gas grenades directly at a man who he claimed had fired at him. Agents could have shot tear gas grenades at escaping Davidians to drive them back into the burning building and still claim they had never fired a shot.

Hostile FBI snipers or agents in tanks out of television camera range could have shot one or more Davidians fleeing the back of the burning building—especially if they thought individuals were armed. If any agents shot Davidians, the law enforcement "code of silence" probably would prevent other agents from "snitching" on them.

Davidians and Agents Outside the Building

While Mount Carmel was still burning, CNN and other news outlets reported that as many as twenty Davidians were seen fleeing out the back of Mount Carmel. Such claims ceased as soon as the FBI announced there were only nine survivors.

Based on the missing four-and-a-half minutes of infrared video tape, and the fact that tanks seem to be pushing dark oblong objects into the back of the gymnasium soon after, Michael McNulty believes video tape caught FBI snipers shooting several Davidians trying to escape the building before the fire, forcing the FBI to speed up demolition. He demands the FBI account for all ammunition, spent and intact, issued to FBI snipers on April 19.[88]

Also, speculation continues to center on agents seen outside Mount Carmel before and during the fire, such as the agents seen gassing the tornado shelter in the morning, the alleged agent seen walking in front of the building as the tank finishes smashing in the front doors, and agents alleged to be wearing Scott breathing apparatus who were outside their tanks capturing Davidians during the fire.

"Systematic" Gunfire Heard During the Fire

In the FBI SWAT team video contained in "Waco, the Big Lie Continues," sounds of systematic gunfire are heard at approximately 12:15 P.M. while most of the building is still standing. The Justice report mentions FBI agents heard "systematic gunfire" at around 12:25 P.M. and "a distinct pattern of gunfire from inside the compound at approximately 12:30 A.M., when only a small portion of the structure remained intact."[89] Since the bodies of Davidians who committed suicide were found in a number of locations and most bodies had only one wound, it is unlikely that Davidian suicides could have produced "systematic" gunfire in any "distinct pattern." However, such gunfire could have been produced by FBI agents shooting in at Davidians.

Justice Department's Immediate Claim Davidians Shot

Some find it suspicious that three days before the medical examiner released any findings that Davidians had died of gunshot wounds, Justice Department Director of Public Affairs Carl Stern announced to the press that two bodies bore bullet wounds to the head. On April 21, 1993, Stern claimed one victim was "virtually blown away" and that the clothing of one man allegedly shot in the ear was "singed, indicating that he was trying to flee the fire." (Of course, this might also be evidence FBI snipers shot the escaping man.)[90]

The very next day medical examiner Nizaam Peerwani said he had "no evidence" of the wounds and that autopsies had not been completed. Texas Governor Ann Richards' spokesperson Chuck McDonald expressed dismay about the Justice Department's hasty conclusions.[91] It was not until April 24 that Peerwani first confirmed that any bodies bore gunshot wounds—a man and woman on top of the concrete room.[92] Some wonder how the Justice Department knew Davidians had gunshot wounds even before the medical examiner announced the fact.

Questions About Some Autopsy Results

Three bodies the government states were found in the kitchen/serving area have prompted some suspicion. Phillip Henry's official autopsy revealed he had two major gunshots, in the chest and head. A 9-millimeter bullet was found in his body, like those used by law enforcement, but it had "insufficient detail for comparison of bullet." Mary Ann

Borst, who was found in front of the concrete room, died of gunshot wounds to the back, something that would not be expected in a suicide or mercy killing.

Jimmy Riddle, who had been shot in the head, also was found in the kitchen/serving area. He was identified through finger prints, something that one would assume would be obliterated by fire. (Two women buried under debris in the concrete room also were identified through fingerprints.)[93] If Riddle had been killed outside and his body bulldozed back into the fire, it might well have been less damaged than those inside the building for the duration of the fire.

There have been persistent rumors that FBI snipers entered Mount Carmel and shot David Koresh and Steve Schneider. These rumors are disproved by Davidians who say they saw them right before the fire. Because Koresh was shot in the forehead, "execution style," and Schneider in the mouth, "suicide style," Dr. Peerwani surmised that Steve Schneider killed David Koresh and then himself—in the first floor communications room. FBI agents and news reporters would go on to repeat this "suicide pact" story—without mentioning that both had carbon monoxide in their systems and were trapped on the second floor.[94]

Other Evidence and Allegations

There have been rumors that fire survivor Derek Lovelock claimed that Davidians trying to exit the back were shot down. Prosecutors let Lovelock return to England when he promised he would testify as a prosecution witness; but the government never requested he return. Some believe prosecutors feared he would repeat that allegation on the stand.[95]

Graeme Craddock told the grand jury that as he exited the chapel window, "I heard these gunshots being fired, I didn't know what reason. I knew they were coming from somewhere."[96] His inability to pinpoint the gunfire creates suspicions that some came from FBI snipers.

Shortly after the fire, famed pathologist Cyril H. Wecht conducted an independent autopsy on the bodies of Koresh and Steve Schneider. Wecht fed the sniper rumor when he stated that because Koresh's bullet wound was in the middle of the forehead, he did not "'rule out' the possibility that Koresh and Schneider were shot by outside snipers."[97] Also, Wecht claimed Schneider's bullet wound was in the back of the head, indicating "he did not shoot himself."

Ramsey Clark's civil lawsuit alleges that not only did the FBI incapacitate Davidians with CS gas, but FBI agents then entered the building and shot Davidians. Clark himself told a reporter that agents "walked in there after the fire had started and shot people, some of whom were alive, on the ground."[98] However, survivor testimony contradicts this theory. Considering all the above, it is likely speculation will continue that agents shot Davidians either inside or outside the building.

AUTOPSY RESULTS

Davidians claim that seventy-six people, including two unborn children, died during the fire. The following table shows the results of medical examiner Nizaam Peerwani and staff's autopsies of those who died in the fire as of mid-1994.[99]

Because of other errors in autopsies, all this information remains suspect.

I have grouped autopsy results according to cause of death and location of body. Not all numbers originally assigned were eventually connected to individuals. Because parts of the same body were sometimes given more than one number, there are more numbers than people who actually died in this listing. (Because I did not have access to all final autopsy reports, this listing is incomplete. According to Davidian survivors, after final autopsies, two Martin and two Martinez children were not specifically identified before burial.)

Note that "bunker" is the above ground concrete room and "auditorium" is probably the gymnasium. Also, many of those listed as having died in the first floor kitchen/ serving area, in the communications room, or in front of the "bunker" may in fact have died trapped on the second floor. Therefore, a question mark has been placed beside these locations.

Table 11-1

INCOMPLETE AUTOPSY FINDINGS			
#29	B. Elliot	F, 31	1st Fl. Hallway?	Burns/Smoke
#3	F. Houtman	M, 61	Auditorium	Burns/Smoke
#6	W. Martin	M, 42	Auditorium	Burns/Smoke
#4	S. Sonobe	M, 35	Auditorium	Burns/Smoke
#40	G. Summers	M, 28	Top Bunker	Burns
#36	D. Jones	M, 38	Top Bunker	Burns
#38	R. Saipaia	F, 24	Top Bunker	Burns
#15	A. Davis	M, 30	Kit/Serving?	Burns
#5	M. Wendel	M, 37	Comm. Room?	Burns
#8	D. Koresh	M, 33	Comm. Room?	Gunshot/head
#7	S. Schneider	M, 48	Comm. Room?	Gunshot mouth
#31A	A. Gyrfas Summers	F, 17	In Bunker	Gunshot/chest
#31B	Gyrfas fetus		In Bunker	Maternal demise
#56	A. Martinez	F, 11	In Bunker	Gunshot/head
#47A	N. Gent	F, 24	In Bunker	Gunshot/head
#47B	Gent fetus		In Bunker	Maternal demise
#66	L. Sylvia	F, 40	In Bunker	Gunshot/back, thorax
#53		F, 5-6	In Bunker	Gunshot/left chest
#67-8		?, 1	In Bunker	Gunshot/head
#34	F. Sonobe	F, 34	In Bunker	Gunshot/head
#35	S. Doyle	F, 18	In Bunker	Gunshot/head
#45	M. Borst	F, 38	Front bunker?	Gunshot/back
#20	J. Riddle	M, 32	Kitchen?	Gunshot/forehead
#43	L. Farris	F, 24	Kit/Serving?	Gunshot/head
#44	J. Little	M, 28	Kit/Serving?	Gunshot/left chest
#21	P. Henry	M, 22	Kit/Serving?	Gunshot/chest/head
#22	S. Henry	M, 26	Kit/Serving?	Gunshot/forehead
#39	N. Hipsman	F, 36	Top Bunker	Gunshot/head/chest
#41	N. Vaega	M, 36	Top Bunker	Gunshot/head
#37	A. Bennet	M, 35	Top Bunker	Smoke/CO
#27	D. Fagan	F, 60	1st Fl. Hallway?	Smoke/CO
#25	Y. Fagan	F, 30	1st Fl. Hallway?	Smoke/CO
#24	B. Monbelly	F, 31	1st Fl. Hallway?	Smoke/CO
#26		F, 15-19	1st Fl. Hallway?	Smoke/CO
#28		F, 50	1st Fl. Hallway?	Smoke/CO
#42	P. Cohen	M, 28	Top Bunker	Smoke/CO
#23	S. Benta	F, 31	Kit/Serving?	Smoke/CO
#10	S. Murray	F, 29	Kit/Serving?	Smoke/CO

INCOMPLETE AUTOPSY FINDINGS

#	Name	Sex, Age	Location	Cause
#9	C. Sellors	M, 50	Kit/Serving?	Smoke/CO
#11	S. Jewell	F, 42	Kit/Serving?	Smoke/CO
#14		F, 30-39	Kit/Serving?	Smoke/CO
#16		F, 22-28	Kit/Serving?	Smoke/CO
#17		F, 22-40	Kit/Serving?	Smoke/CO
#18		F, 17-35	Kit/Serving?	Smoke/CO
#19	T. Norbrega	F, 48	Kit/Serving?	Smoke/CO
#12	J. Andrade	F, 19	Front bunker?	Smoke/CO
#71	M. Jones Thibodeau	F, 28,	Front bunker?	Smoke/CO
#2	L. Malcolm	M, 26	Stage/chapel	Smoke/CO
#1	R. Friesen	M, 76	Stage/chapel	Smoke/CO
#51A	M. Schneider	F, 2	In Bunker	Smoke/CO
#54	J. Martinez	F, 30	In Bunker	Smoke/CO
#52	J. Martinez	M, 8	In Bunker	Smoke/CO
#30	K. Andrade	F, 24	In Bunker	Smoke/CO
#49	M. Wayne Jr.	M, 20	In Bunker	Smoke/CO
#32	J. McBean	M, 27	In Bunker	Smoke/CO
#64		F, 1	In Bunker	Smoke/CO
#65	H. Sylvia	F, 1	In Bunker	Smoke/CO
#67-1		F, 5-6	In Bunker	Smoke/CO
#67-4	B. Koresh	M, 1	In Bunker	Smoke/CO
#67-5	P. Gent	F, 1	In Bunker	Smoke/CO
#69		?, 1	In Bunker	Smoke/CO
#72		F, 4-5	In Bunker	Smoke/CO
#73		?, 1	In Bunker	Smoke/CO
#75		F, 25-35	In Bunker	Smoke/CO
#57	S. Koresh	F, 6	In Bunker	Suffocation
#67-2	C. Koresh	M, 8	In Bunker	Suffocation
#67-6	R. Sylvia	F, 13	In Bunker	Suffocation
#70	C. Andrade	F, 1	In Bunker	Suffocation
#51B	J. Schneider	F, 41	In Bunker	Suffocation/buried
#67-3	R. Koresh	F, 24	In Bunker	Suffocation/buried
#61	R. Morrison	F, 29	In Bunker	Suffocation/buried
#55	A. Martinez	F, 12	In Bunker	Suffocation/buried
#59		F, 14-19	In Bunker	Trauma/Head
#63	Jones twin	F, 1	In Bunker	Trauma/Head
#13	D. Martin	F, 41	Front bunker	Trauma/Fall
#33	D. Gent	M, 3	In Bunker	Stabbed/(or trauma)
#74		F, 7-8	In Bunker	Unknown

Chapter Eleven: FBI Tank Attacks
Led to Fire and Death

1. June 16, 1995 trial transcript: 136–137.
2. Clive Doyle and Rick Sherrow, private communication, May, 1995.
3. *Newsweek*, May 3, 1993: 25; Clive Doyle, private communication, May, 1995.
4. Trial transcript: 6624, 6376.
5. Mary Jordan and Sue Anne Pressley, "Examiners Work to Identify Bodies," *Washington Post*, April 23, 1993.
6. Trial transcript: 6370; Clive Doyle, private communication, August, 1994.
7. David Thibodeau interview, "Current Affair," May 3, 1993.
8. Justice Department report: 231; Fire report: 9.
9. Trial transcript, 5897–98.
10. Ibid., 5819–22.
11. Justice Department report: 330–31.
12. Ibid., 294.
13. Trial transcript: 5926–28.
14. Justice Department report, Fire report: 5.
15. Michael Rezendes, "2 versions emerge of disaster at cult compound," *Boston Sunday Globe*, April 25, 1993: A12.
16. Jaime Castillo, private communication, January, 1995.
17. David Thibodeau, private communication, May, 1995.
18. Associated Press wire story, April 22, 1993, 08:26 EDT.
19. Rick Sherrow, private communication, May, 1995.
20. Justice Department report: 294.
21. Trial transcript: 6370–73; Clive Doyle, private communication, May, 1995.
22. Ibid., 5907.
23. James L. Pate, "Government's Waco Whitewash Continues," *Soldier of Fortune*, February, 1994: 56.
24. Trial transcript: 5839–40, 5861, 5884–85.
25. Trial transcript, 5940, 5942, 5944, 5946.
26. Ibid., 5019.
27. Ibid., 5862.

28.   Sue Ann Pressley and Mary Jordan, April 23, 1993: A16; Mary Jordan and Sue Anne Pressley, "40 Bodies Found in Waco Ruins," *Washington Post*, April 22, 1993: A16.

29.   Ibid., 6212–13.

30.   Justice Department report: 294.

31.   Ibid., 837; Caddell and Conwell lawsuit (February 25, 1995): 55; Clark lawsuit: 43; Gordon Novel, private communication, March, 1995; Rick Sherrow, private communication, May, 1995.

32.   Trial transcript: 5162, 5322, 5332.

33.   Ibid., 5039, 5121, 5189.

34.   Ibid., 5839–40, 5884–85; April, 1995.

35.   Ibid., 5505–08, 5578.

36.   Ramsey Clark lawsuit: 44.

37.   Erik Larson, "High-Heat Arson Fires Swiftly Raze Buildings But Leave Few Clues," *Wall Street Journal*, October 7, 1993: A1.

38.   Justice Department report: 304–07.

39.   Louis Sahagun and J. Michael Kennedy, April 21, 1993: A6.

40.   Justice Department report: 296.

41.   Reuters wire story, "Davidian started fire, agent testifies," *Washington Times*, February 8, 1994; trial transcript: 5242.

42.   Trial transcript: 5433.

43.   Justice Department report: 300.

44.   Sam Howe Verhovek, April 21, 1993: A1.

45.   Trial transcript: 5483–93.

46.   Justice Department report: 300.

47.   Clive Doyle, private communication, August, 1994.

48.   Justice Department report: 300–01.

49.   Trial transcript: 6371–72; Graeme Craddock, private communication, January, 1995.

50.   Marjorie Thomas testimony, November 17–18, 1993: 189.

51.   "Prosecution Completes Case Against 11 Koresh Followers," *New York Times*, February 16, 1994; trial transcript: 6305.

52.   "Tape Transcripts from Agents' Bug Indicate Fire Plans," *San Antonio Express*, February 15, 1994; Paul McKay, February 15, 1994.

53.   Trial transcript: 6243.

54.   Diana R. Fuentes, "Davidian Told Grand Jury of Arming before the Raid," February 16, 1994: 4A.

55.   Ken Fawcett, James Pate, Jack DeVault, and Sarah Bain, private communication, June, 1994.

56. Trial transcript: 6195, 6293–96, 6327, 6350–64.
57. Kathy Fair, "Cult members 'executed' prosecutors say" *Houston Chronicle,* January 13, 1994: 6A.
58. Trial transcript: 6305–06.
59. Ibid., 6322–23, 6283.
60. Ibid., 6314–15.
61. Ibid., 6311.
62. Clive Doyle, private communication, August, 1994; Justice Department report: 300-01; trial transcript: 6212–13.
63. Trial transcript: 6292–96, 6304–10, 6326–27.
64. Ibid., 6200.
65. Ibid., 6228, 6237.
66. William Sessions on ABC news special "Waco: The Decision to Die," April 20, 1993.
67. Michael Rezendes, "2 versions emerge of disaster at cult compound," *Boston Sunday Globe*, April 25, 1993: 12.
68. Trial transcript: 7120–21.
69. Michael deCourcy Hinds, "For Experts, Fire Tapes Provide Rare Evidence," *New York Times*, April 28, 1993: A16.
70. *Washington Times*, April 23, 1993.
71. Marjorie Thomas testimony, November 17–18, 1995: 76.
72. Michael Rezendes, "2 versions emerge of disaster at cult compound," *Boston Sunday Globe*, April 25, 1993: 12.
73. David Thibodeau interview, "Current Affair," May 3, 1993.
74. "The Waco Incident" video; Jaime Castillo, private communication, January, 1995.
75. Mount Carmel Survivors "Mount Carmel Alert," June, 1994; Gordon Novel, private communication, January, 1995.
76. Trial transcripts, 5278, 5399.
77. Justice Department report: 298–99; private communications with survivors.
78. Renos Avraam, private communication, June, 1994; June 16, 1994 trial transcript: 134.
79. NBC "Dateline," June 15, 1993; trial transcript: 121.
80. "Inquest: 28 Davidians were shot," *Washington Times*, September 25, 1994.
81. Sue Anne Pressley and Mary Jordan, "Cultists May Have Been Forced to Stay," Washington Post , April 21, 1993: A1.
82. David Thibodeau interview, "Good Morning America," May 17, 1993.

83.   Ruth Riddle interview, NBC's "Dateline," June 15, 1993.

84.   Sam Howe Verhovek, "Investigators Puzzle Over Last Minutes of Koresh," *New York Times*, May 5, 1993: A18.

85.   Michael Hedges, "Search for corpses starts," *Washington Times*, April 22,1993: A1.

86.   "Mark Potok, "Davidian trial's hoopla mirrors strange case," *USA Today*, January 11, 1994: A3; "Court TV" newscaster reports January 10 and 11, 1993.

87.   Lee Hancock, "No easy answers, law authorities puzzle over methods to end Branch Davidians siege," *Dallas Morning News*, April 15, 1993.

88.   Michael McNulty, private communication, April, 1995.

89.   Justice Department report: 6, 298.

90.   Mary Jordan and Sue Anne Pressley, April 22, 1993: A1, A16.

91.   Mary Jordan and Sue Anne Pressley, "Examiners Work to Identify Bodies," *Washington Post,* April 23, 1993: A1.

92.   Mary Jordan and Sue Anne Pressley, " 'Gunshot Wounds to the Head' Killed 2 Found in Cult Compound," *Washington Post*, April 25, 1993: A20.

93.   Steven R. Reed, February 27, 1994: 21A; Justice Department report: 320–21.

94.   Sam Howe Verhovek, *New York Times*, February 27, 1994: A26; David Koresh autopsy, Nizaam Peerwani, M.D. and James O' Brien, M.D.; Steven Schneider autopsy, Charles M. Harvey, M.D. and Marc Krouse, M.D.

95.   Jack DeVault: 23.

96.   Trial transcript: 6372.

97.   Sue Anne Pressley, "Koresh Wound Not Typical of a Suicide, Doctor Says," *Washington Post*, May 18, 1993: A3.

98.   Evan Moore, "Law suit accuses FBI of shooting cultists, bombing compound," *Houston Chronicle*, February 28, 1995; Ramsey Clark lawsuit: 43.

99.   Justice Department report: 313–28; trial transcript: 5970–85; Mark England, February 16, 1994; 40 final autopsy reports.

12

The FBI-Justice Department-White House Cover-up

> *This is a systematic character assassination by the FBI to eliminate all of the crime scene. What they're doing is, they're destroying the crime scene. This is the biggest lie ever put before the American people! Bill Clinton wants to use a scapegoat, like the attorney general [does]. I don't buy it!*
>
> **Brad Branch as Mount Carmel burned**[1]

Throughout these last chapters, ample evidence has been presented that the FBI and Justice Department seemingly lied to the public and covered up crimes against the Branch Davidians—crimes which still could lead to criminal charges against some agents and officials for excessive use of force, conspiracy to violate civil rights, obstruction of justice, and negligent or even intentional homicide. In this chapter more evidence of a systematic cover up by these agencies and by the Clinton White House will be presented.

FBI POST-FIRE DISINFORMATION

Jack Zimmermann laments, "Within thirty-five minutes, the Justice Department announced from Washington that two 'cultists' <u>confessed to starting the fire.</u> That Monday night . . . the truth was released: <u>No one</u> had confessed to any such thing. How many heard the retraction?"[2] And indeed this was reported on CNN while the fire was still smoldering: "A spokesman for Attorney General Janet Reno says that . . . two of those cult members have admitted that they are the ones who started the fire." This was just one of many examples of self-serving FBI and Justice Department disinformation released immediately after the fire.

During SAC Bob Ricks' April 19 pre-fire press briefing and post-fire press conference and SAC Jeff Jamar's April 20 press conference, the agents spewed forth some of the most outrageous disinformation. These included already described lies that Koresh never intended to write his book, Steve Schneider threw the phone outside the building, Davidians fired hundreds of rounds at tanks, the FBI was unable to fix the phones, agents watched Davidians start the fire, Davidians confessed to starting the fire, and Davidians shot those trying to escape.

Ricks also asserted that Koresh "wanted to have as many people killed as possible. That's why it was called Ranch Apocalypse." Ricks said Koresh "was demanding provocation to get in a fight with us. . . . We believe they were preparing for another armed standoff." Ricks repeatedly speculated that "the children had been injected with some kind of poison to ease their pain."

Ricks also contradicted himself. During the morning briefing, Ricks stated that Davidians worldwide, as well as those who had left Mount Carmel, assured the FBI there would be no suicide pact. Right after the fire Ricks revealed for the first time that Davidians had discussed a suicide pact on March 2.

Ricks claimed that Koresh had "lied" when he supposedly had told the FBI that the children were safe in bunkers. "His last act to America was yet another lie." But several minutes later Ricks stated the contrary, "They bunkered down the kids the best they could. . . . We believed they were inside the cinder block room to protect themselves from the gas."

Ricks described the last big tank smashing deep into the building so that the FBI could put gas into the cinder block room: "We finally made entry into that area and gassed it." But just a few minutes later he denied this was any kind of assault. "We never went in."

In his press conference Jeff Jamar claimed David Koresh was not writing his book, that three people observed Davidians starting the fire, that Koresh had had the children killed, that Davidians killed others trying to escape. Ricks and Jamar both falsely claimed that FBI agents saved escaping Davidians from suicide. They claimed Renos Avraam stayed on the roof until he caught fire and was saved by FBI agents—even though video footage clearly shows him jump off and walk away unharmed and unaided. And they claimed that Ruth Riddle's attempt to escape FBI agents was a suicidal attempt to re-enter the burning building.

Ricks and Jamar sent their lies up the chain of command through then-Assistant Director of Criminal

Investigation Larry Potts. FBI Director William
Sessions repeated Ricks' and Jamars' disinformation in
April 19 and 20 CNN, ABC, and other interviews.
However, Sessions stressed that FBI experts and David
Koresh himself had told the FBI "he did not intend to
commit suicide," and the fire and the suicide were a
"surprise."[3]

During the 1993 House Judiciary Committee
hearing, FBI officials and agents continued the
disinformation campaign, repeating these stories and
others. At that time Ricks added the new charge that
when a released child heard his father and Koresh were
dead, he said, "I don't care. No more beatings." Ricks
said the children had asked if their new home had a
"beating room." However, social workers have not
revealed any such child's statement.

While the FBI has forbidden its agents to speak
to the press, in August, 1993, Bob Ricks charged at a
private meeting that Steve Schneider had shot Koresh
out of anger. "In the end, he probably realized he was
dealing with a fraud. After [Koresh] had caused so much
harm and destruction, he probably now wanted to come
out, and Mr. Schneider could not tolerate that situation."[4]
All this disinformation convinced the public the
Davidians were the suicidal maniacs the FBI wanted
Americans to believe they were.

On April 21, 1993, on "Larry King Live,"
Davidian David Thibodeau's attorney Gary Richardson
criticized the FBI's disinformation campaign: "I've dealt
with the FBI before, having been a former U.S. attorney.
I've worked with them and I've worked against them,
and the thing I do know . . . is that they are going to do

everything they possibly can to try to convince the public that they are justified in their actions. . . . They do things, and as a former U.S. attorney I can tell you, they do things and then they sweep them under the carpet and try to come out looking lily white."

RENO/CLINTON DISINFORMATION AFTER THE FIRE

In the days after the fire, Attorney General Janet Reno, President Clinton, and their representatives all emphasized "humanitarian" reasons for the assault, ones that presumably would play well with the public. However, they also blamed everything on David Koresh.

Reno Disinformation

Janet Reno began a media blitz where she explained the prime reasons for the assault were the "fatigue" of the Hostage Rescue Team and ongoing evidence that "babies were being beaten." However, in an April 20 briefing for reporters FBI Director William Sessions said his agency had "no contemporaneous evidence" of child abuse during the siege.[5] Reno quickly buckled under and confessed she had erred.

And she falsely claimed Davidians would not report on the children's welfare. On April 19, on ABC's "Nightline," Janet Reno claimed that despite the FBI's sending in video tapes, "We did not receive verification that the children were okay." She refused to admit what the Justice Department concedes, such tapes were sent out on March 8 and March 28.

Reno repeatedly asserted in her press conference and on several television programs: "I approved the plan. I am responsible. The buck stops here." Dick DeGuerin told a reporter, "I'm very pleased that we have an Attorney General, finally, after 12 years, who will accept responsibility. But it's *so* refreshing, it's such a *shock* to have that, that when she grabbed the blame for herself, it deflected any other inquiry. . . . [However, Reno] said, 'I'll take the blame, but it's all Koresh's fault.' Well, that's not really taking the blame."[6]

Janet Reno's public relations effort was extremely successful. Justice Department spokesperson Carl Stern asserted that while on April 19 the reaction from those who contacted the Justice Department was ten to one against the assault, on April 20, eight out of ten said they agreed with Janet Reno![7] Two *USA Today/ CNN/Gallup* polls taken right after the April 19 fire reflect the public reaction. In the first, only 13 percent of those responding objected to the February 28, 1993 BATF raid; 52 percent supported the raid.[8] And 93 percent of respondents backed the FBI's assault on the Branch Davidians, despite the fact that it ended in "an apparent mass suicide by fire."[9]

Clinton Disinformation

The press and public's harshest criticism of Bill Clinton was his not taking responsibility as quickly and definitively as did Janet Reno. According to Elizabeth Drew in her book *On the Edge: The Clinton Presidency,* Clinton originally tried to give the impression that he had heard about and approved the gassing plan only the day before it occurred. In fact it was days earlier, Wednesday, April 13, when Nussbaum and Lindsey told Clinton about the plan, before Reno even had approved it.[10]

During his April 20 press conference, Clinton finally took responsibility, and like Reno, he emphasized, "It's because of the children. They have evidence that those children are still being abused, and that they're in increasingly unsafe conditions."[11]   Of course, by the time Clinton made this statement, the children were all dead.

Clinton attacked Koresh. "The bureau's efforts were ultimately unavailing because the individual with whom they were dealing, David Koresh, was dangerous, irrational, and probably insane. . . . Mr. Koresh's response to the demands for his surrender by Federal agents was to destroy himself and murder the children who were his captives as well as all the other people there who did not survive."[12]

During the press conference Clinton growled that Janet Reno should not have to resign "because some religious fanatics murdered themselves." At a press conference two days later he asserted, "I do not think the United States government is responsible for the fact that a bunch of fanatics decided to kill themselves." According to Elizabeth Drew, Clinton tried to intimidate the press from asking any more questions about the FBI's actions when he belligerently answered one reporter's question: "We know that David Koresh had sex with children. Does anybody dispute that? Does anybody dispute that? Where I come from, that's child abuse."[13]

After the Oklahoma City bombing, Clinton again attacked Davidians, charging on CBS's "60 Minutes" on April 23, 1995, "Before that raid was carried out, those people murdered a bunch of innocent law-enforcement officials who worked for the federal government.... And when that [April 19] raid occurred, it was the people who ran their cult compound at Waco who murdered their own children. Not the federal officials. They made the decision to destroy all those children that were there."

Justice Department outside expert Alan A. Stone, M.D., criticized Clinton's statement, saying, "President Clinton seemed to argue on '60 Minutes' that the ultimate fate of the Branch Davidians weeks later, during the final gas assault by the FBI, was somehow morally justified by what happened to the ATF agents who were killed in the botched initial surprise assault."[14]

Why Have Reno and Clinton Supported the Cover up?

In its October 12, 1993, editorial, "The Waco Whitewash," the *New York Times* wrote, "the report is silent on the most glaring deficiency of the tragic episode: the lack of judgement at the top and the reasons for it." As the top law enforcement personnel in the nation, it is likely Clinton and Reno supported FBI officials' rationale—the maintenance of "law and order." Columnist Paul Craig Roberts commented, "If the Branch Davidians could hold out, others might get the same idea. Heavens, people might stop paying their taxes. There was too much rebellion in the defiance of authority."[15]

Moreover, Clinton and Reno doubtless needed to cover up their own inexperience and incompetence in dealing with aggressive and devious FBI officials and agents. Former Black Panther Eldridge Cleaver writes: "The sin of Clinton and Reno is not that they conceived and perpetrated this dastardly carnage, but that their response to it was that of weak rulers who are captives of the power they are supposed to wield, as opposed to the masters of power, who would have pulled the plugs, kicked ass from Washington to Waco, and rolled bureaucratic heads for days. Clinton and Reno closed ranks with their culpable underlings, as is the wont of tyrants, even though these particular underlings were hangers-on from the Reagan/Bush regime. They sided with the power perpetrators against their weak and powerless victims."[16]

Finally, we cannot discount the possibility the BATF, and especially the FBI, intimidated both Clinton and Reno into covering up for their crimes. The FBI probably has a good deal of "dirt" on Bill Clinton and his friends. Treasury Department reviewer Henry S. Ruth, Jr., a former Watergate prosecutor, told a national television audience that the FBI has not been "held accountable, in the way other agencies have been held accountable. And part of this again goes back to the magic of J. Edgar Hoover and the mystique he created and the fear he created among the political apparatus in Washington."[17]

FBI AND BATF CRIME SCENE COVER-UP

The FBI's disregard for preserving the "crime scene" only increased after the April 19 fire. The BATF was deeply involved in this cover-up.

April 19 Destruction of Evidence

By now it seems clear that the FBI's gas and tank attacks themselves were a successful effort to cause massive destruction and destroy evidence. The FBI claims that once the fire started it held back the fire engines in order to protect fire personnel from Davidian gunfire. However, it is more likely that they wanted to ensure that Mount Carmel—and all its bullet-pocked walls and roofs—was completely burned and destroyed before allowing fire trucks near it.

Just to make sure no evidence survived, FBI tanks plowed it into the fire. CNN news footage shows tanks pushing the last standing two-story wall into the fire. Network footage replayed in both "Waco, the Big Lie" videos clearly shows several tanks equipped with bulldozer blades repeatedly and systematically pushing the remaining debris into the flaming rubble.

Despite questions from the press and attorneys, the FBI has never bothered to give the American people an explanation for this systematic destruction of evidence. In response to a defense attorney's question at trial, R. J. Craig explained that at one point he was "dragging burning timber out of the area" of the buried bus in case anyone was trying to escape down into it.[18]

FBI and BATF Really Controlled the Crime Scene

While Texas Rangers, who had been deputized as federal marshals by U.S. attorneys, were technically in control of the "crime scene" after the fire, it is clear FBI agents were really in control. News footage shows FBI and BATF agents and other uniformed personnel all over the scene right after the fire. At trial, Texas Ranger David Byrnes, who was in charge of the investigation, revealed that Rangers started taking over the scene "around 3:00 P.M.," two hours after the fire was over.[19]

The Justice report admits the FBI provided substantial assistance to the Texas Rangers in combing through the crime scene and collecting evidence.[20] The

Justice report reveals that one BATF firearms and explosives expert collected evidence after the fire; the Treasury report mentions several.[21]

At trial, Texas Ranger Fred Cummings acknowledged the BATF bomb squad was there on April 19 and 20. Cummings also revealed FBI laboratory people helped him decide what evidence was significant enough to be collected, as opposed to being thrown in the big trash dumpster. Cummings revealed the trash was hauled off before defense attorneys had the opportunity to inspect it.[22] During CNN coverage of Bob Ricks' afternoon press conference, a live video feed from the site showed a large "U-Haul" truck pull up to the smoking ruins. At trial this was revealed to be an FBI-rented truck for removing evidence.[23] We only can wonder how much important evidence of BATF and FBI crimes ended up in the dumpster or the U-Haul truck.

Texas Rangers were not sufficiently careful in overseeing collection of evidence. As we have seen, some evidence, like half of the two front doors and the phone line, was never found. The small building next to the water tower was not checked for evidence until April 25, six days after the fire—and after Graeme Craddock told authorities he had left a possibly live grenade there. Another allegedly live grenade was found in clothing left by Davidians an entire day after yet another allegedly live grenade was found in nearby clothing.

FBI or BATF agents even stole valuables from the ruins. Texas Ranger Johnny Waldrip confirmed that after the fire, Rangers found an unopened church safe containing more than $50,000 in cash, gold coins, spools of platinum, and personal valuables. Rangers turned the safe over to the FBI—but it never showed up on the FBI evidence list.[24]

Defense attorney Dan Cogdell commented that it was mere "window dressing" to have the Texas Rangers put in charge of the criminal investigation. "It's stretching it to say they are bringing any kind of true independent judgement. They are in charge, but federal agents are dissecting the crime scene and cross-checking all the evidence."[25]

Whatever little separation there was between state and federal officials quickly ended. The *New York Times* reported that in "an apparent shift in policy" the evidence from Mount Carmel would be shipped to FBI laboratories. The *Times* noted that originally officials conducting the fire investigation "said that they were using private laboratories in an effort to avoid any appearance of conflict of interest that might arise from a federal laboratory making conclusions about evidence in a case in which federal agents' actions were being questioned." The Texas Ranger spokesperson told him "if you are concerned about a conflict of interest, you should talk to the U.S. Attorney's office." However, when he tried to do so, Justice Department spokesperson Carl Stern told him, "All the shifts in police [sic] I know of, are the ones you invented."[26] At trial, FBI weapons expert James Cadigan conceded that the Texas Rangers did in fact have facilities adequate to analyze all information.[27]

May 12, 1993, Bulldozing of Remaining Evidence

Two weeks after the release of the "independent" fire investigators' report, but before Branch Davidian attorneys could send in their own fire investigators, bulldozers rolled across the burned rubble of Mount Carmel Center. SAC Jeff Jamar defended this action. "They're just filling holes so people won't fall in the pits. That's just part of taking care of the scene." Texas Rangers said bulldozing was necessary so the Texas Health and Water departments could begin work at the site. However, the Department did not do the work until the summer of 1994.

Bulldozers also smashed and crumbled the concrete room, destroying evidence that a roof cave-in killed several people, and moved around what little evidence remained. Attorney Jack Zimmermann said, "I guess what it does, it forever prevents any checking on the ATF's rendition that the fire was intentionally set."[28] Defense Attorney Jeff Kearney told reporters, "Government can say what they want now and there's little physical evidence to dispute it."[29]

July, 1994 Cleanup of Property

The Texas Natural Resource Conservation Commission delayed cleaning up Mount Carmel, including removing several inches of topsoil allegedly contaminated with lead from bullets, until mid-1994. In the spring of 1994, KPOC-TV investigators discovered that the autopsy reports of forty-eight Davidians revealed lethal doses of cyanide. Noting that cyanide is a byproduct of burning CS gas, Davidians obtained a court order allowing them to obtain soil samples from Mount Carmel just days before the soil—possible evidence of FBI crimes—was to be removed. Details of the findings were not available at publication.

FIRE INVESTIGATION COVER-UP

The Justice report asserts that Texas Rangers assembled a team of independent fire investigators to determine the cause of the fire.[30] However, at trial Captain David Byrnes, head of the Texas Rangers' investigation, testified that he himself did not put the fire investigation team together. Considering that he was deputized by and working for the U.S. attorneys office, we must assume someone in that office actually chose the fire investigation team.[31]

Head of Team Was BATF Sympathizer

The head of the supposedly independent fire investigation team was Paul C. Gray, assistant chief of the Houston Fire Department. However, Gray had close ties to the BATF. He had served as a member of the BATF's National Arson Response Team and taught classes for the BATF agents. And his wife was a secretary in the BATF's Houston office. Not surprisingly, BATF officials recommended him for the job.[32] At trial fire investigator Bill Cass stated he also had worked with the BATF in previous fire investigations.[33]

Attorney Jack Zimmermann revealed, "From 1982 to 1990, [Gray's] office was on Imperial Valley Drive, in the ATF office. . . . He carried a card that identified himself as a special agent of ATF. He handed that card out to people when he interviewed witnesses."[34] Finally, Gray had socialized with BATF agent Steve Willis, who was killed February 28, and attended his funeral.[35]

Zimmermann writes that Paul Gray asked Zimmermann and Dick DeGuerin to aid in his investigation. The attorneys told Gray that because of his close ties to the BATF they could not participate unless Texas Rangers asked them to do so. Otherwise, "Dick DeGuerin and I would not lend our credibility to the anticipated report." In response, Gray called an unscheduled press conference for that same day and announced that the fire was started by the "cultists."[36]

Zimmermann immediately criticized Gray's conclusion that Davidians set the fires. "Until I see the evidence from an independent, impartial expert, I choose to believe the firsthand account of eyewitnesses who were in the center who said there was no fire started by the Branch Davidians."[37]

Gray Withheld Evidence From Other Investigators

At trial Bill Cass, one of the three fire investigators called to the stand, revealed that Paul Gray actually had withheld from other members of the fire investigation team important evidence that a fire started in the gymnasium. Gray showed investigators infrared video taken only from noon on, evidently not showing them the 11:59:16 A.M. photograph which displays an obvious heat plume in the gymnasium. Cass acknowledged that he had not noticed—and Gray had not pointed out to other investigators—the 12:08:17 and 12:08:22 P.M. flashes in the window of the gymnasium's dog run. Gray also withheld from investigators the fact that the official FBI log entries revealed that FBI observers reported seeing fire at the back of Mount Carmel Center right after tanks collapsed the gymnasium.[38]

Cass revealed that Gray, who took responsibility for investigating the flammability of CS gas, did not tell other investigators that manufacturers warn the gas is flammable. The fire report, based on Paul Gray's "research," repeatedly misidentifies the gas used as the more toxic "CN" gas. And Gray asserts, "We are of the opinion that this fire was not caused by nor was it intensified by any chemicals present in the tear-gassing operation."[39]

Cass confessed that he personally had not made a time study of the fire's start or progression and relied on Gray's interpretation.[40] Gray's withholding evidence suggests that the government believes it was the action of its tanks that started the fire in the gymnasium.

Under cross-examination fire investigator Andrew Armstrong conceded that he took Gray's word for it that clothing, wood, carpet, and other samples he tested for flammables did in fact come from the area Gray claimed they did.[41] Finally, fire investigator James Quintiere confessed that while he met with other investigators right after the fire in Waco, he did not read any of their reports or use them to draw his conclusions about the spread of the fire. He did not reveal if this was because Gray withheld such information from him.[42]

Gray never directed investigators to interview fire survivors, something done routinely in other fires. At trial fire investigator Bill Cass admitted he had not spoken to any survivors, including David Thibodeau or Derek Lovelock, two fire survivors who were not under indictment. However, he did speak to Davidian Donald Bunds who was cooperating with authorities but was not at Mount Carmel during the siege or fire. When asked if he had spoken to survivors, investigator James Quintiere said, "absolutely not."[43]

Fire Report Distorted Evidence

Despite the video footage of the damage to the building done by tanks and the extensive survivor testimony to their attorneys about people being trapped by falling debris, blocked stairways, caved-in walls, and rapidly spreading smoke and fire, the fire report concludes: "Considering the observable means of exit available, we must assume that many of the occupants were either denied escape from within or refused to leave until escape was not an option."[44]

The fire report notes that fuel containers were found in the ruins, and flammable liquids were found on survivors shoes and clothes, without mentioning that Davidians were dependent on flammable fuel after the FBI turned off electricity and that it was spilled during the April 19 raid. It infers that any flammables found at the scene were present only for purposes of arson.[45]

The fire report attempts to debunk what it calls "another theoretical explanation reported by the media," i.e., that tanks rupturing "a propane cylinder or flammable liquid container" started the fire. It does not reveal that survivors blamed tanks knocking over lanterns. The fire report claims, "if this had happened, an immediate vapor air explosion or flash fire would have occurred involving the vehicle itself. It did not happen."[46] However, the report ignores the possibility that tanks smashing down walls and pushing around debris could knock over a lantern without coming into contact with any fire caused by the accident.

The report states, "This investigation establishes that these fires occurred in areas significantly distant from each other and in a time frame that precludes any assumption of a single ignition source or accidental cause."[47] In his April 26, 1993, press conference, Gray told reporters, "We believe it was intentionally set by persons inside the compound."[48]

However, Gray and the fire report deny the obvious: that a last barrage of tank attacks occurred in separate locations within the three-minute period during which the fires began; that even one fifty-ton tank smashing deep inside a rickety wooden building filled with dozens of lighted lanterns could start two or three fires in separated parts of a building; and that one fire could have raced around a flammable-laden building filled with natural flues.   At trial, fire investigator Bill Cass admitted he never before had to take into consideration the effect of several fifty-ton tanks smashing repeatedly into a home within a five-minute period.[49]

During his press conference, Paul Gray claimed, "I do believe that a person could have survived the fire. I could speculate that there was ample room in the open pit area for everybody to have gotten into."[50] However, this statement directly contradicts what Gray put in his own report regarding the buried bus that served as a tunnel to the open pit or tornado shelter: "It is also possible that the escape route planned included the aforementioned tunnel system accessible through an opening in the floor at the west end of the building. A significant amount of structural debris was found in this area indicating that the breaching operations could have caused this route to be blocked."[51]

JUSTICE DEPARTMENT COVER-UP

Justice Department officials—especially Attorney General Janet Reno and Webster Hubbell— were involved much more deeply in the disastrous decisions at Waco than were their Treasury Department counterparts who approved the original BATF raid. And their actions resulted in far more deaths—seventy-six people, twenty-three of them children. Moreover, President Clinton approved the April 19 assault "on the record" and may have had "off the record" communications with Webster Hubbell and others. Therefore, the Clinton White House and the Justice Department were motivated to conduct a much more systematic cover up of errors and crimes than was the Treasury Department.

Possible Cover-up of Clinton's Role

As mentioned previously, President Bill Clinton's close friends Assistant to the Attorney General Webster Hubbell, Deputy Secretary of the Treasury Roger Altman, White House Counsel Bernard Nussbaum, and Deputy Counsel Vince Foster all were involved in Waco decision-making. Vince Foster committed suicide in July, 1993. The other three have resigned because of investigations into possible illegal Clinton fundraising and business dealings associated with the Madison Guaranty Savings and Loan Association and the Whitewater Development Corporation—the "Whitewater" affair.

Despite several in-depth media investigations of Foster's death, it was not until May of 1995, an FBI interview was released in which Foster's widow admitted that the standoff in Waco had caused Foster "a great deal of stress," that he was "horrified" by the outcome and that he thought it was "his fault."[52] This puts a new light on his claim that "the FBI lied in their report" to Janet Reno, since he may have been referring to their tricking her into approving their gassing plan. It also raises questions about whether any Waco-related files secretly were removed from Foster's office after his death.

In the summer of 1994 it was revealed that Roger Altman had alerted his close friend Bill Clinton to the status of "Whitewater" investigations as early as March, 1993—despite his earlier assertions to Congress that he knew nothing about efforts to alert Clinton until late 1993. Because so many believed Altman lied to Congress to cover up for his crony Clinton, he resigned his Treasury Department position in August, 1994. Clinton then gave Altman a low visibility White House job.[53]

On December 6, 1994, Independent Counsel Kenneth Starr announced that Webster Hubbell had pled guilty to defrauding Rose law firm clients, including two government agencies, of $390,000 through "phony expenses and inflated fees." Facing up to ten years in prison for his crimes, Hubbell cooperated with the Independent Counsel in the separate Whitewater investigation.

FBI background checks on Hubbell before his confirmation, which were ongoing during the siege at Waco, supposedly turned up nothing about the law firm's allegations against Hubbell—even though these were several months old. The FBI "will likely do an internal review" as to why the background check did not reveal this information. We must wonder if this is some of the "dirt" FBI agents or officials held back to bully Hubbell and Clinton into condoning and covering up for the massacre of the Davidians.[54]

Presidential Advisor Bruce Lindsey, who also was involved in Waco decision-making, was a senior partner at a law firm which received hundreds of thousands of dollars in bond counsel fees from the Arkansas Development Finance Authority. Allegedly doing business with the Authority was a form of "payoff" for Clinton supporters. Whitewater independent counsel Kenneth Starr considered, but declined, to indict Lindsey for violating federal banking laws.[55]

Many suspect that Clinton-Altman-Hubbell-Foster-Lindsey cronyism might extend to covering up errors or crimes related to the massacre of the Davidians, such as whether Altman conveyed any secret messages from BATF raid leader Bill Buford to Clinton; whether Hubbell had some outside-the-chain-of-command contact with Clinton throughout the siege and on April 19; whether Hubbell helped withhold David Koresh's April 14 promise-to-surrender letter from Reno; whether Hubbell, Foster, and Lindsey had any improper role in Waco decision-making; whether Hubbell knew about possible Davidian plans to pursue a fiery defense against tanks; and whether Hubbell approved the decision to proceed with the demolition that led to the April 19 fire.

Justice Department Attempted to Forgo Full Investigation

President Clinton appointed Phillip B. Heymann, a Harvard Law School professor who had been nominated to be Deputy Attorney General, to lead the Justice Department investigation. However, in May, 1993, the *New York Times* reported that the not-yet-confirmed Heymann told an interviewer that investigators would not look at the decision to assault Mount Carmel with tanks and tear gas and that "Department officials have not yet decided whether even to pose questions to Ms. Reno." Heymann stated the report would not "be the ultimate truth about what happened." Other unnamed officials "concluded that nothing could be gained by looking more closely at her order to carry out the assault."[56]

The day after the story appeared, and after several congressional representatives criticized this revelation, the Justice Department contended that Heymann "had erred" and that there would be a full investigation. The most revealing reason given was that Heymann's "remarks reflected a division within the Justice Department about how closely it should look at the events, with some high officials arguing forcefully that the inquiry should be more limited, to focus only on what should be done in future cases."[57]

Review Team and Outside Expert Conflicts of Interest

It is questionable whether Deputy Attorney General Heymann or Assistant to the Attorney General Richard Scruggs, working as they did under Attorney General Janet Reno, could do any independent investigation of errors in Justice Department or FBI decision-making or actions. The most noted conflict of interest was Heymann's appointing another former head of the Justice Department's Criminal Division, Edward S. G. Dennis, Jr., to be the chief reviewer of the government's procedures, decisions, and actions in Waco. (Dennis also oversaw the investigation of the Philadelphia police department's bombing of MOVE in 1985.) This choice came under scathing attack by William Safire who noted that Dennis was in charge of the botched investigation of Banca Lavoro and its relation to Iraq-gate: "Ms. Reno's Criminal Division directed Atlanta prosecutors to shoot down the explosive case with a plea bargain, avoiding a public trial that would have exposed the machinations of the Bush-Thornburgh-Dennis crowd. How could Ed Dennis not be grateful? His judgment about the Waco fiasco: 'there is no place in the evaluation for blame, and I find no fault.' One hand whitewashes the other."[58]

No Testimony Taken Under Oath

Deputy Attorney General Phillip B. Heymann told reporters the review group did "not have the authority to issue subpoenas or grant immunity but could refer findings of wrongdoing for criminal prosecution."[59] Presumably, this means that agents and officials were not interviewed under oath. The Justice Department report makes no reference at all to these issues. Some FBI agents or officials who testified before congressional committees were not sworn in, and they still could be prosecuted were it proved they had lied to Congress.

Review Team Withheld Information From Outside Experts

The Justice Department review team withheld damaging information from the Justice Department's panel of ten outside experts and even from its chief overseer, Edward Dennis. This included, of course, all and any previously mentioned missing physical evidence and withheld audio and video tapes. This also included information about CS gas, the early March memoranda prepared by FBI experts Smerick and Young advising the FBI not to harass the Branch Davidians, and David Koresh's April 14, 1993, promise-to-surrender letter.

Alan Stone complained to one reporter that when he asked for information on CS gas, the FBI provided him only "ambiguous and irrelevant material . . . even after the fact, the FBI and the Justice

Department have never acknowledged the true import of the C.S. dangers."[60] On the May 15, 1995, "McNeil Lehrer News Hour," he spoke in stronger terms, charging: "I feel the FBI has stonewalled me. . . . I believe they haven't been candid with me . . . I asked for material and I got nothing by gobblygook."

Only experts Nancy Ammerman and Alan Stone even mention the March, 1993 Smerick and Young memorandum. However, Nancy Ammerman learned of them from speaking personally with Peter Smerick. And Alan Stone, who withheld his report until he received all the information he requested, refers to the Justice Department originally withholding them from outside experts when he writes: "The evidence now available to me indicates that, contrary to my previous understanding and that of the other panelists, the FBI's Investigation Support Unit and trained negotiators possessed the psychological/behavioral science expertise they needed to deal with David Koresh and an unconventional group like the Branch Davidians. . . . Panelists may have been misled, as I was, by FBI officials at the original briefings who conveyed the impression that they considered David Koresh a typical criminal mentality and dealt with him as such."[61]

It is clear that Koresh's promise-to-surrender letter also was never shown to the outside experts. Only Nancy Ammerman refers to the letter.[62] However, she notes that she got her copy from Dr. James Tabor, not from the Justice Department.[63]

In his report, Lawrence E. Sullivan, director of Harvard's Center for the Study of World Religions, quotes at length from Koresh's April 9 and 10 letters to the FBI, trying to find evidence that Koresh would have come out—yet he never mentions the April 14 promise-to-surrender letter. He also quotes extensively from an earlier, defiant letter, which he was given at a Justice Department briefing of the experts. "In the briefing the letter seems to play the role of a last straw, measuring Koresh's intransigence and provoking the FBI to escalate their interventions."[64] If that letter was presented as the "last straw," doubtless it was also presented as the last letter.

The Justice Department evidently even withheld the letter from the review team's chief overseer, Edward Dennis. In his lengthy report Dennis refers only to the April 9 and 10 letters and Koresh's April 14th phone call.[65]

Failure to Report to Congress on Tampering with 911 Tapes

For the June 9, 1993, House Appropriations subcommittee hearing, an FBI agent gave a committee staff member an excerpted tape of the 911 calls between Lieutenant Larry Lynch and Davidians Wayne Martin, David Koresh, and Steve Schneider.[66] The tapes had been edited into a thirty-minute tape which Waco police said gave a "false impression of how the events occurred."[67]

If one compares the transcript of the tape in the hearing record to the Treasury Department's minute-by-minute February 28 chronology, one finds the tapes actually have been re-sequenced. The section where

Wayne Martin complains about helicopters shooting at him, at approximately 10:05 A.M., has been moved until after David Koresh calls 911 at 10:34 A.M.—after the helicopters withdrew from the scene. This might be evidence that someone wanted to discredit Martin's claims and cover up the BATF's illegal shooting.

No Fault Finding For FBI or Justice Department Errors or Crimes

At the October 8, 1993, press conference where the Justice Department released the report, chief reviewer Edward Dennis stated, "I find no fault in the performance of law enforcement during the standoff and the tear gas assault." He asserted "speculation regarding them coming out is irresponsible." Likewise, Deputy Attorney General Phillip Heymann said, "We can't come out with a scapegoat when there's no severe blame to be placed."[68]

Reporters at the press conference asked Heymann if the Justice report was a "whitewash," especially compared to the Treasury Department report. Heymann answered that the Treasury report found "recklessness (in the initial raid) followed by a coverup." He asserted that in the FBI and Justice Department's handling of the Davidians, the "underlying facts are different," i.e., there was no recklessness and cover up.[69] Attorney General Janet Reno said: "I'm always concerned about the perception of a whitewash. But I don't go out to seek *mea culpas* and I don't go out to seek [a report that says] we didn't do anything wrong. I go out to seek the truth."[70]

Outside expert Alan A. Stone disagreed, writing: "There is a view within the FBI and in the official reports that suggests the tragedy was unavoidable. This report is a dissenting opinion from that view."[71] Nevertheless, a number of newspapers, including the *New York Times* and the *Washington Times* labeled it a "whitewash."[72]

Failure to Discipline or Prosecute Agents or Officials

The Justice Department has taken no official action against agents or officials related to their actions at Waco. FBI Director Sessions was fired for other reasons in mid-1993. In late 1993 the FBI quietly replaced Hostage Rescue Team commander Richard Rogers. Several other high officials have retired or been moved out of Washington as FBI Director Louis Freeh replaced them with his own team. However, while Freeh suspended Assistant FBI Director James Fox for violating repeated judicial admonitions to refrain from commenting on the World Trade Center bombing to the news media, he has taken no action against FBI agents involved in the deaths of seventy-six Davidian men, women, and children.[73] It seems Freeh places a higher value on bureaucratic control than on human life.

Failure to Recommend Prosecutions in Weaver Case

There has been more press and congressional criticism of the FBI's handling of the Randy Weaver case for several reasons: there was less publicity surrounding the Weaver case and therefore less anti-Weaver government disinformation; there was no attorney general like Janet Reno to assume the blame, even as she effectively blamed the victims; there was no way to pin the killing of Vicki Weaver on Randy Weaver; and the FBI and Weaver prosecutors made sloppier mistakes in covering up evidence of federal agent crimes. Despite this criticism, the Justice Department and the FBI could not afford to prosecute, or even harshly discipline, the FBI agents and officials in charge of the Randy Weaver siege because these were the same individuals in charge at Waco: former FBI Director William Sessions, former FBI Deputy Director Floyd I. Clarke, Assistant Director for the Criminal Investigative Division Larry Potts, and HRT commander Richard M. Rogers.

In July, 1993, the Justice Department began an investigation into possible criminal misconduct on the part of FBI agents and officials. Some members of the Hostage Rescue Team, including Richard M. Rogers, refused to cooperate with investigators. Larry Potts, the senior FBI official who would have had to approve the new rules of engagement, told FBI investigators he did not remember giving Rogers a clear go-ahead to change them. However, in the Justice Department report Eugene Glenn, the FBI's on-site commander, swore to investigators that Mr. Potts did approve the rules of engagement, as did Richard Rogers.[74]

Released in December, 1994, the three-hundred-page report recommended criminal charges against the responsible agents, i.e., Richard Rogers and sniper Lon Horiuchi who shot Vicki Weaver. The report stated: "The rules of engagement not only departed from the FBI's standard deadly force policy, but also contradicted the Constitution of the United States." However, the Justice Department's Office of Professional Responsibility reviewed the report and concluded that the agents had not committed crimes and should face only disciplinary action. Janet Reno consulted the department's civil rights division which similarly concluded criminal prosecutions were not warranted. This was despite the fact that Idaho prosecutor Randall W. Day was considering prosecuting Potts, Rogers, Horiuchi and Federal Marshals Arthur Roderick and Lawrence Cooper for murder.[75]

The Justice Department turned the matter over to Louis Freeh for consideration of disciplinary measures. On January 6, 1995, Freeh announced that twelve agents and officials would be disciplined with measures ranging from letters of censure to a maximum of fifteen-day suspensions. Larry Potts received a letter of censure for his "failure to provide proper oversight with regard to the rules of engagement." HRT commander Richard Rogers received a letter and ten-day suspension. Lon Horiuchi was not disciplined at all. It has been noted widely that the letters of censure are the same reprimand that Louis Freeh gave himself for losing his FBI cellular phone. Deputy Attorney General Jamie Gorelick approved Freeh's decision.[76]

In May, 1995, FBI Director Freeh, with the approval of Janet Reno, promoted Potts to Deputy Director, the second highest position in the FBI. This disturbed many members of the public, press, Congress—and even of the FBI. Senator Larry Craig of Idaho said, "I expressed concern that to promote a person whose failure to act in a constitutionally appropriate way resulted in the loss of life . . . flew in the face of public sentiment. This relates to public concern about government agencies being responsible." And FBI Salt Lake City FBI Chief Eugene Glenn, the Weaver site-commander, immediately wrote a letter to the Justice Department challenging the FBI's investigation and Pott's veracity. The Justice Department agreed to investigate further.[77] However, it remains unlikely that Janet Reno's Justice Department will prosecute for the Weaver murder those who are covering up the even more damning massacre of the Branch Davidians.

DAVIDIAN TRIAL CONTINUED THE COVER-UP

The January-February 1994, trial of eleven Branch Davidians for conspiracy to murder federal officers and weapon charges was yet another cover up of federal crimes against the Davidians. The judge was under investigation by the Justice Department for the first half of the trial. Federal prosecutors, appointed by and under the ultimate control of Attorney General Janet Reno and Associate Attorney General Webster Hubbell, repeatedly withheld evidence from the defense, condoned the BATF's and the FBI's tampering with or destroying evidence and improperly influenced witnesses.

Despite the judge and prosecutors' best efforts to stifle the Davidians' ability to present an adequate defense, the jury found all Davidians completely innocent of the most serious charges; conspiracy to murder, and aiding and abetting murder of, federal officers. Three were found completely innocent and released. However, the judge's faulty instructions, faulty juror forms, and juror error resulted in eight Davidians being convicted of crimes resulting in a total of 240 years imprisonment.[78] Davidians are appealing the verdicts and sentences.

Prejudiced Judge Frustrated Defense Efforts

U.S. District Judge Walter Smith, 54, presided over the trial. Smith has a reputation for being pro-prosecution and imposing the maximum sentence on defendants. Something sure to make Smith even more pro-government is that during the trial he was under investigation by the Justice Department for allegedly lying under oath during a civil suit trial. Smith had testified for the defendant, a newspaper and broadcasting company being sued for libel by a political opponent, former McClellan County District Attorney Vic Feazell. In the fall of 1993, Feazell filed a formal complaint against Smith for perjury because two "facts" to which Smith testified were proved to be false. These potentially career-ruining charges were hanging over Smith through the first half of the trial. In early February, 1994, the Justice Department "exonerated" Smith of the charges.[79] After this episode, Smith doubtless felt he was indebted to the Justice Department.

Defense attorneys charged that because Judge Smith allowed prosecutors to try defendants together, supposedly to save money, some defendants could not get a fair trial. Such "group trials" overwhelm the defense attorneys of usually indigent clients so they cannot present an adequate defense. Prosecutors swamp juries with "conspiracy facts" so they will not look at the paltry evidence against each defendant.

Judge Smith took the improper and possibly illegal step of restricting public access to the names of all potential jurors in the federal jury wheel for the Western District of Texas, a total of 16,000 individuals. He acknowledged his fear members of the Fully Informed Jury Association (FIJA) would send potential jurors their literature about jury rights—including the right of the jury to find defendants innocent if they disagree with the law or feel that the government acted improperly. Smith admitted he had heard "an organization" planned on distributing leaflets to potential jurors about "how they should ignore the law and follow their conscience."[80]

Judge Smith took the unusual, but not improper, step of sending out questionnaires to three hundred eligible jurors and then, based on their responses, choosing from those the eighty who would be subjected to questioning and challenge by attorneys.[81] Smith inquired about potential jurors' religious beliefs and asked: "Do you believe persons other than law enforcement officers should be permitted to own firearms?" Smith would not allow defense attorneys to see jurors' answers to this and other leading questions, telling them questionnaires would be bundled and could be reviewed only during appeals.[82]

Declaring he would "not allow the government to be put on trial," Judge Smith forbid defense attorneys from mentioning self-defense, or asking questions, presenting evidence or calling witnesses who could prove self-defense. This was despite the fact the Davidians' primary defense against all charges was that under statutory and common law the BATF's excessive force on February 28, 1993 gave the Davidians the right to use armed force in self-defense. Only in closing arguments did Smith allow mention of self-defense. Jury forewoman Sarah Bain complained to a reporter about the withholding of evidence of self-defense, "I feel that we were improperly used."[83]

Judge Smith repeatedly squashed defense efforts to introduce important evidence, including about the Davidians' legitimate fear of attack, their peaceful pre-occupations, BATF's flawed raid plan, Kathryn Schroeder's testimony that other Davidians told her they heard firing from helicopters, Jaime Castillo's statements to a Texas Ranger that he did not shoot on February 28, portions of the 911 tape where Davidians refer to helicopter attacks and their right to defend themselves.[84]

Judge Smith put up procedural roadblocks to prevent defense attorneys from calling the BATF and FBI agents most knowledgeable about and responsible for the aggressive BATF and FBI assaults on the Davidians. And he restricted David Koresh's gun dealer and business partner's testimony to a written statement "stipulated," i.e., approved, by prosecutors.[85]

Defense attorneys declined to call their most important witnesses, the defendants themselves. They knew the judge would not allow them to answer questions about BATF's attack on them and their attempts to defend themselves, so the only answers they could have given would have been self-incriminating.

Prosecutors Helped Plan Assaults

Assistant U.S. Attorneys Bill Johnston, 34, and John Phinizy, 46, were prime motivators of the original BATF investigation. The Treasury Department report alleged Johnston insisted the BATF use a paramilitary raid against the Davidians. The subject of whether he too should be a witness and whether his desire to cover up his own errors might lead to prosecutorial misconduct was a frequent subject of debate early in the trial.

Ray Jahn, 50, who was named lead prosecutor, was formerly a special counsel to, and had been good friends with, FBI Director William Sessions. The Justice Department had consulted with Jahn regarding their plans to gas Mount Carmel. Attorney Mike DeGeurin was so disturbed by this fact that he asked for Jahn to be dismissed as a prosecutor because he was a potential witness. The judge refused his request.[86]

Prosecutors Withheld Important Evidence

In several motions for mistrial, defense attorneys accused the government of repeatedly violating the Brady and Jencks rules, which require prosecutors to give defense attorneys adequate opportunity to inspect all evidence before it is presented in court. Prosecutors remained unfazed by evidence lost, destroyed, or tampered with by the BATF, the FBI, or other government agencies. The most flagrant examples include:

- The BATF and the FBI claimed they could not find one of the two steel double front doors which might have proved that BATF shot a first barrage of bullets at the unarmed David Koresh, critically wounding the unarmed Perry Jones.

- The medical examiner claimed that Perry Jones' only gunshot wound was to the mouth, despite Davidian claims—including those alluded to by prosecution witness Kathryn Schroeder—that the unarmed Jones was mortally wounded by BATF gunshots as he stood at the front door.

- Despite BATF officials' initial claim that BATF agents had taken video of the first minutes of the February 28 raid, prosecutors supported the BATF's claim that in the first minutes of the raid, BATF equipment both in the undercover house across the street and in the helicopters had not been operating.

- Prosecutors did not tell the defense in advance that several BATF agents had changed their testimony from that first given defense attorneys, including regarding whether anyone had yelled search warrant, had seen David Koresh in the door, or had shot dogs in the first minutes of the raid. Their new testimony was much more damaging to the Davidians.

- Prosecutors did not tell Livingstone Fagan's attorney in advance that two agents would testify that Fagan had shot at them. Only after BATF Agent Evers testified that Livingstone Fagan had shot him did prosecutors turn over to Fagan's attorney evidence that cast doubt on that testimony—a copy of the photo lineup Texas Rangers had shown the agent in March of 1993. Next to the photo of Fagan, Evers had written, "unsure if identified from shooting or TV." Even Judge Smith criticized the prosecution for withholding this evidence.[87]

- Prosecutors disclosed only on the morning of Kathryn Schroeder's testimony that Texas Rangers had a transcript of her original March, 1993, statement to them. Her statement clearly was different from testimony prosecutors gave defense attorneys. Schroeder then admitted on the stand that she had lied to authorities.

- Prosecutors would allow a defense attorney's weapons expert to inspect allegedly illegal machine guns only by looking at them through their plastic wrappings. The government has proved to no one outside law enforcement that these weapons were illegal. This adds to suspicions that prosecutors and FBI weapons experts falsely claimed that some or all legal weapons were illegal ones—or that agents converted some legal weapons to illegal ones in BATF or FBI laboratories.

Prosecutors Intimidated and Influenced Witnesses

Prosecutors intimidated two Davidian women, Kathryn Schroeder and Marjorie Thomas, into testifying against other Davidians. They threatened to use the (often dubious) accusations of Davidian Victorine Hollingsworth, an elderly woman from England who turned against David Koresh after leaving Mount Carmel in March, 1993. Hollingsworth claimed Thomas, who was badly burned in the fire, carried a weapon during the siege. (No other Davidian facing only that accusation was prosecuted.)

Hollingsworth claimed that Schroeder carried a gun during the February 28 raid. Prosecutors also told Schroeder they had a BATF witness who would testify to seeing gunfire coming from her room. Fearful this evidence would lead to a life sentence and separate her forever from her four children, Schroeder cooperated with prosecutors. At this point Hollingsworth and the agent withdrew their allegations against Schroeder.[88]

Prosecutors obviously coached Hollingsworth at trial. She testified with confidence that she had seen various individuals carrying guns during or after the February raid. However, when one attorney read aloud her statement to Texas Rangers taken shortly after she left Mount Carmel in March, the transcript showed that Hollingsworth was very confused and unsure about who was carrying guns or of the difference between a handgun and a rifle.[89]

Prosecutors may have influenced witness Bradley Rogans, a twenty-three year old serving three eight-year sentences on drug-related charges. Rogans testified he befriended defendant Renos Avraam for almost a week at a Texas jail and that Avraam made incriminating statements about carrying and aiming an automatic weapon. Later it was revealed that Rogans had spent only one day at that facility and was paroled the next day.[90] During closing arguments Carroll inferred that Rogans had lied, calling him "an evidence-tampering, three-time felon, twenty-three years old, paroled the next day."[91]

Defense attorneys accused prosecutors of coaching prosecution witnesses, in part to cover up their own misdeeds. Early in the trial FBI agent James Cadigan made the dramatic statement, "I have not seen that many firearms or that quantity of ammunition outside a firearms munitions plant." An angry defense attorney asserted that his testimony had been "rehearsed." Cadigan admitted, "I have discussed my testimony with the prosecution."[92] While prosecution witnesses all met at least once with prosecutors, twenty or more federal agents scheduled to testify attended a November, 1993, pre-trial meeting with prosecutors. Doubtless they received more coaching, plus a subtle reminder that they must all hang together—or some might hang separately.[93]

Paltry and Questionable Evidence Against Convicted Davidians

Most, but not all, of the Davidians identified as carrying a gun on February 28, 1993, were prosecuted. Those who only were accused of having carried a gun during the siege, including David Thibodeau, Rita Riddle and Derek Lovelock, were not prosecuted. Besides the not entirely credible evidence presented by the three Davidian prosecution witnesses, federal agents, and a "jailhouse snitch," the most significant evidence against three defendants was their own truthful testimony to Texas Rangers after they left Mount Carmel. There was no credible testimony that any Davidian carried an illegal automatic weapon on February 28 or during the siege; Kathryn Schroeder did allege she herself carried one. What follows is the paltry and dubious evidence against eight Davidian prisoners, mostly related to self-defense against the seventy-six BATF agents who shot machine guns, threw dangerous flash-bang grenades, and even fired from a helicopter on February 28, 1993.

Renos Avraam, 31, a British businessman of Greek heritage, joined the Davidians in 1991 and escaped the fire. Evidence presented against him was Marjorie Thomas saw him with a gun during the siege;

Kathryn Schroeder alleged Avraam told her he fired a gun February 28 and manned a .50-caliber gun during the siege; Bradley Rogans alleged Avraam confessed that he had a fully automatic weapon, that he was a good shot and that he had aimed his gun; an FBI agent testified he saw Avraam drop a pistol off the roof as he was escaping, but a Texas Ranger said he found no such pistol anywhere near where the gun would have fallen.[94]

Brad Branch, 36, a Navy veteran and technician and frequent visitor to Mount Carmel, left during the siege. Evidence presented against him was Marjorie Thomas said she saw him with a gun on February 28th and heard him claim he had shot someone; Victorine Hollingsworth said she heard Branch say "something like . . . 'One nearly got me and I got one,' " but that he was defending the women and children.[95]

Jaime Castillo, 27, a California musician, joined the Davidians in 1988 and escaped the fire. Evidence presented against him was Marjorie Thomas saw him with a gun February 28; Kathryn Schroeder saw him with an AK-47 during the siege but did not know if it was automatic; Texas Ranger Gary de los Santos testified Castillo said he had three different guns on February 28; a BATF agent testified Castillo kept a gun pointed on her and other armed agents as they helped a wounded agent in the court yard. (The judge would not allow jury to hear that Castillo also told the Ranger that he had hid on the floor during the gun battle, he had seen Winston Blake dead on the floor, or that he did not point his gun at the female agent.)[96]

Graeme Craddock, 34, an engineer from Australia, had been at Mount Carmel a year and escaped the fire. Evidence presented against him was Kathryn Schroeder saw him with a gun on February 28; Marjorie Thomas saw him with a gun during the siege; he gave testimony to a Texas Ranger and a grand jury that he had a gun on February 28 but did not fire it and that David Koresh gave Craddock what he said was a live grenade; he admitted that he left the grenade in the concrete building next to the water tower.[97]

Livingstone Fagan, 36, a British minister and father of two, left during the siege to be spokesperson for the group. His wife Yvette and mother Doris died during the fire. Evidence against him was Schroeder saw him with a gun February 28; Hollingsworth claimed Fagan said he shot an agent who was shooting at him; two BATF agents gave questionable testimony Fagan had shot at them outside the building; however, Hollingsworth testified she saw another black man, now deceased, in the place where agents claim they saw Fagan; two defendants similarly could have testified that man was not Fagan, had it not been a group trial. A BATF agent said the black man shooting looked like a large man—Fagan is a small man.[98]

Paul Fatta, 37, a Hawaiian businessman, father of one and long-time Davidian, was at a gun show in Austin on February 28. Evidence presented against him was government allegation two guns Fatta purchased had been converted to illegal automatics; Kathryn Schroeder testified that other Davidians—but not Fatta—later converted some guns to illegal machine guns.[99]

Ruth Riddle, 31, a Canadian member for several years, who escaped the fire with David Koresh's first chapter of the Seven Seals. Her husband Jimmy Riddle died on April 19. Evidence against her was Thomas and Schroeder saw her with a gun February 28; she admitted to authorities that she gave her rifle to another Davidian during the shootout.[100]

Kevin Whitecliff, 34, father of two from Hawaii, had been at Mount Carmel a year and left during the siege. Evidence presented against him was Marjorie Thomas said he claimed he said he had shot someone; Kathryn Schroeder alleged he told her he shot at helicopters which Davidians say were firing on the building.[101]

Judge's Faulty Instructions Led to Convictions

Judge Smith gave the jurors a sixty-seven-page "Court's Instruction to the Jury" setting out the charges and the specific rules of law which they should use in determining innocence or guilt. Jury forewoman Sarah Bain complained after the trial that Judge Smith had never informed the jury that they might request relevant evidence that had not been presented. She said, "If I knew we could ask for missing evidence, I would've done so then." She particularly was concerned that prosecutors had presented only the search and arrest warrants at trial, and not the affidavits. She said jurors had looked for them among the "ton of paperwork," but never found them.[102]

On February 26, 1994, jurors found all eleven Davidians innocent of the first count of the indictment, conspiracy to murder federal agents, and of the second count, aiding and abetting murder of federal agents. Three Davidians were acquitted of all charges. Judge Smith did find sufficient evidence that Davidians had acted in self-defense to allow defense attorneys to bring up in final arguments and to include self-defense as a defense against the charges of murder of federal agents. Jurors believed Davidians did in fact act in self-defense. Jury forewoman Sarah Bain said the one-hour 911 tape— which jurors specifically asked to hear again in the jury room—was the most impressive evidence to jurors that Davidians had acted in self-defense.[103] One juror told a reporter, "When we heard all that testimony, there was no way we could find them guilty of murder. We felt provocation was pretty evident."[104]

Unfortunately, with the agreement of defense attorneys, Judge Smith had added a new charge to the second count—aiding and abetting voluntary manslaughter. (Most Davidian defendants did not find out about the new charge until just before verdicts were read and were angry about its being added.[105]) Despite defense attorneys requests that he do so, Smith did not instruct the jury on any grounds by which defendants might be found innocent of this charge, i.e., self-defense. Sarah Bain admits that the lack of any defense instruction forced jurors to find five Davidians—Renos Avraam, Brad Branch, Jaime Castillo, Livingstone Fagan, and Kevin Whitecliff—guilty. She said jurors believed aiding and abetting voluntary manslaughter was a minor charge that would earn them little time beyond that served.[106] In fact, the maximum sentence is ten years.

In his instructions to the jury, Judge Smith twice explicitly tied count three, using or carrying a firearm during and in relation to the commission of a crime of violence, only to count one, conspiring to murder federal agents. However, the jury did not read the instructions very carefully and the connection between the charges was not specified on the verdict form on which the jury relied. Confused jurors thought they were finding seven Davidians—Renos Avraam, Brad Branch, Jaime Castillo, Graeme Craddock, Livingstone Fagan, Ruth Riddle, and Kevin Whitecliff—guilty of carrying a weapon during the crime of aiding and abetting voluntary manslaughter. Again, jurors thought this was a minor charge for which Davidians would receive short sentences.[107] In fact, the maximum sentence is thirty years. Sixty-nine-year-old juror Jeanette Felger told a reporter, "I would never have voted that way if I had known it was connected to count one."[108]

Smith admitted to defense attorneys this weapons verdict was inconsistent, but refused to send the jury back to reconcile the verdicts, insisting "that portion of the verdict simply cannot stand. . . . So, the Court will set that finding aside." Prosecutors did not object.[109] Because Smith set the finding aside, defendants did not exercise their right to "poll" the jury and see if each one did in fact support the final verdict.

However, on February 28, 1994, prosecutors asked Smith to reinstate the weapons verdicts. On March 9, 1994, in his *Memorandum Opinion and Order*, Smith did so, citing previous case law. Smith argued he only had spoken "prospectively in terms of a future written order" about setting the verdict aside, since he was unsure of the law in this area.

Jurors also found Graeme Craddock guilty of possession of an unregistered hand grenade despite the fact the grenade was found six days after the fire. Despite the lack of any evidence that Paul Fatta was involved in illegally converting weapons, jurors believed the government's testimony that the guns bought by Fatta had in fact been converted to illegal machine guns, and found him guilty of manufacturing and conspiring to manufacture machine guns. Afterwards jury forewoman Sarah Bain acknowledged that she herself was beginning to wonder if prosecutors and government weapons experts lied about the weapons.[110]

Judge Imposed Maximum Sentences

Despite the jurors' belief Davidians should get little time for the "minor charges" on which they convicted them, and letters from two jurors requesting leniency, Judge Smith threw the book at the Davidians. Judge Smith claimed that Davidians did indeed engage in a conspiracy to cause the death of federal agents, shot first at the BATF, and murdered other Davidians— effectively rejecting the jurors' finding that they were innocent of any such conspiracy.[111] Smith gave the five convicted Davidians the maximum sentence, ten years.

Smith also agreed with prosecutors' arguments that the government can argue someone carried a machine gun, even if it was not part of the original indictment. They cited the "fortress theory"—that a defendant found in a place where a large number of weapons have been accumulated can be assumed to have had access to all those guns, legal and illegal. Until this time the fortress theory only had been used in drug cases. Judge Smith found that all defendants had "constructive possession" of automatic weapons and sentenced seven Davidians to a total of 170 years.[112]

Final sentences were as follows: Renos Avraam, forty years; Brad Branch, forty years; Jaime Castillo, forty years; Graeme Craddock, twenty years; Livingstone Fagan, forty years; Paul Fatta, fifteen years; Ruth Riddle, five years; and Kevin Whitecliff, forty years. Prosecution witness Kathryn Schroeder later received a three-year sentence.

Davidian Appeals for Justice

Six Davidians, Renos Avraam, Brad Branch, Graeme Craddock, Jaime Castillo, Paul Fatta, and Kevin Whitecliff, immediately appealed the verdicts and sentences. All retained their original attorneys except Jaime Castillo who engaged weapons expert Steve Halbrook. Halbrook helped win the June, 1994 *Staples vs. the United States* court case which protects gun owners who unwittingly come into possession of an illegal weapon. Ruth Riddle, who had received a reduced sentence of five years, did not appeal, fearing judges might comply with any prosecution request and increase her sentence. Livingstone Fagan, who faced a rigged trial with government witnesses who lied about him and a judge who effectively prevented witnesses from testifying on his behalf, expressed his contempt by refusing to appeal his forty-year sentence. (However, should other Davidians' appeals succeed, in part or in full, Riddle and Fagan would have avenues of legal recourse.)

Five Davidians are appealing for new trials or dismissal of verdicts for the aiding and abetting manslaughter charge based on the judge's failure to instruct the jury as to any defense for the manslaughter charge; presentation of insufficient evidence to justify the verdicts. They are appealing for dismissal of the weapons charge based on the fact that Title 18 924(c)(1) clearly specifies that the defendant must be "convicted" of the first crime (i.e., conspiracy to murder in the Davidians' case) before they can be convicted of using a firearm in relation to the crime; the fact Judge Smith stated he would "set aside" the charge and then reinstated it, a possible case of double jeopardy. If those arguments fail, they ask for reduced sentences based on the fact that Davidians were not indicted for or convicted of possession or use of machine guns; the lack of evidence any Davidians carried illegal weapons; the sentences' inconsistency with the June, 1994, *Staples vs. the United States* case which holds that the government must prove an individual knew he or she was in possession of an illegal weapon. Two Davidians are basing their call for dismissal of the grenade and automatic weapons charges against them on insufficient evidence.

After the verdicts were announced, jury forewoman Sarah Bain went on a number of radio talk shows to protest Judge Smith's actions in the case. Bain told one reporter, "The federal government was absolutely out of control there. We spoke in the jury room about the fact that the wrong people were on trial, that it should have been the ones that planned the raid and orchestrated it and insisted on carrying out this plan who should have been on trial."[113]

THE DAVIDIAN PRISONERS

Renos Avraam   Brad Branch   Jaime Castillo

Graeme Craddock   Livingstone Fagan   Paul Fatta

Ruth Riddle   Kathryn Schroeder   Kevin Whitecliff

Chapter Twelve:
The FBI-Justice Department-White House Cover-up

1.   Brad Branch interview, CNN, April 19, 1993.
2.   Jack B. Zimmermann, Esq., paper, "The Legacy of Waco: The Demise of ATF and Justice Department Integrity," 1993.
3.   William Sessions interview, CNN, April 19, 1993; ABC Special "Waco: The Decision to Die," April 20, 1993.
4.   "FBI agent suggests Koresh was killed by vengeful aide," *Dallas Morning News*, September 5, 1993.
5.   Stephen Labaton, "U.S. Opens Up to Avoid Backlash on Cult Attack," *New York Times*, April 22, 1993: B13.
6.   Steve McVicker, July 22, 1993.
7.   Stephen Labaton, April 22, 1993: B13.
8.   "Poll: Most supported first raid," *USA Today*, April 21, 1993: A3.
9.   Mark Mayfield, "Poll: 93% blame Koresh," *USA Today*, April 21, 1993: A1.
10.   Elizabeth Drew, *On the Edge: The Clinton Presidency* (New York: Simon & Schuster, 1994): 131.
11.   Stephen Labaton, "Officials Contradict One Another on Rationale for Assault on Cult," *New York Times*, April 21, 1993: A1.
12.   Federal News Service transcription of April 20, 1993 press conference.
13.   Elizabeth Drew: 133.
14.   Jerry Seper, "Reviewer disputes Clinton on Waco," *Washington Times*, April 27, 1995.
15.   Paul Craig Roberts, "Rallying Round Reno," *Washington Times*, May 7, 1993.
16.   Eldridge Cleaver, "Waco: Bill Clinton's Bay of Pigs," in James R. Lewis, editor: 235–36.
17.   "American Justice" program, "Attack at Waco," August 3, 1994.
18.   Trial transcript: 5539.
19.   Ibid, 610.
20.   Justice Department report: 308–09.
21.   Ibid., 228; Treasury Department report: 128.
22.   Trial transcript: 1080–81, 1087–88.
23.   Ibid., 617.
24.   James L. Pate: 49; trial transcript: 6847.

25.   Michael deCourcy Hinds, "Arson Investigators Say Cult Members Started Fire," *New York Times*, April 27, 1993.
26.   Michael deCourcy Hinds, April 28, 1993: A16.
27.   Trial transcript: 1244–47.
28.   "Cultist's lawyer calls bulldozing of site a cover-up," *Washington Times*, May 13, 1993.
29.   Sue Anne Pressley and Mary Jordan, April 21, 1993.
30.   Justice Department report: 329.
31.   Trial transcript: 602, 668.
32.   J. Michael Kennedy, "Waco Cult Set Fire, Texas Officials Say," *Los Angeles Times*, April 27, 1993: A7; Michael deCourcy Hinds, April 27, 1993.
33.   Trial transcript: 5852–55.
34.   James L. Pate, October, 1993: 75.
35.   James L. Pate, November, 1993: 74–75.
36.   Jack B. Zimmermann, Esq., paper, 1993.
37.   Associated Press wire story, April 27, 1993, 04:10 EDT.
38.   Trial transcript: 5839–46.
39.   Justice Department report, Fire report: 8.
40.   Trial transcript: 5836–37, 5847, 5859–62, 5869.
41.   Ibid., 5748.
42.   Ibid., 5932.
43.   Ibid., 5811, 5816, 5834, 5951.
44.   Justice Department report, Fire report: 9.
45.   Ibid., 3.
46.   Ibid., 9.
47.   Ibid., 3.
48.   Hugh Aynesworth, "Koresh followers set fires," *Washington Times*, April 27, 1993.
49.   Trial transcript: 5819-22.
50.   "Cultists had tunnel to escape fire, arson prober says," *Washington Times*, May 1, 1993: A5.
51.   Justice Department report, Fire report: 10.
52.   Jerry Seper, "Foster felt Waco was 'his fault,' " *Washington Times*, May 23, 1995: A1, A13.
53.   Frank J. Murray, "Altman gets close to the heat," *Washington Times*, March 3, 1994: A1, A10; Susan Schmidt, "Altman Testimony Disputed," *Washington Post*, July 24, 1994: A1; "Act 2," John McCaslin, *Washington Times,* September 23, 1994.

54.   Jerry Seper, "Hubbell pleads guilty to fraud," *Washington Times*, December 7, 1994, A1: A16; Sharon LaFraniere and Pierre Thomas, "Surprised Colleagues Discover 'a Webb Hubbell nobody knew,'" *Washington Post*, December 7, 1994; Susan Schmidt, "Hubbell Pleads Guilty to Fraud Charges," *Washington Post*, December 7, 1994: A1, A18.

55.   Jerry Seper, "Whitewater probe grows to include state agency," and "State agency Major Source of funds for Clinton backers," *Washington Times*, January 24, 1994: A1, A9; Susan Schmidt, "Lindsey Avoids Key Charges," *Washington Post*, May 20, 1995.

56.   Stephen Labaton, "Inquiry Won't Look at Final Waco Raid," *New York Times*, May 16, 1993: A20.

57.   Stephen Labaton, "Justice Inquiry Will Now Examine Assault on Cult," *New York Times*, May 18, 1993.

58.   William Safire, "Waco, Reno, Iraq-gate," *Washington Post*, October 14, 1993.

59.   Michael deCourcy Hinds, "Toll is Lowered for Sect Dead to Around 72," *New York Times*, April 30, 1993: A12.

60.   Jerry Seper, "Reviewer disputes Clinton on Waco," *Washington Times*, April 27, 1995.

61.   Alan A. Stone, M.D., report to Justice Department, 1993: 12.

62.   Nancy Ammerman, report to Justice Department, 1993: 8.

63.   Nancy Ammerman, private communication, February, 1994.

64.   Lawrence E. Sullivan, report to Justice Department, October 8, 1993: 5–6.

65.   Edward S. G. Dennis, Jr., report to Justice Department in *Recommendations of Experts for Improvements in Federal Law Enforcement after Waco*, October 8, 1993: 26.

66.   June 9, 1993, House Appropriations subcommittee hearing: 99–129.

67.   Associated Press story, "FBI tape of Waco talks probed," *Washington Times*, June 17, 1993.

68.   Jerry Seper, "Tragedy Blamed on Cult: Reno Says Report is Not a Whitewash," *Washington Times*, October 9, 1993.

69.   Michael Kirkland, "Justice Department rejects charges of Waco 'whitewash,'" United Press International, October 14, 1993; "No sanctions expected in Waco raid," *Washington Times*, October 14, 1993.

70.   Michael Isikoff, October 9, 1993: A10.

71.   Alan A. Stone, M.D., report to the Justice Department, 1993: 46.

72.   "The truth about Waco, still untold," *Washington Times*, October 13, 1993; "The Waco Whitewash," *New York Times*, October 12, 1993.

73.   Kirk Lyons, private communication, June, 1994; Michael Isikoff, "FBI Director Suspends Head of New York office," *Washington Post*, December 22, 1993.

74.   David Johnston and Stephen Labaton, "F.B.I. Shaken by Inquiry into Idaho Siege," *New York Times*, November 25, 1993; "Senior FBI official disputes Potts over orders in Weaver shootout," *Washington Times*, March 6, 1995.

75.   Jerry Seper, "Craig hits holdup on probe report," *Washington Times*, November 22, 1994: A3; Pierre Thomas, "FBI to Consider Disciplining Agents in '92 Idaho Shootout," *Washington Post*, December 1, 1994: A1, A24; Jerry Seper, "Five federal agents could face murder charges in Idaho raid," *Washington Times*, December 25, 1994: A3.

76.   Jerry Seper, "FBI disciplines 12 in Weaver case," *Washington Times*, January 7, 1995: A5; Jerry Seper, "FBI official called unfit," *Washington Times*, April 14, 1995.

77.   Jerry Seper, "Reno Promotes Censured FBI boss," *Washington Post*, May 3, 1995; Ruth Marcus, "FBI Chief Gets His Man for No. 2 Post," *Washington Post*, May 7, 1995: A6; Pierre Thomas, "Probe of FBI Siege Questioned," *Washington Post*, May 12, 1995.

78.   This section is a condensation of a much longer, fully footnoted version and has been selectively footnoted.

79.   Hugh Aynesworth, "Waco judge: 'Smart' and 'vindictive,' " *Washington Times*, January 30, 1994: A6; Hugh Aynesworth, "Waco judge cleared of lying in opponent's trial," *Washington Times*, February 6, 1994.

80.   Lone Star FIJA Press Releases, January 3, 1994 and January 11, 1994.

81.   Jack DeVault: 41; January 6, 1994, trial transcript: 5, 6, 13.

82.   Jack DeVault: 43; Jack Devault, private communication, November, 1994; January 6, 1994, pre-trial transcript: 15–16.

83.   January 6, 1994 trial transcript: 45–46; January 10, 1994 trial transcript: 4–5, 81–83; defense attorney Steven Rosen on CNN Court News, January 10, 1994; Egon Richard Tausch article, 1994; Benedict D. LaRosa, "The Branch Davidian Trial: An Interview with Sarah Bain, Forewoman," *Fully Informed Jury Association News*, June 24, 1994.

84.   Transcript: 410–11, 457–58, 579, 3058–61, 3269–70, 3379, 3396, 4115, 4628–29, 6359, 6362, 6479–85.

85.   Trial transcript: 4826–28, 6841–44, 7262.

86.   Ibid., 754.

87.   Ibid., 1657–68.

88.   Ibid., 4126–27, 4240; "Koresh Follower Pleads Guilty to Resisting Officer," *New York Times*, September 12, 1993.

89.   Trial transcript: 4157–58.

90.   Ibid., 6083–92.

91.   Ibid., 7166.

92.   Ibid., 1199–2001, 2768.

93.   Ibid., 2503, 2988.

94.   Marjorie Thomas testimony, November 17–18, 1993: 56–57; trial transcript: 4492, 4517, 5379–80, 5450–52, 6086–92, 7166.

95.   Majorie Thomas testimony, November 17–18, 1993: 45, 48–51; trial transcript: 574, 579, 4099, 4153.

96.   Majorie Thomas testimony, November 17–18, 1993: 45; trial transcript: 2972–77, 3058–60, 3096, 4500-01.

97.   Majorie Thomas testimony, November 17–18, 1993: 46; trial transcript: 4502, 6076, 6352, 6375, 6390–92.

98.   Trial transcript: 1541–42, 1590–92, 2548, 2641–42, 2683, 4129.

99.   Trial transcript: 1170, 1179–82.

100. Majorie Thomas testimony, November 17–18, 1993: 45; trial transcript: 4387, 4496, 5507.

101. Majorie Thomas testimony, November 17–18, 1993: 48–51; trial transcript: 4515.

102. Benedict LaRosa, June 24, 1994.

103. Sarah Bain, private communication, June, 1994.

104. Dick Reavis, "Waco: Justice Takes a Holiday," *Soldier of Fortune*, October, 1994: 39.

105. Livingstone Fagan paper, August, 1994: 20; private communication with five Davidian prisoners, June 19, 1994; Jack DeVault: 182–83.

106. Associated Press, "Cult Jurors Rip Government's Action in Raid," *Austin American Statesman*, March 1, 1994: B3; Sarah Bain, private communication, June, 1994; Sarah Bain, June, 1994, letter to Judge Walter J. Smith.

107. Benedict D. LaRosa, June 24, 1994; Sarah Bain, private communication, June, 1994.

108. Dick Reavis, October, 1994: 39.

109. Trial transcript: 7409–10.

110. Benedict D. LaRosa, June 24, 1994; Sarah Bain, private communication, October, 1994.

111. June 17, 1994 trial transcript: 201–02.

112. Ibid., 205–19.

113. Dean M. Kelley, "Waco: A Massacre and Its Aftermath," *First Things*, May, 1995: 37.

13

Congressional Hearings
Continued the Cover-up

*If only the Congress would open up again what
happened at Waco and lay everything on the
table. God, if our government would be honest
with us for a change, then the people would
not have to feel this kind of anger. We could
trust. That's why people are so frustrated.*

David Thibodeau[1]

The initial disgust with the government's
actions felt by millions as they watched the fires kill so
many Davidian men, women, and children, quickly
turned to rage at Koresh and his followers as FBI agents
and officials, Attorney General Janet Reno, and
President Bill Clinton defended their actions and
attacked David Koresh. The press and public bought
the whole package of lies and distortions about the
BATF raid, the fifty-one day siege and the April 19 fire.
Janet Reno's hard-bitten, "I made the decision. The buck

stops here," transformed a decision based on FBI false information, and Reno's "cursory review" of that information, into a heroic moral act.

1993 CONGRESSIONAL HEARINGS REVEALED LITTLE

The U.S. Congress, which is supposed to protect citizens against such abuses of executive power, bought the lies as well. As notorious poll watchers, congressional members could not ignore polls claiming 93 percent of the public backed the FBI's action. During the April 22, 1993, Senate Appropriations Subcommittee on Justice, State and Judiciary hearing Democratic Senator Bob Kerry (D-NE) told Reno, "I think the vast majority of Americans support the President's explanation of what happened and are enthusiastically supportive of the way you handled the situation."

A few representatives spoke out against federal actions after the fire. Representative Harold Volkmer (D-MO) charged that the initial attack on the Davidians was part of a pattern of "Gestapo-like tactics" at the bureau. "I fail to see the crimes committed by those in the Davidian compound that called for the extreme action of BATF on February 28 and the tragic final assault."[2] Representative John Conyers (D-MI) branded the April 19 attack a "military operation" and called it a "profound disgrace to law enforcement in the United States." He told Janet Reno, "you did the right thing by offering to resign. I'd like you to know that there is at least one member of Congress who is not going to rationalize the innocent deaths of two dozen children."[3]

However, most representatives largely applauded the efforts of the BATF and the FBI. They asked few searching questions that could have brought out the truth about government crimes. Absurdly, even the television movie "In the Line of Duty: Ambush at Waco," which was aired in May, 1993, before one of the most important hearings, managed to uncover important facts which Congress never discovered: that Davidians were working with a licensed gun dealer, that they used legal "hellfire" devices that make guns fire more rapidly, that BATF tried to bypass the sheriff's office because of the social worker's allegations of "leaks," and that a Davidian in a postal truck was alerted accidently to the impending raid by a newsperson.

What was truly frightening about the April 22, 1993, House Ways and Means Subcommittee hearing was that, compared to several committee members, BATF Director Stephen Higgins looked like a staunch civil libertarian. After presenting a number of affidavits, Higgins stated, "We had a feeling that something illegal was occurring. The Davidians, as you can see from the affidavit, legally were ordering various parts and components . . . . What we were trying to establish was: were they violating the laws?" Committee Chair J. J. Pickle (D-TX) cut Higgins short, declaring: "But, Mr. Higgins. You knew that. That was not the question. You knew they were doing that. You knew they were violating the law."[4]

Later Representative Rick Santorum (R-PA) expressed his concern that the BATF had been "outgunned" during the "assault" and wondered, "is there a problem with your funding as far as your capability of weapons?" Higgins felt pressed to remind him that "outgunned" was an "unfortunate choice of words in that we did not go there to engage in a gun battle, that is not the way we conduct law enforcement in this country." He even reminded representatives, "We . . . as law enforcement do not have the right to fire through walls and ceilings and roofs.[5] Of course, Davidians and their attorneys accuse BATF agents of doing just that—but no one on the subcommittee ever had an inkling of that fact.

Early in the most in-depth hearing, the April 28, 1993, House Judiciary Committee hearing, any pretense Congress would delve into BATF and FBI crimes was shattered when C-Span microphones and cameras caught committee chair Jack Brooks (D-TX) joking with FBI agents appearing as witnesses: "You know what I'd a done?" asked Brooks. "The first night, I'd a run everybody off, quietly put a bomb in that damned water tank. Put tear gas in there. If they wanted to shoot, kill 'em when they came out. If they didn't want to shoot, put 'em in a paddy wagon. It'd been over by twelve-thirty. That's what Brooks would do!" And during the hearing Brooks made it very clear why he felt so free to make such a joke—he said he had already "read the verdict" on David Koresh in the Gallup poll.

Appearing at the hearings were BATF Director Stephen Higgins, Attorney General Janet Reno, FBI Director William Sessions, and a phalanx of FBI officials and agents, including Jeff Jamar, Bob Ricks, and Dick Rogers. Details of the disinformation and propaganda disseminated at this hearing have already been examined here.

Webster Hubbell's May 19, 1993, Senate Confirmation hearing transcript reveals that the Senate Judiciary Committee members did not ask Webster Hubbell a single question about the massacre of the Branch Davidians, despite his crucial decision-making role. Senator Arlen Specter (R-PA) did ask Hubbell if he had had any direct contact with Clinton regarding any issues before the Department of Justice. Hubbell answered that the only topic they discussed was appointment of a Supreme Court justice. Considering Hubbell's subsequent guilty pleas for fraud, including against government agencies, his honesty here must be questioned.

The House Appropriations Subcommittee on the Treasury's June 9, 1993, hearing focused solely on the BATF's actions. Committee chair Democrat Steny Hoyer (D-MD) began the hearing by blaming the deaths of BATF agents and the fire on Koresh. Representative Jim Lightfoot (R-IA) quickly upped the ante, saying, "Just because Adolf Hitler is dead, just because David Koresh is dead, just because people of that ilk are no longer on the face of the earth, does not mean there are not others out there just like them."[6]

The most newsworthy revelation of the hearing was the playing of the 911 tapes, the first unveiling of this evidence of the Davidians' terror and BATF agents' brutality to the public. After hearing the tape of distraught citizens begging for police to "call it off" and shouting that they were being fired upon by helicopters, committee chair Steny Hoyer commented: "First of all, we do not play this tape for the veracity of the representations made by either Mr. Koresh or Wayne Martin. I want everybody to know that. We are not publishing this because we think the representations they made were correct. As a matter of fact, we specifically do not believe they were accurate, and we believe those were misrepresentations."[7] Ten months later, the Davidian jury in San Antonio took the 911 tapes much more seriously.

1995 HOUSE HEARINGS
RAISED MORE SUSPICIONS

In November, 1994, Republicans took control of both the United States Senate and House of Representatives for the first time in forty years. Members of the new Congress, many elected by pro-Second Amendment constituents, vowed to reopen hearings into BATF and FBI actions against the Davidians. The Oklahoma City bombing reinforced their desire for hearings—if only to debunk "conspiracy theories."

Not surprisingly, the Clinton administration resisted the hearings which were co-sponsored by subcommittees of the House Judiciary and House Oversight and Reform Committees. On the May 14, 1995, "Face the Nation," White House Chief of Staff Leon Panetta pronounced those calling for hearings "despicable." Treasury Secretary Robert Rubin publicly begged Congress not to use the hearings to undermine law enforcement. He later requested Democrat Bill

Brewster of Oklahoma, a member of the committee, not ask questions that would "make the administration look bad."[8]

Mean-spirited White House and congressional Democrats sabotaged the ten-day hearings in July, 1995. The Republican majority had to fight to get access to White House documents. The Justice Department gave them 48,000 jumbled documents with no index. The Justice Department refused to allow a highly reputed engineering firm to x-ray the Davidians' weapons to discover if they had in fact been converted when the department learned the National Rifle Association was paying the firm. (Republicans rejected the Justice Department offer to bring the guns to Washington and conduct its own x-ray analysis; perhaps they suspected the department would merely use the guns as a propaganda photo-opportunity, while not properly testing them.) The Defense Department failed to provide post-fire reports on whether tanks, at which the FBI alleged Davidians had shot on April 19, actually showed any evidence of bullet damage. And, of course, the Justice Department was unable to comply with Congressional requests to provide the missing half of the front door or the missing February 28, 1993, video tape.

Most of the ninety-four witnesses the Republican majority called were culpable agents and officials or their apologists. Only eight gave firsthand accounts of the Davidians' side of the story. Unlike during the Davidian trial, during which defense attorneys at least could cross-examine witnesses, there were no knowledgeable individuals able and willing to counter point-by-point federal agents' and officials' innumerable and repeated exaggerations and lies. Since so many of these still face potential criminal charges, it is not surprising some may have committed the relatively minor offense of lying to Congress to cover up their crimes.

Republican committee members, many of them former prosecutors or law enforcement agents, were intimidated by the Democrats' shrill accusations that Republicans were using the hearings to undermine law enforcement and rehabilitate David Koresh. The focus of the hearings became not law enforcement abuses of citizens' rights, but how to bolster the credibility of law enforcement. At the end of the hearings Republican co-chairs Bill Zeliff (R-NH) and Bill McCollum (R-FL) asserted the hearings had "put to rest conspiracy theories."

However, this assertion is illusionary. The 1995 House hearings brought out little information not already available to the public, much of it included in this book. Many important questions and issues never were raised. And the new information revealed only supports the "conspiracy theory" advanced herein: FBI and Justice Department official turned a blind eye while FBI agents in Waco sabotaged negotiations with Davidians in order to give the FBI an excuse to destroy evidence that BATF agents murdered six Davidians during and after their reckless February 28, 1993, raid.

FBI negotiation tapes released just before the hearings show that Davidian Steve Schneider told negotiators: "There were a lot of people that got to look out those windows and saw first hand what happened at that approach to the door. They saw. These people get the idea that those on the outside want to do us all in so there's no evidence, period, as to what happened. That they might want to burn the building down. They want to destroy the evidence. Because the evidence from the door will clearly show how many bullets and what happened.... If this building stands, and the reporters, the press, get to see the evidences, it's going to be seen clearly what happened and what these men came to do." And he worried, "The press are so far back that you guys could come and blow us away and give any kind of a story you want to."

Democrats and law enforcement witnesses did conduct a highly successful campaign to demonize David Koresh and the Davidians. The first day of the hearings Democrats threw their biggest "stink bomb" when they presented fourteen-year-old Kiri Jewell and her father David. For the first time Kiri made public her allegation that David Koresh had sexually molested her when she was ten years old. Ambushed Republicans were ignorant of the facts that Kiri had refused to press charges against David Koresh, that even the Department of Justice admitted her statement was insufficient probable cause to indict Koresh, or that her father had put her on the "Donahue" show during the siege as he negotiated to sell her story to television. After the hearing Jewell exposed Kiri to more public scrutiny, doubtless for profit, on two nights of the tabloid television show "Inside Edition."

Throughout the hearings Democrats repeatedly referred to Jewell's testimony, as well as other questionable accusations, as if these excused every law enforcement action against Davidians. The nefarious influence of "cult busters" like Marc Breault, David Jewell, and Rick Ross on BATF and FBI decision-making never once was mentioned during the hearings. The now-deceased Murray Mirons' anti-cult bias never was exposed.

BATF and FBI agents and officials, as well as Treasury and Justice Department officials, continued this pattern of demonization. They repeatedly used fantastic worst-case scenarios to excuse their actions: Davidians *might* assassinate anyone who attempted a peaceful service of warrant; Davidians *might* attack the citizens of Waco; Davidians *might* commit mass suicide if there were a siege; Koresh *might* start systematically shooting other Davidians; Davidians *might* break out of Mount Carmel with a gun in one hand and a child in another; Davidian supporters *might* blow up a dam or attack federal agents. Representatives rarely challenged these absurd law enforcement fantasies.

Republicans were angry to learn the BATF ignored David Koresh's July, 1993 invitation to BATF, through gun dealer Henry McMahon, to inspect his guns. They solicited from a number of expert and law enforcement witnesses opinions that such an invitation always should be accepted, if only as a means of gathering information for a search warrant. One representative castigated Treasury official Ron Noble for not mentioning the invitation in the official Treasury Department report.

Republicans challenged the need for a paramilitary raid to serve the search warrant. They established that BATF agents had misled the military by claiming that there was a methamphetamine laboratory at Mount Carmel in order to receive training from Joint Task Force 6—training they could obtain only if there was a drug nexus. However, none of the BATF raid commanders would confess to having lied to the military. Meanwhile, Special Forces officers denied either illegally teaching BATF agents techniques like room clearing or attending the raid dressed in "civvies."

U.S. Attorney Bill Johnston denied any role in planning the raid—contrary to the Treasury Department report's assertion and his own statements at trial—or that he witnessed the February 28 raid. Raid co-commander Chuck Sarabyn's excuse for having no written plan was the fact that the raid was moved up one day. He claimed commanders of the six different teams did not have a chance to merge their separate plans.

Issues regarding raid co-commanders Phillip Chojnacki and Chuck Sarabyn dominated the BATF raid panel—and distracted from the issue of the unnecessary brutality of that raid. Had they had lied about not knowing surprise had been lost? Why did BATF rehire them despite their lies? Why did BATF destroy the files regarding their actions? Did Sarabyn really carry the warrants, as he claimed? (He said he left them in his truck where "they got all shot up," inferring they were not recovered after the FBI towed the truck away.) The Justice Department, looking for some bone to throw to critics of the government's actions, may yet prosecute Sarabyn and Chojnacki for lying to the Treasury review. However, if the agents do have information that could seriously harm BATF or the Clinton administration, they again may escape any real discipline.

BATF agents repeated lies about an "ambush" in which dozens of Davidians assaulted them with machine guns, .50-caliber rifles and grenades. No one challenged them on the lack of physical evidence that these weapons were used. When tearful BATF agent Jim Cavanaugh cried that Davidians had "cannons" and BATF had "popguns"—i.e., only 9-millimeter handguns—no one reminded him that other witnesses had testified BATF agents carried high-powered AR-15 rifles and MP-5 submachine guns.

The issue of whether agents had fired from helicopters was explored, without any systemic presentation of the evidence that they had, and without a discussion of Davidians' assertions that four died from that gunfire. Davidians David Thibodeau and Clive Doyle, who saw evidence of helicopter gunfire after the fact, were allowed to describe what they and other Davidians saw; surviving Davidians who actually witnessed shooting from the helicopters were not called as witnesses.

One document indicating agents considered using such gunfire was found among thousands turned over to Congress. A handwritten note by some unknown Treasury Department review official read: "HCs [helicopters] as a diversion. Simultaneous gunfire. Worked in Seattle. Three to four hundred meters from boundary. Hover. Practiced at Hood." (Assumedly a reference to Fort Hood, where BATF agents trained.)

BATF agent Davy Aguilera revealed that, contrary to one BATF official's assertion, BATF agents in the Blackhawk had had their weapons loaded. He also disclosed agents had been told they would be permitted to fire in self-defense. When asked if any agents had fired, he answered, "No." Raid co-commander Phillip Chojnacki responded to the same question with, "Not to my knowledge." Melvin Watt (D-NC) presented statements from the rest of the agents in the Blackhawk that they had not fired.

Treasury official Ron Noble asserted the Treasury Department had investigated the issue of firing from helicopters thoroughly—even though the allegation was never mentioned in the department's official report. By refusing to take the steps necessary to find out the truth about firing from helicopters, committee members committed their most blatant act of complicity in cover-up.

One important revelation was that the Department of Justice halted its post-February 28 raid shooting review because agent stories "did not add up." Officials were worried that the interviewers were generating "exculpatory" material that could help the Davidian defendants at trial. One memo expressed hope that the memories of those agents not interviewed would "dim" before trial. Davidian attorneys, Texas Rangers, and others charged that this was an unprecedented attempt to interfere with the right to a fair trial. Should Davidians receive a re-trial, or should there be another round of appeals, this memorandum surely will become an issue.

Another document discovered by staffers revealed that on the morning of February 28 an unnamed BATF agent in Waco informed BATF's Washington office that the BATF raid had been speeded up because of David Koresh's "comments" to the undercover agent. Treasury official Ron Noble tried to explain this away as an after-the-fact record, of no consequence.

Two evidences of BATF and FBI solidarity emerged during the hearing. Tank driver James McGee emotionally testified: "I'd like to pay tribute on behalf of the Hostage Rescue Team to those four ATF agents who sacrificed their lives for this country. And I'd also like to offer my condolences to their families and also to those agents, those seventeen-plus who were wounded by hostile fire at the Branch Davidian compound." And social worker Joyce Sparks revealed that while an FBI agent had contacted her about helping women and children if there were a gas assault, it was definitely a BATF agent who called her back later the same day and said her involvement was canceled. Representatives did not follow up on this damning evidence of BATF involvement in the gassing plan.

Despite the use of tanks to destroy Mount Carmel, there was no real challenge to their legality once military representative assured Congress that the tank artillery was not armed. Congress discovered for the first time that British Special Air Service members advised FBI agents about their actions in Waco. Special Air Service is involved in repressive British civilian law enforcement in Northern Ireland. Republicans demanded Janet Reno look into the matter.

The House hearing did elicit abundant evidence that FBI agents sabotaged negotiations. Former FBI behavioral scientist Peter Smerick explained that his superior John Douglas told him that FBI Director William Sessions was unhappy with his analysis and favored stepped-up tactical harassment. He felt a "self-imposed" pressure to please his superiors and alter his memorandum. However, Sessions himself denied he supported increased harassment and suggested representatives find out where the opinion credited to him really originated.

Smerick also admitted that there were a number of incidents where the FBI destroyed Davidian property after Davidians had cooperated with them. And FBI siege commander Jeff Jamar revealed that there was a Hostage Rescue Team member in the room with the negotiators at all times—supporting Davidians' contentions that tactical agents used information from negotiators to sabotage negotiations.

Dick DeGuerin disclosed that David Koresh told him that he would surrender to the Texas Rangers. The Rangers said they would accept such a surrender if DeGuerin arranged it with the FBI. But, as usual, the FBI rejected any such third-party efforts, no matter how credible or promising.

Testimony on the fifth day of hearings by DeGuerin, attorney Jack Zimmermann, and theologians Phillip Arnold and James Tabor effected a minor turn-around. Representatives received convincing evidence that Davidians' religious convictions were sincere, that they did intend to exit as soon as Koresh finished his short book about the Seven Seals, and that the FBI had lied when they assured Koresh and his attorney they would permit him to finish his book. Several committee members studied transcripts of Koresh's repeated statements in the last days that he was working on his book and eager to exit Mount Carmel and stand trial.

They were impressed by Koresh's statements, "I'll be out. Yes. Definitely. . . . It's clarified. Lock, stock, and barrel it," and by his jokes to negotiators, "I'll be in custody in the jailhouse. You can come down there and feed me bananas if you want," and "Did you take a shower for me?"

Representatives grilled siege commander Jeff Jamar, chief negotiator Byron Sage and HRT commander Richard Rogers about who ordered them to go ahead with the gas and tank assault despite this evidence Davidians would soon exit. Jamar asserted to skeptical Republicans that he got no pressure from FBI or Justice Department officials and that the decision to go ahead was his. Subsequent testimony by Jamar, Sage, and Rogers seemed to support Jamar's contention—and the theory that agents in Waco were allowed full reign by, rather than tightly controlled by, their FBI and Justice Department superiors.

Jamar and Sage both contended that they gave little weight to Koresh's April 14 promise-to-surrender letter because Koresh "always" talked about the Seven Seals and coming out and that this was just one more Koresh lie. Jamar asserted Steve Schneider told negotiators that he had no idea when Koresh would finish the First Seal and that Judy Schneider declared it might take her a year to finish typing the manuscript. However, Republicans familiar with the negotiation transcripts countered that Koresh was working on the Second Seal, that Steve Schneider had seen pages from the First and said he could quickly edit them, and that Judy Schneider merely had made a sarcastic comment about how long it would take her to type the manuscript

using a manual typewriter. They noted that on April 17
Koresh had promised to send out the First Seal to the
FBI in a few days.

Jamar first tried to challenge the authenticity
of the First Seal brought out by Ruth Riddle. He then
claimed he had to execute the gas plan because he did
not have a hard copy to show the "on-site commanders"
as proof that Koresh was writing the book. When
Republicans did not buy these excuses, Jamar fell back
on FBI paranoia—the FBI had to launch their assault
because Davidians might suddenly break out of Mount
Carmel shooting or might commit mass suicide.

Byron Sage admitted he provided little
information to his superiors about what even
representatives began to call "Koresh's promise to
surrender." He sent a copy of David Koresh's April 14
surrender letter solely to FBI analysts in Washington
who sent it to FBI consultant Murray Miron. Only this
analysis was forwarded to FBI officials and Attorney
General Janet Reno. It was revealed that Webster
Hubbell had initiated the April 15 call to chief negotiator
Byron Sage after Justice Department officials learned,
probably from a newspaper, of Koresh's promise to exit
after writing the Seven Seals. Sage conceded he
mentioned no agreement with Koresh and did not read
Hubbell the contents of the letter. Hubbell asserted that
Sage inferred they had abandoned all negotiations—
Sage replied that Hubbell had misunderstood him.

Jamar admitted that while he believed there was
a 99 percent possibility Davidians would fire on tanks
and that the FBI would speed up the gas and tank attack,
he had not shared his certainty with FBI or Justice

officials. Former FBI and Justice officials Larry Potts, Floyd Clarke, and Webster Hubbell asserted that had they known this, they might have reconsidered the plan. Despite this blatant evidence of ill-intent, Republicans refused to label Jamar's and Sage's actions anything more than bungling.

On the last day of the hearing the sole witness was Attorney General Janet Reno. Representative McCollum systematically shot down her stated reasons for approving the gas and tank assault: that negotiations were at an impasse, children were being abused, the Hostage Rescue Team was becoming fatigued and she feared a violent breakout or suicide by Davidians. Similarly, Mark Souder (R-IN), reviewing the dangers of the gas and tank attack to the children, asserted he could not believe she approved the plan for the good of the children.

Pushed to the wall, Reno admitted, "You are right. The reason we did it was that they were dangerous people and they weren't coming out." Nevertheless, she denied that her reasons for approving the plan had anything to do with what one FBI memorandum spotlighted—weakening of the FBI's authority.

Janet Reno continued to defend FBI agents and officials, despite mounting evidence that they had withheld information from or misled her. In her eagerness to excuse her decision, Reno asserted at least three times that Steve Schneider had said it might take six months or six years to finish the manuscript. Finally, Representative McCollum put a stop to her false charge by informing her that there was no such statement in the transcript.

It was discovered that in the April 12 briefing book given Janet Reno that the FBI falsely claimed studies showed the gas would not seriously harm children. However, even Dr. Harry Salem, who had advised Reno, admitted that there were only two studies of children exposed to the gas; they had been exposed for only a few hours, not forty-eight hours. In earlier testimony, chemistry professor George Uhlig held that CS gas could render a poorly ventilated room "similar to one of the gas chambers used by the Nazis at Auschwitz." Bob Barr (R-GA) had displayed the autopsy photo of a six-year-old girl who died in the concrete room of the kind of inflammation of the throat and lungs caused by over-exposure to CS gas. John Mica (R-FL) forced the embarrassed Reno to admit that she did not know that the children did not have gas masks.

Steven Schiff (R-NM) questioned Janet Reno's repeated claims that only the FBI HRT could protect the perimeter against the extremist militia groups which were threatening to attack Mount Carmel, to either support or destroy Davidians. (This was a reference to Linda Thompson's tiny April 3, 1993, "unorganized militia" demonstration.) Given recent publicity about militia activities, Reno obviously was trying to make political hay out of what was in 1993 a minor issue.

Representative McCollum closely questioned Reno on whether she knew siege commander Jamar believed there was a 99 percent chance the Davidians would fire. Reno hesitated, then fumbled into admitting her ignorance: "We expected them to fire, perhaps, in certain instances, or we wouldn't have put the people in the armored vehicles." (At one point, defending the FBI's use of military tanks, Reno callously compared the tanks to "a good rent-a-car.")

However, Reno successfully avoided answering another important question—did she know that once Davidians fired the FBI would quickly accelerate the gassing plan and even proceed to demolition? In a dramatic earlier exchange, Larry Potts, under aggressive questioning by John Shadegg (R-AZ), conceded that the FBI's destruction of the gymnasium was part of the speeded-up plan to demolish the building. Potts angrily declared that Janet Reno's April 12 briefing book outlined that plan and FBI agents had full authority to implement it. Predictably, Jamar and Rogers denied that they were in fact beginning demolition.

Little was learned about decision-making on April 19. Chief negotiator Byron Sage admitted that the FBI thought the Davidians were "not into suicide per se, but sacrifice." In effect, Sage admitted FBI agents knew the Davidians would not be driven out of the building, no matter how fierce the government's gas and tank attacks.

Representatives were confused about what time Attorney General Reno left the FBI Operations Center on April 19 and did not press her to reveal to whom she spoke after she left. Despite their attempts to link Bill Clinton to the operation, Republicans never asked her about her 11:00 A.M. eastern time phone call to him, which she mentioned during the April 28, 1993, House Judiciary hearing.

In contrast to Reno's claim during that hearing that she told the FBI to call off the attack if the children were endangered, she now admitted she was reluctant to call it off. "I don't know what the FBI would have done if I'd done so when their lives were at risk." And she let the FBI talk her into leaving the Operations Center, buying their argument it would "attract attention" if she canceled her speech.

While many representatives seemed convinced that the FBI had proceeded to a demolition of the building, most still accepted unquestioningly the FBI and Justice Department assertion that Davidians started the fire. They barely challenged Jamar's and Sage's false accusations that Davidian survivors admitted Davidians started the fires or FBI agent John Morrison's claim he had seen a Davidian start a fire—despite his testimony under cross-examination at trial that he did not know what the suspect Davidian was doing. Representative McCollum conceded that after reading the government-created April 19 surveillance transcripts he still could imagine innocent interpretations of Davidian conversations about spreading and pouring fuel. Nevertheless, he later concluded that Davidians started the fire.

Fire investigators Paul Gray and James Quintiere presented selectively edited infrared and television video and fire report evidence that the Davidians started the fire. Quintiere did concede the fire started on the second floor just ninety seconds after the tank ripped out the corner of the building directly below it. (Unlike the duplicitous Gray on "Nightline," Quintiere admitted that both front and side windows belonged to the same room.) Quintiere challenged accusations that the fire started there accidentally, asserting the infrared video would have picked up any accidental fire from the moment of its inception. Of course, he never claimed that the infrared video picked up the early inception of the fires he alleged Davidians started.

Former army and BATF fire investigator Rick Sherrow, who has been consulting in Davidian civil suits, also was on the panel. He criticized the government for destruction of, and withholding of, evidence concerning how the fire started. And he criticized Gray and Quintiere for their ignorance of the flammability and toxicity of CS gas and methylene chloride and their rejecting evidence of accidental fire.

Davidian Clive Doyle denied that Davidians started the fire—though he did admit that early in the siege a few Davidians had discussed making molotov cocktails to defend themselves against the tanks. And he put to rest theologians' theories that Davidians thought they could set Mount Carmel on fire and, through faith in God, survive the fire. Doyle replied that only God could create such a salvational "ring of fire."

Four skeptical representatives repeatedly questioned FBI siege commander Jeff Jamar, Larry Potts, and Janet Reno on why the three FBI monitors listening to the surveillance device inside Mount Carmel could not hear suspicious-sounding Davidian conversations about spreading and pouring fuel. The three variously replied that there was too much background noise, that the conversations only could be heard when they were enhanced, and that no notations of such conversations appeared in the FBI monitors' logs. (Davidian defense attorney Tim Evans earlier had revealed that defense attorneys never did receive those monitor logs. Neither, evidently, did the House Committee.) Richard Rogers, Jamar, and Reno all argued that agents would have called off the attack and pulled back the tanks immediately if they had had any idea that Davidians were planning to burn down Mount Carmel.

However, in his first day of testimony, Byron Sage made the ambiguous statement that in the first minutes of the gas attack, "The microphones indicate two things—they immediately donned gas masks and they immediately began to spread fuel." Later in the hearing, Jeff Jamar made the more incriminating statement that tanks were trying to gas further inside the building because "there was information that they apparently were able to go places where they didn't need masks. We either heard that on the over hears, it was reported." ("Over hear," of course, would be the surveillance device, heard by monitors. They reported to Jamar.) Obviously the three monitors must be questioned on this and their logs reviewed.

Republicans tried mightily to find evidence that President Bill Clinton had some improper influence on the fatal decision to gas Mount Carmel. Attorney General Janet Reno explained that a memorandum instructing Acting Attorney General Stuart Gerson to inform Clinton of any aggressive tactical actions was a product of Clinton's concern about an unknown Republican holdover. Friend-of-Bill Webster Hubbell denied repeatedly that he and Clinton had discussed the Waco situation informally and improperly—this despite an Associated Press article claiming Hubbell had revealed he was giving Clinton updates on Waco and despite a memorandum in which Treasury official Ron Noble asserted Hubbell would take the matter up with Clinton if the Treasury Department's review did not downplay BATF errors.

Representatives learned that deceased White House assistant counsel Vince Foster was the White House contact given to Texas Rangers by the Texas Governor's office and that Foster's "Waco file" allegedly contained only a memorandum forwarding to Treasury the "Waco, the Big Lie" video. When Janet Reno was questioned about whether Foster's statement on his "suicide note" about the FBI lying to the Attorney General referred to Waco, she explained it related to "Travelgate." Republicans found no smoking gun proving Clinton's involvement.

Early in the hearing Frederick Heineman (R-NC) declared, "We as a Congress are on trial here. We have to be credible to the people. Because if we are not credible about the oversight of government agencies, then who is?" However, the hearings did little to reassure millions of Americans that Congress will punish federal agents, even when they commit mass murder.

In emotional testimony attorney Jack Zimmermann told of a phone call from the sobbing mother of Davidian and Israeli citizen Pablo Cohen who died in the April 19 fire. Zimmermann recalled, "Then she described for me, an Israeli Jew talking to an American Jewish lawyer, watching that gas be inserted into that building, watching an American tank knock down an American house and then it burst into flames. Can you imagine the images in an Israeli's mind with the Holocaust survivors in Israel? . . . I could not explain to her how that happened. And her comment was, 'I thought he would be safe in America.' " Millions of Americans also want to ensure there are no more such Holocausts in America.

"WACO, NEVER AGAIN"

In his paper "Mount Carmel: The Unseen Reality," Davidian Livingstone Fagan writes: "Whilst not everyone is required to go through our experience at Mount Carmel, everyone is required to give a response of approval or disapproval." Fagan speaks in terms of spiritual salvation, yet his words also can be applied to national salvation. For the government's massacre of the Davidians created a great divide among Americans, one ripped open even wider by the Oklahoma City bombing. On one side are those who know a great wrong was done and want to know the truth and see justice done. On the other are those who lay all blame on the Davidians, passively accept the government's explanation—or worry that a thorough investigation would rattle the political establishment.

As a person who spent thirty hours a week for eighteen months writing on the subject, I know the mass of confusing and sometimes conflicting testimony and evidence that must be sifted through. Only an independent counsel with a full staff of attorneys and investigators empowered to take testimony under oath and grant immunity from prosecution can get to the truth. And only such a thorough investigation will convince millions of Americans that the federal government will not permit another massacre like that of the Branch Davidians.

Citizens must continue to demand Congress appoint an independent counsel to fully investigate the crimes against the Branch Davidians by BATF and FBI agents and officials, Treasury and Justice Department officials, federal prosecutors and a federal judge—and the all pervasive cover-up of those crimes. And citizens must work for justice for surviving Davidians, i.e., immediate freedom for the nine unjustly prosecuted, convicted, and sentenced Davidian prisoners, Renos Avraam, Brad Branch, Jaime Castillo, Graeme Craddock, Livingstone Fagan, Paul Fatta, Ruth Riddle, Kathryn Schroeder, and Kevin Whitecliff.

As one who only has begun to read the Bible, I find Isaiah 42:6–7 to be particularly compelling for those who have learned the truth about what really happened at Mount Carmel:

I, the Lord, have called you with a righteous purpose
and taken you by the hand;
I have formed you, and appointed you to be a light
to all peoples, a beacon for the nations,
to open eyes that are blind,
to bring captives out of prison,
out of the dungeons where they lie in darkness.

Chapter Thirteen: Congressional Hearings
Continued the Cover-up

1. CBS's "48 Hours," May 4, 1995.
2. Associated Press wire story, April 26, 1993, 01:26 EDT.
3. Michael Isikoff, "Reno Strongly Defends Raid on Cult," *Washington Post*, April 29, 1993.
4. April 22, 1993, House Ways and Means Subcommittee hearing transcript: 90.
5. Ibid., 97.
6. June 9, 1993 House Appropriations Subcommittee hearing: 2, 3.
7. Ibid., 130.
8. John Mintz, "Treasury Chief Airs Concern over Probe of Waco Raids," *Washington Post* (July 5, 1995); N.R. A. Special Report, "The Waco Hearings: Day 3," July 21, 1995.

Index

INDEX

493